Aramaic in Postbiblical Judaism and Early Christianity

Duke Judaic Studies Series
Volume 3

Series Editor
Eric M. Meyers

Editorial Board
Kalman P. Bland, Malachi Hacohen,
and Joseph Shatzmiller

Previously Published

1. *Galilee through the Centuries: Confluence of Cultures,* edited by Eric M. Meyers
2. *Liturgy in the Life of the Synagogue: Studies in the History of Jewish Prayer,* edited by Ruth Langer and Steven Fine

Aramaic in Postbiblical Judaism and Early Christianity

Papers from the
2004 National Endowment for the Humanities
Summer Seminar at Duke University

Edited by

Eric M. Meyers *and* Paul V. M. Flesher

Winona Lake, Indiana
Eisenbrauns
2010

© Copyright 2010 by Eisenbrauns.
All rights reserved.
Printed in the United States of America.

www.eisenbrauns.com

Library of Congress Cataloging-in-Publication Data

National Endowment for the Humanities. Summer Seminar (2004 : Duke University)
  Aramaic in postbiblical Judaism and early Christianity : papers from the 2004 National Endowment for the Humanities Summer Seminar at Duke University / edited by Eric M. Meyers and Paul V. M. Flesher.
     p. cm. — (Duke judaic studies series ; v. 3)
  Includes bibliographical references and indexes.
  ISBN 978-1-57506-178-8 (hardback : alk. paper)
  1. Aramaic language—Congresses. I. Meyers, Eric M. II. Flesher, Paul Virgil McCracken. III. Title.
  PJ5201.N38   2010
  492.2—dc22
                                                                  2009053664

The paper used in this publication meets the minimum requirements of the American National Standard for Information Sciences—Permanence of Paper for Printed Library Materials, ANSI Z39.48-1984. ♾™

This volume is dedicated to our friend and beloved colleague

Lucas Van Rompay

whose contributions to the study of Aramaic language and texts—especially the Syriac dialect and its literature—have helped make the fields of Near Eastern studies and Eastern Christianity a key curricular element of religious and historical studies of the ancient world.

Contents

Acknowledgments ix
Abbreviations x
Introduction xiii

Awakening Sleeping Texts

Reconsidering the *Letter* of Mara bar Serapion 3
   David Rensberger, *Interdenominational Theological Center*

"Transgressive": Meaning and Implications of ܘܠܐ (ʿwlʾ) in
   Jewish Syriac Text and Translation 23
   Sigrid Peterson, *University of Pennsylvania*

The Composition of the *Qenneshrē Fragment* 33
   Michael Penn, *Mount Holyoke College*

A Note on an Aramaic Date Formula Found
   at Nabratein and Zoar 49
   Eric M. Meyers, *Duke University*

When? "After the Destruction of the Temple" 55
   Paul V. M. Flesher, *University of Wyoming*

The Details of Language

The Function of the Active Participle in the Aramaic of Daniel . . 69
   Tarsee Li, *Oakwood University*

Tracing the History of a Legal Term of Art: The Word *azarah*
   in Biblical, Tannaitic, and Targumic Literature 105
   Madeline Kochen, *University of Michigan*

The Adverb אולי ("Perhaps") in the Piety and Prophecy
   of the Hebrew Bible and Early Versions 127
   William Reader, *Central Michigan University*

Translating the Hebrew Particle כי אם into Aramaic and English:
   An Exploration through the Targums and the Peshitta 173
   Blane W. Conklin, *University of Texas*

Recasting:
Making an Old Text New

The Use of the First Person in the *Genesis Apocryphon* 193
    Stephen A. Reed, *Jamestown College*

Syntactic Double Translation in the *Targumim* 217
    Michael Carasik, *Philadelphia*

The Fish Grows Bigger: Angelic Insertions in Targums
    Neofiti and Pseudo-Jonathan 233
    David L. Everson, *Xavier University*

Hapax legomena and the Development of Proto-Onqelos:
    The Case of Genesis 245
    Kyong-Jin Lee, *Yale University*

The Wisdom of the Sages: Rabbinic Rewriting of Qohelet 269
    Paul V. M. Flesher, *University of Wyoming*

Indexes 281
    Index of Authors 281
    Index of Scripture 285
    Index of Other Ancient Sources 292

Acknowledgments

The essays in this volume came into being during a six-week residential seminar in the summer of 2004. Held at Duke University and directed by the editors, the seminar focused on Aramaic in Postbiblical Judaism and Early Christianity and was sponsored by the National Endowment for the Humanities, to which we are sincerely grateful. Duke University, through its Department of Religion and Center for Judaic Studies, hosted the participants and the guest lecturers. The department's administrative staff of Nancy Hurtgen, Gay Trotter, and Sandra Woods smoothed the organizational bumps involved in this undertaking and helped the visitors' stay go easily. Duke's Divinity School Library and Perkins Library (now Perkins/Bostock Library) granted the seminar participants access to their holdings, resources, and helpful librarians. Thanks go especially to Roger Lloyd, head of the Divinity School Library. For sharing their expertise with the seminar, we would like to thank Michael Sokoloff, Douglas Gropp, Tina Shepardson, and Hayim Lapin. The book's preparation was greatly assisted by the computer work of Alan Todd and Yael Wilfand of Duke University and of Kerry Luck Torry of the University of Wyoming. Some of the long-distance difficulties of the editing process were made easier by the University of Wyoming; its Religious Studies Program; and Clayleen Rivord, its administrative assistant. The editors are personally grateful to their wives, Carol Meyers and Caroline McCracken-Flesher, who supported us during the intense weeks of the seminar and the long period of editing with both encouragement and advice.

This volume is dedicated to Lucas Van Rompay, whose active and delightful engagement with the seminar inspired us and gave us a boost of energy during the long evening sessions. His teaching talents encouraged the participants in their language studies, and his enthusiasm for the material brought them the desire to understand it. He gave to us the same abilities and energy that he provides so willingly to his students and to his involvement in the international field of Syriac studies.

—Eric M. Meyers and Paul V. M. Flesher

Abbreviations

General

1QapGen	*Genesis Apocryphon*
1QM	*War Rule*
Arak.	*Arakhin*
AZ	*Abodah Zarah*
b.	*Bavli, Babylonian Talmud*
BB	*Baba Batra*
Bek.	*Bekhorot*
Ber.	*Berakhot*
Bik.	*Bikkurim*
BM	*Baba Mesia*
BQ	*Baba Qamma*
CG	Fragments of Palestinian Targums found in the Cairo Geniza
col(s).	column(s)
Ed.	*Eduyyot*
Erub.	*Erubin*
FT	Fragment Targums to the Pentateuch
Git.	*Gittin*
Hag.	*Hagigah*
Hal.	*Hallah*
HB	Hebrew Bible
HL	*Hapax legomenon/a*
Hor.	*Horayot*
Hul.	*Hulin*
JBA	Jewish Babylonian Aramaic
JLA	Jewish Literary Aramaic
JPA	Jewish Palestinian Aramaic
JPS	Jewish Publication Society version
Ker.	*Keritot*
Kil.	*Kilayim*
KJV	King James Version
LJLA	Late Jewish Literary Aramaic
LXX	Septuagint
m.	Mishnah
Maas.	*Masserot*
Mak.	*Makkot*
Maksh.	*Makhshirin*
Meg.	*Megillah*

Abbreviations

Miq.	*Miqvaot*
MQ	*Moed Qatan*
MS	*Maaser Sheni*
MT	Masoretic Text
Naz.	*Nazir*
NEB	New English Bible
Ned.	*Nedarim*
Neg.	*Negaim*
Nez.	*Nezikin*
Nid.	*Niddah*
NJPSV	New Jewish Publication Society Version
NRSV	New Revised Standard Version
NT	New Testament
Ohal.	*Ohalot*
Or.	*Orlah*
OT	Old Testament
Pes.	*Pesahim*
PJ	Targum Pseudo-Jonathan to the Pentateuch
PRE	*Pirqe d'Rabbi Eliezer*
Pss. Sol.	*Psalms of Solomon*
Qidd.	*Qiddushin*
Qod.	*Qodashim*
RH	*Rosh Hashshannah*
RSV	Revised Standard Version
Sanh.	*Sanhedrin*
Shab.	*Shabbat*
Sheb.	*Shebiit*
Sheq.	*Sheqalim*
Sir	Sirach/Ben Sira
t.	*Tosefta*
Taan.	*Taanit*
Tem.	*Temura*
TJ	Targum Jonathan to the Prophets
TN	Targum Neofiti to the Pentateuch
TO	Targum Onqelos to the Pentateuch
Toh.	*Tohorot*
TQ	Targum to Qohelet
TY	*Tebul Yom*
Uq.	*Uqsin*
Wis	Wisdom of Solomon
y.	*Yerushalmi*, Jerusalem Talmud, Palestinian Talmud
Yad.	*Yadayim*
Yeb.	*Yebamot*
Zeb.	*Zebahim*
Zer.	*Zeraim*

Reference Works

ANF   *The Ante-Nicene Fathers: Translations of the Writings of the Fathers down to* A.D. *325*. Edited by A. Roberts et al. 10 volumes. Buffalo, NY: Christian Literature, 1885–96

AS   *Aramaic Studies* [formerly *JAB*]

BDB   Brown, F.; S. R. Driver; and C. A. Briggs. *A Hebrew and English Lexicon of the Old Testament*. Oxford: Clarendon, 1907

CAL   Comprehensive Aramaic Lexicon (http://cal1.cn.huc.edu/)

DJD   Discoveries in the Judaean Desert

GKC   Gesenius, W.; E. Kautsch; and A. E. Cowley. *Gesenius' Hebrew Grammar*. 2nd ed. Oxford: Clarendon, 1910

HALOT   Köhler, L., and W. Baumgartner. *The Hebrew and Aramaic Lexicon of the Old Testament*. 2 vols. Leiden: Brill, 2001

HUCA   *Hebrew Union College Annual*

JAB   *Journal for the Aramaic Bible*

JBL   *Journal of Biblical Literature*

JJS   *Journal of Jewish Studies*

JNSL   *Journal of Northwest Semitic Languages*

JQR   *Jewish Quarterly Review*

JSJ   *Journal for the Study of Judaism*

LSJ   Liddell, H. G.; R. Scott; and H. S. Jones. *A Greek-English Lexicon*. 9th ed. Oxford: Clarendon, 1940. [Available online, http://www.perseus.tufts.edu/]

STDJ   Studies on the Texts of the Desert of Judah

TAD   Porten, B., and A. Yardeni. *Textbook of Aramaic Documents from Ancient Egypt*. 4 Volumes. Hebrew University Department of the History of the Jewish People, Texts and Studies for Students. Jerusalem: Academon, 1986–99

Introduction

For nearly half of the first millennium B.C.E., Aramaic formed one of the languages of international government in the Near East. Three major empires—Assyria, Babylonia, and Persia—used Aramaic as a language of government. From the 700s B.C.E. to the late 300s B.C.E., Aramaic was the international language of administration, diplomacy, and trade—the "English" of the ancient Near East.

With the arrival of Alexander the Great in the Near East, Greek supplanted Aramaic as the language of empire. But Aramaic did not disappear. Although it gradually broke apart into dialects, in many regions of the former Persian Empire, Aramaic became an important local language. Indeed, Aramaic became the lingua franca of peoples in the regions of Palestine, Syria, and Mesopotamia.

In Palestine, Aramaic comprised one of the three languages used by Jews, along with the older Hebrew and the newly arrived Greek. While Greek continued to be used as the governing language for Palestine well into the Byzantine period, use of Aramaic as the native language overcame Hebrew by the second century C.E. in all but the religious sphere. And even in religious matters, Aramaic was being used by the second century B.C.E. and gradually became more important. As a result of this fact, a wealth of important writings in Aramaic has survived, from apocryphal and rabbinic texts to numerous translations of Scripture (*targumim*) and liturgical texts, as well as legal documents, letters, and inscriptions. Aramaic in Palestine remained a popular language for several centuries, up to the coming of Islam and the introduction of the Arabic language in the seventh century.

In the decades following the destruction of Jerusalem and its Temple in 70 C.E. and the failure of the Bar Kokhba Revolt in 135, large numbers of Jews migrated from Palestine to Babylonia. While they brought to Babylonia their own dialect of Aramaic, upon their arrival they also found eastern dialects of Aramaic and Jews speaking them. This set into motion a process, which over time resulted in Babylonian Jews' using three different dialects of Aramaic, one of which eventually formed the linguistic basis for the Babylonian Talmud, along with Hebrew.[1]

In Syria and northern Mesopotamia, a large region north of Palestine that lay between Palestine and Babylonia on the Fertile Crescent, Aramaic also

---

1. P. V. M. Flesher, "The History of Aramaic in Judaism," in *The Encyclopedia of Judaism* (ed. J. Neusner, A. J. Avery-Peck, and W. S. Green; 2nd ed.; Leiden: Brill, 2005) 1:85–96.

developed into an important local language. The city of Edessa provided the center for the best-attested Aramaic dialect, namely, Syriac. As Christianity began to grow, especially after its legalization under Constantine in the fourth century, Syriac took on a new role. While most Christians in the Mediterranean world adopted Latin and/or Greek for religious purposes, those in Syria used Syriac. This Aramaic dialect became the language of the Syrian Christian churches and played a major role in the formation of Christianity in the lands nearest its origins during its first millennium. The churches translated Scripture into Syriac, as well as using the language for commentaries, sermons, and liturgical works. It was also used in letters, legal documents, and a wide variety of inscriptions.

Given the importance of Aramaic in the ancient Near East, one would expect that it would be a major research focus for American scholars interested in that area. This is not quite the case. Most United States researchers who work on the ancient Near East are trained in some form of biblical studies. On the one hand, that means that most graduate students and seminarians have taken some Aramaic, usually during a course on "Biblical Aramaic" placed within a Biblical Hebrew sequence. On the other hand, outside of the Jewish seminaries and a few elite graduate programs, the majority of these students never get beyond this introduction. They receive a small sample of Aramaic studies but not enough to obtain a complete picture.

With this situation in mind, the editors of this volume—Eric Meyers and Paul Flesher—organized a seminar for scholars who wanted to build on their first experience with Aramaic and learn more to help them in their study of Judaism and Christianity. In the summer of 2004, this idea grew into a National Endowment for the Humanities Summer Seminar at Duke University, directed by the two of us. As its title indicates, the seminar focused on "Aramaic in Postbiblical Judaism and Early Christianity." Its goal was to give scholars who wanted more than a taste of Aramaic an opportunity to gain further abilities and to establish a foundation for further study. The six weeks of intense study included both language and text study in Jewish Literary Aramaic, Jewish Palestinian Aramaic, and Syriac, as well as frequent seminars in the history, religion, and literature of texts written in these dialects.[2] The directors were ably assisted by Lucas Van Rompay, whose involvement in the seminar made him like a third codirector—and a much-appreciated one at that. Other scholars visited to lend the participants their expertise: Michael Sokoloff, Douglas Gropp, Tina Shepardson, and Hayim Lapin.

This volume comprises essays written as a result of that seminar. Most were written in residence, and all were done in discussion with the seminar's

2. Despite the obvious importance of Jewish Aramaic in Babylonia, we decided it lay outside the limits of a six-week seminar. Learning the Aramaic of the Babylonian Talmud not only requires a mastery of the language but developing an expertise in talmudic discourse—the latter task being beyond the ability of most neophytes in the short time available.

Introduction xv

participants and faculty. The essays are arranged into three groups: Awakening Sleeping Texts, the Details of Language, and Recasting: Making Old Texts New.

Awakening Sleeping Texts

Texts that have been discovered—whether through archaeological excavation or library research—often wait decades for their relevance to be recognized by the scholarly world. Sometimes they can languish for over a century without attracting significant attention. This is particularly true for texts that see publication without great fanfare or publicity. Whereas the Dead Sea Scrolls were trumpeted by the international press almost from the beginning (after which many were hidden from the scholarly world for nearly four decades), the texts featured in this section were published in the course of scholarly activity without significant attention by the press. Each essay in this section takes one of these texts and aims to awaken academic interest in further research by placing it into a new context and visualizing it through a new angle.

The section opens with David Rensberger's article "Reconsidering the *Letter* of Mara bar Serapion," an early Syriac composition written within the intellectual world of Hellenistic philosophy rather than the dominant Christian perspective of so much Syriac writing. Originally published in 1855 by William Cureton, the manuscript attracted little attention until recently. Indeed, during the preparation of this volume, Rensberger's essay circulated in an unpublished form and became part of an awakening interest in the *Letter* on both sides of the Atlantic. Through that scholarly synergy, it now anticipates an annotated edition.[3] In his essay here, Rensberger makes several key points about the *Letter*'s character. The *Letter* presents itself as a final missive from a man imprisoned by the Romans under false charges to his son, giving last words of guidance. While some previous scholars thought the *Letter* was a pseudepigraphon written by a Christian (including its publisher, Cureton), Rensberger shows that its character should be taken at face value and not seen as a false front for Christianity. He argues that the guidance presented is a mix of Hellenistic philosophy and the wisdom of "Western Asia," as Rensberger terms the Levant. In the end, he suggests that the *Letter* may originate from around Palmyra, perhaps in the second century.

This section's second essay comes from Sigrid Peterson, "'Transgressive': Meaning and Implications of ܥܘܠ (*'wl'*) in Jewish Syriac Text and Translation." Peterson's research focuses on Jewish pseudepigraphic works in Syriac, and here she works to refine the nuances of the Syriac term ܥܘܠ as it is rendered into English in a translation of the Syriac *Sixth Maccabees*. She makes

---

3. A critical edition and translation of the *Letter* of Mara bar Serapion is forthcoming: Mara Bar Serapion, *Letter to His Son* (ed. Annette Merz, David Rensberger, and Teun Tieleman; Sapere 17; Tübingen: Mohr Siebeck).

the case that in *Sixth Maccabees* it means "transgressive" (as in "committing a transgression") rather than simply "lawless," a meaning that also helps illuminate several passages in another Jewish pseudepigraphic text, the Syriac version of the *Psalms of Solomon*. *Sixth Maccabees*, as it is now known, first appeared in a volume edited by R. L. Bensly and W. E. Barnes in 1895, under the title *"Memra* by an Unknown Hand." Peterson's previous work has helped it become recognized as *Sixth Maccabees*, and she has prepared an edited text and an annotated translation.[4]

Michael Penn's essay, "The Composition of the Qenneshrē Fragment," studies a Syriac text that was originally published over 100 years ago by F. Nau and that has since been largely ignored. Penn's essay here provides an analysis of the text's organization and dating as part of his work toward an edition, translation, and commentary. Although the manuscript presents the *Qenneshrē Fragment* as a single text, Penn makes a strong case that the text we now possess was originally three separate documents (with fragments of a fourth), each with its own setting and approach to narration. They are unified by interest in the demonic possession of monks in the North Syrian monastery of Qenneshrē and the demons' subsequent exorcism. Penn dates the combined document to the eighth century C.E.—the time period for two of its sections—while the third may stem from the late seventh century.

Eric Meyers's contribution, "A Note on an Aramaic Date Formula Found at Nabratein and Zoar," begins with a Hebrew text—inscription, actually—rather than an Aramaic text. This is the synagogue inscription found at Nabratein. Although a squeeze impression was published by E. Renan as early as 1864, it remained largely unstudied until N. Avigad's analysis in 1960. More than 45 years after Avigad's publication, Meyers's essay finally brings the Nabratein inscription into a larger context, showing that its dating formula links it to the Aramaic Jewish tombstones at Zoar. The dating formula uses the destruction of the Jerusalem Temple as its beginning point and counts out the years since that time. This approach to dating shows, Meyers argues, the Jews responding to the increasing Christian pressure on their community after Constantine and into the early Byzantine period. As the Christian reckoning of time from Christ's birth became more widespread, these Jewish communities responded with a dating formula based within their own religious tradition.

Paul Flesher's essay "When? 'After the Destruction of the Temple'" continues this interest in the dating formula found at Nabratein and Zoar by surveying its history from the Mishnah through an inscription found in Lebanon

---

4. S. Peterson, "Sixth Maccabees: Introduction, Translation, and Notes," in *More Old Testament Pseudepigrapha* (ed. Richard Bauckham and James R. Davila; Grand Rapids, MI: Eerdmans, forthcoming). The text can be found in S. Peterson, *Martha Shamoni: A Jewish Syriac Rhymed Liturgical Poem about the Maccabean Martydoms* (Ph.D. diss., University of Pennsylvania, 2006).

to medieval marriage agreements and a targumic *tosefta*. It turns out that the Nabratein inscription is the only Hebrew use of this inscription; all others are in Aramaic. Flesher's study of the texts finds that they are linked together by the influence of Jewish Palestinian Aramaic.

The Details of Language

The essays in this section focus on grammatical or lexical aspects of Jewish and Christian forms of Aramaic. The section begins with a morphosyntactical study in the early form of Jewish Literary Aramaic found in Daniel and is followed by lexicographical studies in the targumic forms of Aramaic, the last two of which include the Peshitta. While the first study enables us to understand the development of the Aramaic verb, the last three set out the different ways in which the Aramaic-writing targumists related to the Hebrew context and the Vorlage in which they wrote.

Tarsee Li's essay "The Function of the Active Participle in the Aramaic of Daniel" takes a decidedly linguistic approach. Although somewhat technical, Li's essay provides an important corrective to the impression that students receive when they take a course in "Biblical Aramaic," in which the linguistic features of Daniel and Ezra are presented together as a single, unchanging description of this textually named dialect. Instead, Li treats Daniel as a moment in the diachronic growth of Aramaic and shows how it reveals a stage in the language's transformation from its Imperial form to the forms that it will take in later centuries. Drawing upon the guidelines of morphosyntactic change worked out by Bybee and her colleagues in their multilanguage comparative work, often referred to as "grammaticalization," Li shows that Daniel's participle has shifted from the progressive function that it had in earlier Aramaic, and it now functions as an imperfective, on the way to its transformation into a present tense, which it forms in later dialects.

In her essay "Tracing the History of a Legal Term of Art: The Word *azarah* in Biblical, Tannaitic, and Targumic Literature," Madeline Kochen examines the meaning of the Late Biblical Hebrew term *azarah* as it develops into Mishnaic Hebrew. In contrast to the older Classical Biblical Hebrew term *ḥatzer*, which constitutes a general term for "court" or "courtyard," *azarah* first appears in Later Biblical Hebrew with the primary meaning of "Temple court." This distinction carries through into the rabbinic era of Mishnaic Hebrew as well. As Kochen shows, this development finds a parallel in Aramaic. The Aramaic equivalent *azarta* becomes known during the period of Middle Aramaic, roughly at the same time as Late Biblical Hebrew, and carries the restricted meaning of "Temple court." The more general term in Aramaic is *darta*. This close parallel in the linguistic and legal use of the two terms, argues Kochen, shows the close ties between the rabbinic and the targumic worlds.

William Reader provides a comparative study of the way the different biblical versions—Septuagint, targums, and Peshitta—treat the Biblical Hebrew term אוּלַי in his essay, "The Adverb אוּלַי ('Perhaps') in the Piety and Prophecy of the Hebrew Bible and Early Versions." Although organized as a word study, the essay's results provide evidence for the character of and the relationships among the different targums as well as their (non-)relationship to the Peshitta. The primary result of Reader's study is that Targum Onqelos, Targum Jonathan, and the Palestinian Targums all treat the Hebrew term as requiring a consistent Aramaic equivalent. This outcome stands in stark contrast with the LXX and the Peshitta, which translate אוּלַי by several different terms, revealing no consistent pattern. Onqelos and Jonathan nearly always render אוּלַי as מא אם, while Targum Neofiti and the other Palestinian Targums use the equivalent of דלמא. Interestingly, Targum Pseudo-Jonathan reveals its dependency on both types of targums. It follows TO's usage for the first 27 chapters of Genesis and then into Numbers consistently uses TN's term, דלמא, and finally finishes with its own translation equivalent, לואי. Furthermore, when Reader examines TN's and PJ's use of "perhaps" in added material not in the biblical text, he finds that both use דלמא. Furthermore, in passages unique to Pseudo-Jonathan (that is, not found in Scripture, TO, or TN), he finds that PJ uses TN's term, דלמא, suggesting in part the underlying Palestinian character of PJ's dialect.

Blane Conklin's study of the way the Hebrew particle כי אם is rendered in the targums and the Peshitta provides results that in part parallel Reader's results of his study, while at other points diverge from it. In his essay "Translating the Hebrew Particle כי אם into Aramaic and English: An Exploration through the Targums and the Peshitta," Conklin shows that the Peshitta and the targums take different approaches to addressing this term. The study is complicated because sometimes the Hebrew text treats כי אם as two independent particles, while at other times it treats them as a single, unified term. The translations recognize these different uses. Conklin shows that, when the Hebrew text treats the כי אם construction as two independent particles, all the targums to the pentateuchal and the prophetic books prefer to render it with one similar construction, while the Peshitta approaches the same passages in 13 different ways. By contrast, when the Hebrew text treats the two terms as a single, compound particle, all the translations choose to standardize. The Peshitta has its own approach, while Targums Onqelos and Jonathan have theirs, in contrast to the Palestinian Targums. Interestingly, Pseudo-Jonathan follows Onqelos's approach quite closely and shows little interest in the way the Palestinian Targums render it.

Recasting: Making an Old Text New

What does it mean to recast an older text into a new form, or to retell an old story in a new way? At a theoretical level, this question opens a myriad of hermeneutical responses. But when specific texts are brought into evidence, broader theories rapidly narrow down into particular areas. Given the range of the term *recast*, it should not be surprising that the four kinds of texts studied in this section reveal four different aspects of recasting. These differences range from a deliberate attempt to change the meaning of a text's key concepts—similar to filling wine bottles with Kool-Aid—to an effort to preserve one language's multiplicity of meaning in another language—that is, to prevent change during the translation process. While perhaps not as broad as a theory of recasting, the four examples in the essays here provide solid examples that reveal the flexibility and breadth of this concept.

In his essay "The Use of the First Person in the *Genesis Apocryphon*," Stephen Reed examines the techniques of the *Apocryphon*'s recasting of Scripture's third-person narratives into the first person and explores the manner in which they alter the story. Reed finds that, despite the length of the passages over which this shift occurs, the *Apocryphon*'s author did not use the transformation for what Moshe Bernstein would term "authoritative" reasons: the *Apocryphon* does not use the first person to have the biblical heroes provide new revelation, as does the testamentary literature and the targums, nor does the text use it to bring in matters of biblical interpretation, like the targums. Instead, the first person appears as a device to enhance the literary character of the story, giving more insight into characters, their internal reactions, and their motivations as well as enhancing the plot. Reed sees the *Apocryphon*'s use of the first person as similar to Bernstein's category of "convenient" pseudepigraphy, in which the change provides a new perspective from which to tell the story.

It is widely recognized that one translation technique frequently found in the targums is the providing of two (or more) translations of a single word. In his essay, "Syntactic Double Translation in the Targumim," Michael Carasik demonstrates a newly recognized, related translation technique of providing two translations for a single syntactic construction. Just as the double translation of a word stems from a term with multiple meanings, so also the syntactic double translation stems from a phrase that can be syntactically decoded in more than one way. In each case Carasik analyzes, the targumist has seen this grammatical multiplicity and has provided a translation to reflect each possibility. To demonstrate how widespread this technique is, Carasik brings examples from all the different pentateuchal targums, as well as targums of the Prophets and the Writings.

David Everson turns his focus to the angelic world envisioned by the pentateuchal targums of Neofiti and Pseudo-Jonathan in his essay, "The Fish Grows Bigger: Angelic Insertions in Targums Neofiti and Pseudo-Jonathan." Looking closely at the titles and the names of angels—as well as their role in revelation, their numbering, and their divine status—Everson shows that Targum Pseudo-Jonathan has a much more extensive concern with and development of angels and their lore. He argues that PJ's angelology parallels the angelology found in later rabbinic literature, once again highlighting the links between the targumic and rabbinic literature. Everson argues in the end that the targum's additional information about angels brings Scripture into closer alignment with the rabbinic world view.

In "*Hapax legomena* and the Development of Proto-Onqelos: The Case of Genesis," Kyong-Jin Lee sets out to examine the treatment of *hapax legomena* in the targums and to test whether this treatment reveals or mitigates against the existence of a Proto-Onqelos targum that underlies both Targum Onqelos as it now stands and the Palestinian Targums. Limiting herself to the book of Genesis, Lee begins by examining the scholarly treatment of the biblical *hapax legomena*. Turning to the targums, Lee discovers that, of the 18 absolute hapaxes in Genesis, 10 of them share the same interpretation across all pentateuchal targums, from Targum Onqelos to the Palestinian Targums to Targum Pseudo-Jonathan, even as the targums massage the surrounding text in different ways. This high degree of similarity, Lee argues, shows that there was a targumic translation/interpretation underlying all three targum traditions from which they all drew. This common source is Proto-Onqelos.

Paul Flesher studies the way the later rabbinic world deals with the emphases of the biblical wisdom literature in his essay, "The Wisdom of the Sages: Rabbinic Rewriting of Targum Qohelet." In its earliest centuries, the rabbinic movement ignored wisdom and its questioning character. After rabbinism gained more confidence, it took up wisdom directly. Flesher's study shows how in the Targum of Qohelet the rabbis reshaped the meaning of wisdom into the rabbinic concept of Torah: to be a sage means to be a master of Torah, while the act of following wisdom was transformed into the practice of *halakah*. Qohelet's radical questioning of the meaning of life and death, of the rewards of righteousness and wickedness became a targumic treatise on how the righteous—the sages who practice Torah—are rewarded after death with eternal life in the Garden of Eden.

Eric M. Meyers and Paul V. M. Flesher
Durham and Laramie
July 1, 2008

Awakening Sleeping Texts

Reconsidering the *Letter* of Mara bar Serapion

David Rensberger

The little *Letter* of Mara bar Serapion was first published by William Cureton 150 years ago.[1] It drew some attention in the nineteenth century but very little at all in the twentieth. This is a shame, because the letter raises interesting questions for a number of historical fields, including the Roman East, early Christianity, and Hellenistic philosophy, as well as for the study of early Syriac and related Aramaic dialects.

Because it is so little known at present, I will briefly survey the letter and its problems, discuss the one work of scholarship on Mara that has appeared in recent years, and finally address some problems in the letter that are of particular interest for the study of Aramaic. I hope to make progress toward unraveling these problems here; but their definitive solution is not yet at hand.

The Letter *of Mara bar Serapion*

General Survey

The text is a letter from a man named Mara bar Serapion to his son, Serapion. Judging from what we read in the letter, Mara was a citizen of Samosata who, along with a number of his townspeople, had been taken prisoner by the Romans. He is writing what may be his last letter to his son, who is in the care of a guardian or tutor. Mara encourages Serapion to study Greek philosophy, as he himself has done ("It has been through Greek learning that I have discovered all these things"), and to make use of it to guide his life, especially now that such a difficult situation has overtaken him.[2]

---

1. Cureton, *Spicilegium Syriacum*, Syriac pp. 43–48, English pp. 70–76 (with notes on pp. 101–2).
2. All translations from the *Letter* of Mara bar Serapion are my own.

Mara's letter is thus part personal message from father to son, poignant and at times nearly passionate; and part philosophical epistle, full of advice about how to live one's life in a way that will not fall prey to passions and desires (especially for wealth) but will be conducive to tranquility and self-possession. It shows how a reasonably cultured man of Aramaic background in the early centuries C.E. might acquire some training in Hellenistic philosophy with a strongly Stoic flavor and express it in Syriac in a way that represents but by no means slavishly imitates Greek rhetorical forms and τόποι, while maintaining a relationship with Semitic wisdom traditions.

The letter offers a corrective to our usual ways of perceiving and understanding the Greco-Roman encounter with Western Asia at a couple of points.[3] We have no shortage of examples of people of Semitic backgrounds who embraced Greek culture, sometimes transforming their own heritage in the process (for example, Philo of Alexandria) and sometimes rejecting it altogether (such as Lucian from Mara's hometown, Samosata), but in any case doing their writing in Greek. Here, however, we have someone who sought to express what he had learned from the Greeks in Aramaic, producing a form of the characteristic Hellenistic fusion in the West Asian rather than the European language. This seems to me to represent an impulse that was to be formative, if not in some ways decisive, for the Syriac-speaking Christianity that was probably arising as Mara wrote. Mara did not create this impulse, but he is one of its earliest exemplars and is a non-Christian writer at that.

Second, we are used to seeing the Roman conquest of Western Asia from the Roman point of view. The primary exception is the Jewish resistance to Rome, which scholarship tends to treat as a special case, either in its own right or as a precursor to Christianity. In Mara's letter we have a non-Jewish testimony, however brief and obscure, from the side of the conquered, a document in a Semitic language expressing the grief and pain of the loss of friends and homes, while inculcating a stance of courage in the face of disaster. Mara hopes that the Romans will act justly and set him and his companions free. But if they do not (and we receive the impression that this is more likely), he is prepared to accept his death with equanimity—an equanimity learned, ironically, from the philosophers of the West.

The Text

The letter exists in one manuscript, British Library Add. 14658. It was first published in 1855, along with several other documents from the same manuscript, by William Cureton in his *Spicilegium Syriacum*.[4] It seems to be among the earliest literary texts preserved in Syriac, and it is one of the very

---

3. I use the term *Western Asia* in preference to the more familiar *Near East* or *Middle East* as a more accurate and less Eurocentric designation for the region.
4. In addition to Cureton's edition, I have also been able to consult a microfilm of the manuscript itself.

few texts of this sort that are not Christian; indeed, it may be the *only* original Syriac literary text of its age that is not Christian. The interpretation of the letter is made more difficult by the apparent carelessness of the copyist, resulting in a number of phrases whose sense is extremely difficult to puzzle out. Perhaps we should not be too hard on the scribe, however, since there is evidence to suggest that he was working under unusual conditions: it seems likely that the letter was originally composed not in the Syriac Estrangela script but in a different Aramaic script, so that it had to be transliterated and not just copied. This issue will be discussed in detail below.

The Historical Setting

The letter appears to be set in the period of the Roman expansion and conflict with the Parthian Empire in Western Asia, but it is difficult to be more precise than that. The young Serapion, of course, knew what the general circumstances were, so that his father only had to fill him in on details. The result, as usual in studying ancient documents, is that there is considerable room for ambiguity. Mara speaks of friends who left Samosata grieving for their exile and their loss of family members, whether through enforced absence or through death. He goes on to relate, obscurely, how "we" secretly set out to join this or some other group on its way to Seleucia, all of them caught up both in grief and in fear that they might "have one trouble added to another," which may mean fear that they might lose their own lives. Later, he recalls some kind of civic dispute or rumor campaign when Samosata was in its glory days. He mentions the fact that he is currently in prison and expresses his hope that the Romans will recognize the loyalty that he, and perhaps his companions, have displayed and grant him freedom and return home rather than putting him to death.

Cureton (who assumed that the letter's author was a Christian) flirted with a date late in the first century but concluded that a setting in the Roman expedition against the Parthians in the 160s C.E. was more likely. (He also speculated that Serapion might be the Serapion who became bishop of Antioch around 190, but no one has followed him in that.)[5] Friedrich Schulthess in 1897 discussed the possible datings in greater detail but held (improbably, I think) that it was internal Samosatan politics and not Roman assault that led to Mara's exile, allowing a date anywhere up to the end of the third century.[6] Fergus Millar gives serious consideration to the possibility of a date in the 70s of the first century, when the Romans first took control of Samosata and doubts that it could be later than the late second century, when this control was firmly established and defended.[7] This seems to be about as much as can be said about the letter's date; in Millar's words, "Searching in incomplete

---

5. Cureton, *Spicilegium Syriacum*, pp. xiii–xiv.
6. Schulthess, "Brief des Mara," pp. 376–80.
7. Millar, *Roman Near East*, pp. 461–62.

narrative sources for suitable contexts for enigmatic items of evidence is a notoriously treacherous process."[8] Kathleen McVey, however, has proposed that the letter is actually a Christian fiction of the fourth century.[9] I will take up this hypothesis below.[10]

Mara's Philosophy and Rhetoric

The philosophy that Mara urges on his son is of the sort that was commonplace in the early years of the Roman Empire—so common that Schulthess could describe it confidently and in detail as Stoic, while McVey can deny anything specifically Stoic about it and declare it Middle or Neo-Platonic.[11] The basic focus is on the acceptance of what life brings and on the pursuit of things of enduring worth rather than wealth or possessions. I think McVey somewhat underplays the Stoicism of the text, considering a passage such as the following:

> Let whatever you are able to acquire suffice you; and if you are able to do without possessions, then you will be called happy, for then also no one will be envious of you. Remember this, too, that nothing will disturb your life very much except possessions; that after his death no one was ever called a man of possessions. For frail humans are enthralled by desire for possessions, never realizing that one lives with one's possessions like a chance passerby. They are in a state of terror because their possessions are uncertain; for they have abandoned what is theirs, and go in search of what is not theirs.

Nevertheless, it may be that, by the probable date of this text, Stoic themes such as αὐτάρκεια and distinguishing what is and is not truly one's own had simply become the common property of philosophers. Mara does make use of one quite distinctive technical term, which I will discuss below, a term that seems to be virtually unique to himself.

The letter shows acquaintance with a number of standard Greco-Roman rhetorical τόποι, including those on exile, friendship, and wealth and love of money. At points the letter exhibits diatribal style, and of course the use of the letter form itself to give philosophical advice was well known.[12] In all this, it seems clear that Mara benefited from the education he points to with pride near the beginning of the letter: "It has been through Hellenistic learning [ܝܘܠܦܢܐ ... ܝܘܢܝܐ] that I have discovered all these things."

---

8. Ibid., p. 461.
9. McVey, "Fresh Look."
10. Two articles that appeared after this essay had been completed date the letter shortly after 73 C.E.: Ramelli, "Gesù tra i sapienti" (I am grateful to Prof. Lukas Van Rompay for bringing this article to my attention), and Merz and Tieleman, "Letter of Mara bar Sarapion" (arguing both from Mara's philosophical position and from his membership in the elite of Commagene, who were shocked at their overthrow by the Romans).
11. Schulthess, "Brief des Mara," pp. 381–91; McVey, "Fresh Look," pp. 261–62, 270.
12. Stowers, *Letter Writing*, pp. 36–40.

Nevertheless, it seems to me that Mara has not by any means abandoned the literary and intellectual traditions of Western Asia in his enthusiastic embrace of Hellenism. Unlike Lucian, and more like many Jewish and Christian writers, he apparently wanted to create a fusion that combines the best of both cultures; and he does so in Aramaic. So for instance, right before the passage on possessions just quoted, we read:

> I have seen myself that
> as prosperity increases,
>   so also adversities arise;
> and where luxuries are conveyed,
>   there also griefs collect;
> and where wealth abounds,
>   there are many bitter agonies.

Even more strikingly, in describing the grief of the exiles from Samosata, Mara writes:

> For they thought of their fathers with tears,
>   and of their mothers with sobs;
> they sorrowed for their brothers,
>   and grieved for the brides they left behind.

A few lines later, we read:

> Then our grief grew fearfully strong,
>   and our weeping at our loss became great indeed;
> and our groaning grew dense as fog,
>   and our trouble more immense than a mountain.

The rhythms and parallelism here (which I have emphasized by the use of poetic lines) sound biblical to the Western ear because they sound Semitic. Formally speaking, they could come from the book of Lamentations or from Proverbs; or they could come from *Ahiqar*. This is not the voice of Hellenistic philosophy but that of the Semitic wisdom tradition speaking in its own accents.

I do not believe this is accidental or the result of thoughtlessness. I suspect that Mara was intentionally combining two rhetorical traditions and intellectual cultures, giving pride of place to Hellenism but allowing each to enrich the other, precisely because he saw common values such as modesty, self-restraint, and acceptance of fate in both of them. One can only wonder what he might have produced had his circumstances allowed it. He seems to have had no direct influence on those who came after him. Yet, as I suggested above, his project of fusing Greek with Aramaic literary and cultural traditions may have been an early exemplar of the way that Syriac Christianity would follow. As confirmation of this, one may note the work of Bardaiṣan of Edessa, perhaps a slightly later contemporary of Mara, whose dialogue on fate follows a similar method—and is preserved in the same manuscript as Mara's letter.

A Christian Pseudepigraphon?

As I mentioned above, Kathleen McVey, in a contribution to the 1988 Symposium Syriacum, has proposed that the *Letter* of Mara bar Serapion is nothing more than a Christian fiction intended to strengthen claims about Jesus by presenting the opinions of a philosophically trained pagan writer. She does so by focusing on one of the most intriguing and puzzling features of the letter, which I have not mentioned to this point.

Twice Mara lists a series of historical examples to prove a point. The first, demonstrating that those who are successful and prosperous by the world's standards are likely to fall, names Darius, Polycrates, Achilles, Agamemnon, Priam, Archimedes, Socrates, Pythagoras, and Palamedes.[13] The second is worth quoting in its entirety.

> What else can we say, when the wise suffer violence at the hands of tyrants, their wisdom is taken prisoner by delation, and for all their enlightenment they are dispossessed with no opportunity for defense? For what benefit did the Athenians derive from putting Socrates to death? For they received the punishment for it in the form of famine and plague. Or the people of Samos from the burning of Pythagoras? For in one hour their entire country was covered with sand. Or the Jews [from the killing] of their wise king? For from that very time their sovereignty was taken away from them. God rightly exacted punishment on behalf of the wisdom of these three. For the Athenians starved to death, and the people of Samos were covered by the sea without pity, and the Jews, massacred and chased from their kingdom, are scattered through every land. Socrates, because of Plato, did not die; nor did Pythagoras, because of the statue of Hera;[14] nor did the wise king, because of the new laws he gave.

What to make of this is far from clear. The "wise king" of the Jews seems almost certainly to be Jesus. But why is he not named? Could the reference be instead to, say, Solomon, or perhaps Moses the great lawgiver?[15] Yet there is no tradition of Jewish culpability for the death of these figures. Cureton thought that Mara was writing at a time when it was simply too dangerous to speak openly of Christianity; but he assumed that the author was himself a Christian without giving any evidence for it and also assumed the now disproven concept of widespread Roman persecution of Christians from an early date.[16]

McVey's case that the letter is a Christian pseudepigraphon rests primarily on three points: that the theme of the persecution of the wise occurs in Chris-

---

13. The examples here, if not quite all Greek, are all drawn from Greek history, and Millar notes this as "a prime example of how the historical perspective of educated people in the Near East was determined by Greek tradition" (*Roman Near East*, p. 462).
14. Confusing the philosopher with a sculptor of the same name.
15. Philo treats Moses as king precisely in connection with his role as legislator: *Life of Moses* 2.2–4; *On Rewards and Punishments* 53–55.
16. Cureton, *Spicilegium Syriacum*, pp. xiii–xiv; against Cureton, see McVey, "Fresh Look," p. 271.

tian apologetic beginning in the second century, and is found in Syriac in Aphrahat; that the role of Jesus as lawgiver was central in early Christian apologetic; and that the destruction of Jerusalem and the dispersion of the Jews became a major theme of anti-Jewish polemic in the fourth century.[17] To these she adds that "Mara inveighs against the exposure of unwanted children and expresses bemused admiration for 'those who raise children not their own,'" the critique of exposure being a well-known theme of Christian apologetic.[18] She also suggests the *Sibylline Oracles* and the insertion of an admiring reference to Jesus into the works of Josephus as parallels to the pseudepigraphic practice that she posits for "Mara," that of presenting praise of Jesus by a supposedly pagan, and well educated, writer.[19]

On the whole, however, I do not believe that McVey has made her case. The persecution of the wise is, as McVey herself shows, a widespread theme in pagan and Jewish philosophy, Stoic and otherwise.[20] It is hardly distinctive of Christian apologetic. With regard to exposure, Mara does not "inveigh against" it at all. The context is as follows.

> What then can we say of the delusion that makes its home in the world and leads it so laboriously along, so that as [the world] sways like a reed in the wind we are shaken back and forth with it? For I am astonished at the many who expose their children, and I am amazed at the others who bring up children who are not their own. There are people who acquire wealth by labor; and yet I am amazed at the others who come into possession of what is not their own. Consider then, and see that we are going on a journey of delusion.

The point is the folly of relying on "possessions" like wealth or even family, when we have no way of making them truly our own. Exposure of children is not criticized any more than adoption is admired.

The central issue is what Mara says about Jesus (assuming that the reference really is to him) and the Jews. These statements certainly seem to have a Christian origin; but do they point with certainty to a Christian author in the fourth century? There are really two questions here: must the statements come from the fourth century; and do they require that the letter's author be a Christian (and so a pseudepigrapher), or could they come from a non-Christian writer who had Christian informants?

McVey herself shows, with examples from Origen and Justin Martyr, that Christian claims that the Jews lost their homeland and autonomy in 70 C.E. as divine retribution for the rejection of Jesus were known already in the second century.[21] We may add Tertullian, who says of the Jews, "Scattered

---

17. Ibid., pp. 263–71, summarized on p. 271.
18. Ibid., p. 271.
19. Ibid., p. 272. There she also considers and rejects the possibility that the letter is simply a school exercise.
20. Ibid., pp. 264–65.
21. Ibid., p. 268, citing Origen, *De principiis* 4.1.3; Justin, *1 Apol.* 53.2–3. Indeed, a claim that Jewish sovereignty was destroyed on account of this rejection appears as early as the Gospel of Matthew (Matt 22:7, cited by McVey, p. 268).

abroad, a race of wanderers, exiles from their own land and clime, they roam over the whole world without either a human or a heavenly king" (*Apol.* 21), words very close to those of Mara. Tertullian goes so far as to claim that Judea only came under Roman rule because of its rejection of Christ (*Apol.* 26).[22]

McVey claims that it was only in the fourth century that Jewish dispersion and loss of autonomy became *central* to Christian polemic. But why does this need to have been *central* for Mara to have heard of it in the second century, not far from the time of Justin, Tertullian, and Origen? Indeed, by the fourth century Mara's assertions would seem quite tame if measured against the railings of Ephrem, John Chrysostom, and others.[23] It seems at least as reasonable to suppose that the letter's author is a pagan who has some vague and incomplete information about Jews derived ultimately from Christian propaganda, which he has used without a great deal of discernment. He knows there are Jews who not only have lost their sovereignty but are dispersed around the world, and he has heard that they are in these circumstances because of their treatment of a "wise king" they once had.[24] As for the "wise king" himself, however, Mara seems not even to know his name. Considering the inadequacy of his knowledge about even Pythagoras, it seems more likely that he leaves the king anonymous because of lack of information than that this is some kind of ruse.

In fact McVey never really explains this failure to name the "wise king," saying only that "a Christian is inherently more likely to portray Jesus as the 'wise king' of the Jews who 'thanks to the new laws he made is not dead.'"[25] But is that inherently likely? Christians may have described Jesus as a lawgiver and king, but it seems far from likely to me that that is how a Christian writer, even when writing in the name of a pagan philosopher, would speak of Jesus' *immortality*. Taking McVey's own examples, the Christian interpolations in the *Sibylline Oracles*, despite the general allusiveness of their form, refer to Jesus by such titles as "Christ, the Son of the immortal, most high God" (1.331; compare 6.1–2); "the heavenly Son of God" (1.364); and "Logos with the Father and the Holy Spirit" (7.69), not to mention the acrostic spelling out ΙΗΣΟΥΣ ΧΡΕΙΣΤΟΣ ΘΕΟΥ ΥΙΟΣ ΣΩΤΗΡ ΣΤΑΥΡΟΣ in 8.217–250. With regard to his immortality, they speak explicitly of his resurrection and ascension (1.379–381; 8.313–314).[26]

As for the Josephus interpolation (at *Ant.* 18.63–64), its precise extent is debated, but at least the following seems likely to have been added with ref-

---

22. The translation is that of S. Thelwall in *ANF* 3:34.
23. For Ephrem, see Shepardson, *In the Service of Orthodoxy*; idem, "Anti-Jewish Rhetoric"; idem, "Exchanging Reed for Reed." For others, see, for example, Simon, *Verus Israel*, pp. 212–23.
24. The text does not actually even speak of their killing the wise king, which is only inferred from the context with its references to Socrates and Pythagoras.
25. McVey, "Fresh Look," p. 271.
26. All citations and translations are from Treu, "Christian Sibyllines."

erence to Jesus: "if indeed one may call him a man"; "this man was the Messiah"; and "for he appeared to them on the third day alive again." We may also add the *Acts of Pilate*, perhaps of fourth-century date in something like their present form, but apparently alluded to in some early form already by Tertullian (*Apol.* 21). In this text, Pilate writes a letter to the Emperor in which he reports the resurrection of Jesus.[27] These examples are enough to show that Christian pseudepigrapha attributed to non-Christians consistently made open reference to the name and titles of Jesus and to his resurrection. This is completely different from the murky allusion in Mara's letter and from the way Mara grounds the immortality of the "wise king" in the laws that he gave.

In general, it seems to me that there is just too little in this letter that points to a Christian fiction. Why would a Christian pseudepigrapher put so much effort into detailing a nonexistent historical setting and then obscure the details of the main point, including even the name of Jesus—as if acknowledging that his reputation was less than the reputations of Socrates and Pythagoras? While Mara's philosophical denunciation of wealth might suit an ascetic Christianity well enough, we might also expect a denunciation of sexual desire, of which there is none. Lastly, Mara's attitude toward death is that of a pagan influenced by Stoicism: "if the decision has fallen in favor of what must be, we will receive nothing more than the peaceful death that is laid up for us." There is neither hope for immortality nor regret that immortality cannot be obtained.

The *Letter* of Mara bar Serapion simply does not work as a Christian pseudepigraphon of the fourth century (or earlier). I believe that it must be accepted as what it appears to be: the work of a Syriac-speaking pagan with some philosophical education who happens to have heard something about the Christian opinion concerning the situation of the Jews and has assimilated it into his own system of thought without completely understanding it (compare his egregious confusion about Pythagoras). This "something" may well be part of the reason for its preservation in a manuscript containing primarily Christian translations of and commentaries on Greek philosophical works, but it does not make the letter a Christian work. In the absence of other evidence for a later date, there seems no adequate reason not to accept its apparent date in the second century.

Aramaic Issues in the Letter *of Mara bar Serapion*

Several of the issues associated with this letter are of particular interest to students of Aramaic. Here I will discuss the original script of the text, several linguistic matters, and one particular technical term.

---

27. Scheidweiler, "Gospel of Nicodemus"; for the letter, see p. 527.

Original Script

Perhaps the oddest thing in this unusual little text is something that has been noticed in previous scholarship but never adequately accounted for, an item that may be a significant clue to the date and origin of the letter. The sole manuscript contains what must be one of the worst scribal errors ever committed. In column 2 of folio 184r, we find the following reading:

ܘܡܠܟ ܥܠ ܚܒܪܚ ܟܠܢܫ

Leaving out the corrupt third word, this means, "Everyone ridicules...." The corrupt word should, of course, read ܚܒܪܗ, "his neighbor"; but the final *he*, representing the third-person masculine-singular possessive suffix ("his"), has been replaced by a *ḥet*, resulting in a meaningless collocation of letters. A confusion between these two letters, however, is simply not possible in Syriac Estrangela script. Cureton took note of this fact but did not pursue the obvious conclusion, that the text must at some point have had a Vorlage in some other Aramaic script.[28] In addition, we find another confusion that is common enough in other Aramaic scripts but not in Estrangela, confusion between *waw* and *yod*: in fol. 183r, col. 1, ܕܒܡܪܕܝܬܐ ܗܘ ܕܛܘܥܝܝ ܡܗܠܟܝܢܢ ("that we walk in instruction of delusion") is certainly an error for ܕܒܐܘܪܚܐ ܕܛܘܥܝܝ ܗܘ ܡܗܠܟܝܢܢ ("that we walk on a journey of delusion").

Even in the earliest preserved Estrangela texts, the difference between ܘ and ܝ, let alone between ܚ and ܗ, is great enough that confusion between them is really not feasible.[29] Granted the incredible inattentiveness of a copyist who could write the meaningless ܚܒܪܚ for ܚܒܪܗ, it is nonetheless clear that he must have been working from a non-Estrangela archetype, i.e., one written using something more like the "square" script familiar from Jewish Aramaic texts. Unfortunately, there is no evidence of Syriac texts ever having been written in such a script.

An interesting light is thrown on this issue by Joseph Naveh's hypothesis regarding the development of Estrangela. He postulates a script used in the eastern Aramaic region in the last three centuries B.C.E. in two varieties, formal and cursive. Hatran and Mandaic scripts developed from the formal variety, while Palmyrene and Syriac developed from the cursive. Four inscriptions from the first centuries B.C.E. and C.E. seem to be in a script that, according to Naveh, is not yet either Palmyrene or Estrangela, which he believes to be a survival of the "Seleucid Aramaic" ancestor to both those scripts.[30] A few samples of cursive Palmyrene may suggest that confusion

---

28. Cureton, *Spicilegium Syriacum*, p. 101. Schulthess made the correction in his translation ("Brief des Mara," p. 372) but offered no comment.

29. In Drijvers and Healey, *Old Syriac Inscriptions*, note the following: pls. 20, 27, 40, 58; and the table of letter forms on pp. 5–10.

30. Naveh, *Early History of the Alphabet*, pp. 149–53. Naveh is following in part an idea of Segal, "Some Syriac Inscriptions," pp. 31–34. For one of the inscriptions, see Drijvers and Healey, *Old Syriac Inscriptions*, pp. 157–59, and pl. 46.

between ה and ח (and between ו and י) would have been possible in such a script.[31] Whether or not one accepts Naveh's posited "Seleucid Aramaic" script, the existence of a script or scripts standing between Palmyrene and Estrangela in which early Syriac texts could have been written seems at least plausible. Perhaps, then, the original autograph of Mara's letter was written in such a script, and the letter was subsequently transcribed into Estrangela. In the course of the transcription, errors occurred owing to the similarity of certain letters in the autograph. Conceivably these errors included not only the confusions noted above but others not so readily evident.

In this discussion, I have presumed that the *language* of the letter was always Syriac, but this raises another interesting question. Though its language has been identified as Syriac ever since the letter's discovery and publication, the text emanates from Samosata and not Edessa. Traditionally, however, Syriac has been defined as the dialect of Aramaic that originated in Edessa and then became the common literary language of Aramaic-speaking Eastern Christianity. Then is the Aramaic of second-century Samosata Syriac? The distance between the two cities is only 40 kilometers or so (25–30 miles). Is this close enough geographically to allow us to presuppose linguistic identity? Or should the difference in script suggested by the evidence of this one text lead us to consider the possibility of a different dialect as well? Variations in dialect as well as script might perhaps account for some of the text's other difficulties. The question whether Mara's Aramaic should be considered Syriac will have to await a detailed linguistic study. For present purposes, I will continue to call it Syriac, but it might be best to think of this as a judgment not yet fully validated.

If the letter was written in a Palmyrene-like script, might this indicate that Mara picked up some of his education in Palmyra? That would be possible, of course, but there is hardly enough evidence here even to suggest it. Indeed, the entire preceding discussion may seem quite a lot to hang on one or two textual corruptions. However, *some* solution to the problem of the bizarre scribal confusion between ܝ and ܣ must be advanced, and since it cannot be explained as an inner-Estrangela mistake, a Vorlage in a non-Estrangela script seems the most reasonable hypothesis, though it then raises other questions about linguistic and intellectual context.

Linguistic Issues

The language of the letter is Syriac, but there are several specific points worth noting. Apart from proper names, there are only a few Greek words. Early on, when Mara has indicated his indebtedness to Hellenistic learning and is encouraging Serapion to follow the same course, we find ܐܣܟܡܐ (σχῆμα), ܐܓܘܢ (ἀγών), and ܦܝܠܣܘܦܘܬܐ (φιλοσοφία). In the introduction to

---

31. See the table in Segal, "Some Syriac Inscriptions," p. 32; and Starcky, "Inscriptions archaïques," pl. 1, esp. inscriptions B and D (p. 510), and the table in fig. 1, p. 521.

the examples of martyred philosophers, Mara uses ܛܪܘܢܐ (τύραννος); and ܩܐܪܣܐ (καιρός) is used elsewhere in the sense "battle." All in all, this is not much for someone who claims to have learned everything he knows from the Greeks, and it may indicate both Mara's purpose of expressing Greek wisdom in Syriac and a fairly early date for the letter. Another indication of early date may be the fact that the absolute state still seems to be a living feature of the language, employed in uses that are not simply "frozen," e.g., ܠܙܒܢ ܙܥܘܪ ("for a little while"); ܛܐܒܐ ܕܚܒܪܝܗܘܢ ("news of their comrades"); ܡܕܡ ܒܝܫ ("something bad").³²

One usage seems to be distinctive of Mara, whether as a dialectal variant or just as a matter of personal style. Three times he introduces a short clause with -ܕ and then completes the -ܕ not with the expected imperfect tense verb but with an infinitive with prefixed -ܠ:

ܠܗܠܝܢ ܓܝܪ ܐܬܝܠܕܘ ܒܢܝܢܫܐ ܕܠܣܘܓܦܢܐ ܕܙܒܢܐ ܠܡܥܪܥ
ܐܢ ܨܒܝܬ ܕܬܣܬܟܠ ܟܠ ܡܕܡ ܠܡܚܟܡܘ
ܘܐܢ ܡܨܐ ܐܢܬ ܕܕܠܐ ܩܢܝܢ ܠܡܗܘܐ

These expressions may be translated (overly literally, to demonstrate the point at issue):

> For to these things people are born, <u>that</u> the disasters of time <u>to</u> encounter
> If you wish <u>that to</u> understand things thoroughly
> And if you are able <u>that to</u> do without possessions

In each of these cases, one would have looked for a finite verb rather than the infinitive: "that they may encounter"; "that you may understand"; "that you may do." We might consider these copyist's errors or slips of the pen on Mara's own part, but since there are three of them this seems unlikely. Evidently this is habitual with Mara, but it is simply not grammatical in Syriac.³³ Is it a peculiarity of his own, or does it belong to the particular dialect of Syriac that he spoke? Unless it turns up elsewhere, it may be Mara's own little quirk; but it is so ungrammatical that it may be impossible to be sure of its origin.

Technical Terminology: "Time" as "Fate"

Mara apparently uses the commonplace word ܙܒܢܐ, "time," in a distinctive way as a technical term in his philosophy. This use has been a matter of dispute, so let me briefly lay out the evidence.

In several instances Mara uses the word in its ordinary sense, "time."

---

32. Schulthess ("Brief des Mara," p. 368 n. 8) wanted to make the second phrase either ܛܐܒܐ ܕܚܒܪܝܗܘܢ or ܛܐܒ ܚܒܪܝܗܘܢ, i.e., either determined state plus -ܕ or construct without -ܕ, to accord with developed Syriac idiom, which no longer used the absolute plus -ܕ in this way.

33. Nöldeke, *Kurzgefasste syrische Grammatik*, p. 285 (§364B), describes the usage of -ܠ ܐܝܬ followed by an infinitive to express purpose, etc. But this is neither the form nor the usage here.

ܙܒܢ ܩܠܝܠ, "for a short time"
ܒܟܠܙܒܢ, "at all times"
ܐܘܕܝܢ ܕܝܢ ܒܙܒܢ, "we acknowledged at the time"

Once, Mara uses ܙܒܢܐ as an allusion to death: ܒܙܒܢܐ ... ܕܐܟܚܕܐ ܠܚܕ ܙܒܢܐ, "that we are all equally ... brought to the same time." Elsewhere, however, we find ܙܒܢܐ treated as something that brings misfortune.

> things in the world dissolve, ܕܙܒܢܐ ܡܫܚܠܦܘܬܐ ܓܝܪ ܐܢܝܢ ܣܘܥܪܢܐ, "for they are simply the ups and downs of the times"
> ܕܙܒܢܐ ܣܘܪܚܢܘܗܝ, "the disasters of time"
> ܒܙܒܢܐ ܡܨܛܪܝܢ ܐܝܟܢܐ, "and as if complaining against time"

"Complaining against time" in this last expression seems like an odd idea, and it begins to seem that what is really meant is not time but *fate*. And fate clearly seems to be the meaning in half a dozen other places in the letter, of which I will give just two examples. In the first instance, Mara offers his son advice for occasions when something bad happens to him:

> ܠܐ ܬܬܚܝܒ ܒܪܢܫܐ ܘܠܐ ܬܪܓܙ ܥܠ ܐܠܗܐ ܘܠܐ ܥܠ ܙܒܢܟ ܬܬܚܡܬ

Do not lay the blame on a person, do not be angry at God, do not rail against your time/fate.

For the second instance, it will be worthwhile translating the entire context. At the end of the text, after the conclusion of the letter itself, we find a nice little philosophical anecdote or χρεῖα, what form critics of the New Testament Gospels call a "pronouncement story" or "apophthegm."

> One of his friends asked Mara bar Serapion while fettered next to him, "On your life, Mara, tell me what seems funny to you, that you're laughing!" Mara replied, "I am laughing at time/fate, which has repaid me evil though it owed me none."

Schulthess recognized the sense "fate" in these passages and used this as evidence that Mara was a Stoic.[34] McVey, on the other hand, points out that such a use of ܙܒܢܐ is "lexically unattested," citing Brockelmann's *Lexicon Syriacum*.[35] It may not be entirely unattested, however. In the Syriac *Acts of Judas Thomas*, chap. 8, we find the expression ܐܠܘ ܙܒܢܐ ܠܐ ܚܒܠܢܝ. William Wright rendered this, "if fate had not ruined me."[36] The Greek version of these apocryphal acts (chap. 99) apparently found this difficult to render,

---

34. Schulthess, "Brief des Mara," p. 383.

35. McVey, "Fresh Look," p. 262. Likewise Payne Smith, *Thesaurus Syriacus*, vol. 1, cols. 1077–78, lists no meaning "fate" for ܙܒܢܐ, not even in the quotations from Syriac lexicographers.

36. Syriac in Wright, ed., *Apocryphal Acts*, 1:266; English translation, ibid., 2:231. (I am indebted to Lukas Van Rompay for this reference.) Paul Bedjan, who compared Sachau MS 222 with Wright's edition based on British Library MS Add. 14,645, has the same reading (*Acta Martyrum*, p. 101).

one group of manuscripts reading ἡ ἐμὴ κακηγορία κατέστρεψέν με, "my slander overthrew me," and another omitting the expression altogether.³⁷

Thus Mara may not be absolutely the only Syriac writer to have used ܙܒܢܐ to mean "fate." And however unusual this use of ܙܒܢܐ may be, this is certainly Mara's meaning. Even if one translated ܙܒܢܐ consistently as "time" throughout the letter, eventually one would reach the point where "time" was being used in English to mean "fate." Certainly the *attitude* toward "time" that Mara inculcates is very much that which Hellenistic philosophers, especially Stoics, inculcated toward fate. ܙܒܢܐ may bring disasters, but it cannot touch what is essential to individuals who are wise. Its perversities are to be borne calmly and without complaint, as the inevitable concomitants of human life.³⁸

It is not hard to see the semantic development from time (as that which brings about change in human life) to fate (as the cause of human circumstances, especially bad ones). Exactly how and why Mara developed this usage, however, is another of the letter's difficult puzzles. It does not seem to be one of the things he learned from his study of Hellenistic philosophy. Greek lexica do not list a meaning "fate" under either χρόνος or καιρός, and F. E. Peters's discussion of the various ways of understanding χρόνος in Greek philosophy makes no mention of an identification or any other type of relationship between time and fate.³⁹

Interestingly, however, there is a distinct parallel to be found in pre-Islamic Arabic poetry. There *zamān* (cognate with ܙܒܢܐ) and *dahr*, both meaning "time," were often used in a sense similar to "fate," and especially for ill fate or misfortune, which is exactly how Mara uses ܙܒܢܐ.⁴⁰ It is worth noting also that there seems to have been a pre-Islamic Arab cult of *'Aud*, "time," but also "fate," perhaps alongside that of *Jadd*, "fortune, fate" (cognate with Aramaic גדא).⁴¹ The connection of time with fate in this context was such that Muhammad even forbade his followers to revile *dahr*, as being the same as reviling God.⁴² At first glance, this is strikingly reminiscent of Mara's admonition to his son not to revile persons, God, or ܙܒܢܐ/fate when something bad happens. Indeed, Schulthess held that for Mara fate and deity are

---

37. Maximilian Bonnet suggested reading κακομοιρία, "ill fate," for κακηγορία (*Acta Philippi et Acta Thomae*, p. 211).

38. Ramelli, "Gesù tra i sapienti," translates ܙܒܢܐ as "*destino*" (once "*sorte*") and locates Mara specifically in a neo-Stoic intellectual environment, with many connections to Roman Stoics.

39. E.g., LSJ 2008-9 (χρόνος), pp. 859-60 (καιρός); Peters, *Greek Philosophical Terms*, pp. 30-33.

40. Nöldeke, "Arabs," pp. 661-62 (I am indebted to Sami Aydin for this reference, and for the reference to Watt in n. 42 below); see also Lane, *Arabic-English Lexicon*, 3:923.

41. Nöldeke, "Arabs," p. 662.

42. Lane, *Arabic-English Lexicon*, 3:923; Watt, "Dahr."

one and the same, citing passages from Seneca to the same effect.[43] This is not quite correct, however. Mara overwhelmingly refers the giving of good things to ܐܠܗܐ and of bad things to ܙܒܢܐ. Time/fate is the cause of struggles, evils, and miseries, including specifically the misfortunes of Mara and his friends. God is the source of the good character of the wise and provides them with help. Indeed, immediately after Mara urges on Serapion the kind of mind-set that does not revile God or fate, God is said to be the giver of precisely this frame of mind. Thus it is not piety that causes Mara to counsel against reviling God or fate, since he does not fully identify the two. Rather, it is the aim, typical of Hellenistic philosophy, of attaining an imperturbable disposition in the face of life's ordeals. One may, however, suppose a pious motivation for the distinction that Mara makes between ܐܠܗܐ as beneficent and ܙܒܢܐ as bringing woes.

There is one other possibly relevant cultural domain in which time and fate were identified, and that is Zervanite Zoroastrianism. Zurvān, the primal and supreme deity, is both time (*zamān*, often used for Zurvān) and fate. In this theology, the finite universe and finite time are born from the infinite (Zurvān being both infinite and finite time), and in the finite world Zurvān is manifested as fate. "Zurvān of the long dominion," finite time, is essentially identical with fate.[44] Mara's identification of time with fate (using ܙܒܢܐ, which may be derived from *zurvān/zamān*) seems intriguingly similar. However, ܙܒܢܐ is not personal for Mara and shows no signs of being a deity, nor is there anything resembling the Zervanite mythology or theology in this letter. Thus there is no reason to think of a direct connection with Zervanism.

Nevertheless, Mara's usage does seem to be a further, if quite minor, attestation of an identification of time and fate found in multiple cultural and religious contexts in Western Asia in the first few centuries C.E. This reminds us once again that, though Mara may parade his Greek learning, he is very far from rejecting his own West Asian religious and cultural heritage. Rather, he apparently seeks a fusion of the two. In the case of time and fate, Mara seems to apply a Hellenistic attitude toward fate to a concept of it (or at least a terminology for it) that is attested not in Hellenic or Hellenized sources but in Arabia and Persia.

The word ܙܒܢܐ is thus a technical term for "fate" for Mara, even though it seems to be so for almost no one else writing in Syriac. This is an instance in which one needs to be guided more by context than by etymology and standard usage. Mara clearly expects Serapion to understand him; but Serapion was his son and presumably familiar with his idiom. It is somewhat more surprising that he is pictured using the term when speaking to his fellow-prisoners in the little anecdote with which the text ends. Evidently the story

43. Schulthess, "Brief des Mara," p. 383.
44. Zaehner, *Zurvan*, pp. 55–59, 229, 254–55, 265–66.

portrays Mara as finding a teachable moment there and not hesitating to use his own distinctive vocabulary.

It may be that Mara, working at the development of an Aramaic means of expressing Hellenistic philosophical ideas, simply found no distinctive word readily available to express the concept of "fate" as he understood it. Later Syriac writers would turn to words having to do with apportioning (ܚܠܩܐ) or with cutting or decreeing (ܓܙܪ, ܚܬܝܪ). These suggest a rather personalized conception of fate, as does the mythologized Iranian Zurvān. By using ܙܒܢܐ without deifying it, Mara pictured fate in more impersonal terms, as simply the inevitable working of time on human lives. In this respect, it is interesting that he did not choose ܓܕܐ, both "fortune" and the god of fortune, which would have corresponded admirably to the Greek τύχη. By using ܙܒܢܐ Mara seems deliberately to seek an impersonal and nondeified terminology for fate. In this way, he was able to draw a distinction between ܙܒܢܐ as bringer of ills and God as source of benefits.

Conclusion

Mara bar Serapion of Samosata seems to have been a man of Hellenized and Romanizing Western Asia who had immersed himself in a philosophy based strongly on Stoicism but without abandoning or obliterating his grounding in traditional West Asian thought. A couple of curious features of his letter—a copyist's error suggesting a non-Estrangela Vorlage, the use of ܙܒܢܐ to mean "fate"—may point in the direction of Palmyra, with its mixture of Aramaic and Arabic populations, as significant for Mara. The connection of Paul of Samosata, perhaps a century after Mara's time, with the royal house of Palmyra is one indicator of links between the two cities. It seems possible that Mara deliberately sought to create a fusion of Hellenistic and West Asian philosophies to be expressed in Syriac. His acquaintance with Christianity must have been slender; but his one surviving writing suggests that Christian writers in Syriac were not the only ones in that cultural milieu who were active in creating such a fusion. On the other hand, Mara's use of "time" in a technical sense that was not taken up by later Christian philosophers and theologians implies either that they were unaware of his work or that they did not consider it useful, at least in this respect.

However, the presence of Mara's letter in the British Library manuscript Add. 14,658 may indicate that an early Syriac compiler found in Mara something akin to the Christian philosophical endeavor. William Wright dated this manuscript to the seventh century.[45] Of the first 13 works in what is preserved of the manuscript, at least 9 are original works or translations from the Greek certainly or probably made by Sergius of Resh ʿAina (sixth century), many of them dedicated to his friend, the bishop Theodore. The first 10 works are

---

45. Wright, *Catalogue of Syriac Manuscripts*, 3:1154.

largely Aristotelian; then come 4 works relating to astrology (including two Bardaiṣanite tracts, the *Book of the Laws of Countries* and a list of names of the signs of the zodiac). The remaining 12 works are a mixture of philosophical works (Socratic, Platonic, Pythagorean, and others) and Christian apologies (by Ambrose and Pseudo-Melito).[46] The philosophical works in the manuscript as a whole are mainly technical writings having to do with matters of logic and science; but near the end of what is preserved, there are some collections of ethical maxims.[47] Thus the manuscript seems to consist of a collection of Sergius's writings and translations for Theodore, supplemented by works on related topics, and concluding with something of a miscellany. The Christian works (Bardaiṣan, Ambrose, and Pseudo-Melito) all have a philosophical bent, dealing with fate and the falsity of pagan religions.

We seem to have here a collection of works intended for Syriac-speaking Christians studying Greek philosophy. Mara's letter may have been included for a variety of reasons: because it encourages philosophical study and Greek learning as such, because of the Stoic-tinged ethical advice it offers, because of what it says about acceptance of fate, because it appears to mention Jesus. Perhaps as important as any of these may be its character as a presentation in Syriac of the fruits of an attempt at merging Hellenistic and traditional West Asian wisdom.[48]

46. The intended identity of this Ambrose is uncertain; it is not Ambrose of Milan. In Greek, the apology is falsely attributed to Justin Martyr (*Oratio ad Gentiles*).
47. Wright, *Catalogue of Syriac Manuscripts*, 3:1154–60.
48. A critical edition and translation of the *Letter* of Mara bar Serapion with interpretative essays on its historical, philosophical, linguistic, literary, and religious contexts and implications is in preparation by Annette Merz, David Rensberger, and Teun Tieleman and is anticipated to appear in 2010.

Bibliography

Bedjan, P. *Acta Martyrum et Sanctorum Syriace*. Vol. 3. Paris: Harrassowitz, 1892. Repr., Hildesheim: Olms, 1968.

Bonnet, M., ed. *Acta Philippi et Acta Thomae, accedunt Acta Barnabae*. Vol. 2 of part 2 of *Acta Apostolorum Apocrypha*. Edited by R. A. Lipsius and M. Bonnet. Hildesheim: Olms, 1903. Repr., Darmstadt: Wissenschaftliche Buchgesellschaft, 1959.

Cureton, W., ed. and trans. *Spicilegium Syriacum: Containing Remains of Bardesan, Meliton, Ambrose, and Mara Bar Serapion*. London: Rivingtons, 1855.

Drijvers, H. J. W., and J. F. Healey, eds. and trans. *The Old Syriac Inscriptions of Edessa and Osrhoene: Texts, Translations and Commentary*. Handbuch der Orientalistik: Der Nahe und Mittlere Osten. Leiden: Brill, 1999.

Lane, E. W. *An Arabic-English Lexicon*. Edited by S. Lane-Poole. London: Williams and Norgate, 1863.

McVey, K. E. "A Fresh Look at the Letter of Mara Bar Sarapion to His Son." Pp. 257–72 in V *Symposium Syriacum 1988 Katholieke Universiteit, Leuven, 29–31 Août*

1988. Edited by René Lavenant. Orientalia Christiana Analecta 236. Rome: Pontificium Institutum Studiorum Orientalium, 1990.
Merz, A., D. Rensberger, and T. Tieleman, eds. Mara Bar Serapion, A Letter to His Son. Sapere 17. Tübingen: Mohr Siebeck, 2010.
Merz, A., and T. Tieleman. "The Letter of Mara bar Sarapion: Some Comments on Its Philosophical and Historical Context." Pp. 107–33 in Empsychoi Logoi—Religious Innovations in Antiquity: Studies in Honour of Pieter Willem van der Horst. Edited by A. Houtman, A. de Jong, and M. Misset-van de Weg. Leiden: Brill, 2008.
Millar, F. The Roman Near East, 31 BC–AD 337. Cambridge: Harvard University Press, 1993.
Naveh, J. Early History of the Alphabet: An Introduction to West Semitic Epigraphy and Palaeography. 2nd rev. ed. Jerusalem: Magnes, 1987.
Nöldeke, T. "Arabs (Ancient)." Pp. 659–73 in vol. 1. of Encyclopaedia of Religion and Ethics. Edited by James Hastings, in collaboration with John A. Selbie and Louis H. Gray. Edinburgh: T. & T. Clark, 1926. Repr., New York: Scribner's, 1962.
———. Kurzgefasste syrische Grammatik. 2nd rev. ed. Leipzig: Tauchnitz, 1898. Repr., Darmstadt: Wissenschaftliche Buchgesellschaft, 1966.
Payne Smith, R. Thesaurus syriacus. Oxford: Clarendon, 1879–1901.
Peters, F. E. Greek Philosophical Terms: A Historical Lexicon. New York: New York University Press, 1967.
Ramelli, I. "Gesù tra i sapienti greci perseguitati ingiustamente in un antico documento filosofico pagano di lingua siriaca." Rivista di Filosofia Neoscolastica 97 (2005) 545–70.
Scheidweiler, F. "The Gospel of Nicodemus, Acts of Pilate and Christ's Descent into Hell." Pp. 501–36 in vol. 1 of New Testament Apocrypha. Rev. ed. Edited by Wilhelm Schneemelcher. Translated by R. M. Wilson. Louisville, KY: Westminster/John Knox Press, 1991.
Schulthess, F. "Der Brief des Mara bar Sarapion (Spicilegium Syriacum ed. Cureton p. 43 ff.): Ein Beitrag zur Geschichte der syrischen Literatur." Zeitschrift der Deutschen Morgenländischen Gesellschaft 51 (1897) 365–91.
Segal, J. B. "Some Syriac Inscriptions of the 2nd–3rd Century A.D." Bulletin of the School of Oriental and African Studies 16 (1954) 13–36.
Shepardson, C. C. "Anti-Jewish Rhetoric and Intra-Christian Conflict in the Sermons of Ephrem Syrus." Pp. 502–7 in Papers Presented at the Thirteenth International Conference on Patristic Studies Held in Oxford, 1999. Edited by M. F. Miles and E. J. Yarnold. Studia Patristica 35. Leuven: Peeters, 2001.
———. "'Exchanging Reed for Reed': Mapping Contemporary Heretics onto Biblical Jews in Ephrem's Hymns on Faith." Hugoye 5 (2002) 15–33.
———. In the Service of Orthodoxy: Anti-Jewish Language and Intra-Christian Conflict in the Writings of Ephrem the Syrian. Ph.D. dissertation, Duke University, 2003.
Simon, M. Verus Israel: A Study of the Relations between Christians and Jews in the Roman Empire (135–425). Translated by H. McKeating. Littman Library of Jewish Civilization. Oxford: Oxford University Press, 1986.
Starcky, J. "Inscriptions archaïques de Palmyre." Pp. 509–28 in vol. 2 of Studi orientalistici in onore di Giorgio Levi Della Vida. Pubblicazioni Dell'Istituto per l'Oriente 52. Rome: Istituto per l'Oriente, 1956.

Stowers, S. K. *Letter Writing in Greco-Roman Antiquity.* Library of Early Christianity. Philadelphia: Westminster, 1986.

Treu, U. "Christian Sibyllines." Pp. 652–85 in vol. 2 of *New Testament Apocrypha.* Rev. ed. Edited by Wilhelm Schneemelcher. Translated by R. M. Wilson. Louisville, KY: Westminster/John Knox Press, 1991.

Watt, W. M. "Dahr." Pp. 94–95 in *The Encyclopaedia of Islam, New Edition.* Edited by B. Lewis, C. Pellat, and J. Schacht. Leiden: Brill, 1965.

Wright, W. *Catalogue of the Syriac Manuscripts in the British Museum Acquired since the Year 1838.* London: British Museum, 1870–72.

———, ed. and trans. *Apocryphal Acts of the Apostles.* London: Williams and Norgate, 1871.

Zaehner, R. C. *Zurvan: A Zoroastrian Dilemma.* Oxford: Clarendon, 1955.

"Transgressive":
Meaning and Implications of ܥܘܠ ('wl') in Jewish Syriac Text and Translation

SIGRID PETERSON

I

The word ܥܘܠ occurs unusually frequently in several places in Syriac literature.[1] Two of these are discussed in the present paper. The first is in the anonymous *memra* posthumously published by William E. Barnes in 1895. This text is now known as *Sixth Maccabees* (6 *Macc.*), and the word ܥܘܠ occurs 17 times in it. The other place is in the Syriac version of the *Psalms of Solomon*, in which ܥܘܠ occurs 26 times (not counting variations such as ܥܘܠܬܐ).[2] This paper compares implications of previous understandings and English translations of the word and proposes that this particular Syriac word has a meaning that has not been properly translated until now.

The comparison necessarily focuses on Trafton's English translation of ܥܘܠ as "lawless," in the *Psalms of Solomon*. Otherwise, let me say here that his edition of the *Psalms of Solomon* is in general informative and exemplary. In his examination of the correspondence of the Syriac version of the *Psalms of Solomon (Pss. Sol.)* to the Greek version, which also includes a translation,

---

Author's note: I coined the term *Jewish Syriac* in response to the question of Ann Matter and Robert Kraft; they kept asking me, "What religion is this text?"—referring to what is now *Sixth Maccabees*. As I apply the term, it encompasses the Peshitta Old Testament, the Syriac translation of *Psalms of Solomon*, and the original Syriac compositions *Sixth* and *Seventh Maccabees*. Other Jewish pseudepigrapha known from Syriac would also be included. The *Pseudo-Clementines* would not belong. There is an extensive discussion of this classification in my dissertation, *Martha Shamoni*.

1. See the online entries for "ܥܘܠ3" and "ܥܘܠ2" in the CAL for guidance on pronunciation.

2. For the *Psalms of Solomon*, see Trafton, *Syriac Version*. For the Syriac text of what is now called *Sixth Maccabees*, see Bensly, "Memra." An annotated English translation of *Sixth Maccabees* that I have prepared will appear in Bauckham and Davila, eds., *More Old Testament Pseudepigrapha*.

23

Trafton almost always translated ܥܘܠܐ as "lawless" or "lawlessness." This meaning is accorded minor importance in the *Compendious Syriac Dictionary* of Jessie Payne Smith, and her suggestion of this meaning is not carried forward in Brockelmann's authoritative Syriac-Latin dictionary, the *Lexicon Syriacum*.[3]

Use of ܥܘܠܐ in Sixth Maccabees

In 6 *Maccabees*, ܥܘܠܐ is used almost entirely to describe and execrate Antiochus Epiphanes, the "unjust judge," at the torture and execution of the Maccabean martyrs. A gloss, such as "lawless one" or "villain, wicked one" can be used to translate ܥܘܠܐ in all but three places.

Clearly Antiochus Epiphanes was a "wicked person," which would be a usable epithet, except that ܪܫܝܥ also has a claim on the meaning "wicked person" and sometimes occurs in a parallel of emphasis with ܥܘܠܐ. "Lawless one" has several advantages: Antiochus was of Greek-speaking background, and ἀνομίας, "without the law," was a label for tyrants in the lexicon of Socrates; Antiochus did not respect Jewish law or allow for its continued observance; Antiochus was outside the law in the sense that Jewish law did not apply to him as a Gentile. Surely one could call him "lawless."

Use of ܥܘܠܐ in Syriac Psalms of Solomon

The choice of Barnes in his translation of 6 *Maccabees*, then an anonymous *memra*, was generally to call Antiochus "unjust," and the ironic "unjust judge" features in his translation.

There is another precedent in translation practice; Trafton used the word "lawless" to translate ܥܘܠܐ in his close examination of the *Psalms of Solomon* in Syriac in comparison with Greek, which included a translation of the extant Syriac version.

There is, it is true, an implicit sense of lawlessness in the Peshitta of Ps 1:1, and elsewhere, that the wicked person (ܥܘܠܐ) walks not in the way of the law, but the worthy person studies it day and night.[4] So it is implied that the wicked person (ܥܘܠܐ) does not have the law or is lawless, but wickedness and lawlessness are not explicitly connected in OT Ps 1:1.

As we will see further below, by using "lawless" for his translation term, Trafton appears to follow the Greek, rather than the Hebrew base that he assesses to have been the foundation for each version, the Syriac as well as the Greek.

---

3. As this article went to press, Michael Sokoloff's *Syriac Lexicon* (Winona Lake: Eisenbrauns, 2009) became available. For Brockelman's single gloss on ܥܘܠܐ, the Latin "scelestus," Sokoloff supplied "wicked, offensive" (1080, col. B). The second meaning, "offensive," is a broader term that encompasses much of what I have suggested and discussed as "transgressive"—that is, offensive to the laws and mores, or transgressing them—wicked in a particular sense.

4. Equivalent in Hebrew and in Syriac.

II

Historical and Theological Implications of Translating "Lawless"

The multiple theological intonations of "lawless" stem from the second letter of Paul to the Thessalonians, 2 Thess 2:1–10. There, the "man of lawlessness" (v. 3, ἀνομία) is described as a necessary concomitant of the end times; and according to Helmut Koester, he is "described in traditional terms of Jewish apocalypticism."[5] In later Christian exegesis, this man of lawlessness (v. 10, ἀδικία) is the Antichrist.

In finding the historical precedents that presage the Antichrist, Antiochus Epiphanes became the *type* of the Antichrist, the lawless man who was the human example of the "man of lawlessness" of apocalyptic times.

It is, however, as simple, historically, to see Antiochus Epiphanes as the ruler who epitomized the Classical Greek philosopher's idea of ἀνομία, the specific ability of a ruler to compromise the observance of the laws and customs. One thinks, for example, of Creon in the Greek tragedy *Antigone*, by Sophocles. A summary descriptor of Antiochus and of Creon as rulers might be "transgressive (of laws and customs)." The memory of Antiochus IV Epiphanes was projected upon later rulers whose actions, particularly persecutory actions, resembled his, and the epithet "lawless" was applied to these later rulers also, both those who were real and those who were imaginary.

So, whether or not it applies to the meaning of ܥܘܠܐ in *Psalms of Solomon* and 6 *Maccabees*, the word "lawless" has a particularly encrusted history that disinclines one to its use in an English translation of an earlier text. After these generalities, we will look more closely at the relationship between Greek usage and its relationship to Trafton's frequent translation, "lawless," in the places where the Syriac has ܥܘܠܐ.

Trafton

In comparing the Syriac version of the *Psalms of Solomon* with the more fully attested Greek version of the *Psalms of Solomon*, Joseph Trafton used "lawless" or "lawlessness" to translate ܥܘܠܐ and also thoroughly annotated its use in both the Syriac version and the similar Greek.[6] Trafton, it should be noted, did not concentrate on this Syriac word as a source of evidence; he made extensive comparisons between Greek and Syriac at a number of levels. He eventually concluded, on evidence and against prevailing scholarly opinion, that both *Psalms of Solomon* in Syriac and *Psalms of Solomon* in Greek were, independently, translations from Hebrew Vorlagen, as mentioned above.

---

5. Koester, *Introduction to New Testament*, 2:250.
6. As did several other translators before him.

Based on Trafton's extensive presentation of evidence, I concur with his finding regarding the Hebrew base of both Syriac and Greek versions of the *Psalms of Solomon*. Without making any comments on theological readings of the *Psalms of Solomon*, Trafton gathered and presented evidence on the relatedness or nonrelatedness of the Syriac and Greek versions. As a consequence, he made very close comparisons concerning ܥܘܠܐ. For example, his first note on the word he translates as "lawless" is at *Psalms of Solomon* 2 (that is, the second psalm), note 1. The verse begins, as Trafton translates, "In his arrogance the lawless one cast down strong walls on the feast day." His note to this lemma reads:

> 1. Lit. "In the arrogance of the lawless one, he . . . ." Gk has "When the sinner behaved arrogantly, he . . ." [sentence omitted]. Sy ܥܘܠܐ ("lawless one") corresponds to Gk ἁμαρτωλός ("sinner") sixteen times in the *Pss. Sol.* (2:1, 17, 38 [twice], 39 [twice]; 3:11, 13, 15; 4:27; 13:4, 5, 6, 7; 15:7, 9; 17:26). Six times Gk has παράνομος (4:21, 27; 12:1; 14:4; 16:8 [παρανομέω]; 17:27), twice ἄδικος (15:6; 17:24), and twice ἄνομος (17:13, 20). ἁμαρτωλός corresponds elsewhere to ܚܛܝܐ (1:1; 4:2; 12:8; 13:2, 10; 14:4; 15:7, 11, 13 [twice], 15; 16:2, 5; 17:6, 27, 41), and to ܪܫܝܥܐ (4:9).[7]

Thus Trafton gives an index of the Syriac to the Greek words found throughout the *Psalms of Solomon*, plus one index of locations where one Syriac word other than ܥܘܠܐ, found in the Syriac, corresponds to just one word of the Greek words in his list. That is, while ἁμαρτωλός, "sinner," corresponds to ܥܘܠܐ 16 times, it corresponds to ܚܛܝܐ another 16 times, and corresponds once to another Peshitta word from the Hebrew, ܪܫܝܥܐ, according to Trafton. By using ἁμαρτωλός, "sinful, hardened in sin," so frequently, the Greek translator suggests lawlessness in the sense of moral depravity.

Of the other Greek words that Trafton lists, ἄδικος denotes a person who is "doing wrong, unrighteous, unjust." In similar vein, παράνομος signifies "transgression of law, decency or order" or "above/beyond/outside the law." Regardless of word correspondences, the Syriac of *Psalms of Solomon* at several places describes a person who *does* ܥܘܠܐ. In the pairing of ἄδικος and παράνομος, the former is a condition: someone is, through and through, unjust or unrighteous. In contrast, the second meaning of ἄδικος and the meaning of παράνομος both suggest a person who performs ܥܘܠܐ. This construction, ܥܘܠܐ (CAL #3) signifying the person who does ܥܘܠܐ (CAL #2), is a form of description based in Hebrew and on the Jewish Scriptures.[8]

In another note, Trafton lays out further Greek correspondences to the Syriac word ܥܘܠܐ, as follows:

> [MSS] 253, 655, and 659 have the plural: "injustices" (the other MSS have "evil things"). Sy uses ܥܘܠܐ three times in this psalm: in v. 3 the corresponding Gk

---

7. Trafton, *Syriac Version*, p. 31 n. 1.
8. That is, CAL, sense and pronunciation #3, or sense and pronunciation #2. Lemma search for "(wl".

word is ἀνομία (cf. 1:8, 15:9, 11), in v. 9 it is ἀδικία (cf. 17:36), and here it is ἄδικος (cf. 4:12; 12:6). Elsewhere in the PssSol, ἀνομία corresponds to ܚܛܗܐ (2:3, 13) and ܥܘܠ, and ἄδικος corresponds to ܥܘܠ ("wicked person" — 15:6; 17:24). On the use of ἀδικία in the PssSol, see note 33 on PssSol 3.[9]

While Trafton's note is confusing when taken out of context, I cite it to show that there are several Greek words with various nuances that the Greek translator used to express the Hebrew underlying the *Psalms of Solomon*. We do not know how similar the Greek and Syriac Vorlagen were; what we may suggest is that the more limited Syriac correspondences (a) admitted of more nuance or (b) were fixed in relationship to a more limited number of Hebrew words.

The use of ܥܘܠ in *Psalms of Solomon* and 6 *Maccabees* supports the first alternative above and will be discussed below. By contrast, the use of ܥܘܠ in 7 *Maccabees* is an example of the second alternative above — the fixed, almost stereotypical relationship to specific cognate Hebrew words.[10]

The next section will discuss the implications of nuances found in Greek and Syriac texts.

III

The Greek words ἁμαρτωλός, ἄδικος, παράνομος, and ἄνομος are each of a semantic domain representing transgression against laws and norms, the prevailing complaint of the community that first wrote, collected, and preserved the *Psalms of Solomon*, probably in Hebrew. The confusion of multiple Greek words occurring in the same places as Syriac ܥܘܠ seems to indicate an expansion of usage for the Syriac word, possibly implied in Peshitta OT Psalms, especially Psalm 1.

Apparently "lawless" and "wicked" and "sinner" are approximately equal variations on "these people are not like us; they are not righteous and just and good and all that." As in the Psalms of the Peshitta OT, they "do wrong." Whether they do this knowingly or not is unclear. When called upon to judge, they are unjust. When called upon to stick to community norms, they are sinners.

We come to some understanding, from Trafton's notes on the Syriac, that the frequent and consistent application of "lawless" in his translation has no exact correspondence in Greek. Further, when used to translate Syriac ܥܘܠ

---

9. Trafton, *Syriac Version*, p. 100 n. 12.
10. The *Seventh Book of Maccabees* (7 *Macc.*) is a short prose text in Syriac that, like other pseudepigrapha transmitted in Christian circles, is a slightly modified version of a Jewish text. This is a complex oversimplification of issues that have been thoroughly explored separately in Robert Kraft's collected essays, *Exploring the Scripturesque*, and in James R. Davila, *Provenance*. For the Syriac text of 7 *Maccabees*, see Barnes, "Maryam." A new translation of 7 *Maccabees* by Sevile George Mannickarottu and Sigrid Peterson, with introduction and notes by Sigrid Peterson, is forthcoming in Richard Bauckham and James R. Davila, eds., *More Old Testament Pseudepigrapha*.

in Jewish texts such as *6 Maccabees* and *Psalms of Solomon*, "lawless" is misleading. It does not necessarily apply to people who are outside the covenant of Jews with God. It inaccurately applies to people who have their own laws and mores, just not those of this group.

Neither Peshitta Psalms nor *Psalms of Solomon*, with one exception, uses ܪܫܥܐ in specific descriptions of named persons. The exception occurs in *Psalms of Solomon* 17, the so-called messianic psalm, which seems to describe a person and his actions as follows:

17:13 The lawless one devastated our land so that no one was living in it;
   They destroyed the young ones and the old ones and their children together.
17:14 In the beauty of his wrath he sent them away to the west,
   And he also did not spare the ruler of the land from scorn.
17:15 The enemy was boasting in a foreign manner,
   And his heart was foreign from our God.[11]

This usage of ܪܫܥܐ in *Psalms of Solomon* links to the way the Syriac word is used in *6 Maccabees* to identify Antiochus Epiphanes. The first translator of *6 Maccabees* generally used "unjust one" to characterize Antiochus, and such consistency allowed her or him to translate the ironic phrase "unjust judge" and apply it to Antiochus. This is not bad; it does not accuse Antiochus of being "lawless" in his own culture and norms. It does not insist that he is the *type* of the Antichrist, the Lawless One of 2 Thess 2:2–10. What fails to happen, though, is to convey a sense that, no matter how true to his own lights and cultural norms Antiochus (or, supposedly, the unnamed Pompey in *Psalms of Solomon*) might have been, from the point of view of the writers of *Psalms of Solomon* and *6 Maccabees*, the ruler's actions were evil. He was a "wicked person." Hence the adjectives are piled on, in *6 Maccabees*; in *Psalms of Solomon* it is the use of extended description that makes the evil fairly specific.

The word group in English that conveys this desecration of boundaries by a foreign ruler is "transgressor" or "violator." One of the Greek words in Trafton's notes specifically on ܪܫܥܐ is παράνομος. This word occurs 6 times in the Greek text of *Psalms of Solomon* at points corresponding to the Syriac ܪܫܥܐ. Unlike the more frequent correspondences (of some sort) of the Syriac ܪܫܥܐ to ἁμαρτωλός "sinner," the Greek word παράνομος *only* occurs in places in the Greek text that correspond to places in the Syriac text where the word used is ܪܫܥܐ, except as noted below in the discussion of *Psalms of Solomon* 12. Of course, ܪܫܥܐ is used more frequently, and, as we have seen, corresponds to other Greek words and probably translates several different underlying Hebrew words, as in Psalms.

Substituting "transgressor" or "violator" for "lawless" would give the following results in the 6 cases of correspondence of παράνομος with Syriac ܪܫܥܐ, modifying Trafton's translation:

   11. Trafton, *Syriac Version*, p. 157.

4:11 And his eyes are upon a house in calmness like a snake,
To destroy the wisdom of each one with words or <u>transgressions</u>.[12]

Here there is a contrast between words and acts, where lawlessness does usually imply specific actions, but it is a less pointed contrast.

4:21 May the flesh of those who show partiality be scattered by beasts,
And the bones of the <u>transgressors</u> before the sun in disgrace.[13]

Here the thematic meanings of unjust judgment parallel to violation of the law seem to apply.

4:27 And the Lord will save them from deceitful and lawless men,
And he will save us from every stumbling block of the <u>transgressors</u>.[14]

Here Trafton suggests that ܥܘܠܐ, occurring twice, reflects a Hebrew original that has ܥܘܠܐ in both places; Greek has ἁμαρτωλός and then παράνομος.

12:1 O Lord, deliver my soul from the perverse and violating man,
And from the whispering and <u>transgressing</u> tongue.[15]

In this psalm, and only here, παράνομος corresponds to another Syriac phrase, ܥܒܪ ܢܡܘܣܐ, "to transgress or violate the Law," and Trafton translates "transgressor" at each place the phrase occurs: 12:1, 12:3, and twice in 12:4. See further discussion of this unusual phrase below.

14:4 But not such are the sinners and the <u>transgressors</u>.[16]

Are sinners and transgressors parallel and similar in meaning, or parallel and contrastive? Since a group is indicated, I would vote for an *inclusio*, a contrast in meaning between the two words.

16:8 Do not let the beauty of a <u>transgressing</u> woman cause me to slip, nor any sin which there is.[17]

Here, the parallelism is from a specific instance to the more general and contradicts the separation of transgression and sin in the example just above.

17:27 To destroy the <u>transgressing</u> nations with the word of his mouth.

There is nothing particularly illuminating in the usage in our last example, except to say that "lawless" would not have applied to the nations at the time of the writing of *Psalms of Solomon*. Phenomena such as proselytizing and the presence of god-fearers in synagogues during this time indicate the

---

12. Ibid. Underscore represents my substitution in Trafton's English translation. This usage is continued below.
13. Ibid., p. 60.
14. Ibid., p. 60 and p. 71 n. 78.
15. Ibid., p. 114.
16. Ibid., p. 131.
17. Ibid., p. 145.

acceptance among Jews of the Diaspora that non-Jews *generally* followed the Noachian commandment to establish systems of laws and were therefore not lawless, per se.

A final point about παράνομος in *Psalms of Solomon*: unlike the other correspondences of Greek with Syriac, this word—and its cognates—corresponds *only* to ܥܘܠܐ, according to Trafton's notes to his translation of *Psalms of Solomon*. This one-to-one correspondence indicates an additional meaning for our Syriac word, that of "transgression of law, decency or order," the meaning for the Greek word. The only doubt arises from the use of ܥܠ ܚܘܒܗ, only in Psalm 12, as we saw above, a direct indication that something is against the law. The Syriac word ܚܘܒܗ is associated with Christian use, does not occur elsewhere in *Psalms of Solomon*, and seems to herald an interpolation stretching from 12:1b through 12:5. Thus the psalm may actually have been composed to read as follows:

> 12:1 O Lord, deliver my soul from the perverse and violating man,
> 12:6 And may the Lord keep the soul of the righteous, which hates the transgressor,
> And may the Lord establish the man doing peace in the house of the Lord.

There is good continuity between 12:1 and 12:6; incidentally, all the usages of ܚܘܒܗ ܥܠ disappear and no longer trouble us, and παράνομος, "transgression," corresponds only to ܥܘܠܐ.

IV

Does this meaning assist in translating ܥܘܠܐ as it occurs in 6 *Maccabees*? To make the question clear, here is a sample of the first four times it occurs.

> 1 (106) Then the transgressor, the execrable, commanded (them)
> To strip off the clothes from the modest martyr.
> 2 (162) Then the evil transgressor commanded his worthless servants
> That they should bring and arrange in front of them all sorts of torments.
> 3 (179) "Bring your tortures, O evil and transgressive tyrant,
> Apply your harsh scourgings, depraved foolish brute."
> 4 (392) Then he heard these things (that went) to such a degree (of defiance)
> And he thirsted for slaughter, the wicked and impure Antiochus.

The use of "wicked" in the fourth translation here takes us back to sections I and III, for the meaning that is well established by the parallels and context of Ps 1:1 of the Peshitta. The implied meaning that the wicked do not appreciate the law, do not "meditate on the Law day and night," has become more explicit with the confrontation with foreign rulers who transgress the laws and customs of the Jews.

V

It has taken us a long way around to come to a fairly small point, that in translating the Syriac word ܥܘܠܐ as a person or as an action or quality, the lexicon should reflect a third meaning, that of "transgressor" and "violation." I base this conclusion on an examination of Syriac texts with reference to the nuances available from Greek translation. It appears that, in the transition from Hebrew to Syriac, ܥܠܐ expanded in usage and gained an additional, though related, meaning. I have presented the case that ܥܠܐ functioned as the Syriac equivalent of Greek παράνομος, literally, "contrary to law and custom, beyond the law," and may perhaps be represented in English as "transgressive."

Bibliography

Bauckham, R., and J. R. Davila, eds. *More Old Testament Pseudepigrapha*. Grand Rapids, MI: Eerdmans, forthcoming.

Bensly, R. L. "*Memra* by an Unknown Hand" [ܡܐܡܪܐ ܕܠܐ ܝܕܝܥ]. [This text is now known as *Sixth Maccabees* and is available at http://ccat.sas.upenn.edu/~petersig/macc6syriac/BenslyText/]

Barnes, W. E. *The Fourth Book of Maccabees and Kindred Documents in Syriac, First Edited on Manuscript Authority by the Late Robert L. Bensly*, with an introduction and translations by W. E. Barnes. Cambridge: Cambridge University Press, 1895. [See especially: (1) "ܡܐܡܪܐ ܕܠܐ ܝܕܝܥ" on pp. ܡܗ–ܣܚ. with the English translation "(D) Memra by an Unknown Hand," pp. xlviii–lxxii; (2) "ܬܫܥܝܬܐ ܕܡܪܝܡ ܫܡܘܢܐ ܘܫܒܥܐ ܒܢܝܗ̈" on pp. ܝܗ–ܟܚ. with the English translation "(B) The Story of Maryam (Shamoné) and Her Seven Sons: Martyred on the First of Ab," pp. xxxv–xliv.]

Brockelman, C. *Lexicon Syriacum*. 2nd edition. Halle: Max Niemeyer, 1928.

Davila, J. R. *The Provenance of the Pseudepigrapha: Jewish, Christian, or Other?* JSJSup 105. Leiden: Brill, 2005.

Efron, J. "The Psalms of Solomon, the Hasmonean Decline and Christianity." Pp. 219–86 in *Studies on the Hasmonean Period*. Leiden: Brill, 1987.

Koester, H. *Introduction to the New Testament*, vol. 2: *History and Literature of Early Christianity*. New York: de Gruyter, 1982, 2000.

Kraft, R. L. *Exploring the Scripturesque: Jewish Texts and Their Christian Contexts*. Leiden: Brill, 2009.

Mannickarottu, Sevile George, and Sigrid Peterson. "Seventh Maccabees: Translation," in *More Old Testament Pseudepigrapha*. Edited by Richard Bauckham and James R. Davila. Grand Rapids, MI: Eerdmans, forthcoming.

Payne Smith, J. *A Compendious Syriac Dictionary*. Oxford: Clarendon, 1903. Reprinted Winona Lake, IN: Eisenbrauns, 1998.

Peterson, S. *Martha Shamoni: A Jewish Syriac Rhymed Liturgical Poem about the Maccabean Martyrdoms (Sixth Maccabees)*. Ph.D. dissertation, University of Pennsylvania, 2006.

———. "Seventh Maccabees: Introduction and Notes," in *More Old Testament Pseudepigrapha*. Edited by Richard Bauckham and James R. Davila. Grand Rapids, MI: Eerdmans, forthcoming.

———. "Sixth Maccabees: Introduction and Translation," in *More Old Testament Pseudepigrapha*. Edited by Richard Bauckham and James R. Davila. Grand Rapids, MI: Eerdmans, forthcoming.

Sokoloff, Michael. *A Syriac Lexicon: A Translation from the Latin, Correction, Expansion, and Update of C. Brockelmann's* Lexicon Syriacum. Winona Lake, IN: Eisenbrauns / Piscataway, NJ: Gorgias, 2009.

Trafton, J. L. *The Syriac Version of the Psalms of Solomon: A Critical Evaluation.* Society of Biblical Literature Septuagint and Cognate Studies 11. Atlanta: Scholars Press, 1985.

The Composition of the *Qenneshrē Fragment*

MICHAEL PENN

In 1907, François Nau published an edition and French translation of a Syriac work that he entitled the *Qenneshrē Fragment*.[1] The extant text tells the story of possessed monks, miraculous relics, re-embodied saints, tortured demons, and a cross-wielding Muslim emir. Since 1907, there has appeared only a single article concerning this intriguing Syriac document that may preserve one of our earliest witnesses to the way that Syriac Christians depicted Muslims.[2]

I am currently working on a new edition, English translation, and commentary of the *Qenneshrē Fragment*. One question that my research addresses is when this text was originally written. The following article contains some initial forays into this issue as well as some tentative conclusions regarding the date of the *Qenneshrē Fragment*'s composition.

A Demonic Past

The *Qenneshrē Fragment* takes up five folios of a larger manuscript now found in Berlin and catalogued as Sachau 315. This codex was signed by the scribe Jesus, son of Isaiah, who copied it in 1480/1481 at the Mar Gabriel Monastery of Qartamin.[3] In addition to the body of the text, there are several scribal notes copied in the margins as well as some emendations to the main text. Unfortunately, our copy of this work is not complete, and we are missing

---

Author's note: I wish to express my gratitude to Paul V. M. Flesher and especially to Lucas Van Rompay for their assistance with this article, as well as to the National Endowment for the Humanities for helping fund this project.

1. Nau, "Notice historique," pp. 114–35. This document was first catalogued by Sachau, *Verzeichniss*, pp. 523–24.
2. Reinink, "Die Muslime."
3. Ibid., p. 336.

a number of folios before and after the extant text. The modern reader must begin partway through the story, and the text ends before completing the tale.

The surviving narrative is set at the North Syrian monastery of Qenneshrē on the Euphrates, founded in the early sixth century by John bar Aphtonia. The monastery's received history includes a particularly colorful episode. Two medieval works, the *Chronicle of 1234* and the work of Michael the Syrian (d. 1199), both give accounts of a mid-seventh-century demonic infestation at the monastery of Qenneshrē. According to the *Chronicle of 1234*, magicians in a neighboring town discovered a bronze figurine that contained 60,000 demons. The magicians transferred these demons to the monks of Qenneshrē. The possessed monks began insulting the saints with slurs such as "long-bearded" (in reference to John bar Aphtonia) and "dried up, beardless one" (Ephrem).[4] Michael the Syrian presents another version of this story. A magician sent demons into a monk who killed the magician's dog and into other monks who swam in ponds outside the monastery of Qenneshrē instead of attending to the divine offering. In response to these possessions, Daniel of Edessa obtained the right hand of the deceased Severus of Samosata in order to exorcize the possessed Qenneshrē monks.[5] The original author (or authors) of the *Qenneshrē Fragment* was also familiar with a version of this demonic tale that forms the central trope for the document's narrative.

Fragment or Fragments?

Given that the only surviving witness to this text is incomplete, given that the document has numerous marginal glosses, given that François Nau titled the document *Qenneshrē Fragment*, and given that the plot so frequently concerns itself with bodily fragments, it is surprising that the few scholars who have examined this document most often treat the work as a unified whole. Even a cursory summary of the manuscript's content suggests that the text that Jesus, son of Isaiah, copied in the late fifteenth century may already have been a compilation of several earlier accounts. This, of course, complicates the question of when the *Qenneshrē Fragment* was written. Does this question ask, When was the final document, including all its layers of marginalia, finalized? Or perhaps, it means, When was the body of the text fixed in close to its present form? Alternatively, if a later redactor combined several earlier documents to make the *Qenneshrē Fragment*, When were each of these documents written?

Although each of these questions is important, for the purposes of this article I want to concentrate on the last: Regardless of when a later editor may have combined and modified earlier texts, when were these earlier texts themselves written? My choice here is mainly motivated by the issue of prac-

---

4. *Chronicle 1234* in Chabot, *Chronicon*, pp. 267–68.
5. Michael the Syrian 11.8 in Chabot, *Chronique*, pp. 420–21.

The Composition of the Qenneshrē Fragment

Table 1: Dividing the *Qenneshrē Fragment* into Narrative Sections

Section	Folios	Characters and Plot	How Section Is Distinct from Others
Zero	58a	Theodore inquires about the scourging of a demon.	Narration is from Theodore's point of view.
One	58a–61a	Athanasius, Severus, John bar Aphtonia, Ephrem, and martyrs torture insolent demons.	Point of view shifts to a monk of Qenneshrē. Ends with allusion to John 20:30.
Two	61a–62a	Daniel and a holy man (also Daniel?) interrogate demons.	Point of view shifts to first-person voice of Daniel and third-person narration. Torture is no longer for torment but for information.
Three	62a–63b	Daniel, Bishop of Edessa, and an unnamed young man bring relics. The Muslim Emir ʿAbdallah questions the demons and exorcises one with the true cross.	Point of view shifts to a Miaphysite monk, first-person voice of Daniel, and then third-person narration. Now only Chalcedonian monks are possessed.

ticality. The surviving work preserves several literary and textual seams that are jarring enough to justify dividing the work into four sections. Because divisions of this sort are helpful to the modern reader, I have summarized them in chart form (see table 1). These sectional divides may also delineate the remnants of separate documents that only later were combined with each other. If they were originally independent textual sources, by the time a redactor "pasted" these sections together, each may already have had its own complicated textual history. Nevertheless, I feel the extant text does not preserve sufficient evidence either to identify clearly or to date any further subsections with much certainty.[6]

The *Qenneshrē Fragment* begins with section zero. I use the number zero because the surviving text preserves only part of a story and thus does not contain much information that would allow us to date this section's composition. The extant section zero begins in the midst of what originally was a larger story concerning Theodore, the Miaphysite patriarch of Antioch (d. 667). It commences with the phrase "and I Patriarch Theodore . . ." and continues to have Theodore, in his own words, tell of his encounter with Satan scourging a man possessed by a demon. Theodore asks one of the friends of the possessing demon (the friend also being a demon, of course) if Satan is torturing the demon himself or the demoniac who is possessed by the demon. The demon

---

6. Although our rationales occasionally differ, Reinink ("Die Muslime," pp. 337–40) and Hoyland (*Seeing Islam*, pp. 144–47) divide the text in a manner similar to the way I divide it. Reinink provides additional subdivisions.

friend tells Theodore that it is the demon, not the demoniac (literally, the demon's "house"), who is being tortured. After Satan pounds the demon's head with a hammer of fire, the demon flees, and the narrative shifts to the next story. Because none of the other *Qenneshrē Fragment* accounts are told in Theodore's voice, this first episode may have been more strongly connected to the tales that originally preceded it than to those that follow.

Immediately after Theodore's narrative comes section one. Although it is possible that section one simply continues section zero, there are several reasons for suspecting that it comes from a different source. The most telling is the abrupt shift in point of view. No longer do we have an account from Theodore's first-person voice; instead the text comprises a generally third-person presentation of plot with the narrator occasionally breaking frame to make a brief first-person intervention. Whenever using the first person, the narrator depicts himself as one of the monks from Qenneshrē (e.g., "we sent for the right hand of Severus," "And when that brother asked me . . ."). As a result, unlike section zero that presents itself as an autobiographical account by the patriarch Theodore, section one reads as a more omniscient account, with the narrator occasionally referring to himself in the first person when he alludes to his own involvement in the story line.

Section one consists of a series of narrative episodes. Each episode shares a similar structure: a deceased saint (or at least a relic from a saint) comes to the monastery, one or more demons insult the saint, the saint tortures the insolent demons, and the story then shifts to another saint. The first episode speaks of Athanasius, the Miaphysite patriarch of Antioch (d. 631). Like many of the characters in the *Qenneshrē Fragment,* by the time of the story's setting, Athanasius has already been dead for some years. This inconvenience, however, will not hinder his reembodied apparition from intervening in the demons' affairs. After Athanasius prevents the demons from throwing a possessed man into a fire, the demons complain that they are afflicted by Athanasius's continual asceticism and prayer.

The demons' woes continue when the monks of Qenneshrē (including the narrator) acquire the right hand of Athanasius's brother Severus, the late bishop of Samasota (d. 641). As Severus's hand comes to the monastery, fire springs out from this relic, blinding the demons. The dead monks buried near the monastery then rise up, greet Severus, are blessed by him, and return to their graves. Severus next exorcises a possessed woman and joins his brother, Athanasius, in prayer.

The narrative then jumps to a story concerning the monastery's founder, John bar Aphtonia (d. 538). In this account, a demon insults the length of John's beard, and John responds by torturing the demon who slighted his facial hair. John then exorcises a possessed monk, gives the monk the Eucharist, and suddenly John disappears. When the formerly possessed man asks the narrator if he had seen John, the narrator lies, saying that he did in order not to upset the recently exorcized monk.

Next, a demon chief chides one of the Qenneshrē monks for carrying a relic of Ephrem (d. 373). The demon begins to insult Ephrem himself, whom the demon addresses as a withered, parched worm. In response, Ephrem rolls the demon from wall to wall, twists the demon's hands and feet around each other, and flails him with fire. After further tortures, the demon is driven away and dissipates like smoke.

In the next episode, another set of demons who did not learn from their predecessors' mistakes begin to insult four Christians martyred by the Emperor Julian (d. 363). The martyrs in turn torture the demons. This story cycle ends with a brief reference to additional exorcisms and the narrator proclaiming that the saints did many further wonders that are not written in this book.

Several textual clues suggest that the next set of stories originally came from a source different from those found in section one. First, the text's proclamation that there were many other miracles not written in this book (most likely an allusion to John 20:30) seems to mark a clear ending to section one. Second, the incidents that follow break the previous pattern of demons insulting the saints and the saints torturing the demons in revenge. Instead the later stories focus on the interrogation of demons and the information they reveal. Finally, section two is separated from the former stories by a shift in person. Unlike the previous tales that are told by a monk from Qenneshrē, the next set of stories begins with the first-person voice of Bishop Daniel (either Daniel of Edessa, d. 684, or Daniel of Aleppo, fl. early ninth century). Section two consists of three episodes: the first is told from Daniel's point of view, the second is an omniscient narrative involving an unnamed holy man (who may be Daniel), and the final episode explicitly returns to Daniel but in this case is told in the third person.

Section two begins with a demon explaining to Daniel that many of those who are nominally under Daniel's authority are actually the demon's allies. Daniel binds the demon with oaths and forces him to begin naming these conspirators. Daniel learns that a deacon from Serug possesses one of the demon's books. Daniel summons the deacon and burns the deacon's magical book. The deacon then repents. Unfortunately for Daniel, the demon has learned his lesson, and he will not reveal to the bishop any other of his allies.

The narration then shifts to the third person. An unnamed holy man (perhaps Daniel?) binds demons with oaths and interrogates them. In response to a series of questions, the demons state that they prefer Jews to pagans, Julianists to Nestorians, that they cannot distinguish between Chalcedonians and Nestorians, and that Sataniel himself led the Council of Chalcedon. The next episode shifts back to Daniel, but this time it is told in the third person. In this final episode, a demon complains to Daniel that in the present day Miaphysites are serving the Eucharist in the monastery of Qenneshrē.

Section three consists of the final set of extant stories. Here the point of view briefly returns to that of a Miaphysite monk (although there is no indication that this is the same monk who narrated section one), then to a brief first-person account by Daniel, and finally to a third-person account by an unspecified narrator. Despite their differing vantage points, together these episodes form a fairly coherent, linear narrative that takes place in the court of the Muslim emir ʿAbdallah b. Durrai (fl. 660s). The content of these last extant episodes, however, suggests that they originally came from a source different from sections one and two. Unlike the first two sections of the *Qenneshrē Fragment*, where the possessed monks were Miaphysites, section three insists that only Chalcedonian monks were possessed.

Section three begins with a flashback to an earlier time, when Chalcedonians had taken possession of the monastery of Qenneshrē. According to one of the demons, at this point it was the demons who gave the Eucharist to their friends, the Chalcedonians! This serves as background for ʿAbdallah's investigating whether an unnamed magician sent the demons into the monastery.[7] As part of his inquiry, the emir wants to interrogate the possessed monks. ʿAbdallah questions the head of the demons and discovers that indeed the magician did send them into the monastery, and there the demons suffered many afflictions from the saints.

The narrative then shifts into the first-person voice of Daniel, bishop of Edessa, who has with him a bag from one of the saints. Fire comes out of the bag, beginning to burn the demon, and the demon reveals that the saint's presence has prevented him from possessing the emir. Next, a young man arrives with a ring that contains a piece of Jesus' cross. ʿAbdallah then uses this ring to appraise the true cross's efficacy. The emir puts the ring with the cross splinter upon his own staff and approaches a demon, who then cries out. ʿAbdallah then removes the relic from his staff and replaces it with his own signet ring. This time when he approaches the demon, the demon jumps up and grabs the emir's ring. The emir then puts the ring with the true cross back on his staff, touches the possessed man, and exorcises the demon. At this point, the extant text breaks off with the phrase "Clergy from Nisibis came...."

Although a threefold (fourfold, if one counts section zero) division of the *Qenneshrē Fragment* is helpful for the modern reader, this schema is not without drawbacks. The most obvious is that each of these sections could be divided by episodes into further subsections. Although this is certainly true, if one further partitions the text, any sort of correspondence between modern division and potential source documents will most likely be lost. It seems unlikely that an ancient redactor had over one dozen different texts in front of him, most only a few sentences long, and each directly corresponding to a single episode in the final compilation. Given the inherently probabilistic

---

7. The text speaks of the Chalcedonian occupation of the monastery of Qenneshrē occurring under Domitanus, which most likely began in 599 (Frend, *Monophysite Movement*, pp. 334–35). As pointed out by Reinink ("Die Muslime," pp. 339–40 n. 21), if the text sees ʿAbdallah's inquiry as contemporary with Chalcedonian control of the monastery of Qenneshrē, its chronology is off by about half a century.

nature of almost any form of source criticism, it seems wisest to stay with a division into what appear to be fairly well-delineated sections rather than to take the next step and try to reconstruct the various subcomponents of an admittedly already-hypothetical set of source documents.

Conversely, there are several reasons for questioning whether the above schema necessitates the earlier existence of independent written sources that a later redactor "pasted" together: (1) Much of my justification for dividing the text as I do relies on shifts in the narrative point of view or inconsistencies in terms of plot. Is it possible that instead of there having been a final redactor of three or more documents who did a very poor job of covering his tracks we have a single author who was not very interested in narrative consistency but simply wove together an almost postmodern pastiche? Alternatively, perhaps abrupt shifts in narrative voice or plot details resulted from a single author combining multiple oral accounts that he heard over an extended period of time, as opposed to "pasting" together written documents.

(2) There are several items that unify these sections. Daniel appears in the first person in both sections two and three. Occasionally section three seems to allude to plot elements of earlier sections (for example, the demons claim that they suffered torture from "those broken ones and that bearded one," the same appellations used to describe various holy men in sections one and two). Although throughout the work there are several words used to speak of torture (e.g., ܬܫܢܝܩܐ, ܐܘܠܨܢܐ) and demons (e.g., ܕܝܘܐ, ܫܐܕܐ), there is no clear preference between sections so that one section only uses one of these words and another section only its synonym. Even more striking is that both sections one and two have the demons refer to a monastery as "a mill," an altar as a "hole" and the Eucharist as "chaff."[8] Of course these similarities could have motivated an editor to combine three or more documents together in the first place. Alternatively, they could be due to a redactor's modifying his sources so they fit together better.

(3) If a later redactor combined three separate written documents, why did he not do a better job of editing them? Although a similar objection can be raised against almost any attempt at source criticism, at least when dealing with a sacred text (e.g., the Pentateuch and the Documentary Hypothesis) one has recourse to the possibility that, since the component documents may already have gained some sort of authoritative status, the final redactor hesitated to modify them to the point of complete harmonization. Its unlikely that a redactor would have as much respect for various accounts of a possessed monastery. This leads to a bit of a catch-22. If the final editor cared about consistency, why did he not more carefully redact his sources? If he was not concerned with uniformity, are what I have identified as seams really the result of "pasting together" earlier sources, or are they simply artifacts of a single author's inconsistent story?

---

8. Nau, "Notice historique," pp. 126, 131.

Fortunately, in terms of estimating the composition date for the *Qenneshrē Fragment*, these issues do not need to be resolved fully. If, as I initially suggested, the *Qenneshrē Fragment* is a composite text, then each of the original texts needs to be dated separately. In this case, one should establish a set of *terminus ante quem* and *terminus post quem* parameters for each extant section. On the other hand, if one is persuaded by the above alternatives and the *Qenneshrē Fragment* was written by a single author, dating the document becomes much easier; it would have been composed after the latest *post quem* clue found in the extant manuscript and before the earliest *ante quem* indication in the text. In what follows, I will initially treat each section as an originally independent text so that I can address what, for dating the text, is a worst-case scenario.

Some Initial Parameters

Establishing the *terminus post quem* for the *Qenneshrē Fragment* is initially fairly easy. The document refers to numerous historical personages. These include Theodore (d. 667) in section zero, Severus (d. 641) in section one, Bishop Daniel (either of Edessa, d. 684, or Aleppo, fl. early ninth century) in section two, and ʿAbdallah b. Durrai (fl. 660s) in section three. Whether a unified or a composite text, the result is the same: the *Qenneshrē Fragment* could have been written no earlier than the late seventh century. There are, however, two issues that potentially could raise the *terminus post quem* to a time later than the seventh century: (1) possible dependence on other versions of the story of demonic possession at Qenneshrē, and (2) the references to Bishop Daniel in sections two and three of the *Qenneshrē Fragment*.

The frame story of the *Qenneshrē Fragment* shares several details with both the *Chronicle of 1234* and Michael the Syrian. For example, as in the *Chronicle of 1234*, in the *Qenneshrē Fragment* the demons insult John bar Aphtonia's beard and call Ephrem "dried up." Similar to Michael the Syrian, the *Qenneshrē Fragment* speaks of obtaining Severus's hand from the monks of Mar Jacob at Kayshum, calls Severus "broken one" (or "breaker"), and refers to Daniel, bishop of Edessa. Michael the Syrian explicitly attributes his story to Dionysius of Tel Maḥrē (d. 845), whose chronicle is no longer extant. Because the *Chronicle of 1234* also often quotes from Dionysius, both later documents could depend on the work of this mid-ninth-century Miaphysite patriarch for their accounts of demons at Qenneshrē. Might the *Qenneshrē Fragment*'s tale of possession also rely on Dionysius's chronicle and therefore have been written after the mid-ninth century?

Although this remains a possibility, the large number of differences between the *Qenneshrē Fragment*'s version and the details found in the *Chronicle of 1234* and Michael the Syrian suggest that this late date is unlikely. In the places where the plots overlap, the details are different. Although two of the insults found in the *Chronicle of 1234* are repeated in the *Qenneshrē Frag-*

ment, most of them (such as Paul the "skin head" or Thomas "one-ball") are not.[9] In the *Chronicle of 1234*, the monks insult the icons of the saints, not their reanimated relics; in the account by Michael the Syrian, Daniel plays a very different role in the narrative, appearing only in places where he is absent in the *Qenneshrē Fragment* story and showing up in the *Qenneshrē Fragment* only in episodes unattested by Michael. In addition, the majority of episodes found in the *Qenneshrē Fragment* are not in the other documents. This pattern of occasional agreement on general plot and character names seems much more indicative of shared oral traditions than literary dependence and provides poor evidence of a direct connection between Dionysius of Tel Maḥrē and the *Qenneshrē Fragment*.

The *Qenneshrē Fragment*'s references to Bishop Daniel could also affect the *terminus post quem*. Daniel is found three times in the extant text: twice in section two and once in section three.[10] In section two, he is referred to as Daniel of Aleppo in the main text, but in both cases the word Aleppo is crossed out and is changed in the margins to Edessa. In section three, the main text speaks of Daniel of Edessa. Because Daniel of Edessa lived in the mid-seventh century and Daniel of Aleppo in the early ninth, resolving the question which Daniel did the text originally refer to has a clear impact on dating this document.

In his brief analysis of the *Qenneshrē Fragment*, Robert Hoyland presents a hypothesis to account for these changes. He suggests that a scribe already having one or more accounts of demonic possession at Qenneshrē (our section three or perhaps sections one and three) discovered another document that spoke of a Daniel's (in this case Daniel of Aleppo) interrogation of demons. The scribe mistakenly assumed that all these demon documents were originally concerning Daniel of Edessa, and therefore he "corrected" the two Daniel of Aleppo references when he combined these sources.[11] If Hoyland's theory is correct, it still would give us no additional information about the date of sections one and three, but it would require that both the original composition of section two and the combination of sections two and three occurred no earlier than the ninth century.

---

9. But even the two shared insults are worded differently in the two documents. Although both have a demon refer to Ephrem as "dried up" (ܢܫܝܒ), the *Chronicle of 1234* speaks of him as a "dried up, beardless one." The *Qenneshrē Fragment* reserves the term "beardless one" for other holy men and instead has the demon call Ephrem a "dried up deaconlet" and later a "parched worm." Similarly, while both documents have the demons insult the length of John bar Aphtonia's beard, the phrasing of the insults differs. The documents' tendency to vary in detail, even at the few points where the general plot is the same, provides another indication that shared oral traditions more likely account for these works' similarities than direct literary dependence.

10. Nau, "Notice historique," pp. 129, 131, 132.

11. Hoyland, *Seeing Islam*, p. 146.

Alternatively, the scribal marginalia in section two could be correct: originally section two referred to Daniel of Edessa, this was then corrupted to Daniel of Aleppo, and finally it was corrected by a later scribe back to Daniel of Edessa. Although less elegant than Hoyland's solution, there are several arguments that support this possibility: (1) As detailed below, section two's reference to the Julianists implies that this section was originally written before the ninth century. (2) Section two refers to a deacon in Serug who is under Daniel's authority. This makes perfect sense if Daniel is from Edessa. Serug, however, is far removed from the jurisdiction of Aleppo. (3) Later in the Sachau 315 manuscript, there is another reference to Aleppo that geographically makes little sense but that would work well if instead the reference originally was to Edessa.[12]

Because the *Qenneshrē Fragment*'s dependence on Dionysius of Tel Maḥrē seems improbable and the reference to Daniel of Aleppo could be a later textual emendation, the *terminus post quem* of the main text of the *Qenneshrē Fragment* should remain at the late seventh century. But what about the other textual emendations and scribal marginalia? Obviously these could occur only after the main text's composition. It is unclear if all of these changes were initially made by a single scribe (whether Jesus or one of his predecessors) or if they were made by multiple scribes at different periods of time. The references to Daniel of Aleppo (whether it was original to part of the text or was a later scribal alteration) show that at least some textual modifications occurred after the early ninth century. The appearance in the marginalia of Arab loanwords gives further evidence to ninth century or later changes.[13]

Narrowing the Parameters

Jesus bar Isaiah notes that he copied this document in AG 1792 (1480/1481 C.E.), which provides a solid *terminus ante quem*.[14] Thus all portions of the extant text must have been completed between the late seventh and the late fifteenth centuries. But an 800-year expanse is not a very satisfying date for a text. Can we do any better than this? Although none of the following arguments is indisputable, I suggest that the extant text does provide several additional clues that allow us to lower the *terminus ante quem* and establish a more narrow range of probable dates for the initial composition of the *Qenneshrē Fragment*(s).

Greek Learning

In section one, a demon chastises the monks of Qenneshrē for having a relic of Ephrem, stating: "Are you not ashamed? You are holy men and Greeks

---

12. Ibid., n. 105.
13. Reinink, "Die Muslime," p. 340 n. 24.
14. Sachau, *Verzeichniss*, p. 530; Nau, "Notice historique," p. 113; Reinink, "Die Muslime," p. 336.

and famous ones but he brings one dried up deaconlet both a Syrian and a foreigner."[15] Some of the passage's humor comes from the demon's *hutzpah* in insulting Saint Ephrem, and this prepares the reader for the next passages, which contain Ephrem's slapstick revenge. Comprehending the insult itself, however, depends on the reader's recognizing the contrast drawn between Ephrem, the most famous author of Syriac literature, and the monastery of Qenneshrē, famous for Greek learning. The demon is making fun of Hellenophiles who are appealing for help to the epitome of Syriac learning. The joke, however, only works as long as Qenneshrē is associated with Greek scholarship.[16] This rings true in the sixth, seventh, and early eighth centuries, when Qenneshrē was renowned for Greek learning and housed Miaphysite luminaries such as Thomas of Haraclea, who made a Syriac translation of the Bible that more closely followed the Septuagint.[17] It is possible that a later author is relying on his audience's knowledge of how Qenneshrē used to be to get a laugh. It is rare, though, for a joke to require its listeners to transport themselves back in time in order to get the punch line. In other words, section one's humorous exchange makes perfect sense in a seventh- or eighth-century context but seems like a much less comprehensible joke in later time periods.

Julianists

In section two, an unnamed monk interrogates the demons. The narrative of the monk's questions and the demons' answers forms a far-from-subtle polemic against the author's theological opponents. In the course of this inquisition, the demons declare that Sataniel himself ran the Council of Chalcedon. Similarly, the demons proclaim that, although they love the Chalcedonians and the Nestorians, both are so far removed from the truth that the demons cannot distinguish between them. Such comments could delight Miaphysite readers for many centuries to come. There is one remark, however, that seems more time specific. The demons note one group that is dearer to them than even the Nestorians: "'Who is closer to you, the Nestorians or the Julianists?' [asks the holy man]. The demons answered, 'The Julianists because they are all magicians and on account of this we love them

---

15. Nau, "Notice historique," p. 127.

16. A special thanks to Lucas Van Rompay for first bringing this argument to my attention.

17. Nau, "Notice historique," p. 112; Watt, "Portrait of John Bar Aphtonia," pp. 156, 159, 168; Wright, *A Short History of Syriac Literature*, p. 84. By the late eighth century, there appears to be a general decline in the use of Greek. Manuscript evidence reflects this shift. Several late eighth-century and ninth-century manuscripts are palimpsests with Syriac written over Greek (see Brock, "Syriac Attitudes to Greek Learning," p. 29 n. 140). For example, the *Chronicle of Zuqnin* reuses folios from six different Greek Bibles (see Harrak, *Chronicle of Zuqnin*, pp. 1–2; and Van Rompay, "Past and Present Perceptions," par. 36).

greatly.'"[18] Given the long tradition of polemic between the Miaphysites and the Nestorians, discovering a group that the author dislikes more than the Nestorians is quite surprising. So who are these Julianists?

In the 520s and 530s, there arose a controversy surrounding the theology of the Miaphysite Julian of Halicarnassus. Julian claimed that from the moment of his conception Christ's body was incorruptible, a doctrine that many felt was too docetic.[19] As a result Julian and his followers were considered heretics by many of their fellow Miaphysites, and we possess numerous Miaphysite tractates against the Julianists. In the midst of this vehement, intra-Miaphysite debate, it would not be surprising for a Miaphysite author to claim that demons like the Julianists even better than Nestorians. The Julianists, however, flourished only until the eighth century, and we rarely hear of them in later centuries. Similarly, even the preservation of anti-Julianist manuscripts quickly died down. For example, of the eight manuscripts in the British Library that contain anti-Julianist writings, according to the paleographic judgment of Wright, one of them was copied in the ninth century, one in the eighth or ninth century, and the other six in the eighth century or earlier.

As with the joke in section one, it is possible that the author assumes his audience will take on the perspective of seventh-century Miaphysites even if they themselves are living in a later time period. It seems much more likely, however, that section two's anti-Julianist polemic would be written in the midst of the Julianist controversy as opposed to being written long after the controversy had died down.

Mhaggrâyâ

Section three is the only part of the *Qenneshrē Fragment* that refers to Muslims. In particular it speaks of ʿAbdallah ibn Darraj, a Muslim official in charge of the administration in Kufa in the 660s and calls him "ʿAbdallah bar Darrai, the emir and governor of Bet Nahrin." Scholars such as Robert Hoyland argue that the *Qenneshrē Fragment*'s correct dating of ʿAbdallah's rule (that is, he is a contemporary with Daniel of Edessa and the patriarch Theodore) and its proper reference to him as a governor indicate that the *Qenneshrē Fragment* was not written long after the events it depicts.[20] Although suggestive, this argument is far from conclusive. Especially given the obsession of many Syriac chroniclers with listing Muslim rulers and their frequent success in keeping the dates roughly on target, it does not seem that only a seventh-century author would know that Daniel and ʿAbdallah were contemporaries. Although such details give the document an air of authenticity, they do little to guarantee a seventh-century composition.

18. Nau, "Notice historique," p. 131.
19. Grillmeier and Hainthaler, *Christ in Christian Tradition*, pp. 79–111.
20. Hoyland, *Seeing Islam*, p. 145.

This section's discussion of Muslims may, however, give another hint regarding its date of composition. When section three first introduces the character of the emir, it specifies that he is a ܡܗܓܪܝܐ (*mhaggrâyâ*). Although most often translated as Muslim, ܡܗܓܪܝܐ is just one of many designations that could have been used to describe ʿAbdallah's ethnic and religious affinities. Seventh-century documents such as the *Record of Arab Conquest of 637*, the *Chronicle of 640*, the *Letters of Ishoʿyhab III*, the *Chronicle of Khuzistan*, the *Maronite Chronicler*, the *Canons of George I*, and the *Chronicle of John Bar Penkaye* most often refer to one we would call a Muslim as ܐܪܒ (Arab). Other terms that seventh-century documents use include ܐܝܫܡܥܠܐ (Ishmaelites), ܒܪ ܐܝܫܡܥܠܐ (Sons of Ishmael), ܒܪ ܗܓܪ (Sons of Hagar), and ܣܪܩܘ (Saracens).

Only two seventh-century authors, Ishoʿyhab III and the scribe responsible for the colophon of BL Add. 14,666, however, use the term *mhaggrâyâ*.[21] Only in the eighth century does the term *mhaggrâyâ* becomes one of most popular terms for a Muslim, when it is found in the writings of Jacob of Edessa, the *Caliph List of 724*, the account of *John and the Emir*, the *Chronicle of 775*, the *Canons of Giwargi*, and a scribal addition to the letter of Athanasius of Balad.[22] It will also appear in ninth-century sources such as the *Life of Theodotus of Amida* and the writings of Moshe bar Kepha.[23]

Because there are two seventh-century witnesses to the term *mhaggrâyâ*, the *Qenneshrē Fragment* may simply provide us the third such attestation. But, given that this term is infrequently used by seventh-century authors but quite popular starting in the eighth century, its appearance increases the probability of a post-seventh-century author for this section.

Dating a Demonic Text

Previous scholars such as Patricia Crone, Michael Cook, and François Nau claimed that the *Qenneshrē Fragment* consisted of Daniel of Edessa's eye-witness account to events of the mid-seventh century.[24] Even Robert Hoyland writes that it is quite plausible that Daniel of Edessa "was a major source of the fragment and that some account was written down, either by him or at his behest, in the 670s or 680s."[25] In contrast, Gerrit Reinink points

---

21. Duval, ed., *Ishoʿyahb Patriarchae*, p. 97; and the manuscript *British Library Add.* 14,666, f. 56.
22. Brooks, ed., *Chronica Minora II*, p. 155; Nau, "Un colloque," pp. 248, 251, 252; Brooks, ed., *Chronica Minora III*, p. 348; Vööbus, ed., *Synodicon*, p. 4; Nau, "Littérature," p. 128.
23. *Damascus Patr.* 12/18, f. 64b, cited in Hoyland, *Seeing Islam*, p. 159; *British Library Add.* 14,731, f. 11a.
24. Crone and Cook, *Hagarism*, pp. 162–63; Nau, "Notice historique," p. 118.
25. Hoyland, *Seeing Islam*, p. 145. Hoyland later qualifies this statement as "Daniel may well be the main source for the episode of the demoniacs of Qenneshrē, but in this fragment we have only a reworked excerpt of the original narrative" (p. 147).

out numerous problems in assigning the text's authorship to Daniel, though otherwise he makes few comments regarding when the document was written.[26] A better understanding of the possible composite nature of the *Qenneshrē Fragment* as well as the document's allusion to Qenneshrē's fame for Greek learning, its polemic against the Julianists, and its use of the term *mhaggrâyâ* all point toward a later date for the text's composition than the seventh-century time frame that Crone, Cook, Hoyland, and Nau propose.

In sum, an absolute *terminus post quem* is the last third of the seventh century; the absolute *terminus ante quem* is no earlier than the fifteenth century. Nevertheless, the *Qenneshrē Fragment* provides several textual clues that point toward an earlier date. Although none of these is conclusive, taken together they are suggestive. If the *Qenneshrē Fragment* is a unified text, then one can combine the evidence from section three suggesting an eighth century or later date and the evidence from sections one and two that best fit an eighth-century milieu; in this case the *Qenneshrē Fragment* was most likely composed sometime in the eighth century. If, on the other hand, the *Qenneshrē Fragment* is a composite from earlier documents that roughly correspond to my threefold section division, then sections one and two most likely stem from eighth-century sources and section three from a work written after the seventh century.

26. Reinink, "Die Muslime," pp. 340 n. 26, 346.

Bibliography

Brock, S. "From Antagonism to Assimilation: Syriac Attitudes to Greek Learning." Pp. 17–34 in *East of Byzantium: Syria and Armenia in the Formative Period.* Edited by N. G. Garsoïan, T. F. Matthew, and R. W. Thomson. Washington, DC: Dumbarton Oaks, Center for Byzantine Studies, Trustees for Harvard University, 1982.

Brooks, E. W., ed. *Chronica Minora II.* Corpus Scriptorum Christianorum Orientalium 3. Paris, 1904.

———. *Chronica Minora III.* Corpus Scriptorum Christianorum Orientalium 5. Paris, 1907.

Chabot, J. B., ed. *Chronicon ad annum Christi 1234 pertinens.* Corpus Scriptorum Christianorum Orientalium 81. Louvain, 1920.

———. *Chronique de Michel le Syrien, patriarche jacobite d'Antioche (1166–99) 2/3.* Paris, 1924.

Crone, P., and M. Cook. *Hagarism: The Making of the Islamic World.* Cambridge: Cambridge University Press, 1977.

Duval, R., ed. *Ishoʿyahb Patriarchae III Liber epistularum.* Corpus Scriptorum Christianorum Orientalium 11. Louvain, 1955.

Frend, W. H. C. *The Rise of the Monophysite Movement: Chapters in the History of the Church in the Fifth and Sixth Centuries.* Cambridge: Cambridge University Press, 1972.

Grillmeier, A., and T. Hainthaler. *Christ in Christian Tradition: From the Council of Chalcedon (451) to Gregory the Great (590–604),* vol. 2, part 2. Translated by J. Cawte and P. Allen. Atlanta: Westminster John Knox, 1995.

Harrak, A., trans. and ed. *The Chronicle of Zuqnin, Parts III and IV,* A.D. *488–755.* Toronto: Pontifical Institute of Mediaeval Studies, 1999.

Hoyland, R. G. *Seeing Islam as Others Saw It: A Survey and Evaluation of Christian, Jewish and Zoroastrian Writings on Early Islam.* Princeton, NJ: Darwin, 1997.

Nau, F. "Un colloque du patriarche Jean avec l'émir des Agaréens et faits divers des années 712 à 716." *Journal asiatique* 11 (1915) 225–79.

———. "Littérature canonique syriaque inédite." *Revue de l'Orient Chrétien* 14 (1909) 1–49, 113–30.

———. "Notice historique sur le monastère de Qartmin, suivie d'une note sur le monastère de Qennesré." Pp. 114–35 in *Actes du XIVe Congrès international des orientalistes, Alger 1905, Part 2.* Paris, 1907.

Reinink, G. J. "Die Muslime in einer Sammlung von Dämonengeschichten des Klosters von Qennesrin." Pp. 335–46 in *VI Symposium Syriacum 1992.* Edited by René Lavenant. Rome: Pontificio Istituto Orientale, 1994.

Sachau, E. *Verzeichniss der syrischen Handschriften,* vol. 2. Berlin, 1899.

Van Rompay, L. "Past and Present Perceptions of Syriac Literary Tradition." *Hugoye: Journal of Syriac Studies* 3 (2000).

Vööbus, A., ed. *The Synodicon in the West Syrian Tradition II.* Corpus Scriptorum Christianorum Orientalium 375. Louvain, 1976.

Watt, J. W. "A Portrait of John Bar Aphtonia, Founder of the Monastery of Qenneshrê." Pp. 155–69 in *Portraits of Spiritual Authority: Religious Power in Early Christianity, Byzantium and the Christian Orient.* Edited by J. W. Drijvers and J. W. Watt. Religions in the Graeco-Roman World 137. Leiden: Brill, 1999.

Wright, W. *A Short History of Syriac Literature.* London: Black, 1894. Repr. Piscataway, NJ: Gorgias, 2001.

A Note on an Aramaic Date Formula Found at Nabratein and Zoar

Eric M. Meyers

The recent republication of the well-known Hebrew ancient synagogue lintel inscription from Nabratein in the Upper Galilee has led me to think anew about the date formula in it.[1] First discovered in the nineteenth century by Ernest Renan, it was mentioned frequently by subsequent explorers.[2] The lintel inscription was considered an enigma until Naḥman Avigad successfully explained it in 1960.[3] The inscription, using Avigad's translation reads as follows:

למספר ארבא מאות ותישאים וארבא שנה לחרבן הבית ניבנה בשרר חנינא בן ליזר ולוליאנא בר יודן

[According] to the number four hundred and ninety four years after the destruction [of the Temple], the house was built during the office of Ḥanina son of Lezer and Luliana son of Yudan.

My curiosity about the inscription was first raised when I observed the unusual date formula that related the (re)building of the synagogue to the destruction of the Jerusalem Temple in 70 C.E., making the actual date 564 C.E. Most observers of the lintel—a stone with an elaborate laurel decoration and menorah encased in a small wreath, with the inscription beneath them—were struck by the anomaly of what appeared to be a Roman-period architectural fragment with a Byzantine-period inscription. The disconnect between these two rather obvious points was resolved when Avigad suggested that the inscription was added to an earlier architectural piece and referred to the rededication of a once-destroyed or collapsed building.

---

1. See Meyers and Meyers, *Excavations at Ancient Nabratein*, pp. 92–95.
2. Renan, *Mission*, p. 777, pl. 70, 5A–B. For others, see especially the reprint edition of Kohl and Watzinger, *Antike Synagogen in Galilaea*, p. 103 and fig. 19.
3. Avigad, "Dated Lintel-Inscription."

The recent excavations at Nabratein support Avigad's suggestion, especially the coins found in connection with the rebuilt Synagogue 3, which stood from ca. 564 to 700 C.E.[4] The rededication of the synagogue at Nabratein, thus, refers to the final rebuilding and rededication of the building in the time of Justinian. (For the earlier building phases, the reader should consult the final excavation report.)

What no one seems to have noticed along the way is the rarity of the date formula that related the rededication to 70 C.E., instead of the more common formula linking to the creation of the world or some other important moment in Jewish history. To the best of my knowledge, the date formula at the time of Avigad's article was known from only two Aramaic epitaphs on tombstones from the ancient Jewish cemetery near Zoar at the southern end of the Dead Sea.[5] One of the tombstone inscriptions was published in 1925 by Cowley, and then both in 1944 by Ben-Zvi.[6] These early publications noted the general rarity of dated inscriptions written in Jewish script after 135 C.E.[7] J. Naveh repeated the observation as his publications helped bring the total number of Zoar epitaphs with this formula to 25.[8]

Naveh reviewed the entire Zoar corpus of Aramaic tombstone epitaphs and especially its date formulas in his 1999–2000 presentation in *Tarbiz*. His study of the dates of the Zoar corpus reveals an interesting pattern. Using Naveh's corpus numeration as opposed to the epitaph number, 1–5 fall between the years 352 and 393 C.E., numbers 6–20 fall between 408 and 476 C.E., numbers 21–23 from 503 to 505 C.E., and numbers 24 and 25 are not certain, though both would be fifth century.[9] This means that the formula apparently originated well after the onset of the Christianization process of the Roman Empire that began with Constantine the Great and continued in the East till ca. 640 C.E.

One of the more surprising inferences to be drawn from the study of Jewish epigraphy in late antiquity—which perforce requires a serious consideration of the archaeology of the synagogues, towns, and cites of Israel—is that these developments in writing, art, and archaeology, not to mention the literary

---

4. See Meyers and Meyers, *Excavations*, especially the coin catalogue prepared by Gabi Bijovsky in chap. 10, pp. 374–95.

5. For the site of Zoar, see the references in Avi-Yonah, *Gazetteer*, p. 104. For an account of the first three Aramaic tombstones from Zoar, see Naveh, "Another Tombstone."

6. Cowley, "Jewish Tomb-stone"; and Ben-Zvi, "Two Epitaphs."

7. It should also be noted that the epitaphs provide documentary evidence for the existence of a Jewish settlement on the southern shore of the Dead Sea in the fifth century C.E. whose language was Aramaic.

8. Naveh, "Seven Epitaphs." The entire corpus today consists of 25 epitaphs. For all 25 inscriptions, see also: Naveh, "Aramaic Tombstones"; idem, "More Tombstones"; and Stern, "New Tombstones." They are also available on the Web site of the CAL.

9. Naveh, "Seven Epitaphs." See chart on p. 628, where the corpus numbers are listed alongside the epitaph number with the number of years after the destruction.

output of the sages in the land of Israel, especially the Jerusalem Talmud, reveal a positive response or counterreaction to increasing Christianization. This is part of the thesis developed by Seth Schwartz in his recent book, *Imperialism and Jewish Society, 200 B.C.E. to 640 C.E.* While I take issue with many aspects of the book, Schwartz's understanding of the impact of the Christian empire on Jewish life from 350 to 640 C.E. has much to offer.[10] I would even go so far as to call the use of the date formula a kind of nationalist reflex indicating a focal interest on the part of the Jewish community on one of the central moments in Jewish history, the ninth of *Ab*, when both the First and Second Temple were supposedly destroyed, at least according to later traditions.[11] Schwartz puts it most aptly:

> Neither the pagan nor the Christian Roman Empire was founded on an ideology of pluralism. What changed under Christian rule was the emperors' promotion of *religious* uniformity—as opposed to cultural uniformity containing a diffuse and rather vague religious component. Notwithstanding what has just been said, many laws already in the fourth century move far in the direction of identifying Roman citizenship with orthodox Christianity.[12]

By making a tragic day central in their calendar, Byzantine-period Jews in the land of Israel expressed both their solidarity with Jewish martyrs of the past and their desire to define themselves within their own unique history and experience. This may well be the beginning of what subsequently became popularly known as the "lachrymose" theory of Jewish history.[13]

This kind of self-definition of one's place within a specific tradition is reflected also in the repeated use of the sabbatical cycle in the Zoar corpus. Let me cite Naveh's Epitaph C from his 1985 article:[14]

May rest the soul of (Halfu	תתניח נפשה (דחלפו)
the daughter) of . . . , who died	בר(ת) . . . דמית(ת)
on Tuesday, the eleventh	ביום תלת(ה) בחד עשר
day in the month Elul, in the . . . y(ear)	יומין בירח אלול בש(.)
of the sabbatical cycle, that is the year	דשמטתה דהיא שנת
four hundred thirty	ארבע מאה ותלתין
five years after the destruction	וחמש שנין לחרבן
of the Temple. Peace	בית מקדשה שלום
upon Israel, Peace!	על ישראל שלום

10. Such as his understanding of the process of Hellenization; see Schwartz, *Imperialism*, chap. 4, pp. 129–76. Unfortunately, his summary of the archaeology of the period is full of mistakes and problems.

11. Tishʿah Beʾav is commemorated as a full day of mourning in orthodox and conservative communities, the only such day apart from the Day of Atonement. The book of Lamentations is normally read at evening services, though some congregations also do it in the morning. In some communities, worshipers sit on low stools, a sign of mourning, and chant special hymns of mourning, or *qinot*.

12. Schwartz, *Imperialism*, p. 194.

13. That is, viewing Jewish history from the perspective of tragedy and suffering.

14. Naveh, "Another Tombstone," p. 113.

The degree of specificity in this epitaph says a great deal about the community and the family that was responsible for inscribing it, who did so in 505 C.E. Comparing the inscription with others in the corpus, Naveh is able to supply the year of the sabbatical year cycle, namely, "seven."[15]

This small group of Aramaic inscriptions from Zoar thus sheds a small ray of light on a community of Jews about which we know very little. The language in which they are written also provides insight into the time and larger Late-Antique setting in which they were conceived. And finally, they also help us to understand better the lintel inscription from the ancient synagogue inscription at Nabratein, whose history illuminates an era of synagogue (re)building in the Upper Galilee during a period when restrictive laws were being imposed on the local, non-Christian population. Those laws began shortly after Constantine's public adoption of Christianity, when he himself issued a law concerning the Jews as early as 315 C.E. forbidding Christians to attend Jewish worship.[16] Most of the imperial laws concerning the Jews may be found in the Latin *Codex Theodosianus*, promulgated in 438 C.E., and in the Latin and Greek code of Justinian, which dates to 534 C.E. Intermarriage between Jewish men and Christian women was banned by Constantius (337–361 C.E.) and in 388 extended to any intermarriage between Jews and Christians. In the Theodosian code, Jews were banned from public service, and in the new law of Theodosius II, in 439 C.E., a ban on building new synagogues was imposed on the Jewish population.[17] These anti-Jewish laws may well have contributed to the need on the part of the local Jewish community to note important dates in such detail as reflected in the Zoar corpus.

If there is anything surprising about the observation regarding the date formula noted in this article, it is that, given our impressions of what was happening in the land of Israel in Late Antiquity, we might have expected that we would find more communities that would have chosen such a formula for display in their public buildings or in epitaphs on tombstones. That they did not is reason enough at least to hypothesize that things were not as bad for the Jewish community as some of the literary sources suggest. In other words, the kind of floruit we may observe in Byzantine Palestine with regard to synagogues and the demographic picture we may infer from the archaeological record serve as a corrective to our assessment of what was actually happening on the ground. Schwartz concludes from this data that the Jewish community in Late Antiquity reacted and responded to the Christianization of the empire in a way that was both true to their heritage and influenced "by

---

15. Naveh, "Seven Epitaphs." p. 628.
16. See Marcus, *Jew in the Medieval World*, p. 4.
17. These laws are collected in a more scholarly format by Linder, *Jews in Roman Imperial Legislation*.

old Greco-Roman urban ideas about euergetism and honor."[18] Jodi Magness suggests that most synagogues in the land of Israel have been dated too early, and many if not most should be moved up to the Byzantine period.[19] Mordecai Aviam has suggested that the use of *spolia* in the Byzantine period was a way to circumvent the restrictive legislation of the Christian emperors who forbade the building of new synagogues.[20] Whatever the case may be, relating the rebuilding of a destroyed synagogue or the end of the life of an individual to years after the destruction of the Temple in 70 C.E. and to the sabbatical year cycle was one of many ways that the Jewish community emphasized the distinctive past that set them apart from the surrounding population.[21]

18. Schwartz, *Imperialism*, p. 289.
19. Magness, "Question." But see my response in the same volume: Meyers, "Dating of the Gush Halav Synagogue."
20. Aviam, *Jews, Pagans and Christians in the Galilee*, p. 168, where he makes this suggestion in relation to his reexamination of the dating of the Baram synagogue. This is especially interesting in light of the Nabratein lintel, which dates back to the Roman period.
21. Y. Wilfand's article, "Aramaic Tombstones from Zoar," which appeared after this article was prepared, addresses the corpus as a whole and concludes (p. 536) that the concept of afterlife at Zoar "concurs with the rabbinic view of afterlife."

Bibliography

Aviam, M. *Jews, Pagans and Christians in the Galilee*. Rochester: University of Rochester Press, 2004.
Avigad, N. "A Dated Lintel-Inscription from the Ancient Synagogue of Nabratein." *Louis M. Rabinowitz Fund for the Exploration of Ancient Synagogues* 3 (1960) 49–56.
Avi-Yonah, M. *Gazetteer of Roman Palestine*. Qedem 5. Jerusalem: Israel Exploration Society, 1976.
Ben-Zvi, I. "Two Judaeo-Aramaic Epitaphs from the Vicinity of Zoar," *Bulletin of the Jewish Palestine Exploration Society* 10 (1944) 35–38. [Hebrew]
Cowley, A. "A Jewish Tomb-stone," *Palestine Exploration Fund Quarterly Statement* (1925) 207–10.
Kohl, H., and C. Watzinger. *Antike Synagogen in Galilaea*. Osnabrück: Zeller, 1975. [Original: Leipzig, 1916.]
Linder, A. *The Jews in Roman Imperial Legislation*. Detroit: Wayne State University Press for the Israel Academy of Sciences and Humanities, 1995.
Magness, J. "The Question of the Synagogue: The Problem of Typology." Pp. 1–48 in *Judaism in Late Antiquity*, part 3, vol. 4: *Where We Stand: Issues and Debates in Ancient Judaism. The Special Problem of the Synagogue*. Edited by A. Avery-Peck and J. Neusner. Leiden: Brill, 2001.
Marcus, J. R. *The Jew in the Medieval World*. Philadelphia: Jewish Publication Society, 1960.

Meyers, E. M. "The Dating of the Gush Halav Synagogue: A Response to Jodi Magness." Pp. 49–70 in *Judaism in Late Antiquity*, part 3, vol. 4: *Where We Stand: Issues and Debates in Ancient Judaism. The Special Problem of the Synagogue.* Edited by A. Avery-Peck and J. Neusner. Leiden: Brill, 2001.

———, and C. L. Meyers. *Excavations at Ancient Nabratein: Synagogue and Environs.* Meiron Excavation Project Report 6. Winona Lake, IN: Eisenbrauns, 2009.

Naveh, J. "Another Jewish Aramaic Tombstone from Zoar." *HUCA* 56 (1985) 103–16.

———. "Aramaic Tombstones from Zoar." *Tarbiz* 64 (1994–95) 477–97. [Hebrew]

———. "More on the Tombstones from Zoar." *Tarbiz* 68 (1998–99) 581–86. [Hebrew]

———. "Seven New Epitaphs from Zoar." *Tarbiz* 69 (1999–2000) 617–39. [Hebrew]

Renan, E. *Mission de Phénicie.* Paris: Imprimerie Impériale, 1864.

Schwartz, S. *Imperialism and Jewish Society, 200 B.C.E. to 640 C.E.* Princeton: Princeton University Press, 2001.

Stern, S. "New Tombstones from Zoar (Moussaieff Collection)." *Tarbiz* 68 (1998–99) 177–85. [Hebrew]

Wilfand, Y. "Aramaic Tombstones from Zoar and Jewish Conceptions of the Afterlife." *JSJ* 40 (2009) 510–39.

When?
"After the Destruction of the Temple"

Paul V. M. Flesher

Eric Meyers points out the links between two instances of a rare date formula that counts the years beginning with the destruction of the Jerusalem Temple.[1] Beyond those described by Meyers, the inscriptions at Nabratein and Zoar, there are only four other instances of the Destruction Date Formula. These are: a burial inscription from Baalbek, two medieval *ketubbot*, and a targumic *tosefta* to Ezek 1:1. The paucity of examples of this formula gives rise to two questions. First, why is it so rare? Second, how are these instances of the formula connected? We turn immediately to the first question.

The Mishnah's Ban

The destruction of the Jerusalem Temple in 70 C.E. was a calamitous event for Judaism. It permanently removed the site that had been Judaism's sacred center for over 1,000 years, and the only place at which sacrifices to God could be offered (at least in the theology of Jerusalem priests, and later the rabbis).[2] But the founding document of Rabbinic Judaism, the Mishnah, treats the destruction in an ambiguous fashion. Even though many passages discuss Jewish life, belief, or practice after the Temple was gone, the majority of tractates and their contents address matters of Temple practice and speak as if the Temple and its priests are still functioning.

When the Mishnah's framers refer directly to the Temple's destruction, they often do so in a particular manner, namely, to identify the moment in which a particular practice changed. In the 14 Mishnah passages that mention when "the Temple was destroyed" (usually חרב בית המקדש), 11 of

---

1. See his article in this volume.
2. Of course, not everyone agreed with this position, as the temples at Arad and Elephantine indicate.

them refer to such alterations.³ M. *Sukkah* 3:12 refers to the destruction as the time when the carrying of the *lulab* changed, for example, while m. *Menahot* 10:5 uses it to indicate when the waving of the *omer* ended.⁴ Although later rabbinic literature used the phrase to discuss prophecies of the destruction and other topics, it retains this function into the Babylonian Talmud.⁵

The use of the Temple's destruction as a beginning point for reckoning the passage of time, as Eric Meyers highlights for the inscriptions at Nabratein and Zoar, does not appear in rabbinic literature. The one Mishnah passage that refers to the practice emphasizes that it is totally invalid. This passage is m. *Gittin* 8:5.

M. *Gittin* 8:5 centers on the practice of dating legal documents by time systems inappropriate for Jews. Among the list of incorrect dating references appears the destruction of the Temple. This passage constitutes a long and complicated discussion about how the use of an incorrect dating system invalidates a divorce decree. The case begins when a husband divorces his wife with a *get*—a divorce decree—that uses a forbidden time system. Once sent away from her first husband, the now ex-wife goes out and finds another husband. After the second marriage has taken place, the *get* from the first husband is examined, and the mistake is discovered. The incorrect dating system renders the *get* invalid, and so legally the divorce never took place, leaving the woman married to two men and giving rise to a great number of problems.

כתב לשום מלכות שאינה הוגנת לשום מלכות מדי לשום מלכות יון
לבנין הבית לחורבן הבית
היה במזרח וכתב במערב במערב וכתב במזרח
תצא מזה ומזה וצריכה גט מזה ומזה
ואין לה לא כתובה ולא פירות ולא מזונות ולא בלאות לא על זה ולא על זה

- A. [If a man] wrote [and delivered a *get* to his wife and then she went out and married another. Afterwards it was discovered that he had written it] according to [the dating practice of] a kingdom that is not applicable,
- B. [or] according to [the dating practice of] the Kingdom of the Medes,
- C. [or] according to [the dating practice of] the Kingdom of the Greeks,
- D. [or according to the number of years] after the building of the Temple,
- E. [or according to the number of years] after the destruction of the Temple,

---

3. M. MS 5:2; *Sukkah* 3:12; RH 4:1, 4:3, 4:4; MQ 3:6; *Sotah* 9:12 (2×); *Menahot* 10:5; *Arak.* 9:8; and *Ohal.* 18:9.

4. M. *Taan.* 4:6, *Nazir* 5:4, *Sotah* 9:15 (2×), and *Git.* 8:5.

5. For further discussion of the use of the Temple's destruction as a means for numbering time, see Stern, *Calendar*; idem, *Time*.

F. [or] he had been in the east and he wrote "in the west,"
G. [or] he had been in the west and he wrote "in the east,"
H. [then] she goes out from [her first husband] and from [her second husband] (literally, "from this one and from this one"). And she must [obtain] a *get* from [her first husband] and from [her second husband] (literally, "from this one and from this one").
I. There is nothing for her: no *ketubba* [payment], and no increase [from her property controlled by her husband], and no alimony and no compensation—not from [her first husband] and not from [her second husband] (literally, "not upon this one and not upon this one"). (*m. Gittin* 8:5a)⁶

Lines A through G list a number of different ways of dating a legal document, in this case a divorce decree. These include the dating system of non-Jewish nations and empires, dating by the Temple, and false statements about location. Lines H through I detail the difficulties for the woman that arise from this situation in which, through no fault of her own, she finds herself married to two men. The fact that she must now receive divorce decrees from both men—the first because his original *get* was invalid and the second to remove the stain of (accidental) adultery—indicates the gravity of using improper dating.

The point for this study is that the dating formula used at both Nabratein and Zoar, dating from the Temple's destruction, is declared here to be one of the improper ways to date a legal document. The impact upon the woman and her status reveals that this seeming minor matter has grave consequences. This seems to have been taken seriously in the rabbinic world, rather than debated, for there is no use of this date formula found within the rabbinic literature. This contributes to the rarity of its use, as observed by Meyers.

Specifying the Destruction Date Formula

Although the Mishnah refers to the key words of the Destruction Date Formula, it does not use the entire formula. The Mishnah's framers use the Hebrew phrase, לחרבן הבית, "after the Temple's destruction" (literally, "after the destruction of the house"). This phrase constitutes the core of the Nabratein synagogue inscription of 564 C.E. This is the only complete Hebrew inscription, and so it provides the only Hebrew example of the formula. The inscription reads as follows.

למספר ארבא מאות ותישאים וארבא שנה לחרבן הבית ניבנה בשרר חנינא בן ליזר
ולוליאנא בר יודן

6. Hebrew text is from Albeck, *Mishnah*. Translation is my own, although I consulted Neusner, *Mishnah*. The passage goes on to list further consequences that fall upon the woman.

[According] to the number four hundred and ninety four years after the destruction of the Temple, it [i.e., the synagogue] was built, in the office of Ḥanina son of Lezer and Luliana son of Yudan.[7]

The date formula is as follows: it begins with number, followed by the word "year" (שנה) to indicate that the number refers to a number of years, followed by the *lamed*, which functions as the preposition translated "after," followed by the phrase "the destruction of the Temple" (לחרבן הבית).

The Aramaic version of this Destruction Date Formula is quite similar, and is well evidenced by the 29 known Jewish Aramaic inscriptions from Zoar.[8] The inscriptions span slightly more than 300 years, with the earliest from 352 C.E. At 564, the Nabratein inscription was composed during the last century of this period. The versions of the formula found at Zoar have slight variations but largely adhere to a standard pattern. Naveh's Epitaph C gives the formula as:[9]

דהיא שנת ארבע מאה ותלתין וחמש שנין לחרבן בית מקדשה

... that is (דהיא), the year four hundred and thirty-five years after the destruction of the Temple (בית מקדשה).

After the "that is" (דהיא), which links the formula to the preceding material, this Zoar inscription reads as follows: it begins with the term "year" (שנת), followed by a number, and then the word "years" (שנין) in the plural. The familiar *lamed* + "destruction" (חרבן) then appears, and the formula ends with the term בית מקדשה (literally, "sacred house") to designate the Temple. Rather than use the shorter term as in the Hebrew (הבית), or its Aramaic equivalent, it uses the more complete, two-word phrase, But apart from the repetition of שנין/שנת and the use of בית מקדשה instead of הבית, the Hebrew and the Aramaic formulas are the same.

Other examples of the formula from the Zoar inscriptions show slight variations but nothing that changes it in a significant manner. Naveh's Epitaph 10 shows a tendency toward abbreviation in the number.[10]

שנת ג מא ושתין ב שנין לחרבן בית מקדשה

the year 3 hun[dred] and twenty 2 years after the destruction of the Temple.

Naveh's Epitaph 18 is even more abbreviated.[11]

---

7. Avigad ("Lintel-Inscription," pp. 52–53) decided there was a haplography with הבית here. I attempt to translate as written.
8. I have benefited in my analysis of the Zoar material from the unpublished article of Yael Wilfand. I thank her for sharing her essay with me. See Wilfand, "Conceptions of the Afterlife."
9. Naveh, "Another Jewish Aramaic Tombstone," pp. 113–14. In idem, "Aramaic Tombstones," p. 480, Naveh renumbers it as Epitaph 3.
10. Ibid., pp. 490–91.
11. Idem, "More," p. 586.

When? "After the Destruction of the Temple"

שנת רצ שנין לחרבן בית מקדשה

the year 290 years after the destruction of the Temple.

The abbreviations are the only alterations in the formula; the repetition of שנין/שנת remains the same, as does the term for Temple.

The Zoar inscriptions link the Destruction Date Formula to a second formula that established the date of death not in linear time but within the cyclical time of the sabbatical cycle. Here are the two formulas in Epitaph C, linked by the pronoun דהיא.

דמית[ת ביום תלת[ה]]בחד עשר יומין בירח אלול בש[. .] דשמטתה דהיא שנת ארבע
מאה ותלתין וחמש שנין לחרבן בית מקדשה

who die]d on the third day [of the week], 11 days into the month of Elul in the y[ear]of the *shmiṭah* (= sabbatical cycle), that is (דהיא), four hundred and thirty-five years after the destruction of the Temple.

The two formulas are paired in most of the 29 Zoar Jewish Aramaic inscriptions. Epitaph C is one of the more elegant ones. Most do not take the same care with formulas. Epitaph 10 puts the two formulas together without concern for felicity of expression.[12]

דמיתת יום חמישה יז יומין בירח אלול בשתה רביעתה דשאבועה שנת ג מא ושתין
ב שנין לחרבן בית מקדשה

who died on the fifth day [of the week] 17 days into the month of Elul in the fourth year of the sabbatical cycle, the year 3 hun[dred] and twenty 2 years after the destruction of the Temple.

These are the same two formulas seen in the previous inscription. The only two differences are that they call the sabbatical cycle a "week" (שבועה) instead of the *shmiṭah* and that they leave out the connecting pronoun, דהיא. The two formulas do not depend upon each other, but few of the Zoar inscriptions leave it out.

Other Texts with the Destruction Date Formula

Beyond the inscriptions just discussed, the Temple Destruction Date Formula appears only four times: once in a ninth-century inscription found at Baalbek, in two different *ketubbot* from the Cairo Geniza, and in a targumic *tosefta* added into Ezekiel Targum 1:1. Their differing characters require us to examine each one separately.

The Baalbek inscription is also a burial epitaph, which dates the individual's death from the Temple's destruction.[13] It is later than both the

---

12. Idem, "Aramaic Tombstones," pp. 490–91.
13. I follow the text as it appears on the Web site of CAL. The text was published and translated in Naccach, "Epitaph from Bʿalbak." See also the remarks by Naveh in "Aramaic Tombstones," p. 493.

Nabratein and Zoar inscriptions, yet shows links to both. The inscription reads as follows:

עַל שִׁמְךָ זֶכֶר
צַדִּיק לִבְרָכָה
הָדֵין קְבַרְתֵּיהּ
דְּרַבִּי מֹשֶׁה בַּר
אֵלִיָּה דְּאִתְכְּנֵשׁ
מִן עָלְמָא בִּשְׁתַּ[ה]
שְׁתִיתִיתָהּ דְּשָׁבוּעַ[ה]
דְּהִיא שְׁנַת שֶׁבַע
מְאוֹן וְאִישְׁתִּין
וּתְמַנְיָה שְׁנִין לְחֻרְבַּן
הַבַּיִת הוּא יִבְנָא אַתוּ
וִיקִיץ יְשֵׁנַיָּה עַמּוֹ אָמֵן

Upon your name: The memory of the just be blessed! This is the tomb of R. Moshe bar Eliyah who was gathered from (this) world in the sixth year of the septennial cycle (שבועה), that is (דהיא) the year seven hundred and sixty and eight years after the destruction of the Temple (הבית). May He rebuild it and awaken those who are asleep, (namely) his people! Amen.[14]

The Destruction Date Formula follows the Zoar formula closely, with just one exception. Instead of the Aramaic phrase "the holy house" (בית מקדשא), the inscription uses the Hebrew word "the house" (הבית). This was the term used in the Nabratein inscription, as well as in *m. Gittin* 8:5, which forbade this dating expression.

Part of the Sabbatical Date Formula found at Zoar appears here as well, placed just before the Destruction Date Formula, as in the Zoar inscriptions. Here only the year of the sabbatical cycle (= septennial cycle) is given, not the day or the month. It is joined to the following formula by the term דהיא as in Zoar's Epitaph C.[15] Counting 768 years after the Temple's destruction, R. Moshe's death should be dated to 837 C.E.

There are two medieval *ketubbot* found in the Cairo Geniza that use the Destruction Date Formula, and both are rather fragmentary. The first one, which M. A. Friedman dates to the tenth century, has only enough text remaining to entice but not enough to provide much information.[16] Although the text on the document's right side is well preserved, it is missing the entire left side. The only thing we can tell about it is that the Destruction Date Formula was preceded by a Sabbatical Date Formula, as in the Zoar inscriptions. The first two lines are as follows.

14. The translation is from Naccach, "Epitaph from Bʻalbak." Note the citation of Prov 10:7 in lines 2–3 (in Hebrew) and the mostly Hebrew blessing in lines 11–12 after the date formula.

15. In another similarity to the Zoar epitaphs, the Baalbek inscription ends with a blessing in Hebrew. For Zoar Epitaph C, see Naveh, "Another Jewish Aramaic Tombstone," p. 113.

16. Friedman, *Jewish Marriage*, pp. 339–43. Friedman numbers this as #39.

[ב]יום חמשתה בארבעת יומין לי[רח . . .
לחרבן בית מדקדשא קדישא] . . .

[In] the fifth day on the fourth day of the month . . .
after the destruction of the holy Temple . . .

The second *ketubba* is more complete, and Friedman dates it to the eleventh century.[17] The date formula begins on line 6.

[. . .]שתיתיתה דשבועה שנת ארבעה אלפין ושבע מאוון [. . .]
[. . .] שני[ן] לחרבן בית מוקשה קדישה יתבנה ביומינן וביומיהי[ון . . .]

. . . sixth [year] of the Sabbatical cycle. The year four thousand seven hundred . . .
. . . yea]rs after the destruction of the holy Temple. May it be built in our days and the days of our . . .

The first line contains the end of a Sabbatical Date Formula, which is followed by the term "year" (שנת), which introduces a number of years. Given the *lacuna*, however, the date must be translated into the Gregorian calendar with care. At first glance, it looks as if the number of years belongs to the destruction formula, and all that is missing are numerals in the tens and ones digits. (I could imagine a 42 or a 67, for instance.) But if this is the case, then the date is fanciful, for it gives a number more than 4,700 years after the destruction. This would be unusual for a *ketubba*, which is supposed to be a legally binding text, and it would place the date into our own future.

It is more likely that something else is missing. Friedman and others think the date begun in the first line is reckoned from the creation of the earth, followed by a Destruction Date Formula that is missing its numbers.[18] By rabbinic reckoning, the year 4700 is equivalent to 940 C.E. in the Gregorian Calendar, and so the reference would be to a year in the century following 940. This would fit with the range of dates of other materials found in the Cairo Geniza. Friedman argues that the *ketubba* can be dated to 1005 or 1012.

The last example of the Destruction Date Formula comes from a targumic *tosefta* inserted into a manuscript of the Ezekiel Targum at 1:1. This is quite a large addition of approximately 1,250 words. Targumic *toseftot* are notoriously difficult to date but are often thought to be medieval. This one appears in the Manchester manuscript, Gaster 1478.[19]

The Destruction Date Formula appears in the first line, and the writer uses it to date the story he is telling, rather than the moment in which it was written. Since the story is about Hilkiah the high priest and his finding of the

17. Ibid., pp. 1–34. This is Friedman #1.
18. Ibid., pp. 2–4.
19. See Kasher, *Targumic Toseftot*, pp. 180–88. Gaster 1478 is a typewritten copy prepared from a now-lost manuscript with the number of 1040 by Gaster himself, sometime around the start of the twentieth century. See Kasher, p. 306 and the Targum Manuscripts Database at the Theologische Universiteit Kampen (Netherlands) (URL: www.Targum.nl). Thanks to A. Houtman and E. van Staalduine-Sulman for this information.

"original" scroll of the Torah in the Temple during the reign of King Josiah, the story is set in the late First Temple period, not in the rabbinic or geonic periods of the Common Era. The date formula appears by itself and not in conjunction with the Sabbatical Date Formula.

... והוה לסוף ארבע מאה ותלתין שנין לחורבן בית מקדשא בזמן דאשכח חלקיה
כהנא רבא ית סיפרא דאוריתא בבית מקדשא דיוי בעזרתא בהיכלא

... And it came about at the end of four hundred and thirty years after?/before? (-ל) the destruction of the Temple, in the time when (ד-בזמן) Hilkiah the high priest found the scroll of the Torah in the Temple of the Lord, in the Court of the Temple. [My translation.]

This use of the date formula is odd, for it clearly must indicate a date before the Temple's destruction rather than after, and the destruction of the First Temple at that! The formula itself follows the standard pattern: number + "years" (שנין) + ל + "destruction of the Temple." The only thing that is missing from the formula set by the Zoar inscriptions is the opening term "year" (שנת). This is probably replaced by the term "at the end of" (לסוף). Despite this conformity, perhaps the date formula should be interpreted to mean "before" rather than "after," for the story takes place in the time when (ד-בזמן) Hilkiah found the Torah scroll during the reign of King Josiah. This discovery places the story in Josiah's reign (639 to 609 B.C.E.), before the Temple's first destruction and the Babylonian Exile that followed.[20] But this makes no sense either: how could the author or scribe not know the meaning of this preposition?[21] So although this targumic *tosefta* uses the Destruction Date Formula, it fails to do so correctly.

Tracing the Date Formula

Outside of Zoar, the only known location to make a regular use of it, the Destruction Date Formula appears only five times: Nabratein, Bᶜalbek, two *ketubbot*, and the Ezekiel 1:1 targumic tosefta. Since these inscriptions and texts use the same formula, the formula is known. But what links these texts together? How did they all know the same formula?

They do not seem to be linked chronologically or geographically. Only Zoar and Nabratein are in roughly the same time period, the sixth century; but Bᶜalbek was inscribed in 837, the best date for the datable *ketubba* is just

---

20. The date of 430 years is either fanciful or some sort of mistake, for it does not accurately indicate the time between Josiah's reign (639–609 B.C.E.) and the Temple's destruction in 587, just 22 years after Josiah's death. R. Kasher also finds this a puzzling date. See Kasher, *Targumic Toseftot*, p. 184. A. Damsma addresses this issue in her 2008 doctoral dissertation at the University of London, under the direction of W. Smelik, entitled, *An Analysis of Targum Ezekiel and Its Relationship to the Targumic Toseftot*. I thank her for sharing her preliminary findings with me.

21. Of course, the problem could lie in the *tosefta*'s transcription itself, since it is known only from a typescript prepared by Gaster.

after 1000 C.E., and the targumic *tosefta* is probably later. Geographically, the three inscriptions range from Zoar at the south end of the Dead Sea, north to Nabratein in the Upper Galilee, and north again to Bʿalbek in Lebanon.

Nor can we make a claim for unity of language, at least not for Nabratein, since its Hebrew goes against the Aramaic of the rest. But perhaps the Aramaic exempla of this date formula belong to the same Aramaic dialect. While quite a general criterion, a unity of dialect would indicate at least some connecting strand that joins the texts. The Zoar inscriptions belong most appropriately to Jewish Palestinian Aramaic, in particular to what Stephen Kaufman identifies as its inscriptional sub-dialect.[22] Michael Sokoloff includes them in his *Dictionary of Jewish Palestinian Aramaic*. However, there are a few elements that suggest a Jewish Literary Aramaic influence.

Three lexical items point to the Jewish Palestinian Aramaic character of the Zoar inscriptions. First, 10 of the 29 inscriptions begin with the feminine demonstrative pronoun הדה, as in the phrase . . . ד הדה נפשה, "This is the tomb of. . . ."[23] Its spelling is strictly JPA. Both JLA and LJLA use the ʾalep ending, הדא.

Second, the spelling of the word for "hundreds" in Epitaph 15 is מאון.[24] Again, this form appears only in JPA. JLA and LJLA use מאה or מאתן.

Third, in Epitaph 24, the day of burial is designated ביום ערובתה, "on the day of the evening."[25] This is shorthand for "on the day of the evening *of the Sabbath*," or in other words "Friday." This idiom appears elsewhere only in the Yerushalmi and the Palestinian *midrashim*, where it is found with or without the preceding יום. Thus all three of these elements appear exclusively in JPA.

Two terms found in the Zoar inscriptions point to the influence of JLA. First, the uncommon spelling of "sixth" in Epitaph 17 as part of the phrase בשתה שתיתתה דשאבועה, "in the sixth year of the sabbatical cycle."[26] This spelling appears three times in JLA and four times in LJLA, but never in JPA materials.[27]

Second, the different dialects of Jewish Aramaic vary in the orthography of the names of peoples, such as Canaanites, Jews, and Amalekites. So when Epitaph 24 speaks of the deceased as having died בארעהון דחמיראי, "in the land of the Hamirites," the ʾalep-yod ending of the people's name points to JLA and LJLA.[28] JPA usually has yod-yod for this ending, but occasionally yod-ʾalep. The orthography of the Aramaic terms for 10 and 20 likewise points

---

22. Kaufman, "Aramaic," p. 175.
23. See, for example, Epitaphs B and D, 13, 14, 16, and 19. The CAL website has all the epitaphs accessible by number.
24. Stern, "New Tombstones," p. 179.
25. Naveh, "Seven," p. 624.
26. Naveh, "More," p. 581.
27. For JLA, see TO Exod 26:9, TO Lev 25:21, and TJ Ezek 8:1. For LJLA, see PJ Exod 26:9, PJ Lev 25:21, PJ Lev 25:22, and Targum to Song of Songs 1:1.
28. Naveh, "Seven," p. 624.

to a mix of JPA and JLA. Several inscriptions spell these numbers with a *śin* (עשר), which is a JPA spelling that occasionally occurs in JLA, while others spell them with a *samek* (עסר), as occurs in JLA but not JPA.²⁹ So descriptively, the inscriptions at Zoar seem to be predominately Jewish Palestinian Aramaic with some borrowings from Jewish Literary Aramaic.

When we turn to the Bʿalbek inscription, matters are not so clear. Most of the inscription follows common Aramaic forms that indicate no dialect distinctions, at least when it is not using Hebrew. Two numbers that appear in line 9, however, suggest JPA. First, the word for "hundreds" is מאון, which we have seen is an exclusively JPA term. Second, the orthography of the term for 60, namely, אישתין, is a JPA form. The forms beginning with ʾ*alep* or ʾ*alep-yod* appear often in JPA and never in JLA or LJLA.³⁰ So the dialect indicators of the Baalbek inscription place it easily into Jewish Palestinian Aramaic.

When we turn to the most complete *ketubba* (Friedman #1), we see that it was composed predominantly in JPA, but it contains a couple elements that should be attributed to LJLA.

First, line R[ecto]02 has the JPA spelling of "hundreds," מאון. Second, line R23 has the Palestinian orthography הדה for the demonstrative pronoun, rather than the JLA/LJLA הדא. Third, the number 10, which occurs in lines R12, R17 and R18, is consistently spelled in the dominant JPA form, עשר. Fourth, in line R34, the pronoun "I" is spelled in the form native to JPA, with a final *heh* אנה, rather than the final ʾ*alep* common to JLA and LJLA, אנא. Fifth, the plural form of "Jews," יהודיין, which appears in line R27, is spelled with the exclusively JPA double-*yod* ending, rather than the JLA/LJLA ending of ʾ*alep-yod* or ʾ*alep-heh*.

Into this predominantly JPA text, there appear two forms that can be attributed to LJLA. First, the word for "wife" is spelled with a *nun*, a LJLA archaizing form. It appears in line R22 as אנתתיה and in R05 as אנתו, "wifehood." Second, the numeral "sixth" in line R02 has the uncommon LJLA/JLA orthography of שתיתה. So what we seem to have here is a rather late JPA document that has been influenced by LJLA.

The targumic *tosefta* from the Targum to Ezek 1:1, by contrast, possesses a different dialectal character, one like most targumic *toseftot* found in Targum Onkelos or Targum Jonathan. The author has aimed to compose the addition in the targum's dialect of JLA. This is accomplished fairly successfully, but there are elements of other dialects here, either because the author did not know JLA natively or because the version of JLA he or she knew contained those other elements. So the Ezek 1:1 addition in which we found the date formula comes across in general as JLA but with a few elements in it that should be attributed to LJLA or other dialects.

---

29. *Śin* appears in Epitaphs 13, 14, 24, and 27, while *samek* is used in Epitaphs D, 25, and 29.

30. The form of "sixth" with an ʾ*alep* prefix appears in the Chronicles Targum. This targum awaits a detailed investigation of its linguistic character.

It is clear that the *tosefta* to Ezek 1:1 is predominantly JLA from its use of אנא for the first-person pronoun "I"; from the 'alep-yod ending of יהודאי, "Jews"; from the 'alep-heh ending of כסדאה, "Chaldeans"; from the use of חזי as the verb for "to see"; and from the use of אמרא for the feminine-singular *Peal* participle of אמר, "to say." While some of these forms are also found in LJLA (for instance, אנא and אמרא), others are not (such as חזי).

The non-JLA elements include the *tosefta*'s spelling of the word for "vessel, clothing" with an 'alep, מאן. This orthography appears in both JPA and LJLA, but not in JLA (Kasher, line 123). Similarly, the form מבתר, "after," appears several times in the *tosefta* (Kasher, lines 15, 37, 41, 43, 46, 49, 55, and so on). This is short for מן בתר, and both JPA and LJLA alternate the two forms as their translation for the Hebrew אחר and אחרי. This is unlike TO and TJ, which use only בתר as their Aramaic equivalent for this term. There are also several occurrences of כל קביל, "concerning, as opposed to," which is common in Jewish Babylonian Aramaic, although there are a few instances in JPA and even one in Biblical Aramaic. None appears in the JLA of TO or TJ.

So what we have in the end is not an LJLA passage with a heavy dose of JLA, but a JLA passage with the occasional intrusion from JBA and either JPA or LJLA. The result may be understood as a "mixed" dialect, as Kasher states.

Conclusion

It seems that the Aramaic inscriptions that use the Destruction Dating Formula were not written in the same dialect. Working backward through the evidence, the targumic *tosefta* to Ezek 1:1 seems to be a JLA passage, with a few borrowings from JBA and LJLA and/or JPA. The *ketubba* is a JPA document with some LJLA intrusions. The Bʿalbek inscription evidences only JPA. Finally, the Zoar inscriptions seem to be written primarily in JPA, but with some lexical items belonging to JLA. While only the Bʿalbek inscription contains a pure dialect of any kind, they all have a dominant dialect character with a few elements from another dialect (or two).

If we look more selectively, however, it becomes clear that the Aramaic texts and inscriptions that use the date formula correctly all use JPA as the dominant dialect. The one text that uses the formula incorrectly, the Ezek 1:1 *tosefta*, was carefully cast in JLA to fit into Targum Jonathan's dialect. All other inscriptions and texts use the formula properly and are composed with JPA as their dialect, even though some have a few elements identified with JLA or LJLA.

So in the end, the connection among all the accurate examples of this "banned" date formula lies in their shared dialect, Jewish Palestinian Aramaic. Because of this dialect's use in inscriptions, its geographical area of use can be identified, at least in part. Jewish Palestinian's center was the Galilee and the Golan, but it extended along the Jordan Valley (properly the Rift Valley) as far north as Bʿalbek and as far south as southern Judea. Nabratein, with its synagogue and inscription, lies in Upper Galilee, in the heart of the dialect's geographical range. That could explain why the writer of Nabratein's Hebrew inscription knew the formula and could render it in Hebrew. It would also clarify why the Ezekiel *tosefta* did not use it correctly. That is, its author was not familiar with the formula belonging to another dialect and so used it incorrectly.

Bibliography

Accordance Bible Software. http://www.accordancebible.com/.
Albeck, C. *Six Orders of the Mishnah*. Vol. 3. Jerusalem: Mosad Bialek, 1938. [Hebrew]
Avigad, N. "A Dated Lintel-Inscription from the Ancient Synagogue of Nabratein." *Bulletin of the Louis M. Rabinowitz Fund for the Exploration of Ancient Synagogues* 3 (1960) 49–56.
Cook, E. M. *A Glossary of Targum Onkelos*. Leiden: Brill, 2008.
Fassberg, S. E. *A Grammar of the Palestinian Targum Fragments from the Cairo Genizah*. Harvard Semitic Studies 38. Atlanta: Scholars Press, 1990.
Flesher, P. V. M. "A Study Guide for Jewish Palestinian Aramaic." Unpublished manuscript, 2004.
Friedman, M. A. *Jewish Marriage in Palestine: A Cairo Geniza Study*. Vol. 2. Tel-Aviv: Tel-Aviv University / New York: Jewish Theological Seminary, 1981.
Kasher, R. *Targumic Toseftot to the Prophets*. Jerusalem: World Union of Jewish Studies, 1996. [Hebrew]
Kaufman, S. A. "Languages (Aramaic)." Pp. 173–78 in vol. 4 of *Anchor Bible Dictionary*. Edited by D. N. Freedman. New York: Doubleday, 1992.
Naccach, A. F. "A Ninth Century A.D. Judeo-Aramaic Epitaph from Bʿalbak." *Orientalia* 58 (1989) 243–45 and pl. 5.
Naveh, J. "Another Jewish Aramaic Tombstone from Zoar." *HUCA* 65 (1985) 103–16.
———. "Aramaic Tombstones from Zoar." *Tarbiz* 64 (1994) 477–97. [Hebrew]
———. "More on the Tombstones from Zoar." *Tarbiz* 68 (1998) 581–86 and plate. [Hebrew]
———. "Seven New Epitaphs from Zoar." *Tarbiz* 69 (1999) 617–34. [Hebrew]
Neusner, J. *The Mishnah: A New Translation*. New Haven, CT: Yale University Press, 1988.
Sokoloff, M. *A Dictionary of Jewish Palestinian Aramaic*. 2nd ed. Ramat Gan, Israel: Bar Ilan University Press / Baltimore: Johns Hopkins University Press, 2002.
Stern, S. *Calendar and Community: A History of the Jewish Calendar, Second Century BCE–Tenth Century CE*. New York: Oxford University Press, 2001.
———. "New Tombstones from Zoar (Moussaieff Collection)." *Tarbiz* 68 (1998) 177–85 and plates. [Hebrew]
———. *Time and Process in Ancient Judaism*. Portland, OR: Littman Library of Jewish Civilization, 2003.
———, and Misgav, H. "Four Additional Tombstones from Zoar." *Tarbiz* 74 (2005) 137–51. [Hebrew]
Wilfand, Y. "Aramaic Tombstones from Zoar and Jewish Conceptions of the Afterlife." *JSJ* 40 (2009) 510–39.

The Details of Language

The Function of the Active Participle in the Aramaic of Daniel

Tarsee Li

1. Introduction

The active participle in the Aramaic of the biblical book of Daniel has a wide range of functions, ranging from an aspectual progressive to an allegedly aspectless simple past, making it one of the most intriguing features of the verbal morphosyntax of this form of Aramaic. The present study examines its various functions in the light of cross-linguistic diachronic evidence. I conclude that the active participle advanced from a progressive to an imperfective and is on its way to becoming a present. Furthermore, this study also explores the relationship between איתי/הוה + *participle* and *participle* + הוה.

Some relevant views on the function of the active participle in the Aramaic of Daniel may be summarized as follows. For Kautzsch (1884: 138–41), it was primarily a nominal form expressing a state. According to Bauer and Leander (1927: 290–96) the active participle has partly taken over the functions of the prefix conjugation and can function as present, future, or imperfective past. Its temporal relevance can be strengthened or highlighted by איתי or a conjugated form of הוה. In addition, the participle can express the simple past. Rosén (1961) distinguished "linear" verbs from "point" verbs. For "point" verbs, the participle is the past-time narrative tense, whereas for "linear" verbs, the participle denotes the present, and the compound tense containing the copula is both subordinative and future-volitive. According to

---

Author's note: I want to express my thanks to Lucas Van Rompay and Paul Flesher for reading earlier drafts of this article and for their encouragement and insightful suggestions, as well as for sharing their expertise in various Aramaic dialects. The views articulated here and any shortcomings are my own.

I originally submitted a version of this essay in the early stages of my research on the verbal system of the Aramaic of Daniel, which was subsequently published in Li 2009. The present version of this article includes material that appeared in my monograph (2009: 39–57, 79–91) in a slightly updated form.

Rosenthal (1961: 55), the participle was used for expressing the "immediate present," which led to its use for an "action that is simultaneous with the main action," and its frequent use in past time eventually "led further to the free use of the participle as a narrative tense." In addition, it was used to express continuous and habitual action. Muraoka (1966: 157–60) suggested that the participle in Biblical Aramaic is "more or less indifferent to time," that is, its temporal reference is determined by the context. That is, the participle may refer to the past, present, or future, depending on the context. Where the context does not specify a temporal reference, the participle is atemporal. Segert (1975: 381–83) observed that this is also the case of the participle in Old Aramaic, but only in Daniel does it denote independent past time actions. Cohen (1984: 393–432) proposed that the active participle has a durative function. By itself it expresses the durative present, and the addition of הוה adds the tense: durative past with a suffix conjugation הוה and durative future with the prefix conjugation הוה. In discussing the distinction in the past-time functions of the participle and the suffix conjugation, he allowed that the participle by itself can function as a historical present in narrative contexts (as suggested by Bauer and Leander 1927: 294–95), but claimed that this use always follows a suffix conjugation verb (Cohen 1984: 413, 477). According to Blau (1987: 6–10), the participle, the prefix conjugation, and verbless clauses all mark simultaneity in past time after a suffix conjugation form or a temporal adverbial, "without visible functional difference," and reflects the "blend of two systems, . . . the earlier one with the imperfect and the later one with the participle." Gzella (2004: 306–8) lists the functions of the participle as present, performative, future, and narrative past. I should also mention two recent studies that focused on discourse analysis and/or textlinguistics, Toews (1993) and Shepherd (2008), neither of which, however, attempted to explain the morphosyntactic function of the participle. Thus, although there is widespread agreement that the active participle can express the present as well as the past, the nature of its function in these temporal spheres and the diachronic sequence in which these functions developed remain to be explored.

In the present study, I have relied heavily on the typological work of Bybee, Perkins, and Pagliuca (1994), who examined cross-linguistic trends in the grammaticalization of selected verbal grammatical morphemes in 76 languages.[1] Of special relevance to this study is the relationship between pro-

---

1. *Grammaticalization* denotes the study of how certain lexical terms and constructions come to serve grammatical functions and how grammatical items develop new grammatical functions. Although the use of the term itself goes back to Meillet in 1912, studies in grammaticalization did not flourish until the beginning of the 1980s (see Hopper and Traugott 2003: 19–38). Some have criticized grammaticalization theory, preferring to call it an "epiphenomenon" of language change (e.g., Janda 2001: 266) because there are occasional counterexamples (the entire issue of *Language Sciences* 23 was dedicated to a critique of grammaticalization theory; see especially Campbell and Janda 2001; Campbell 2001; as well as the response to these criticisms in Hopper and Traugott 2003: 130–38). For

gressive and imperfective grammatical constructions. Although definitions of "progressive" and "imperfective" aspect vary in the literature on linguistics, the progressive is commonly explained as a subset of imperfective aspect (Comrie 1976: 24–40). A progressive, which is also sometimes called durative, "views an action as ongoing at reference time," whereas an imperfective can express a wider range of meanings, including habitual, iterative, frequentative, etc., as well as ongoing actions (Bybee, Perkins, and Pagliuca 1994: 125–26). Progressives generally occur with dynamic rather than stative predicates. This is because a stative denotes a state that will continue indefinitely unless something puts an end to it, whereas a progressive denotes an action that continues because it is sustained by a constant input of energy. They offer the following two sentences as examples (1994: 126):

1. Sara is reading.
2. *Sara *is knowing* the answer.

Sentence 1 contains a progressive construction with a dynamic verb. Sentence 2 uses a stative verb in a progressive construction and is ungrammatical, which is indicated by the asterisk. At the risk of oversimplification, I would like to illustrate further the relationship between progressive and imperfective with the following examples:

3. Sara was reading the novel.
4. Sara used to read novels.
5. Sara kept on reading the novel.

Sentences 3 to 5 illustrate some varieties of imperfective aspect. Of these, only sentence 3 is progressive, expressing an action in process at reference time. Sentence 4 is habitual, indicating a customary or habitual action, rather than an action in process. And sentence 5 is, depending on context, either iterative, expressing repetition, or continuative, expressing the deliberate continuance of an action. Thus, in languages with an imperfective—that is, a grammatical construction capable of expressing most or all shades of imperfective aspect—the imperfective construction can express any of the meanings of sentences 3 to 5, with the exact shade of meaning being determined by context. Of course, an all-inclusive imperfective can, and often does,

---

more recent discussions on the validity of grammaticalization as a theory, see the contributions in Fischer, Norde, and Perridon 2004; López-Couso and Seoane 2008. Fischer (2007) presented a very balanced discussion, comparing the approaches of generative grammar and grammaticalization theory, discussing their strengths and weaknesses, and suggesting ways in which they can complement each other. It is beyond the scope of this article to address issues regarding grammaticalization as a theory. Nevertheless, it is beyond question that grammaticalization studies have highlighted a number of cross-linguistic tendencies that are relevant for the study of historical linguistics, even if some explanation other than grammaticalization is more appropriate for these tendencies.

coexist with grammatical constructions for more specific types of imperfectivity, such as progressives, habituals, iteratives, and so on. As Bybee, Perkins, and Pagliuca (1994: 126) point out, imperfectives are often restricted to the past, as in the Spanish and French imperfect tenses, but may also be applicable to present and the future, as in Russian. They also consider the present to be a type of imperfective, because it can also express present habitual and gnomic situations.[2]

Progressive expressions originate from a limited number of sources, and most of the progressives in the world derive from locative expressions (Heine 1994). According to Bybee, Perkins, and Pagliuca (1994: 125–75), progressives develop into presents or imperfectives. More specifically, "a progressive restricted to the present by the existence of a past imperfective will become a present tense," while one that is not so restricted will become a general imperfective (Bybee 1994: 250). This path of development is due to the fact that, when a new grammatical entity develops, it is at first more specific than the ones already in use. As the original constrictions gradually erode, the new grammatical expression becomes appropriate in more and more contexts. Thus, a construction that was at first restricted to the expression of a subset of imperfective aspect, for example, the progressive, can eventually expand its range of functions to include the entire imperfective aspect.

Since the active participle originated very early in Semitic, we cannot verify whether or not it originated from a locative expression. However, it is safe to say that at some point in time in the development of ancient Northwest Semitic languages, the active participle came to have a progressive function, as for example in Biblical Hebrew (Hatav 1997: 89–116). Many of the progressives attested in the languages surveyed by Bybee, Perkins, and Pagliuca consist of the verb "to be" in combination with a nonfinite verbal form. However, since the verb "to be" is not obligatory in Semitic nominal clauses, it is easy to see how the active participle by itself could function as a progressive.

It has also been observed that the active participle eventually took over the functions of the prefix conjugation in later Aramaic, as reflected, for example, in its wide range of functions in Syriac (Nöldeke 1904: 211–18). Nöldeke recognized that the Syriac active participle began to be used "in room of the Impf. [sic]" (1904: 216). The process by which the active participle eventually takes over the functions of the prefix conjugation is not an isolated Aramaic, or even Semitic, phenomenon, but is part of a more widespread phenomenon common to many languages, that is, progressives eventually become imperfectives or presents.[3]

---

2. Bybee (1994: 236) does allow for exceptions. The present can be perfective in performatives or in the narration of ongoing events, such as a sports event. Otherwise, presents are imperfectives.

3. For example, Caubet (1991) gives examples of participles with present, present perfect, and future meanings in modern Arabic dialects.

In order to put this research in perspective, though its focus is limited to the Aramaic of Daniel, it is helpful to mention the verbal systems of some other forms of Aramaic. According to Muraoka and Porten (1998), the finite verbal system of Egyptian Aramaic consists of two tenses.[4] That is, the suffix conjugation is basically preterital, and the prefix conjugation is "roughly future" (1998: 192). As for the participle (1998: 203–8), besides nominal and attributive functions, it expresses the actual present, an action that has been going on up to the moment of speaking, and the "historic present" (1998: 204), that is, the present used for the simple past.[5] According to Fitzmyer, the *Genesis Apocryphon* from Qumran (hereafter 1QapGen) exhibits the "ordinary" functions of the verb. That is, the suffix conjugation expresses the "past" and the prefix conjugation the "present or future" (2004: 291), whereas the participle occurs either alone in "nominal sentences," where the time is determined by the context, or with הוה, where the nuance "seems to be that of progressive or continuous past action" (2004: 292).[6] On the other hand, the participle has become a "full-fledged member" of the verbal system of the Aramaic of Targums Onkelos and Jonathan, which consists of the suffix conjugation, the participle, and the prefix conjugation, the latter of which is confined to future and modal uses (Gropp forthcoming: chap. 19). Syriac is typically described as having three tenses, that is, "perfect, imperfect, and participle" (Muraoka 2005: 40). However, since the imperfect is only rarely used as a future in independent clauses, and is more often the complement of another verb, one could conclude that only two of the verb forms are operative in most independent indicative clauses: the suffix conjugation, which is "essentially a past tense," and the participle, which expresses either present or future (2005: 65–66). Syriac also makes extensive use of compound tenses with הוה, which will be discussed separately below.[7]

Determining the total number of active participles in the Aramaic of Daniel is tricky, because the t-stem participles—that is, Hithpeel and Hithpaal—can have both passive and nonpassive (e.g., reflexive, reciprocal) functions. I have included them in the total number, but will indicate below

---

4. Folmer (1995) also has a very thorough study of the Aramaic of this period, but unfortunately does not address the function of the active participle. Apparently, she would agree with Muraoka and Porten that the participle is not part of the finite verbal system. Since Gzella's (2004) study of Imperial Aramaic includes Biblical Aramaic, the present study will interact with his where relevant.

5. For an alternative view that pays attention to dialect differentiation in Egyptian Aramaic, see Cohen (1984: 349–82).

6. Thus, one can infer that he does not consider the participle a full-fledged member of the verbal system.

7. Also of interest is a recent contribution by Rubin on grammaticalization in Semitic languages, which includes a discussion of several aspects of the Semitic verb and a chapter on the present tense marker in modern dialects of Aramaic and Arabic (Rubin 2005: 26–46, 129–52). However, Rubin did not try to describe the verbal system of any one language or dialect.

instances that I consider purely passive. Also, the consonantal text allows many G-stem active participles to be understood as suffix conjugation verbs. Nevertheless, although these will be noted in passing where the information may alter some statistics (e.g., see below under formulaic expressions), the basic conclusions remain unaffected. This results in a provisional total of 231 instances of active participles (*Ketiv/Qere* counted as single instances). Of these, at least 41 occur in combination with הוה or איתי, and will be discussed separately. In the remainder of this article, I will analyze and classify the function of each active participle on the basis of the context. The analysis will distinguish nominal and verbal functions—the latter in terms of tense (past, present, future), aspect (perfective or imperfective, and if imperfective, progressive or nonprogressive), and modality. For obvious reasons, the discussion of aspectual functions will be more extensive.

The examples cited are taken at random, except for those cited because they require special comment. Since many verses contain more than one participle, which in turn do not always have the same function, they are distinguished where necessary by the order of occurrence with the addition of a letter after the verse number (e.g., 5:5a). However, participial expressions with איתי/הוה are counted separately. For instance, in 6:5, the two participles are listed as 1 instance of הוה + *participle* and 1 instance of the participle alone, not as 6:5a and 6:5b.

2. Active Participles without הוה or איתי

2.1. Nominal Functions of the Active Participle

Since participles are verbal nouns, it is no surprise that they have nominal as well as verbal functions. Among the nominal functions of the participle are the following. In 10 instances, a participle is either (part of) the nominal predicate of a verbless (equational) sentence (2:15c, 21a, b, c, d, 22a, b, 47c; 3:22) or stands in apposition to it (2:28).

Daniel 2:47

מן־קשט די אלהכון הוא אלה אלהין ומרא מלכין <u>וגלה</u> רזין

Of a truth, your god is a god of gods, and a lord of kings, and *a revealer* of secrets.

Some of these participles could be alternatively analyzed as general presents (e.g., see Muraoka 1966: 158 on 2:22).

In at least 12 instances, a participle functions substantively in a verbal sentence. These may occur as (part of) the subject (2:27d, 29; 4:4b, 32a; 5:12a, b), the direct object (5:7b), the indirect object (2:21e; 4:16e), or other nominal phrase (4:32c; 5:11; 7:16). In addition, I would also include under this category 2 more instances where the participle should be analyzed as the predicate of the verb "to be" (2:43a; 7:19a), as explained below in the discussion of participles with the verb הוה.

Daniel 4:32

וכל דָארי ארעא כלה חשיבין

And all the *inhabitants of* the earth are accounted as nothing.

In 11 instances, participles function attributively (3:6, 11, 15, 17c, 20, 21, 23, 26a; 7:3b, 5a, 9).

Daniel 3:6

ומן־די־לא יפל ויסגד בה־שעתא יתרמא לגוא אתון נורא יָקדתא

And whoever does not fall down and worship, at that moment he will be thrown into the *burning* fiery furnace.

2.2. The Active Participle in Formulaic Expressions

Turning to verbal uses of the participle, many participles involve verbs of speaking, generally introducing direct speech. Of these, 55 instances (all in main clauses) belong to a special category because of their formulaic nature.[8] Typically, the first verb of this formula is an asyndetic participle (there are also 2 instances introduced by באדין, 5:17; 6:14), though there are also 5 instances where the formula begins with a suffix conjugation verb (2:7, 10; 3:9, 16a; 5:10). The second verb is almost always a participle (the only exception occurs in 5:10, where both verbs are suffix conjugation forms). In the majority of cases, the verbs in question are ענה and אמר.[9]

Daniel 2:5

עָנה מלכא ואָמר לכשדיא

The king *answered and said* to the Chaldeans . . . ,

No distinction in nuance could be detected between occurrences of this formula with a suffix conjugation form as the first verb and those with a participle as the first verb. However, Tropper (1997: 117–18) has argued that in the majority of the instances, the first verb in this formula should be emended to a suffix conjugation form.

Additionally, 9 participles introduce direct speech by themselves, without another verb (3:4a, b; 4:20b, 28a; 6:6, 7, 13a, 16; 7:5b). Conversely, there are also instances of single participles used with verbs of speaking in clauses that do not introduce a direct speech, including אמר (4:4c) and קרא (5:7a) (see also מלל in 7:8, 11, 20).

It is not easy to explain the formulaic use of the active participle with verbs of speaking. I will attempt an explanation in my discussion of the historical

---

8. The list is as follows: 2:5a, b, 7, 8a, b, 10, 15a, b, 20a, b, 26b, c, 27a, b, 47a, b; 3:9, 14a, b, 16a, 19a, b, 24a, b, c, d, 25a, b, 26a, b, 28a, b; 4:11a, b, 16a, b, c, d, 27a, b; 5:7b, c, 13a, b, 17a, b; 6:13b, c, 14a, 17a, b, 21a, b; 7:2a, b. The fact that this use belongs to a special category is widely recognized: see, e.g., Bauer and Leander (1927: 295) and Segert (1975: 383).

9. In a few instances, the formula אמר + ענה does not introduce a direct quotation (e.g., 3:19).

present below (§2.3.7). In this section, I will limit myself to the following observations. Cohen (1984: 414) observed that the verb אמר means "command" in the suffix conjugation but "say" as a participle.[10] However, such a distinction does not explain why other verbs of speaking are also often used as participles. It is possible that the participle is the preferred form for introducing a direct quotation in some forms of Aramaic, and that this usage spread to other instances of verbs of speaking. Moreover, since the infinitive למאמר is only attested with a telic function in Daniel, it is possible that the participle אמר as the second member of the above formula may have a function similar to the Hebrew infinitive לאמר.

The preference of the participle of אמר in introducing direct speech is not limited to the Aramaic of Daniel. According to Muraoka and Porten (1998: 204), many instances of אמר in past time in Egyptian Aramaic may actually be participles. Cohen (1984: 451) also observed that in Targum Neofiti the participle of אמר following another suffix conjugation verb is often used to translate the Hebrew imperfect consecutive ויאמר. Nöldeke (1904: 215) noted a similar use of the active participle of the verb אמר in Syriac, which he calls a "historical present," and which "scarcely ever" occurs with other verbs. Finally, although the formulaic participles in Daniel are usually translated as simple pasts, some of them also have one of the imperfective functions described below.

Regardless of how one might explain the frequent use of the participle in expressions introducing direct speech, the recognition of the formulaic nature of such expressions and the concomitant less frequent use of participles in nonformulaic clauses suggest that it does not occur frequently enough to support Rosén's (1961) claim that it is the narrative tense. There are 87 remaining instances of active participles functioning verbally without הוה or איתי. These instances may be grouped by function as follows.

2.3. The Active Participle as an Imperfective

2.3.1. Past Progressive

The apparently atemporal nature of the active participle (e.g., Muraoka 1966: 157–60) is in keeping with the nature of progressives, since the reference time of progressives is indicated by the context. Some participles with a progressive function occur in main independent clauses (2:31; 3:3a, b, 26d, 27; 5:5a, b, 6; 7:2c, 3a, 10a, b, 21a, b). When these occur in a series, the actions/events denoted are often simultaneous or overlapping.

---

10. He acknowledges exceptions, however. For instance, he concedes that the participle אמר in 3:19 means "command," and the suffix conjugation of אמר in 5:10 means "say." As further examples of the latter, I would add the instances of the suffix conjugation אמר in 2:25 and 7:23, and perhaps also 7:1, 16.

The Function of the Active Participle in the Aramaic of Daniel 77

Daniel 5:5

בה־שעתה נפקו אצבען די יד־אנש וכתבן לקבל נברשתא על־גירא די־כתל היכלא די
מלכא ומלכא חזה פס ידה די כתבה

At that moment, the fingers of a human hand came out. And they *were writing* opposite the lampstand on the plaster of the wall of the royal palace, and the king *was watching* the back of the hand that was writing.

Buth (1987: 483–84) observed that foreground clauses in Daniel are verb initial, though an animate narrative topic may precede the verb. Thus, the two participles cited in the above example are in temporal succession, since the order of the clauses is irreversible. That is, the hand started writing before the king started watching it. However, the overlapping nature of the participles is clear from the fact that the king started watching while the fingers were still writing on the wall. Another example occurs in 3:3, where the participles (both active and t-stem) are typically translated as simple pasts.

Daniel 3:3

באדין מתכנשין אחשדרפניא סגניא ופחותא אדרגזריא גדבריא דתבריא תפתיא וכל
שלטני מדינתא לחנכת צלמא די הקים נבוכדנצר מלכא וקאמין לקבל צלמא

Then the satraps, prefects, and governors ... and all the officials of the province *were gathering together* for the dedication of the statue that king Nebuchadnezzar had set up, and *were standing* before the statue.

Bauer and Leander (1927: 294) cited the above verse as one of the examples of active participles denoting single (nonrepetitive) past-time events. Similar to the previous example, the participial clauses are irreversible. That is, the officials had to gather together before they could stand before the statue. However, the fact that the order of the sentences is irreversible does not preclude them from being temporally overlapping. Since the subject of the verbs is plural, it is reasonable to conclude that the officials did not first finish gathering together before they began to stand before the statue. Thus, the overlapping nature of the actions suggests that these participles are better understood as progressives than as simple pasts.

Often, progressive participles occur in clauses that are either marked as subordinate, such as relative clauses (5:5c), or that are semantically dependent on other clauses, such as circumstantial clauses (5:9a, b, c).

Daniel 5:5

ומלכא חזה פס ידה די כתבה

The king was watching the back of the hand that *was writing*.

Daniel 5:9–10

(9) אדין מלכא בלשאצר שגיא מתבהל וזיוהי שנין עלוהי ורברבנוהי משתבשין
(10) מלכתא לקבל מלי מלכא ורברבנוהי לבית משתיא עללת

Then *as* king Belshazzar *was* greatly *alarmed*, his complexion *was altered*, and his nobles *were perplexed*, the queen entered the banquet hall because of the words of the king and his nobles.

In the above example, the active participle and two t-stem participles form a series of participial clauses conveying the circumstances attending the ensuing suffix conjugation verb.

Not all semantically dependent clauses are circumstantial. I would describe the remaining progressive instances as adverbial for lack of a better definition (3:25d; 4:10, 20a; 6:12; 7:7a, b, c, 19a, b, c).[11]

Daniel 3:25

הא־אנה חזה גברין ארבעה שרין <u>מהלכין</u> בגוא־נורא

Look, I see four men loose, *walking* in the fiery furnace.

Finally, a few instances of formulaic participles introducing direct speech are also progressive in function (e.g., 4:11a, b, 20b; 7:8, 11, 20).

Daniel 4:10–11

(10) ואלו עיר וקדיש מן־שמיא נחת (11) <u>קרא</u> בחיל וכן <u>אמר</u>

Look, there was a watcher and holy one from heaven coming down, *calling* with a loud voice, and *saying* thus: . . .

In spite of the fact that the active participle so often has a progressive function, more often than not it is impossible to ascribe a progressive meaning to it. There are two evidences that the active participle in Daniel is more than a progressive, and has become an imperfective. First, active participles are often formed from stative verbs (e.g., שנה 7:3; דמה 3:25; 7:5; ידע 2:8; 5:23; יכל 2:27; 3:17; 4:15, 34; 6:5; כהל 2:26; 4:15; 5:8, 15). Second, active participles often have imperfective functions beyond the progressive, as explained below.

2.3.2. Past Habitual or Iterative/Frequentative

In a few instances, active participles are habitual or iterative/frequentative. The term *habitual* refers to customarily repeated actions, *iterative* refers to repeated actions that have a well-defined end point, and *frequentative* refers to actions that occur frequently in a specific period of time (Bybee, Perkins, and Pagliuca 1994: 127). Since distinguishing among these three functions is difficult in a dead dialect with a limited corpus, I have grouped together the discussion of possible instances. Habitual participles occur both in the past (6:11a, b, c) and in the present (6:14b), though a present habitual should be classified as a general present, as will be explained later.

Daniel 6:11

וזמנין תלתה ביומא הוא <u>ברך</u> על־ברכוהי <u>ומצלא ומודא</u> קדם אלהה

And three times a day he *kept on kneeling* on his knees, *and praying, and giving thanks* before his God.

---

11. In some instances where the participle is adverbial to a nominal clause, there could be some ambiguity in the analysis (e.g., 4:10, 20a; 7:7a, b, c). That is, the participle could be analyzed either as an adverbial participle in a nominal clause or as a progressive participle in a verbal main clause (compare, however, the instances in 7:7 with those in 7:19).

The participles above describe repeated or customary actions (for example, "three times a day") rather than actions in process. Thus, they are examples of nonprogressive imperfective aspect. The use of a progressive construction to express habitual action is a "major step" toward its development into either present or imperfective (Bybee, Perkins, and Pagliuca 1994: 141).

In at least 4 instances, active participles could be analyzed either as iterative or progressive (3:7a, b, c; 5:8a). Bauer and Leander (1927: 293) cited כדי שמעין in 3:7 as an example of repetition in the past, "whenever they would hear" ("So oft alle Völker . . . hörten"). However, it is more likely that this expression is a progressive, parallel to the later Syriac בד + participle, "as they were hearing."

Daniel 3:7

כל־קבל דנה בה־זמנא כדי שמעין כל־עממיא קל קרנא משרוקיתא קיתרס שבכא
פסנטרין וכל זני זמרא נפלין כל־עממיא ולשניא סגדין לצלם דהבא די הקים
נבוכדנצר מלכא

Therefore, as all people *were hearing* the sound of the horn, pipe, lyre, trigon, harp, and all kinds of music, all the peoples, nations, and languages *were falling down worshiping* the golden image that Nebuchadnezzar the king set up. [or: "whenever . . . would hear . . . would fall down (and) worship . . ."]

Kutscher (1976: 51–58) drew attention to this expression, which he called "predicative," which occurs in Targum Onkelos as כד + participle, in the Babylonian Talmud as כי + participle, and in Galilean Aramaic as מן + participle. In the present corpus, the imperfective force of the expression כדי + participle in the above example can be contrasted with the expression כדי + suffix conjugation, which is not imperfective (6:11, 15). In at least one instance the active participle could be either iterative or inceptive (4:4a). See below.

2.3.3. Past Inceptive

There are 2 possible instances where the active participle is inceptive—that is, it depicts the beginning of an action—though both instances could be otherwise analyzed. The inceptive function is also called ingressive or inchoative in some grammars. One instance occurs in Daniel 4:4a.

Daniel 4:4–5

(4) באדין עללין חרטמיא אשפיא כשדיא וגזריא וחלמא אמר אנה קדמיהון ופשרה
לא־מהודעין לי (5) ועד אחרין על קדמי דניאל

Then as the magicians, exorcists, Chaldeans, and psychics *began to come in*. And as I was telling them the dream, and they could not make known its interpretation, finally Daniel came in before me.

The switch in the tenses of the verb עלל from a participle in v. 4 to a suffix conjugation in v. 5 suggests a switch in aspectual function from imperfective to perfective/past. Thus, the magicians and others "began to come in" (participle) until finally Daniel came in (suffix conjugation). It is also possible to interpret this participle as having an iterative meaning. That is, the magicians and others "were coming in" (that is, one by one) until finally Daniel came in. A progressive interpretation also cannot be ruled out, for example, "as they were coming in. . . ."

Another possible inceptive participle occurs in 5:1.

Daniel 5:1–2

(1) בלשאצר מלכא עבד לחם רב לרברבנוהי אלף ולקבל אלפא חמרא שתה
(2) בלשאצר אמר בטעם חמרא להיתיה למאני דהבא וכספא די הנפק נבוכדנצר אבוהי מן־היכלא די בירושלם וישתון בהון מלכא ורברבנוהי שגלתה ולחנתה

Belshazzar the king made a great feast for his thousand nobles and before the thousand *he began to drink* wine. Belshazzar commanded when drunk to bring the vessels of gold and silver that Nebuchadnezzar his father had brought out from the Temple that was in Jerusalem, so that the king, his nobles, his concubines and maid servants might drink with them.

Though other explanations are possible, an inceptive function fits the sequence of verbs in v. 1–2: the king עבד "made" (suffix conjugation) a great feast, and שתה "began to drink" (participle); when he was drunk, he אמר "commanded" (suffix conjugation) to bring the vessels from the Temple, וישתון "so that they might drink" (prefix conjugation) with them.

2.3.4. General Present

As mentioned above, presents are considered a subset of the imperfective. Just like the imperfective, the present tense can be subdivided into progressive and nonprogressive (habitual/gnomic/generic). That is, for most verbs in most discourse contexts, the actual present can be characterized as a present progressive, and the general present as a present habitual (Bybee 1994: 236–38). Whereas the actual present expresses events occurring at the moment of speech, general presents are statements of timeless facts or general habitual actions. Furthermore, the habitual is the default function of the present (1994: 246). That is, it is normal for a form that expresses the habitual (general) present to also express the progressive (actual) present, except in cases where a progressive present becomes obligatory to express that meaning.

In at least 22 instances, active participles function as general presents. That is, they express factual statements, statements of states that are generally true, or habitually occurring actions that are not necessarily occurring at the moment of speech. The list includes at least 2:38, 40a, b, c, 43b; 3:16b, 17a, 25e, 31; 4:6, 32b, 34d; 5:23b, c, d; 6:14b, 17c, 21c, 26, 28a, b, c. Many of these instances occur in poetic contexts or in relative clauses. Additionally, some instances of participial forms of יכל/כהל (including at least 2:27e; 3:17b; 4:15a, b, 34e) could also be construed as general present, though there is also an element of modality in the latter.[12]

---

12. The instance in 3:17 has also been interpreted as part of a complex verb phrase איתי + *participle*.

Daniel 5:23

ולאלהי כספא־ודהבא נחשא פרזלא אעא ואבנא די לא־<u>חזין</u> ולא־<u>שמעין</u> ולא <u>ידעין</u> שבחת
And you praised the gods of silver, gold, bronze, iron, wood, and stone, who neither *see* nor *hear* nor *know*.

Daniel 6:14

וזמנין תלתה ביומא <u>בעא</u> בעותה
Three times a day, *he makes* his petitions.

As can be seen from the above examples, these participles denote either timeless facts or habitual occurrences, rather than actions in process at the moment of speech. That is, they are general presents rather than actual (progressive) presents.

2.3.5. Actual Present

In a number of instances, the active participle expresses the actual present (2:8c, d, 11, 23a, b, 27c; 3:12a, b, 25c; 4:34a, b, c).

Daniel 4:34

כען אנה נבוכדנצר <u>משבח</u> ומרומם <u>ומהדר</u> למלך שמיא
Now, I Nebuchadnezzar *do praise, exalt, and glorify* the king of heaven.

Admittedly, it is occasionally difficult to distinguish between a general and an actual present (for example, 3:12a, b?).

2.3.6. Performative Present

Performatives are acts of speech that entail the actions contained in the speech act. In English, performatives are generally expressed with the present tense, for example, "I now pronounce you man and wife," or "I hereby declare. . . ." It has been observed that there was a shift in Aramaic and Hebrew from the earlier use of the suffix conjugation to the later use of the active participle for expressing performatives. Gzella (2004: 205–14, 307; 2007: 93–94) suggests that performative participles are first attested in Biblical Aramaic. Rogland (2003: 426–27) also gives examples of performatives with participles in Biblical, Egyptian, and other forms of Aramaic. However, two of the Biblical Aramaic examples involve the participle אמרין (Dan 3:4; 4:28), and, as argued above, participial constructions involving verbs that introduce direct speech are formulaic in nature, and cannot be used to determine the function of other participles in the corpus. As for the other instances (Dan 2:23; 4:34; Ezra 4:16; 7:24), Rogland acknowledges that they "could conceivably be referring to the action as an ongoing process," which is tantamount to saying that they could be simply actual presents. In fact, a performative present is a type of actual present! Nevertheless, although the instances cited are not indisputable, Rogland is probably correct that the period of Aramaic attested in "texts from Egypt and Qumran," which includes Biblical Aramaic, belongs to a phase in which the shift from the earlier suffix-conjugation performatives to the later active-participle performatives was "underway but not yet complete" (2003: 427).

2.3.7. Historical Present

Besides formulaic expression introducing direct speech, there are many other instances where the active participle allegedly functions as a simple past or a "historical present," the common name given to the employment of the present to express past events. However, every one of these instances could be otherwise explained, and some were discussed above under other categories. There are 3 instances of participles of the auxiliary verbs כהל (5:8, 15) and יכל (6:5) that deserve further comment. Two of these are better understood as past imperfectives (5:8; 6:5), and the remaining instance is probably a general present (5:15).

Daniel 5:8

אדין עללין כל חכימי מלכא ולא כהלין כתבא למקרא ופשרא להודעה למלכא

Then all the wise men of the king were coming in but *were* not *able* to read the writing or make known the interpretation to the king.

Rosén (1961: 185) included the above instance in his examples of the participle as a simple past, but the Greek translation which he cited in support consists of the imperfect (Old Greek ἠδύνατο / Theodotion ἠδύναντο). In fact, the participle כהלין may simply express the continuation of the function of the previous participle, עללין. That is, both are iterative (that is, they "kept coming in and not being able to ...") or progressive (i.e., "they were coming in, but were not able to ...").

Daniel 6:5

אדין סרכיא ואחשדרפניא הוו בעין עלה להשכחה לדניאל מצד מלכותא וכל־עלה ושחיתה לא־יכלין להשכחה

Then the supervisors and satraps were seeking to find a pretext against Daniel in regard to the kingdom, but *were* not *able* to find any pretext or corruption.

For some unknown reason, Rosén (1961: 185), in his citation of the above instance, appealed to the Old Greek translation (which is very free in this passage) with the imperfect ηὕρισκον rather than Theodotion's aorist εὗρον, which would have better supported his case. Perhaps the disagreement in the Greek translations is suggestive. Although the participle יכלין could be analyzed as a simple past, it could also be understood as continuing the function of the previous participial expression, הוו בעין (that is, "they were seeking to ... but not able to ..."). The resulting imperfective notion could be either progressive (untranslatable into an English progressive, because it is a stative verb) or iterative (that is, they were repeatedly unable to).

Daniel 5:15

וכען העלו קדמי חכימיא אשפיא די־כתבה דנה יקרון ופשרה להודעתני ולא כהלין פשר מלתא להחויה

And now, the wise men and magicians were brought in before me to read this writing and make known to me its interpretation, but *they cannot* make known the interpretation of the matter.

In the above example, though the participle could be understood as a simple past, it also makes perfect sense as a general present in the context of the king's address to Daniel. Notice the parallel use of כען in vv. 15–16: . . . כען ולא־כהלין . . . , "And now . . . , but they cannot. . . . But . . . , now if you can. . . . ." Therefore, there is no reason not to interpret the instance in the above-cited example as a general present. Thus, it appears that the only undisputable instances of simple past-time active participles in the corpus are restricted to formulaic expressions involving verbs of speaking.

In passing, a word must be said concerning Gzella's (2004: 120–31) long discussion of the participle as a historical present or *Erzählform*, which he presents as a feature of Imperial Aramaic. As it turns out, the only instance that he cites as a clear example outside Biblical Aramaic, other than verbs introducing direct speech, is the following:

TAD B2.8:4–5

אדין מומאה מטאה עליכי וימאתי לי

da *kam* der Eid zu dir und du hast mir geschworen [italics mine]

The above example comes from one of the documents of the Mibtahiah archive, and the context is a divorce quit-claim between her and a man named פיא. Gzella's interpretation seems to be at least partly based on the assumptions that the conjunction אדין must be immediately followed by a perfective/simple past and that participial circumstantial clauses do not precede main clauses. However, there is no reason why the nonverb initial participial clause in the above example cannot be circumstantial to the following suffix–conjugation verb. Thus, a valid alternative interpretation could be:

Then, *as* an oath *was imposed* upon you, you swore to me.

Therefore, other than verbs introducing direct speech, there are no clear examples of the participle functioning as a historical present or narrative tense in Imperial Aramaic outside the book of Daniel.[13]

Finally, the label *historical present* may be inaccurate for Aramaic participial expressions introducing direct speech. The appeal to the category of *historical present* is useful for those who see the active participle as primarily a present tense (e.g., Bauer and Leander 1927: 294–95; Rosenthal 1961: 55; Johns 1972: 25; Cohen 1984: 413, 477; Rogland 2003: 430–32). However, the fact that the majority of instances of active participles function in past time suggests that it is not a present tense but a general imperfective that can

---

13. Gzella's (2004: 130) examples from Ezra 6:14 can likewise be translated as imperfectives: בנין ומצלחין, "they continued building and prospering."

also express the present as part of its imperfective function. Furthermore, Goodwin (1889: 17) noticed that in Classical Greek, in "such expressions as *he said, he commanded,* . . . the action is of such a nature that it is not important to distinguish its duration from its occurrence." That is, the aspectual opposition between the Greek aorist (that is, the past perfective/simple past) and the imperfect (i.e., the past imperfective) was sometimes irrelevant for verbs introducing direct speech, and both aspects could be used interchangeably, their distinction being "occasionally indifferent" (Goodwin 1900: 270). It is possible that this phenomenon occurs in other languages, including some forms of ancient Aramaic. If so, the use of the active participle with verbs introducing direct speech should not be classed as instances of the historical present but as the "occasionally indifferent" use of the imperfective aspect in expressions introducing direct speech. That is, the reason why the active participle of אמר and other verbs introducing direct speech were originally employed in past-time narrative instead of the suffix conjugation was not because the participle was used as a historical present but because the aspectual difference between simple past and past imperfective is often irrelevant for such expressions. Later, when the Aramaic participle became more clearly a present tense, this function persisted as a vestige of earlier usage.

2.4. Nonimperfective Functions That Overlap with the Prefix Conjugation

There are a few instances of the active participle that are best explained not as imperfective but as the result of the active participle's taking over the functions of the prefix conjugation. In at least 3 instances, all occurring in poetic contexts, the participle denotes future events that are not necessarily imperfective (4:22a, b, 29).

Daniel 4:22

ולך טרדין מן־אנשא ועם־חיות ברא להוה מדרך ועשבא כתורין לך יטעמון ומטל שמיא לך מצבעין

And you *will be driven* away from mankind, and with the wild animals will be your dwelling, and you will be fed grass like oxen, and you *will be drenched* with the dew of heaven.[14]

It is interesting to observe in the example above the poetic parallelism between participles and prefix-conjugation verbs. Toews (1993: 305–6) distinguishes mainline predictions with the prefix conjugation from background predictions with the active participle. If so, the latter would have a future progressive/imperfective function as classified in the present study. However, though Toews's suggestion is possible, the few instances where they both occur together in predictive discourse make his case difficult to prove.

14. I translate impersonal plurals as passive because there is no parallel expression in English.

It is possible that the active participle has also begun to take over the prefix conjugation's function of expressing modality, though examples are sparse (excluding participial occurrences of the verb "be able," 2:26, 27; 3:17; 4:15 [2×], 34; 5:8, 15; 6:5) and could be otherwise interpreted. One instance occurs in 4:4d:

Daniel 4:4–5

(4) באדין עֲלָלִין . . . וחלמא אמר אנה קדמיהון ופשרה לא־מְהוֹדְעִין לי
(5) ועד אחרין על קדמי דניאל

Then, as they . . . were coming in, and as I was telling them the dream, and *they were* not *making known* [or, *they could* not *make known*] its interpretation, finally Daniel came in before me.

In the above example, מהודעין, in addition to continuing the progressive or iterative sense of the previous clause(s), may possibly (though not necessarily) also express ability, that is, "could make known."

The participle in 5:23a is probably best understood as expressing purpose.

Daniel 5:23

ועל מרא־שמיא התרוממת ולמאניא די־ביתה היתיו קדמיך ואנתה ורברבניך שגלתך ולחנתך חמרא שָׁתַיִן בהון

And you have raised yourself against the Lord of heaven, and the vessels of his Temple were brought before you, *so that* you, your nobles, your consorts, and your concubines *might drink* wine with them.

Compare the participle in the above example with the parallel expression in 5:2, cited above (p. 80), containing the prefix-conjugation verb instead of the participle. Alternatively, שתין could be understood as circumstantial to the following suffix-conjugation verb, שבחת, that is, "and as you were drinking wine . . . , you praised. . . ." Also possible is Gzella's (2004: 195–96) suggestion that it denotes a present, though "schon länger andauert," that is, "you have been drinking," though less likely, because the suffix-conjugation verbs both before and after the participle suggest that the context is a narration of past-time events.

3. Active Participles in Combination with הוה or איתי

There are 37 instances of active and t-stem participles that occur in connection with הוה.[15] In 2 of these instances, the participle should be analyzed

---

15. The number includes 2 instances where the auxiliary function of the verb הוה is extended to a second participle (5:19; 6:27); that is, they form a continuation of a הוה + *participle* syntagm and function not as independent participles but as part of this syntagm; and 1 instance with words intervening between the participle and הוה (6:3), introduced by the subordinating relative די. Although there are no other examples of words intervening within a הוה + *participle* syntagm in Biblical Aramaic, it is not extraordinary, since such instances also occur in Biblical Hebrew (2 Kgs 17:41; 18:4).

as the predicate of the verb "to be" (2:43; 7:19). The remaining instances consist of 19 occurrences of הוה + *participle* (including 2 instances where הוה combines with two participles) and 16 occurrences of *participle* + הוה. (For the sake of clarity, throughout this study, הוה + *participle* refers to the sequence where the verb "to be" precedes the participle, and *participle* + הוה refers to the sequence where the participle precedes the verb "to be.") Additionally, there are up to 4 instances of איתי + *participle* that should be considered together with הוה + *participle* for reasons that will be explained below.[16] The "periphrastic imperative" attested in some other forms of Aramaic, consisting of an imperative of the verb הוה + *participle* (Greenfield 1969), does not occur in the Aramaic of Daniel.

In passing, mention should be made of a study by Thacker (1963). Based on the assumption that Egyptian and Semitic finite verbs mark aspect rather than tense, he suggests that the verb "to be" acts as a marker of tense when combined with other finite verbs. Likewise, the verb "to be" is a "time-indicator" when combined with the Egyptian infinitive or with a Semitic active participle.

Below, I will argue that, although the addition of הוה to the participle originally functioned as a tense marker, the expression became grammaticalized at the stage of the language attested in the corpus as a complex verb phrase consisting of the renewal of the imperfective. The variation in the order of constituents is due to the fact that the expression is in the early stages of grammaticalization.

3.1. The Complex Verb Phrase הוה + Participle

3.1.1. Progressive

Instances of הוה + *participle* occur in both subordinate and main clauses, as well as with a variety of verbs, both dynamic and stative, transitive and intransitive. They also have a broad range of functions. There is an instance in 6:4 of הוה + *participle* that could be analyzed as either progressive or inceptive.

Daniel 6:4

אדין דניאל דנה הוא מתנצחם על־סרכיא ואחשדרפניא

Then this Daniel *was distinguishing himself* [or *began to distinguish himself*] over the supervisors and satraps.

3.1.2. Habitual or Iterative/Frequentative

In at least 4 instances, הוה + *participle* has a habitual or iterative meaning (5:19a, b; 6:11, 15).[17]

---

16. The number includes an instance where the auxiliary function of איתי may be extended to a second participle (3:14a, b). Although the repetition of the negative particle לא before the second participle may call this interpretation into question, the absence of an explicit subject of the second participle suggests that the two participles may form a compound sentence.

17. In 5:19, הוה governs two participles.

Daniel 6:11

וזמנין תלתה ביומא הוא ברך על־ברכוהי ומצלא ומודא קדם אלהה כל־קבל די <u>הוא עבד</u>
מן־קדמת דנה

And three times a day he kept on kneeling on his knees, praying, and giving thanks to his god, just as *he used to do* before this.

Additionally, a series of 8 instances of הוה + *participle* in 5:19 may be habitual or iterative (5:19c, d, e, f, g, h, i, j).

Daniel 5:19

די־<u>הוה צבא הוא קטל</u> די־<u>הוה צבא הוה מחא</u> די־<u>הוה צבא די־הוה מרים</u> די־<u>הוה צבא הוה</u>
משפיל

Whom *he wished, he would kill*; whom *he wished, he would keep alive*; whom *he wished, he would exalt*; and whom *he wished, he would abase*.

It is instructive to compare the instances in 5:19 above with similar constructions in 4:14, 22, 29; and 5:21, where prefix-conjugation verbs are used instead of participles. The clearest observable difference is that, whereas the instances with prefix conjugation verbs are timeless, the occurrences with suffix-conjugation הוה + *participle* are set in a past time context. Alternatively, these participles could be analyzed as 4 pairs of הוה + *participle*, in which the first clause in the pair is hypothetical (that is, "whomever he wished") or as in more colloquial English, "whoever he happened to want to," and the second clause expresses ability (that is, "he could").[18] Perhaps this ambiguity is related to the fact that both interpretations involve some type of irrealis, since, as Palmer points out, "the habitual past does not relate to specific actions in the past, but to a tendency to act" (2001: 179; see also pp. 55, 190–91).

3.1.3. Inceptive

Muraoka (1966: 159) cited an instance in 6:5 as "inchoative," that is, inceptive, though it is also possible to understand it as iterative (as in Stevenson 1924: 58).

Daniel 6:5

אדין סרכיא ואחשדרפניא <u>הוו בעין</u> עלה להשכחה לדניאל מצד מלכותא

Then the administrators and satraps *began trying* [or, *kept trying*] *to find* a pretext against Daniel with reference to the kingdom.

Another possible instance of an inceptive occurs in 6:4, though a progressive function is also possible (see above).

3.1.4. Future

There is one instance of prefix-conjugation הוה + *participle* with a future function (2:43).

---

18. In these cases, although the first clause in each pair is syntactically a simple relative clause, it functions semantically as if it were a protasis.

Daniel 2:43

די חזית פרזלא מערב בחסף טינא מתערבין להון בזרע אנשא ולא־<u>להון דבקין</u> דנה
עם־דנה הא־כדי פרזלא לא מתערב עם־חספא

And inasmuch as you saw iron mixed with wet clay, they will be mixed in human seed, but they *will* not *(continue to) stick together* one with the other, just as iron is not mixed with clay.

It is possible that the above instance expresses an imperfective future—that is, in this case a continuous future. Gzella (2007: 97) cites an instance of prefix-conjugation הוה + *participle* with future durative or iterative function in Qumran Aramaic (1QapGen 22:22). However, the single instance in Daniel is insufficient to determine whether or not the expression denotes imperfectivity in the future.

3.1.5. Modality

In a number of instances, the prefix-conjugation הוה + *participle* expresses modality. There are 2 instances in purpose clauses (6:3a, b).

Daniel 6:2–3

(2) שפר קדם דריוש והקים על־מלכותא לאחשדרפניא מאה ועשרין די להון
בכל־מלכותא
(3) ועלא מנהון סרכין תלתא די דניאל חד־מנהון די־<u>להון</u> אחשדרפניא אלין <u>יהבין</u>
להון טעמא ומלכא לא־<u>להוא נזק</u>

It pleased Darius to appoint over the kingdom a hundred and twenty satraps to be over the entire kingdom, and over them three administrators, of whom Daniel was one, *so that* the satraps *might report* to them, *so that* the king *might not suffer loss*.

There are at least 2 instances where prefix-conjugation הוה + *participle* occurs in clauses expressing the complement of a command (6:27a, b, להון governs 2 participles).

Daniel 6:27

מן־קדמי שים טעם די בכל־שלטן מלכותי <u>להון זאעין ודחלין</u> מן־קדם אלהה די־דניאל

And it is decreed by me that in all my royal dominion *they must tremble and fear* before the god of Daniel.

The above example shows that the function of a prefix-conjugation הוה + *participle* can overlap that of the prefix conjugation by itself, since the complement of a royal command is often expressed with the latter. For example:

Daniel 5:29

והכרזו עלוהי די־<u>להוא</u> שליט תלתא במלכותא

They made a proclamation concerning him *that he should be* the third ruler in the kingdom.

Additionally, there is a series of 8 instances of suffix-conjugation הוה + *participle* grouped in 4 pairs (5:19c, d, e, f, g, h, i, j), in which the first clause in the pair may be hypothetical, and the second clause expresses ability ("could"). See above, under habitual or iterative/frequentative.

3.2. The Complex Verb Phrase איתי + Participle

There are at least 4 instances of the complex verb phrase איתי + participle.[19] Of these, at least 1 is clearly a general present (2:26).

Daniel 2:26

האיתיך כהל להודעתני חלמא די־חזית ופשרה

Are you able to make known to me the dream that I saw and its interpretation?

Gzella (2004: 197, 203–4) argues that איתי distinguishes the actual present from the general present, or "extratemporalis." That is, it marks the participial expression as actual present rather than general present. Thus, he translates the above instance as, "Kannst du mir jetzt . . . ?" However, in the context, the king is not asking whether Daniel is "now" able to interpret the dream as opposed to yesterday or tomorrow but, rather, whether Daniel is able to interpret it in contrast to the other wise men who are not able to. Therefore, the addition of איתי to the active participle does not distinguish between general and actual present, nor does it make the participle "emphatic" (Johns 1972: 25; see also Bauer and Leander 1927: 331; and Rosenthal 1961: 41), but rather, it makes explicit the temporal reference of a participle, which would otherwise have to be inferred from the context. That is, it serves as a present-tense marker. It is doubtful, however, whether it distinguishes between general and actual present.

The remaining instances are probably also general presents (3:14a, b, 18), though other interpretations are possible. The instances in 3:14 are probably general presents, but could be understood as actual presents.

Daniel 3:14

ענה נבכדנצר ואמר להון הצדא שדרך מישך ועבד נגו לאלהי לא איתיכון פלחין ולצלם דהבא די הקימת לא סגדין

Nebuchadnezzar answered and said to them, "Is it true, Shadrach, Meshach, and Abednego, do *you* not *serve* my gods, nor *worship* the image of gold that I made?"

The remaining instance (3:18), which is continued in the following clause by a prefix-conjugation verb, could be understood as a future, but is probably also a general present. In fact, as Muraoka (1966: 158) observed, both the said expression and the following prefix-conjugation verb are translated with a present indicative in the LXX.

Additionally, there may be another instance in 3:17. However, this is subject to various interpretations (see Bloch 1991 for a brief discussion of some views).

19. See n. 16.

Daniel 3:17

הן אִיתַי אלהנא די־אנחנא פלחין יָכִל לשיזבותנא

If our God, whom we serve, *is able* to deliver us. . . . [or: If *it is so*, our God, whom we serve, is able to deliver us . . .]

If the above example belongs to the list of איתי + *participle* phrases, it also expresses the general present. All other instances occur with a pronominal suffix attached to איתי (that is, איתי + *pronominal suffix + participle*), but if this instance should be included, the actual verb phrase is איתי + *subject + participle*. However, the interpretation of this instance is disputed.

3.3. The Complex Verb Phrase Participle + הוה

In contrast to Ezra, where there are no instances of *participle* + הוה prefix conjugation—that is, all instances are הוה + *active participle* (Ezra 6:8, 9, 10; 7:25, 26)—in the Aramaic of Daniel, הוה/איתי + *participle* outnumbers *participle* + הוה by only a few instances. However, the distribution of the latter is much more restricted. Since only 4 lexemes are attested with this syntagm (חזה 2:31, 34; 4:7, 10; 7:2, 4, 6, 7, 9, 11a, b, 13, 21; הלך 4:26; שכל 7:8; אתה 7:13), it is not possible to decide what types of verbs can occur in this construction.[20] They are attested only in main clauses, and all can be interpreted as having a progressive function.

3.3.1. Progressive

Although all instances of *participle* + הוה can be interpreted as having a progressive function, some instances could also be otherwise interpreted. In at least 5 instances, the progressive function is clear and needs no further comment (2:31; 4:7, 26; 7:2, 13b).

Daniel 4:7

וחזוי ראשי על־משכבי חזה הוית ואלו אילן בגוא ארעא ורומה שגיא

I was looking at the visions of my head on my bed, and look, there was a tree in the middle of the earth, whose height was great.

3.3.2. Reiteration and/or Other Functions

The remaining 11 instances of *participle* + הוה (2:34; 4:10; 7:4, 6, 7, 8, 9, 11a, b, 13a, 21) could be interpreted either as reiterations of earlier progressives or as continuatives. For example:

---

20. Another possible instance, מתערבין להון in 2:43, will be discussed separately below. Furthermore, the complex verb phrase *participle* + הוה only occurs in chapters that narrate prophetic visions, that is, chaps. 2, 4, and 7. However, the significance of this fact is limited, since one expects expressions such as חזה הוית (whether in the form of 1st-person common-singular הֲוֵית or 2nd-person masculine-singular הֲוַיְתָ) to be more characteristic of prophetic visions.

Daniel 2:31–34

(31) אנתה מלכא חזה הוית ואלו צלם חד שגיא צלמא . . . . (34) חזה הוית עד די
התגזרת אבן די־לא בידין ומחת לצלמא על־רגלוהי די פרזלא וחספא הדקתו המון

As for you, O king, you were looking, and look, there was a great image. . . .
You kept on/were looking, until. . . .

In the above example, the phrase חזה הוית in v. 34 could be a reiteration of the same phrase in v. 31, which has a progressive function. Alternatively, it could have a continuative function, that is, "you kept on looking." Although both options are valid, I favor the first one based on discourse considerations. To begin with, a number of instances of *participle* + הוה are followed by temporal clauses introduced by עד די (at least 2:34; 7:4, 9, 11b). Although עד די generally introduces subordinate temporal clauses, in some instances these temporal clauses actually contain the main thought of the sentence. For example:

Daniel 6:25

ולא־מטו לארעית גבא עד די־שלטו בהון אריותא

They had not (even) reached the bottom of the pit, *when the lions overpowered them.*

From a discourse perspective, the juxtaposition of the clauses "they had not reached . . . , when the lions . . ." is equivalent to "before they reached . . . , the lions. . . ." That is, these subordinate temporal clauses seem to be part of the foreground, even though they occur in syntactically subordinate clauses. Therefore, I prefer to interpret sequences of the phrase *participle* + הוה, especially when followed by עד די, as an initial instance with a progressive function followed by one or more instances of reiteration or repetition to segment the narrative and thereby move it forward, similar to back-referencing or resumptive repetition.[21] There is no need to ascribe to these reiterations/repetitions a different aspectual function than the initial occurrence that is being reiterated.

Daniel 7:2–9

(2) חזה הוית עם־ליליא וארו ארבע רוחי שמיא מגיחן לימא רבא (3) וארבע חיון רברבן
סלקן מן־ימא שנין דא מן־דא (4) קדמיתא כאריה . . . חזה הוית עד די . . . (5) וארו חיוה
אחרי תנינה . . . (6) באתר דנה חזה הוית וארו אחרי . . . (7) באתר דנה חזה הוית

21. *Back-referencing*, also called *tail-head linkage*, is a means of providing discourse cohesion between separate narrative segments. The expression is here used somewhat loosely, since technically it means that "something mentioned in the last sentence of the preceding paragraph is referred to by means of back-reference in an adverbial clause in the following paragraph" (Thompson and Longacre 1985: 209). The expression *resumptive repetition* was first coined by H. W. Wiener in 1929 (for more details, see Talmon 1978: 12–17; reprinted in 1993: 117–22). It is a common feature of Semitic narratives that, after an interruption, the main line of thought is picked up again by repeating the last clause(s) before the interruption (Bar-Efrat 1989: 155, 215–16).

(8) ... מִשְׁתַּכַּל הֲוֵית בְּקַרְנַיָּא וַאֲלוּ ... (9) חָזֵה הֲוֵית בְּחֶזְוֵי לֵילְיָא וַאֲרוּ חֵיוָה רְבִיעָיָה ...
עַד דִּי ...

I was looking in my vision by night, and look, there were the four winds of heaven stirring up the great sea, and four great animals coming up out of the sea, different from each other. The first one. . . . *I was looking* until . . . and look, another second animal. . . . After this *I was looking*, and look, another one. . . . After this *I was looking* in the visions of the night, and look, a fourth. . . . *I was considering* the horns, and look. . . . *I was looking* until. . . .

As can be seen from the above example, the expression הֲוֵית חָזֵה—functioning as a reiteration, notwithstanding that it occurs in syntactically main clauses—is equivalent to an unmarked circumstantial clause in terms of the discourse. That is, "I was looking, until/and . . ." is equivalent to, "As I was looking. . . ."

As for the remaining instances of *participle* + הוה that are not followed by עַד דִּי, they tend to be followed either by וַאֲרוּ "look" (7:6, 7, 13a) or וַאֲלוּ "look" (4:10; 7:8), which also continue the foreground of the narrative.[22]

Daniel 4:7, 10

(7) וְחֶזְוֵי רֵאשִׁי עַל־מִשְׁכְּבִי חָזֵה הֲוֵית וַאֲלוּ אִילָן ... (10) חָזֵה הֲוֵית בְּחֶזְוֵי רֵאשִׁי עַל־מִשְׁכְּבִי וַאֲלוּ

I was looking in the visions of my head on my bed, and look . . . *I was looking* in the visions of my head on my bed, and look. . . .

In the above example, there is also a reiteration of the entire clause, though not with the same word order.

In addition, the words לֶהֱוֺן מִתְעָרְבִין in 2:43 could possibly be understood as a complex verb phrase *participle* + הוה.

Daniel 2:43

דִּי חֲזַיְתָ פַּרְזְלָא מְעָרַב בַּחֲסַף טִינָא מִתְעָרְבִין לֶהֱוֺן בִּזְרַע אֲנָשָׁא וְלָא־לֶהֱוֺן דָּבְקִין דְּנָה עִם־דְּנָה הֵא־כְדִי פַרְזְלָא לָא מִתְעָרַב עִם־חַסְפָּא

Since you saw the iron mixed with wet clay, they will *be mixed/mix themselves* with human seed, but they will not stick one with another, just as the iron is not mixed with clay.

As already mentioned, I prefer to analyze the participle מִתְעָרְבִין in the above passage as an adjectival predicate of the verb "to be," that is, "they will be mixed," rather than "they will mix themselves." This is also the understanding of the Greek translators (both the Old Greek and Theodotion), who trans-

---

22. In addition to the instances followed by עַד דִּי listed above, the instance in 7:21 could be interpreted as a longer description introduced by *participle* + הוה and followed by עַד דִּי in v. 22. Also, the two instances in 7:11a, b could be understood as essentially one reiteration. That is, the first *participle* + הוה is followed by an explanatory clause, which is then repeated by the second instance of *participle* + הוה and followed by עַד דִּי. In 7:8, it is possible that מִשְׁתַּכַּל הֲוֵית is not part of the chain of reiterations, since a different verb is used. If so, it is simply another progressive instance, perhaps in a circumstantial clause.

lated the participle with an adjective, συμμειγεῖς. Aside from this debatable instance, the construction *participle* + הוה is attested only with suffix conjugation forms of הוה. Nevertheless, this instance deserves additional comment, because the possibility that it is another instance of the complex verb phrase *participle* + הוה has important implications. In addition to the fact that this instance is not necessarily progressive (though a future progressive function is not precluded), more significantly, the parallel between מתערבין להון and the following להון דבקין could be evidence that the order of the constituents in this expression is not yet fixed, supporting the conclusion that it is still in the early stages of grammaticalization (see further below).

3.4. The Relationship between הוה/איתי + Participle and Participle + הוה

Since the active participle is an imperfective in the Aramaic of Daniel and may have already become so even prior to Daniel, the addition of הוה/איתי before it does not make it continuous/habitual, and so on (see also Muraoka 1966: 158). Rather, the addition of הוה/איתי originally functioned as the addition of a tense marker. That is, a suffix-conjugation הוה adds the specification of past time, a prefix-conjugation הוה adds the specification of either future time or modality, and איתי adds the specification of the present, including general present.

The distinction between הוה/איתי + *participle* and *participle* + הוה in the Aramaic of Daniel has sometimes been ignored (e.g., Muraoka 1966: 157–60; Cohen 1984: passim) or denied (e.g., Rowley 1929: 99).[23] Bauer and Leander (1927: 293–94) proposed that third-person forms of הוה occur in front of the participle, whereas other persons occur after the participle. However, the instance in 4:26 (מהלך הוה) is a counterexample, and their explanation does not account for non-third-person instances of איתי + *participle* (2:26; 3:14, 18). Greenfield considered the latter construction to be exceptional, because the order הוה + *participle* "is expected" but was perceptive enough to notice that "stylistic grounds" do not suffice to explain the reversed order (1969: 206). Indeed, the order of the elements is significant in other forms of Aramaic. Egyptian Aramaic uses primarily הוה + *participle*, whereas *participle* + הוה is reserved primarily for internal passives and some statives and expresses not iteration but a resulting state (Muraoka and Porten 1998: 205–8).[24] Likewise,

---

23. There is hardly any discussion of the complex verb phrase in Toews 1993.
24. For Rowley (1929: 99), the distinction between הוה + *participle* and *participle* + הוה existed neither in Egyptian Aramaic nor in Biblical Aramaic. Muraoka (1966: 157–60) follows Rowley on this point only in regard to Biblical Aramaic. Neither Rowley nor Muraoka distinguished instances with the active participle from those with the passive participle. Coxon (1977: 109) argues against Rowley and asserts that, at least for prefix-conjugation forms of הוה, both Biblical and Egyptian Aramaic normally use הוה + *participle*, reserving *participle* + הוה for passive and reflexive participles.

the construction attested in 1QapGen is הוה + *participle* with nothing intervening (Muraoka 1972: 34). In the Aramaic of Onqelos and Jonathan, the construction occurs as הוה + *participle*, except where it is imitating the Hebrew word order (Gropp forthcoming: chap. 29). Furthermore, in Syriac there is also a distinction between הוה + *participle* and *participle* + הוה (Muraoka 2005: 68), though their respective functions are not the same as in the western Aramaic dialects. Therefore, comparative evidence urges at least an attempt to explain the relationship between הוה/איתי + *participle* and *participle* + הוה in the Aramaic of Daniel.

In terms of simple frequency, the sequence הוה/איתי + *participle* outnumbers the sequence *participle* + הוה by only a few instances. As I argued above, however, since the majority of instances of the latter are cases of reiteration/repetition and since the few attested instances of איתי + *participle* (i.e., איתי + subject / pronominal suffix + *participle*) do not seem to show any variation in word order, I suggest that the sequence הוה/איתי + *participle* is the more common one for the Aramaic of Daniel.

Nevertheless, grammaticalization often results in a restriction of syntactic position, and the "possibility of more than one position may indicate a lesser degree of grammaticalization" (Bybee and Dahl 1989: 61). Therefore, one can posit that, in the early stages, the position of הוה in relation to the active participle was free, but after the syntagm was reanalyzed as a complex verb phrase, the position of the two words eventually became fixed as הוה + *participle* in western Aramaic.[25] Thus, the coexistence of the expressions הוה/איתי + *participle* and *participle* + הוה may be evidence that the expression has not yet grammaticalized to the point where the order of the constituents became fixed. This may mean either that the expression has not yet become a complex verb phrase (that is, הוה/איתי is still only a temporal marker of the imperfective participle) or more likely that a reanalysis has occurred but is still in its early stages.

This explanation is supported by the fact that the complex verb phrase consisting of the verb הוה in combination with the participle was a development of Official Aramaic and was not attested earlier.[26] Therefore, Kaddari's (1983: 45) suggestion that "the order of constituents with *hwh* was not yet fixed" in Imperial (or Biblical) Aramaic cannot be ignored, because new grammatical expressions in the early stages tend to be less restricted in syn-

---

25. Biblical Hebrew attests to a similar phenomenon at an early stage of grammaticalization. Muraoka (1999: 199–200) noted that the use of the periphrastic verb phrase (that is, הוה in combination with the participle) in Biblical Hebrew and Qumran Hebrew was optional, and that whereas the order of the constituents was fixed in Qumran Aramaic, it was not in Biblical Hebrew, where there was no functional distinction between the two. Muraoka (1999: 200–201) also argued that, since this construction existed in early Biblical Hebrew, its existence in late Biblical Hebrew and Mishnaic Hebrew cannot be due to Aramaic influence, though it may have been reinforced later by Aramaic.

26. See Muraoka's (1999: 201 n. 42) comment on Greenfield's citation from the Sefire inscription.

The Function of the Active Participle in the Aramaic of Daniel 95

tactic position.[27] Also, the one attested instance where words intervene between הוה and the participle (6:3), if correctly understood, may be further evidence that the order of the constituents is not yet fixed.[28]

4. Conclusions

Recent advances in the study of grammaticalization suggest that grammatical constructions tend to develop in predictable ways cross-linguistically. The advantage of this insight is that the study of any corpus or dialect, even when studied in isolation, can be viewed in the light of a larger framework of how human languages generally develop. Hence, one can not only describe the various functions of a grammatical construction but also recognize their diachronic significance.

Among the many observable phenomena that are widely common in the historical development of languages, two are especially relevant for the active participle in the Aramaic of Daniel: first, a progressive construction may eventually take over the function of the imperfective or the present; and second, new grammatical constructions begin with a restricted range of functions and eventually acquire a wider range of functions. In the Aramaic of Daniel, the active participle continues to function nominally and as a progressive expressing ongoing actions but has in addition acquired many other imperfective functions, and it is possible that it even occasionally expresses modality. A special function of the participle occurs in formulaic expressions introducing direct speech. Though the participle is frequently used in the expression of the present (general and actual present), the fact that the majority of instances function in past time suggests that it is not a present tense but a general imperfective that can also express the present as part of its imperfective function. Therefore, the active participle in the Aramaic of Daniel may be characterized as an imperfective that arose from an earlier progressive. As such, it has become a full-fledged member of the verbal system.

According to Bybee (1994: 250), "a progressive restricted to the present by the existence of a past imperfective will become a present tense, while a progressive that is not so restricted will become an imperfective—expanding to cover as many functions as possible." Thus, the active participle was a general

---

27. Kaddari also argued in the same study (1983: 43–45) that in both Imperial and Biblical Aramaic the unmarked word order was for the verb הוה to precede the head word, which includes participles, because it can occur in both main and subordinate clauses, whereas the marked word order, *participle* + הוה, only occurs in main clauses. Muraoka (1999: 200) disagrees and doubts that one syntagm is more marked than the other.

28. An alternative possible explanation is that, since הוה + *participle* expresses a wide range of imperfective functions, and *participle* + הוה consistently expresses the progressive, the first may be a renewal of the imperfective and the latter a renewal of the (past) progressive. However, I prefer the view proposed above, because a progressive complex verb phrase *participle* + הוה is not attested in any other form of Aramaic (though it is possible for grammaticalized expressions to fall into disuse instead of further grammaticalizing).

(that is, temporally unrestricted) progressive that developed into a general imperfective rather than a present. However, since the participle by itself was not restricted in time, הוה and איתי were used to locate the imperfective temporally, but this new syntagm was eventually reanalyzed from הוה/איתי [temporal marker] + *participle* to a complex verb phrase הוה + *participle*, at which stage, a past imperfective came to exist in Aramaic. That is, the suffix-conjugation הוה + *participle* was reanalyzed from [*past*] + [*imperfective*] to [*past imperfective*].

The fact that the active participle still functions as a general imperfective in the Aramaic of Daniel is indicated by the fact that the majority of instances occur in the past time rather than the present. That is, although one expects vestiges of earlier functions to remain, the past imperfective function of the active participle cannot be vestigial if it is attested more often than the newer הוה + *participle*. Also, the frequent occurrence of the reverse word order, *participle* + הוה, may be evidence that the order of the constituents has not yet become fixed, and, therefore, the combination of הוה and the active participle as a complex verb phrase is still in its early stages of grammaticalization. Nevertheless, the new past imperfective—that is, suffix-conjugation הוה + *participle*—will eventually replace the past imperfective function of the active participle, which in turn will eventually be restricted to primarily the present tense.

That is, if we could project the development of the verbal system of the Aramaic of Daniel forward in time, suffix-conjugation הוה + *participle* would become the standard construction for the past imperfective, and the active participle by itself would become the present tense, which is exactly what we find in some later forms of Aramaic. Rubin (2005: 31–32) gives examples of how the active participle, after becoming the present tense, can take an enclitic pronoun in later forms of Aramaic. The enclitic pronoun is eventually fused to the participle, and the new form becomes the base of a fully conjugated present-tense verb in Neo-Aramaic. Also, once the active participle becomes the new present tense, the addition of איתי becomes superfluous.[29]

It is expected that there will be disagreements with my interpretation of some passages cited above. Nevertheless, it is hoped that this study will be deemed accurate both in its general approach and in its conclusions. I also hope that this study has demonstrated that a grammaticalization approach holds promise for the analysis of other forms of Aramaic.

---

29. A quick search through Targum Onqelos and Jonathan yielded אית + *participle* only in instances of literal translation of the Hebrew copula יש followed by the participle. Also, according to Wertheimer (2002: 13–14), the Syriac copula or particle of existence ܐܝܬ does not occur with predicative participles.

Bibliography

Bar-Efrat, S.
1989 *Narrative Art in the Bible.* Trans. Dorothea Shefer-Vanson. Journal for the Study of the Old Testament Supplement 70. Bible and Literature Series 17. Sheffield: Almond.

Bauer, H., and P. Leander
1927 *Grammatik des biblisch-Aramäischen.* Halle (Saale): Max Niemeyer.

Bergsträsser, G.
1983 *Introduction to the Semitic Languages: Text Specimens and Grammatical Sketches.* Translated with notes by P. T. Daniels. Winona Lake, IN: Eisenbrauns.

Binnick, R. I.
1991 *Time and the Verb: A Guide to Tense and Aspect.* New York: Oxford University Press.

Blau, Joshua
1987 Minutiae Aramaicae. Pp. 3–10 in *Perspectives on Language and Text: Essays and Poems in Honor of Francis I. Andersen's Sixtieth Birthday, July 28, 1985.* Edited by E. W. Conrad and E. G. Newing. Winona Lake, IN: Eisenbrauns.

Bloch, A. A.
1991 Questioning God's Omnipotence in the Bible: A Linguistic Case Study. Pp. 174–88 in vol. 1 of *Semitic Studies in Honor of Wolf Leslau on the Occasion of His Eighty-Fifth Birthday, November 14th, 1991.* Edited by A. S. Kaye. Wiesbaden: Harrassowitz.

Buth, R. J.
1987 Word Order in Aramaic from the Perspectives of Functional Grammar and Discourse Analysis. Ph.D. dissertation, University of California, Los Angeles.
1990 'edayin/Tote: Anatomy of a Semitism in Jewish Greek. *Maarav* 5–6: 33–48.

Bybee, J. L.
1994 The Grammaticalization of Zero: Asymmetries in Tense and Aspect Systems. Pp. 235–54 in *Perspectives on Grammaticalization.* Edited by W. Pagliuca. Amsterdam: Benjamins.
1998 "Irrealis" as a Grammatical Category. *Anthropological Linguistics* 40: 257–71.

Bybee, J. L., and Ö. Dahl
1989 The Creation of Tense and Aspect Systems in the Languages of the World. *Studies in Language* 13: 51–103.

Bybee, J. L., and W. Pagliuca
1985 Cross-Linguistic Comparison and the Development of Grammatical Meaning. Pp. 59–83 in *Historical Semantics: Historical Word Formation.* Edited by J. Fisiak. Berlin: Mouton.

Bybee, J. L.; R. Perkins; and W. Pagliuca
1991 Back to the Future. Pp. 17–58 in *Approaches to Grammaticalization, Volume 2: Focus on Types of Grammatical Markers.* Edited by E. C. Traugott and B. Heine. Typological Studies in Language 19/2. Amsterdam: Benjamins.
1994 *The Evolution of Grammar: Tense, Aspect, and Modality in the Languages of the World.* Chicago: University of Chicago Press.

Campbell, Lyle
  2001   What's Wrong with Grammaticalization? *Language Sciences* 23/2–3: 113–61.
Campbell, Lyle, and Richard D. Janda
  2001   Introduction: Conceptions of Grammaticalization and Their Problems. *Language Sciences* 23/2–3: 93–112.
Caubet, D.
  1991   The Active Participle as a Means to Renew the Aspectual System: A Comparative Study in Several Dialects of Arabic. Pp. 209–24 in vol. 1 of *Semitic Studies in Honor of Wolf Leslau on the Occasion of His Eighty-Fifth Birthday*. Edited by A. S. Kaye. Wiesbaden: Harrassowitz.
Cohen, D.
  1984   *La phrase nominale et l'évolution du système verbal en sémitique: Études de syntaxe historique.* Leuven: Peeters.
Collins, J. J.
  1993   *Daniel: A Commentary on the Book of Daniel.* Hermeneia. Minneapolis: Fortress.
  2001   Current Issues in the Study of Daniel. Pp. 1–15 in vol. 1 of *The Book of Daniel: Composition and Reception.* Edited by J. J. Collins and P. W. Flint. Leiden: Brill.
Collins, J. J., and P. W. Flint, eds.
  2001   *The Book of Daniel: Composition and Reception.* 2 vols. Vetus Testamentum Supplement 83. Leiden: Brill.
Comrie, B.
  1976   *Aspect.* Cambridge: Cambridge University Press.
Cook, E. M.
  1986   Word Order in the Aramaic of Daniel. *Afroasiatic Linguistics* 9/3: 111–26.
  1992   Qumran Aramaic and Aramaic Dialectology. *Abr-Nahrain Supplement* 3: 1–21.
Coxon, Peter W.
  1977   The Syntax of the Aramaic of Daniel: A Dialectal Study. *HUCA* 48: 107–22.
Dahl, Ö,
  1985   *Tense and Aspect Systems.* Oxford: Blackwell.
Di Lella, A. A.
  1981   Daniel 4:7–14: Poetic Analysis and Biblical Background. Pp. 247–58 in *Mélanges bibliques et orientaux en l'honneur de M. Henri Cazelles.* Edited by A. Caquot and M. Delcor. Alter Orient und Altes Testament 212. Kevelaer: Butzon & Bercker / Neukirchen-Vluyn: Neukirchener Verlag.
  1982   Strophic Structure and Poetic Analysis of Daniel 2:20–23, 3:31–33, and 6:26b–28. Pp. 91–96 in *Studia Hierosolymitana III: Nell'Ottavo Centenario Francescano (1182–1982).* Edited by G. C. Bottini. Jerusalem: Franciscan Printing.
Dobbs-Allsopp, F. W.
  2000   Biblical Hebrew Statives and Situation Aspect. *Journal of Semitic Studies* 45: 21–53.
Emerton, J. A.
  1960   The Participles in Daniel v. 12. *Zeitschrift für de alttestamentliche Wissenschaft* 72: 262–63.

Fassberg, S. E.
1989   The Origin of the Ketib/Qere in the Aramaic Portions of Ezra and Daniel. *Vetus Testamentum* 39: 1–12.
Fischer, Olga
2007   *Morphosyntactic Change: Functional and Formal Perspectives*. Oxford Studies in Syntax and Morphology 2. Oxford: Oxford University Press.
Fischer, Olga; Muriel Norde; and Harry Perridon, eds.
2004   *Up and Down the Cline: The Nature of Grammaticalization*. Typological Studies in Language 59. Amsterdam: Benjamins.
Fitzmyer, J. A.
2004   *The Genesis Apocryphon of Qumran Cave 1 (1Q20): A Commentary*. 3rd ed. Biblica et Orientalia 18/B. Rome: Pontifical Biblical Institute.
Folmer, M. L.
1995   *The Aramaic Language in the Achaemenid Period: A Study in Linguistic Variation*. Orientalia Lovaniensia Analecta 68. Leuven: Peeters.
Goldenberg, G.
1992   Aramaic Perfects. *Israel Oriental Studies* 12: 113–37.
Goodwin, W. W.
1889   *Syntax of the Moods and Tenses of the Greek Verb*. Rewritten and enlarged. Boston: Ginn. [Repr. Eugene, OR: Wipf & Stock, 2003.]
1900   *A Greek Grammar*. Revised and enlarged ed. Boston: Ginn.
Greenfield, J. C.
1969   The "Periphrastic Imperative" in Aramaic and Hebrew. *Israel Exploration Journal* 19: 199–210.
Gropp, D. M.
Forthcoming   *The Aramaic of Targums Onkelos and Jonathan: An Introduction*.
Gzella, H.
2004   *Tempus, Aspekt und Modalität im Reichsaramäischen*. Veröffentlichungen der Orientalischen Kommission 48. Wiesbaden: Harrassowitz.
2007   The Use of the Participle in the Hebrew Bar Kosiba Letters in the Light of Aramaic. *Dead Sea Discoveries* 14: 90–98.
Hatav, G.
1997   *The Semantics of Aspect and Modality: Evidence from English and Biblical Hebrew*. Amsterdam: Benjamins.
Heine, B.
1994   Grammaticalization as an Explanatory Parameter. Pp. 235–54 in *Perspectives on Grammaticalization*. Edited by W. Pagliuca. Amsterdam: Benjamins.
Heine, B.; U. Claudi; and F. Hünnemeyer
1991   *Grammaticalization: A Conceptual Framework*. Chicago: University of Chicago Press.
Heine, B., and T. Kuteva
2002a   *Common Grammaticalization Processes in the Languages of the World*. Cambridge: Cambridge University Press.
2002b   *World Lexicon of Grammaticalization*. Cambridge: Cambridge University Press.
2005   *Language Contact and Grammatical Change*. Cambridge Approaches to Language Contact. Cambridge: Cambridge University Press.

Hopper, P. J.
1991 On Some Principles of Grammaticalization. Pp. 17–35 in *Approaches to Grammaticalization, Volume 1: Focus on Theoretical and Methodological Issues*. Edited by E. C. Traugott and B. Heine. Typological Studies in Language 19/1. Amsterdam: Benjamins.

Hopper, P. J., and E. C. Traugott
2003 *Grammaticalization*. 2nd ed. Cambridge Textbooks in Linguistics. Cambridge: Cambridge University Press.

Huehnergard, J.
1995 What Is Aramaic? *Aram* 7: 265–86.

Janda, Richard D.
2001 Beyond "Pathways" and "Unidirectionality": On the Discontinuity of Language Transmission and the Counterability of Grammaticalization. *Language Sciences* 23/2–3: 265–340.

Johns, A. F.
1972 *A Short Grammar of Biblical Aramaic*. 2nd ed. Andrews University Monograph 1. Berrien Springs, MI: Andrews University Press.

Joosten, J.
1992 Biblical Hebrew *wᵉqaṭal* and Syriac *hwa qaṭel*: Expressing Repetition in the Past. *Zeitschrift für Althebräistik* 5: 1–14.

Kaddari, M. Z.
1983 The Existential Verb *HWH* in Imperial Aramaic. Pp. 43–46 in *Arameans, Aramaic and the Aramaic Literary Tradition*. Edited by M. Sokoloff. Bar-Ilan Studies in Near Eastern Languages and Culture. Ramat-Gan: Bar-Ilan University Press.

Kaufman, S. A.
1974 *Akkadian Influences on Aramaic*. Assyriological Studies 19. Chicago: University of Chicago Press.
1992 Aramaic. Pp. 173–8 in vol. 4 of *The Anchor Bible Dictionary*. 6 vols. Edited by D. N. Freedman et al. New York: Doubleday.

Kautzsch, E. F.
1884 *Grammatik des biblisch-Aramäischen: Mit einer kritischen Erörterung der aramäischen Wörter im neuen Testament*. Leipzig: Vogel.

Kutscher, E. Y.
1969 Two "Passive" Constructions in Aramaic in the Light of Persian. Pp. 132–51 in *Proceedings of the International Conference on Semitic Studies Held in Jerusalem, 19–23 July 1965*. Jerusalem: Israel Academy of Sciences and Humanities. [Reprinted pp. 70–89 in *Hebrew and Aramaic Studies* (Jerusalem: Magnes, 1977).]
1970 The Genesis Apocryphon of Qumran Cave I. *Orientalia* 39: 178–83.
1976 *Studies in Galilean Aramaic*. Translated by M. Sokoloff. Bar-Ilan Studies in Near Eastern Languages and Culture. Ramat-Gan: Bar-Ilan University Press.

Lacocque, A.
1979 *The Book of Daniel*. Translated by David Pellauer. Atlanta: John Knox.

Li, Tarsee
2009 *The Verbal System of the Aramaic of Daniel: An Explanation of the Context of Grammaticalization*. Studies in Aramaic Interpretation of Scripture 8. Leiden: Brill.

López-Couso, María José, and Elena Seoane, eds.
2008 *Rethinking Grammaticalization: New Perspectives.* Typological Studies in Language 76. Amsterdam: Benjamins.

Luzzatto, S. D.
1865 *Elementi grammaticali del caldeo Biblico e del dialetto Talmudico babilonese.* Padua: Bianchi.

Mastin, B. A.
1992 The Meaning of Hᵃlaʾ at Daniel iv 27. *Vetus Testamentum* 42: 234–47.

Morrow, W. S., and E. G. Clarke
1986 The *Ketib/Qere* in the Aramaic Portions of Ezra and Daniel. *Vetus Testamentum* 36: 406–22.

Muraoka, T.
1966 Notes on the Syntax of Biblical Aramaic. *Journal of Semitic Studies* 11: 151–67.
1972 Notes on the Aramaic of the Genesis Apocryphon. *Revue de Qumran* 29: 7–51.
1983 On the Morphosyntax of the Infinitive in Targumic Aramaic. Pp. 75–79 in *Arameans, Aramaic and the Aramaic Literary Tradition.* Edited by M. Sokoloff. Bar-Ilan Studies in Near Eastern Languages and Culture. Ramat-Gan: Bar-Ilan University Press.
1993 Further Notes on the Aramaic of the Genesis Apocryphon. *Revue de Qumran* 61: 39–48.
1995 Linguistic Notes on the Aramaic Inscription from Tel Dan. *Israel Exploration Journal* 45: 19–21.
1998 Again on the Tel Dan Inscription and the Northwest Semitic Verb Tenses. *Zeitschrift für Althebräistik* 11: 74–81.
1999 The Participle in Qumran Hebrew with Special Reference to Its Periphrastic Use. Pp. 188–204 in *Sirach, Scrolls, and Sages: Proceedings of a Second International Symposium on the Hebrew of the Dead Sea Scrolls, Ben Sira, and the Mishnah, Held at Leiden University, 15–17 December 1997.* Edited by T. Muraoka and J. F. Elwolde. Studies on the Texts of the Desert of Judah 33. Leiden: Brill.
2000 An Approach to the Morphosyntax and Syntax of Qumran Hebrew. Pp. 193–214 in *Diggers at the Well: Proceedings of a Third International Symposium on the Hebrew of the Dead Sea Scrolls and Ben Sira.* Edited by T. Muraoka and J. F. Elwolde. Studies on the Texts of the Desert of Judah 36. Leiden: Brill.
2005 *Classical Syriac: A Basic Grammar with a Chrestomathy.* 2nd rev. ed. Wiesbaden: Harrassowitz.

Muraoka, T., and B. Porten
1998 *A Grammar of Egyptian Aramaic.* Handbuch der Orientalistik, erste Abteilung: Der nahe und mittlere Osten 32. Leiden: Brill.

Naudé, J. A.
1994 The Verbless Clause with Pleonastic Pronoun in Biblical Aramaic. *Journal for Semitics* 6: 74–93.

Nöldeke, T.
1904 *Compendious Syriac Grammar.* Translated by J. A. Crichton. London: Williams & Norgate. Reprinted, Winona Lake, IN: Eisenbrauns, 2001.

Palmer, F. R.
   2001   *Mood and Modality*. 2nd ed. Cambridge Textbooks in Linguistics. Cambridge: Cambridge University Press.

Pardee, D., and R. M. Whiting
   1987   Aspects of Epistolary Verbal Usage in Ugaritic and Akkadian. *Bulletin of the School of Oriental and African Studies* 50/1: 1–31.

Péter-Contesse, R., and J. Ellington
   1993   *A Handbook on the Book of Daniel*. United Bible Societies Handbook Series New York: United Bible Societies.

Pfann, S.
   1991   The Aramaic Text and Language of Daniel and Ezra in the Light of Some Manuscripts from Qumran. *Textus* 16: 127–37.

Prinsloo, G. T. M.
   1993   Two Poems in a Sea of Prose: The Content and Context of Daniel 2.20–23 and 6.27–28. *Journal fo the Study of the Old Testament* 59: 93–108.

Qimron, Elisha
   1993   ארמית מקראית. Biblical Encyclopedia Library 10. Jerusalem: Bialik Institute.

Rogland, M.
   2001   Performative Utterances in Classical Syriac. *Journal of Semitic Studies* 46: 243–50.
   2003   Remarks on the Aramaic Verbal System. Pp. 421–32 in *Hamlet on a Hill: Semitic and Greek Studies Presented to Professor T. Muraoka on the Occasion of His Sixty-Fifth Birthday*. Edited by M. F. J. Baasten and W. T. van Peursen. Leuven: Peeters.

Rosén, H. B.
   1961   On the Use of the Tenses in the Aramaic of Daniel. *Journal of Semitic Studies* 6: 183–203.

Rosenthal, F.
   1961   *A Grammar of Biblical Aramaic*. Porta Linguarum Orientalium. Wiesbaden: Harrassowitz.
   1995   *A Grammar of Biblical Aramaic*. 6th rev. ed. Porta Linguarum Orientalium n.s. 5. Wiesbaden: Harrassowitz.

Rowley, H. H.
   1929   *The Aramaic of the Old Testament: A Grammatical and Lexical Study of Its Relations with Other Early Aramaic Dialects*. London: Oxford University Press.

Rubin, A. D.
   2005   *Studies in Semitic Grammaticalization*. Harvard Semitic Studies 57. Winona Lake, IN: Eisenbrauns.

Rundgren, F.
   1960   Der aspektuelle Charakter des altsemitischen Injunktivs. *Orientalia Suecana* 9: 75–101.
   1961   Das altsyrische Verbalsystem: Vom Aspekt zum Tempus. Pp. 49–75 in *Språkvetenskapliga Sällskapets i Uppsala Förhandlingar: Acta Societatis Linguisticae Upsaliensis—Jan. 1958–Dec. 1960*. Uppsala: Almqvist & Wiksell.
   1974   Réflexions sur le participe actif du sémitique. Pp. 195–202 in *Actes du premier congrès international de linguistique sémitique et chamito-sémitique:*

Paris 16–19 juillet 1969. Edited by A. Caquot and D. Cohen. Janua Linguarum, Series Practica 159. The Hague: Mouton.

Segert, S.
1975   *Altaramäische Grammatik mit Bibliographie, Chrestomathie und Glossar.* Leipzig: VEB Verlag Enzyklopädie.
2002   Aramaic Poetry in the Old Testament. *Archiv Orientální* 70: 65–79.

Seow, C. L.
2003   *Daniel.* Westminster Bible Commentaries. Louisville, KY: Westminster John Knox.

Shepherd, Michael B.
2008   *The Verbal System of Biblical Aramaic: A Distributional Approach.* Studies in Biblical Literature 116. New York: Peter Lang.

Stevenson, W. B.
1924   *Grammar of Palestinian Jewish Aramaic.* Oxford: Oxford University Press. [2nd ed. with appendix by J. A. Emerton, 1962.]

Strack, H. L.
1905   *Grammatik des biblisch-Aramäischen: Mit den nach Handschriften berichtigten Texten und einem Wörterbuch.* Leipzig: Hinrich.

Talmon, S.
1978   The Presentation of Synchroneity and Simultaneity in Biblical Narrative. Pp. 9–26 in *Studies in Hebrew Narrative Art.* Edited by J. Heinemann and S. Werses. Jerusalem: Magnes. [Reprinted in Talmon 1993: 112–33.]
1993   *Literary Studies in the Hebrew Bible: Form and Content. Collected Essays.* Jerusalem: Magnes / Leiden: Brill.

Thacker, T. W.
1963   Compound Tenses Containing the Verb "Be" in Semitic and Egyptian. Pp. 156–71 in *Hebrew and Semitic Studies: Presented to Godfrey Rolles Driver.* Edited by D. Winton Thomas and W. D. McHardy. Oxford: Clarendon.

Thompson, S. A., and R. E. Longacre
1985   Adverbial Clauses. Pp. 171–234 in *Language Typology and Syntactic Description: Volume II: Complex Constructions.* Edited by T. Shopen. Cambridge: Cambridge University Press.

Toews, B. G.
1993   *A Discourse Grammar of the Aramaic in the Book of Daniel.* Ph.D. dissertation, University of California, Los Angeles.

Tropper, J.
1997   Lexikographische Untersuchungen zum Biblisch-Aramäischen. *Journal of Northwest Semitic Languages* 23: 105–28.

Weinrich, H.
1964   *Tempus: Besprochene und erzälte Welt.* Stuttgart: Kohlhammer.

Weninger, S.
2000   On Performatives in Classical Ethiopic. *Journal of Semitic Studies* 45: 91–101.

Wertheimer, A.
2002   Syriac Nominal Sentences. *Journal of Semitic Studies* 47: 1–21.

Wesselius, J.-W.
1988   Language and Style in Biblical Aramaic: Observations on the Unity of Daniel ii–vi. *Vetus Testamentum* 38: 194–209.

2001 The Writing of Daniel. Pp. 291–310 in vol. 2 of *The Book of Daniel: Composition and Reception*. Edited by J. J. Collins and P. W. Flint. Leiden: Brill.
2005 The Literary Nature of the Book of Daniel and the Linguistic Character of Its Aramaic. *Aramaic Studies* 3: 241–83.

Tracing the History of a Legal Term of Art: The Word *azarah* in Biblical, Tannaitic, and Targumic Literature

MADELINE KOCHEN

Azarah (עזרה) is not simply a Hebrew word for "courtyard." Since rabbinic times, it has been used consistently by rabbis and scholars to designate a space that was thought to have unique metaphysical characteristics and special ontological status. Unlike the word *ḥatzer* (חצר), a generic term for "courtyard" dating from early Biblical Hebrew, *azarah* is a legal term of art with the very special meaning of "Temple court."[1] It connotes the main (or great) courtyard of the Jerusalem Temple, the area that housed the sanctuary with the Holy of Holies and the sacrificial altar where virtually all Temple-related practices and activities took place. As the operational hub of the Second Temple, this cultic courtyard was believed by the rabbis of late antiquity to be imbued with a divine sacredness associated with the presence of God.[2]

In addition, there were other courts of the Temple to which the term *azarah* is applied that are identified by the demographic of those permitted (and, implicitly, of those not permitted) to enter. There are three of these courts: the Priestly Court (*Ezrat Cohanim* עזרת כוהנים), which was off limits

---

Author's note: I wish to thank the organizers and hosts of the NEH Summer Program in Aramaic, Paul Flesher, Eric Meyers and Lucas Van Rompay, as well as my seminar colleagues for a rewarding intellectual experience. I am very grateful to Paul Flesher for his invaluable help in developing this paper. Special thanks to Rachel Neis and to my teacher, Avi Hurvitz.

1. A *term of art* is an expression, word, or phrase that has a defined meaning when used in a particular epistemic community.

2. 1 Kings 8. See Davies, "Presence of God," which focuses on the centrality of the Temple to the rabbis in a legal sense. For other approaches to this question that were prevalent among Jews in ancient times—(1) the idea that the Temple represents the entire cosmos (in Josephus and Philo), and (2) the idea that the earthly Temple exists concomitantly with a Temple in heaven (in rabbinic literature)—see Klawans, *Purity, Sacrifice and the Temple*.

to non-priests; the Israelite court (*Ezrat Yisrael* עזרת ישראל), open to non-priestly Israelite males; and the women's court (*Ezrat Nashim* עזרת נשים), open to Jewish women, but not to non-Jews.

Translated "enclosure" in BDB, the word *azarah* rarely appears in biblical literature.[3] Linguistically it is characterized as a Late Biblical Hebrew term because its few occurrences in the Bible are in books known to have been written late.[4] As will be shown, its meaning in the biblical appearances is somewhat curious, however, for by the rabbinic period this Hebrew word, as well as its Aramaic cognate *azarta* (עזרתא), has taken on the clearly delineated meaning "Temple court."

This article examines the evidence for the categorizing of *azarah* as a late element in the Bible. This study is undertaken, however, with more than linguistic purposes in mind.[5] It is part of a larger project that looks at *azarah* in rabbinic literature in order to explore the ways in which the rabbis of late antiquity used law and language to construct reality. What is offered here is a focused study of the word *azarah* with an overall goal of addressing broader questions of meaning. Unlike a purely formalistic linguistic study, this approach focuses more closely on context and substance and yields insights into both the semantics of *azarah* and related words, and into the broader relationships between and among the bodies of biblical writings, rabbinic literature, and the targums.[6]

Highlighted here is the rabbis' use of a new and specialized term for Temple court as part of their larger project of inventing sacred space and areas that are juridically *sui generis*. The article demonstrates, for example, that the word *azarah* cannot be said to have straightforwardly replaced the word *ḥatzer* as would a normal classical equivalent or linguistic contrast. Although at first glance we might think that the word *ḥatzer* simply replaced *azarah* (and that the parallel Aramaic term *azarta* was similarly replaced by the word *darta* [דרתא]), the relationship between these words is shown to be more complex. It is through an examination of this complexity that a broader and more nuanced sense of the meanings and functions of these terms is

---

3. BDB 741.
4. See Segal, "Mishnaic Hebrew."
5. Indeed, a number of linguistic questions are not addressed in this article, such as why the word *azarah* became the word for Temple court, and where the sacred-versus-secular distinction between *azarah* and *ḥatzer* originated. Did the special meaning of *azarah* develop in parallel in Hebrew and Aramaic, or did Aramaic (as it seems to) borrow the meaning in the later period? One might also ask whether it is an internal Hebrew development that then affects Aramaic (at least in the targums) or an Aramaic development that moved over into Hebrew.
6. The methodology used in more formalistic aspects of this article is based on that of Avi Hurvitz, who pioneered this type of linguistic study of Late Biblical Hebrew (see, for example, Hurvitz, *Bein Lashon*; and "Continuity and Innovation") and provides an abridged explanation as to why the word *azarah* can be characterized as a Late (postexilic) Biblical Hebrew term. See also idem, "Evidence of Language," p. 41.

derived. Moreover, a close look at the way in which *azarah*, *ḥatzer*, and related terms are translated into and used in Jewish Literary Aramaic reveals an interesting link between targumic and rabbinic projects of exegesis.[7]

A. History and Methodology

1. Biblical Hebrew

Biblical literature constitutes a primary resource for uncovering the early history of the Hebrew language.[8] Although the exact dates of composition for most biblical books remain an area of scholarly debate, there is a consensus that the biblical corpus represents two linguistic stages: Classical (or pre-exilic) Biblical Hebrew, dating from the tenth through the sixth centuries B.C.E., and Late (or postclassical or postexilic) Biblical Hebrew, dating from the fifth to the second centuries B.C.E. In the latter period, some books (for example, Esther, Ezra, and Nehemiah) refer to historical events that can be traced to a late period, while other books signify their lateness by their language (such as Greek words appearing in the book of Daniel) or by their content (as when echoes of Hellenistic philosophy appear in the book of Qohelet).

The next stage in the history of the Hebrew language (postbiblical) is known as Mishnaic (or Rabbinic) Hebrew.[9] The language of tannaitic literature, which is the focus of this article, is sometimes specifically referred to as early Mishnaic or Tannaitic Hebrew.[10]

By starting with a focus on Late Biblical Hebrew, we may uncover terms, such as *azarah*, that serve as bridges between Classical Biblical Hebrew and Mishnaic Hebrew.[11] The methodology for such linguistic dating, pioneered by Avi Hurvitz, compares biblical data to extrabiblical sources in order to detect late linguistic elements.[12] He identifies a number of criteria to support a claim that a particular linguistic element of Biblical Hebrew is late.

---

7. See, for example, Samely, "Is Jewish Literary Aramaic Rabbinic Hebrew?"; Maori, "The Aramaic Targumim and Rabbinic Exegesis"; Flesher, "Pentateuchal Targums."

8. See, for example, Rooker, "Diachronic Study of Biblical Hebrew"; Waldman, *Recent Study of Hebrew*; Rabin, "Biblical Hebrew Linguistics"; Kutscher, *History of the Hebrew Language*, pp. 71–77.

9. See generally Bar Asher, "Mishnaic Hebrew"; Kutscher, "Present State of Research into Mishnaic Hebrew" and "Problems of Lexicography of Mishnaic Hebrew."

10. Although the names of these linguistic categories make reference to specific texts (the Bible and the Mishnah, respectively), these forms of the Hebrew language are found in other texts as well. For example, the Bar Kokhba letters are written in the Mishnaic Hebrew.

11. For more on the character of Late Biblical Hebrew, see, for example, Polzin, *Late Biblical Hebrew*; Hurvitz, *Bein Lashon Lelashon*; idem, "*Hamikra Vetoldot Yisrael*"; idem, "*Leshono Vezmano*"; idem, *Bechanim Leshoniim*.

12. See idem, *Bein Lashon Lelashon*; idem, "Continuity and Innovation." Hurvitz briefly reviews the basis for characterizing the word *azarah* as a Late (postexilic) Biblical Hebrew term in "Evidence of Language," p. 41.

(1) *Late distribution within the Hebrew Bible*: In order to be able to ascribe a word or linguistic element to the late period, one must be able to show that it appears predominantly or exclusively in late books of the Bible. While this distribution pattern is indicative of the late biblical period, it is not enough, by itself, to prove that an element is late.

(2) *Appearance in late extrabiblical sources*: Is the word or element in question prevalent in the later period outside biblical literature? Two types of extrabiblical sources are examined to supply this evidence: (a) *Subsequent late sources*: Since Mishnaic Hebrew essentially followed Late Biblical Hebrew as the next link in the linguistic chain (with the caveat that Dead Sea Scrolls Hebrew shows up at the end of the period of Late Biblical Hebrew), it is important to track and analyze the appearance of the particular word or element in texts written in Mishnaic Hebrew. Prevalence of the term in Mishnaic Hebrew lends credence to the suggestion that, as a Biblical Hebrew term, the element is late. Analysis of how that element is translated or used in the targums or other late sources can provide further insight or proof. (b) *Contemporaneous late sources*: It is also useful to explore extrabiblical sources that are more contemporary with late biblical literature, such as the Elephantine Papyri or Qumran literature. (The word *azarah* does not appear in these sources, so this body of evidence will not come into play here.)

(3) *Existence of a classical equivalent or linguistic contrast*: If possible, it is useful to show that the writers of early biblical literature used a different word or expression to express the same idea as the word or element in question. The absence of a clear linguistic contrast is not dispositive; nor is it necessary to show that the classical equivalent (in Classical Biblical Hebrew) was completely supplanted by the later (Late Biblical Hebrew or Mishnaic Hebrew) linguistic element. The presence of a clear linguistic contrast, however, is another strong indication that the word or element is late.

2. Aramaic and Hebrew

As suggested by their names, the two stages of Biblical Hebrew are divided precisely by the Babylonian Exile of 586 to 538 B.C.E., after which Jews returned to Palestine, having been immersed in Aramaic.[13] This is one obvious way that Aramaic influenced the development of the Hebrew language. In fact, among the Jews in Palestine, the interrelationship between these two languages is extensive and their histories are intertwined.[14]

From the eighth until the four centuries B.C.E., Hebrew was spoken in the land of Judah, which existed within a series of Aramaic-speaking empires (Neo-Assyrian, Neo-Babylonian, and then Persian). Following the exile, the residents of Palestine continued to use Aramaic, and the use of Hebrew began to decline. Nevertheless, Hebrew continued as the vernacular until

---

13. See, for example, Driver, "Hebrew Poetic Diction"; Greenfield, "Review of Wagner."
14. See Flesher, "History of Aramaic."

Table 1: Periods of Hebrew and Aramaic

Century	Hebrew Period	Aramaic Period	Jewish Aramaic Dialects	Jewish Aramaic Texts
10 B.C.E.	Classical			
9				
8				
7		Imperial		
6	Late			
5				
4				
3				
2		Middle	Jewish Literary Aramaic	Daniel
1 B.C.E.				
1 C.E.	Mishnaic			Targums Onqelos and Jonathan
2				
3		Late	Jewish Palestinian Aramaic	Targum Neofiti and other Palestinian Targums
4				
5				
6				
7 C.E.				

the early second century C.E.[15] Aramaic was also used alongside Hebrew up to the rabbinic period, when it finally supplanted Hebrew to become the Jewish lingua franca.[16]

The parallel periodizations of (1) Hebrew, (2) Aramaic, and (3) Aramaic among the Jews in Palestine can be mapped roughly, as in table 1. Noteworthy, for purposes of the article are the following observations about the Hebrew and Aramaic periods and texts:

1. Late Biblical Hebrew overlaps with both Imperial and Middle Aramaic.[17]

---

15. See Alexander, "How Did the Rabbis Learn Hebrew?" pp. 74–75; Saenz-Badillos, *History of the Hebrew Language*, pp. 112–201.

16. Alexander, "How Did the Rabbis Learn Hebrew?" p. 75. The final blow to the continuing use of Hebrew was the Bar Kochba revolt of 135 C.E.

17. There is a small gap of 200–300 years between the period of Late Biblical Hebrew and Mishnaic Hebrew. This period is characterized linguistically as "Qumran Hebrew," "Dead Sea Scroll Hebrew," or "Ben Sira Hebrew." Generally, however, there is no reason to assume that the chronological transition from Late Biblical Hebrew to Mishnaic Hebrew was interrupted during this brief hiatus, and "[t]he characterization of Qumran Hebrew (QH) remains problematic." Alexander, "How Did the Rabbis Learn Hebrew?" p. 74 n. 3.

2. Targum Onqelos to the Pentateuch and Targum Jonathan to the Prophets are written in a form of Jewish Literary Aramaic that is a dialect of Middle Aramaic (200 B.C.E. to 200 C.E.).[18]
3. Mishnaic Hebrew, dating from the early first century C.E. through the end of the seventh century, overlaps with both Middle and Late Aramaic, the period of the Palestinian Targums as well as of the earlier Targums Onqelos and Jonathan.[19]

Thus, from the period of Late Biblical Hebrew to the end of the rabbinic period, both Hebrew and Aramaic existed in Palestine and were used by Palestinian Jews. Sometimes this led to the use of essentially the same word in both languages, as with the Hebrew word *azarah* and the Aramaic term *azarta*.

The give and take between Hebrew and Aramaic during these centuries means that they often influenced each other's semantic development. Thus a comparison of Hebrew and Aramaic texts from the rabbinic period may reveal supporting evidence concerning the development of related terms. To take advantage of this, this essay will compare the Aramaic use of related terms once the semantic development of the Hebrew words has been laid out.

B. Biblical Evidence of azarah

The word *azarah* does not appear at all in Classical Biblical Hebrew. It makes its first appearance in late biblical literature and eventually exhibits widespread use in rabbinic literature. Its only appearances in the Bible occur in the books of Ezekiel and Chronicles. Both of these are late biblical compositions, with Ezekiel (which is treated as a transitional book) coming first chronologically.[20]

There are a total of four appearances of the word *azarah* in the book of Ezekiel, all of which appear to represent a rather technical use of the word as referring to the ledge surrounding the altar. This connotation of the word is not evidenced anywhere else. These usages of *azarah* are as follows:

Ezekiel 43:14

ומחיק הארץ עד העזרה התחתונה . . . ומהעזרה הקטנה עד העזרה הגדולה

And from the bottom upon the ground even to the lower ledge (*azarah*) . . . and from the lesser ledge (*azarah*) to the greater ledge (*azarah*).[21]

---

18. For information on the different bodies of targumic literature, see Alexander, "Targum."
19. As Paul Flesher notes, "[t]he relationship among the various Pentateuchal Targums, Targum Onkelos as well as Palestinian Targums, is a matter of intense discussion." See Flesher, "History of Aramaic," n. 20 and materials cited therein.
20. The book of Ezekiel is regarded as unique in that it "occupies a position mid-way between classical (pre-exilic) and post-classical (post-exilic) Biblical Hebrew" (Hurvitz, "Continuity and Innovation," p. 3 n. 4).
21. All translations of the Hebrew Bible are from the NJPSV.

Ezekiel 43:17

והעזרה ארבע עשרה ארך

and the ledge (*azarah*) shall be fourteen cubits long

Ezekiel 43:20, 45:19

ארבע פנות העזרה

four corners of the ledge (*azarah*)

The only other appearances of the word *azarah* in biblical literature are in 2 Chronicles:

2 Chronicles 4:9

ויעש העזרה הגדולה ודלתות לעזרה

And he made . . . the great court (*azarah*) and doors for the court (*azarah*).

2 Chronicles 6:13

כי עשה שלמה כיור נחשת ויתנהו בתוך העזרה

For Solomon had made a bronze scaffold and had set it in the midst of the court (*azarah*).

In these verses, *azarah* means "Temple court" and refers to Solomon's Temple.

There may be a connection between these two meanings of *azarah*, "Temple Court" and "ledge" of the altar. Just as a courtyard is as an enclosed space, the ledge surrounding the altar demarcates an area in the Temple with sanctity and special legal significance. In other ways, however, the altar, the courtyard, and those things defining their parameters do not seem analogous. In fact, whereas *azarah* is meant to refer to the space inside the court (as opposed to the walls creating the courtyard), Ezekiel uses the word *azarah* precisely to connote the tangible matter forming the perimeter of the altar (upon which, we are told, the blood is to be spilled).

Although it has no explanatory power vis-à-vis the book of Ezekiel, what the later rabbis do with the altar and the *azarah* does suggest a significant connection. They treat the altar and the *azarah* as similar in a very significant way: each was legally considered a unitary area in which was located (a kind of) sacredness. With respect to both the altar and the *azarah*, the rabbis construct intricate rules (about the transmission or loss of) sacredness based on an item's location with respect thereto, such as the invalidation of an item for sacrifice when it is taken out of the space (off the altar or out of the *azarah*). Perhaps the rabbis saw this connection in the different usages of the term *azarah* even if the evolution of the word had no relation to them.

C. azarah *and* ḥatzer

The rules of Temple construction and practice do not appear in the Pentateuch. In constructing these rules, the rabbis turn primarily to two things:

(1) descriptions of the *mishkan* (משכן), or mobile Tabernacle in Exodus, and (2) descriptions of the Temple envisioned by Ezekiel in Ezekiel 40–46. The central role of the *azarah* and, indeed, of the Temple is foreshadowed by the *mishkan* and its courtyard. In both Exodus and Ezekiel, the word used in reference to this parallel space is not *azarah* but *ḥatzer*, the generic term for court or courtyard that is dated to Classical Biblical Hebrew.[22] *Ḥatzer* appears with this common (nonsacred) usage, for example in:[23]

Exodus 8:9

וימתו הצפרדעים מן הבתים ומן החצרות ומן השדה

and the frogs died out of the houses, out of the courts (*ḥatzerot*), and out of the fields.

2 Samuel 17:18

ולו באר בחצרו

And he had a well in his court (*ḥatzer*).

The term *ḥatzer* is used elsewhere in the Bible in connection with Solomon's Temple (the same Temple referred to a few times by the word *azarah* in the book of Chronicles, as noted above). For example, the text makes reference to different types of courts in the Temple:

Inner Court	1 Kgs 6:36	ויבן החצר הפנימית
		And he built the inner court (*ḥatzer*)
	Ezek 8:16	חצר בית ה׳ הפנימית
		the inner court (*ḥatzer*) of God's house
Upper Court	Jer 36:10	בית ה׳ . . . חצר העליון
		in God's house . . . in the higher court (*ḥatzer*)

22. In the Bible, the word *ḥatzer* actually has two "distinctly separate roots and meanings": (1) "enclosure, court," and (2) "settled abode, settlement, village." See BDB; Orlinsky, "Ḥaser," p. 22. This article is only concerned with the appearances of *ḥatzer* in the former sense of "court."

23. It is worth noting, however, that the most prevalent appearances of *ḥatzer* in biblical literature refer to the court of the tabernacle (*mishkan*) or of Ezekiel's Temple. For example, see:

Exodus 27:9

חצר המשכן

court (*ḥatzer*) of the tabernacle

Ezekiel 46:21, 22

ויוציאני אל החצר החיצנה ויעבירני אל ארבעת מקצועי החצר והנה בחצר במקצע החצר חצר
במקצע החצר: בארבעת מקצעות החצר חצרות קטרות

Then he brought me out into the outer court (*ḥatzer*), and caused me to pass by the four corners of the court (*ḥatzer*); and, behold, in every corner of the court (*ḥatzer*) there was a court. In the four corners of the court (*ḥatzer*) there were roofless courts (*ḥatzerot*).

Outer Court	Ezek 10:8	החצר החיצונה
		the outer court (*ḥatzer*)
All Courts	1 Chr 23:28	לעבודת בית ה׳ על החצרות ועל הלשכסב
		for the service of God's house, in the courts (*ḥatzerot*) and in the chambers

There is one fascinating instance of overlap in the biblical use of the terms *azarah* and *ḥatzer* in biblical literature. 2 Chr 4:9 employs both of these terms in the same sentence, each in reference to a court in Solomon's Temple:

2 Chronicles 4:9

ויעש חצר הכוהנים והעזרה הגדולה ודלתות לעזרה

And he made the court (*ḥatzer*) of the priests, and the great court (*azarah*), and doors for the court (*azarah*).

It is hard to make sense of the uses of both *azarah* and *ḥatzer* in this verse. It might seem that *azarah* and *ḥatzer* are used interchangeably in referring to Temple courts.[24] On the other hand, a careful reading of the verse reveals that the word *ḥatzer* is used only in connection with the sub-court of the priests (something later to be called *azarah*), whereas *azarah* is used twice to refer to the main Temple court near which the priests' court was located. Yet, there is a problem with assuming that the words *azarah* and *ḥatzer* were consciously used to refer to different courts (the great court, *azarah*; versus a sub-court, *ḥatzer*). Other verses in Chronicles do not bear out this distinction. For example, in 2 Chr 7:7 and 20:5, *ḥatzer* seems to be referring to the great court, and in 2 Chr 23:8 (quoted above), the word *ḥatzer* is used to refer to "all the courts in God's house."

The seeming overlap in the use and meanings of the terms *ḥatzer* and *azarah* in 2 Chr 4:9 must be examined in light of the fact that much of what is mentioned in the late book of Chronicles represents the retelling of material previously recounted in the books of Samuel and Kings. A comparison of texts in Chronicles with their synoptic parallels in Samuel and Kings sometimes reveals a shift in language, as a term used in the earlier version is substituted with a different word, often a late element, in Chronicles.[25] This is not the case in Chronicles' use of the term *azarah*; however, something even more telling is revealed when these texts from Chronicles are compared with the book of Kings.

---

24. In the Septuagint, the same word is used to translate the words *azarah* and *ḥatzer* in 2 Chr 4:9, as well as the word *azarah* in 2 Chr 6:13. See Maier, "Architectural History," p. 31.

25. For synoptic parallels, see Endres, Millar, and Burns, eds., *Chronicles*. For an example of this comparative word study, see, for example, Japhet, "Hilufei Shorshei Hapoel."

The passages in 2 Chr 4:6–11, where the terms *ḥatzer* and *azarah* are both used to describe the Temple courts, have no parallels in the corresponding section in the book of Kings (1 Kgs 7:38–40). The same is true with respect to the only other passage in Chronicles (2 Chr 6:12–14) where the word *azarah* is used, again to describe the Temple court. There, too, the parallel passage is entirely missing from the relevant portion of the book of Kings (1 Kgs 8:22–23). Thus, both the place where Chronicles uses the this rare biblical term, *azarah*, and the only place in which both *azarah* and *ḥatzer* are used (possibly interchangeably) to refer to the Temple court are found in passages that are late additions to the story first told in Kings.

Not only are these verses in which *azarah* appears (2 Chr 4:9 and 6:13) late additions to Kings, but they appear to have been added with a particular purpose in mind. The Kings version of the narrative recounted in Chronicles (1 Kgs 8:22) implies that Solomon was standing near the altar inside the court of the priests, an area that was off limits to him as a non-priest.[26] The verses were added in Chronicles to correct this (incorrect?) impression from Kings that Solomon did something forbidden. It is in this regard that the use of the two different terms, *ḥatzer* and *azarah*, might also be explained. 1 Kgs 8:22 (and see 2 Chr 6:12) states that "Solomon stood before the altar of God in the sight of all the assembly of Israel and spread out the palms of his hands to heaven," in a context in which the altar was situated in the area that only the priests could enter. The Chronicler adds a verse at 2 Chr 6:13 that locates Solomon, not in the priests' area, but in the larger Temple court, where he was allowed to stand. This verse uses the word *azarah* to refer to the larger Temple court; 2 Chr 4:9, another verse added by the Chronicler and the only other verse utilizing the word *azarah*, had drawn a contrast by using the two different terms, *ḥatzer* and *azarah*, to make clear the fact that *azarah* (as used in 2 Chr 6:13) was an area separate from the area that was off limits to all but the priests.

Given the question raised earlier as to whether *azarah* and *ḥatzer* are understood as being used interchangeably in 2 Chr 4:9, it is particularly interesting that *azarah* is used in a new text, one that was added precisely to specify that Solomon was in the great court, not in the priests' court.

D. azarah *in Tannaitic Literature*

As noted earlier, in Mishnaic Hebrew, the word *azarah* is a technical term used exclusively to refer to the Temple court. Used on its own, the word *azarah* referred to the main, enclosed area of the Temple, within which was situated the Holy of Holies and the altar. The *azarah* was the Temple's focal point, where almost all of the action took place—from the priestly slaughtering and burning of the animal sacrifices to non-priestly donors' ritually laying

---

26. This point is also made in Maier, "Architectural History."

their hands on the animals, as well as the burning of the incense (inside the sanctuary itself) and almost all of the labor of the Temple.[27] This usage in Mishnaic Hebrew is witnessed in the detailed description of the Temple in Tractate *Middot*. For example,

m. Middot 1:4

שבעה שערים היו בעזרה

There were seven gates in the [Temple] court (*azarah*).

Besides the priestly *azarah*, there were different, smaller courts within the Temple compound, each with its own set of rules limiting those who were permitted to enter (men versus women, priests versus non-priests, etc.). The word *azarah* was also used for these Temple courts. Thus, for example, Mishnah Middot 2:6 describes:

m. Middot 2:6

עזרת ישראל—the court of (*ezrat*) the Israelites
עזרת הנשים—the court of (*ezrat*) the women[28]
עזרת הכהנים—the court of (*ezrat*) the priests
וכל העזרה היתה—the whole [Temple] court (*azarah*) was. . . .

Thus, in Classical Biblical Hebrew, before the Late Biblical Hebrew word *azarah* made its appearance, the word *ḥatzer* was used for all courts, including the court of the *mishkan*. With the full-blown use of *azarah* in Mishnaic Hebrew for Temple court, *ḥatzer* continued to be the generic word for court, but it was no longer applied to the Temple. Examples of the continued generic use of the word *ḥatzer* continued include:

m. Eruvin 6:1

הדר עם עובד גלולים בחצר

One who dwells with idol worshipers in a courtyard (*ḥatzer*)

m. Eruvin 6:3

אנשי חצר

people of the courtyard (*ḥatzer*)

---

27. The holiest part of the Temple was the Holy of Holies, located in the sanctuary within the *azarah*. However, there was virtually no human engagement with that space. The only person allowed to enter the Holy of Holies was the high priest, and he was allowed to do so only once a year. See generally Smith, *To Take Place*.

28. The term *ezrat nashim*, used in certain contemporary Jewish contexts to describe the women's section in a synagogue, might derive from this use of the term *azarah* in rabbinic literature to describe the women's court in the Temple. Indeed, *m. Middot* 2:5 provides, in part, "The women's court (*ezrat hanashim*) had originally been quite bare but subsequently they surrounded it with a balcony so that the women could look on from above while the men were below, and they should not mix together." However, on the apparent lack of a separate women's "section" in late antique synagogues. see Safrai, "Were Women Segregated?"

The early rabbis were reflective in the way they used the terms *azarah* and *hatzer*. M. *Middot* 2:5 perhaps best illustrates that the rabbis were knowing in their use of the unique term *azarah* to refer to what had previously been known by the generic term *hatzer*:

m. *Middot* 2:5

עזרת הנשים היתה . . . שנאמר ויוציאני אל החצר החיצנה ויעבירני על ארבעת מקצועי החצר והנה חצר במקצוע החצר חצר במקצוע החצר: בארבעת מקצעות החצר חצרות קטרות

The <u>women's court</u> (*azarah*) was . . . as it is said (in Ezek 46:21–22), "Then he brought me forth into the outer <u>court</u> (*hatzer*), and caused me to pass by the four corners of the <u>court</u> (*hatzer*); and, lo, in every corner of the <u>court</u> (*hatzer*) there was a <u>court</u> (*hatzer*). In the four corners of the <u>court</u> (*hatzer*) there were small <u>courts</u> (*hatzerot*)."[29]

The Mishnah describes the size of the women's court within the Temple with the contemporary term, therefore: *azarah*. It does so on the basis of a passage from Ezekiel, which the rabbis quote, that calls a Temple court *hatzer*. The substitution of terms is transparently deliberate.

The rabbis' conscious use of the special significance of the term *azarah* is reflected unequivocally in a *beraita* from the Babylon Talmud, which not only illustrates but, indeed, demonstrates the intentionality in the rabbis' use of the two terms *hatzer* and *azarah*:[30]

b. RH 24a

כדתיא: לא יעשו אדם בית תבנית היכל אכסדרא תבנית אולם חצר כנגד עזרה שלחן מנורח כנגד מנורה

[It is forbidden to make a likeness of God's attendants . . .] as it has been taught (in a *beraita*): A man may not make a house in the form of the Temple, or an exedra in the form of the Temple Hall, or <u>a court (*hatzer*) corresponding to the [Temple] court</u> (*azarah*), or a table (*shulhan*) corresponding to the (sacred) table (*shulhan*), or a candlestick (*menorah*) corresponding to the (sacred) candlestick (*menorah*).

The point of this statement is precisely to draw a contrast between sacred Temple items and nonsacred replicas of those things that, we are told here, are prohibited. An *azarah* is contrasted with a *hatzer* precisely to make clear the distinction that essentially comprises this prohibition. This is in sharp contrast to the phrases dealing with the candlestick (*menorah*) and the table (*shulhan*). In these cases, there is no special name associated with these

---

29. M. *Middot* 2:5.
30. A *beraita* is an ostensibly tannaitic rabbinic tradition, that is, one attributed to the early rabbis, before the third century C.E. Although this particular text is presented as a *beraita* and, therefore, as tannaitic, one cannot be certain that this temporal chronological attribution is correct, since the language does not appear in any separate tannaitic corpus.

items when situated in the Temple, so the same word is used to refer to both the Temple table or candlestick and the nonsacred replica.

Hatzer thus cannot simply be described as the classical equivalent or linguistic contrast of the word *azarah*, which, without further elaboration, implies that one word was substituted for the other. Such is the suggestion we are left with from Hurvitz's findings regarding the word *azarah*—that it "gradually replaced the pre-exilic (word) *hatzer*."[31] In fact, the meaning of both terms changed over time. Thus, an examination of the rabbinic texts reveals that, in Mishnaic Hebrew, the word *hatzer* continued in its original meaning except that it ceased to mean (also) courts in the Temple. In turn, the term *azarah* became a special term of art.[32] One specific court—in the Temple—acquired its own distinctive label of *azarah*, precisely to set it apart as an enclosed space such that, because of its sacredness and concomitant special characteristics, it was legally and ontologically different from any other.

E. azarta *in the Targums*

An examination of *azarah* and its place in Aramaic sheds further light on the development of *azarah* as a word that links Mishnaic Hebrew and Classical Hebrew, and as a rabbinic term of art that substantiates and reinforces the rabbinic strategy of drawing directly upon the *mishkan* in Exodus for the (intellectual) construction of the permanent Temple. In light of the findings revealed thus far concerning the Hebrew word *azarah*, we need to address the following questions:

1. How is the biblical word *azarah* translated into Aramaic by the targumists?
2. How is the biblical word *hatzer* (in the sense of "court") translated into Aramaic by the targumists?
3. Are there any other uses (that is, uses that do not represent direct translation) of the relevant Aramaic words disclosed by questions (1) and (2) in the targums?

First, corresponding to the two different meanings of *azarah* in the two books of the Bible in which that word appears—ledge of the altar (in Ezekiel) and Temple court (in Chronicles)—there are two different words used by the targumists when translating those passages into Aramaic.

Targum Jonathan to Ezekiel translates the word *azarah* as used in Ezek 43:14, 17, 20, and 45:19, as *m'samta* (מסמתא). This is the only appearance of

---

31. Hurvitz, "Evidence of Language," p. 43.

32. It is hard to say to what extent *azarah* had this special meaning or connotation in Late Biblical Hebrew, where it does not make many appearances. Although mostly used the way that it was used in Mishnaic Hebrew, *azarah* is also used for the ledge of the altar. Also, it is not clear how and whether there was a different valence to the word *azarah*, as compared with *hatzer* when used for Temple court.

the word *msamta* in all extant Aramaic texts.[33] This may correspond to the fact that the use and meaning of the Hebrew word *azarah* in Ezekiel is not associated with that word anywhere else in Biblical or Mishnaic Hebrew.

For most of the appearances of the word *azarah*, meaning "Temple court," in Chronicles, the targum uses the Aramaic word *darta* ("court").[34] Indeed, where the biblical text uses both *azarah* and *ḥatzer* to refer to a Temple court in 2 Chr 4:9, the targumist uses one word, *darta*, in his translation of both words:

2 Chronicles 4:9

ויעש חצר הכוהנים והעזרה הגדולה ודלתות לעזרה

And he made the court (*ḥatzer*) of the priests, and the great court (*azarah*), and doors for the court (*azarah*).

Targum to 2 Chronicles 4:9

ועבד דרתא דכהניא ודרתא רבתא ודשין לדרתא

He made the court (*darta*) of the priests and the great court (*darta*) and the doors for the court (*darta*).[35]

The word *darta* appears frequently in the targums as a translation for the word *ḥatzer*. It is used consistently by the pentateuchal targums Onqelos and Neofiti for the word *ḥatzer* in the phrase "court of the Tabernacle"; it is used in the Targum to the Prophets in reference to Temple courts and in reference to nonsacred courts.[36]

By contrast, the word *azarta* does not appear often in Aramaic. There are no occurrences in the dialects of Old Aramaic, Imperial Aramaic, or Biblical Aramaic. It makes its first appearance in Middle Aramaic (during a period contemporaneous with Late Biblical Hebrew, where the word *azarah* first appears), appearing only once in a Qumran fragment.[37] The word mostly occurs in Jewish Literary Aramaic, most often in the targums and most frequently in Targum Jonathan.[38] This is a phase of Middle Aramaic that is con-

---

33. The medieval grammarian and biblical commentator Rabbi David Kimḥi (1160–1235) commented on this word in his discussion of Ezek 43:17. He says, "The Targum (translates) 'the *azarah*' (as) '*m'samta*', and I have not seen this word (used) anywhere else." See Commentary of R. David Kimḥi to Ezek 43:17, s.v. *p'not*.

34. The word *prḥ* (פרח) or *kpr* (כפר) is used by the targumists to translate *ḥatzer* when it means "village." See, for example, TN Gen 26:16; Lev 25:31; Deut 2:23 (*kpr*) and similarly in Targum Onqelos. Conversely, it should be noted that in Jewish Literary Aramaic the word *ḥatzer* also means "lobe (of the liver)" (חצר כבדה). See Jastrow, *Dictionary*.

35. McIvor, *Targum of Chronicles*, p. 150.

36. For Temple courts, see Targum to 2 Chr 7:7; 20:5; 24:21; and 29:16; TJ Ezek 40:17; 46:21; TJ 1 Kgs 6:36. For nonsacred courts, see Targum Jer 32:2 and 32:8, where the biblical phrase המטרה חצר ("court of the prison") is rendered דרת בית אסיריא.

37. The New Jerusalem Scroll. For English translation, see G. Vermes, *The Complete Dead Sea Scrolls in English*, 607–10.

38. The fact that the Targums of the Prophets are called *Targum Jonathan* does not definitively indicate that they were written by the same person.

temporaneous with Mishnaic Hebrew, where *azarah* witnesses frequent use. As is true of the Hebrew word *azarah* in rabbinic literature, a search through the online targum texts in the CAL reveals that in every occurrence in the targums, *azarta* refers to a Temple court.

In general, the particular contexts or ways in which the term *azarta* is used fall into four categories:

(1) *Direct translation of* ḥatzer: On only two occasions is the word *azarta* used in the targums the way *darta* is frequently used: as a direct translation of the word *ḥatzer*, the primary biblical word for court.[39] For example,

Isaiah 1:12

כי תבאו לראות פני מי־בקש זאת מידכם רמס חַצֵרָי

When you come to be seen before me, who requires this from your hand, to trample my courts (*ḥatzerai*)?

Targum Jonathan Isaiah 1:12

אתן לאתחזאה דאתון קדמי מן תבע מיכדון דא למיתי לא תדושון עַזְרָתִי

When you come to be seen before me, who requires this from your hand, *that you should come? Do not* trample my courts (*azrati*)![40]

In the nine other instances (discussed below) in which *azarta* is used in Jewish Literary Aramaic (eight of which are in the targums), it is in a text that is not a direct translation of a biblical word.[41]

(2) *Rough "translation":* In two cases that come closest to being translation-like, in that the word corresponds to an explicit referent in the biblical text, the word *azarta*, meaning "Temple court," refers to the word for "altar" (*mizbeaḥ*, מזבח) or the word for "My [i.e., God's] house" (*beti*, ביתי).[42] Both Temple (*beti*) and altar (*mizbeaḥ*) are meant to communicate roughly the same idea as Temple court—a space that possesses special sacred status.

In all of the other uses of the word *azarta*, described below, the targumist is neither translating nor interpreting a biblical word; rather, the word is in language overtly added to the biblical text. In this sense, these uses of *azarta* in the targums function much as the way in which *azarah* is used in Chronicles, where the term is used in verses, or parts of verses, that are new either to Chronicles (as compared with the earlier version in Kings), or to the targum (as compared with the biblical text).

---

39. To be exact, in these two instances the word being translated is *ḥatzerei*/חצרי, "My [i.e., God's] court."
40. Chilton, *Isaiah Targum*. See also TJ Zech 3:7. In all translations of targumic texts in this essay, words in italics represent language not being translated directly from the biblical text but something added by the targumist.
41. See TJ 1 Sam 3:4; TJ Isa 10:32; TJ Ezek 1:1, 43:8, and 44:7; TJ Amos 9:1; TJ Zech 3:7; Megillat Taanit 19; Targum to Song 4:11; and Second Targum Esth 1:2.
42. TJ Amos 9:1 and TJ Ezek 44:7, respectively. Perhaps the former echoes the use of *azarah* as "ledge of the altar" in Ezekiel.

(3) *Explanation or embellishment*: In two instances the word *azarta* appears in what is essentially a parenthetical statement added by the targumist to explain or embellish the biblical text. Thus Ezek 1:1 states:

וַיְהִי בִּשְׁלֹשִׁים שָׁנָה בָּרְבִיעִי בַּחֲמִשָּׁה לַחֹדֶשׁ

And it came to pass in the thirtieth year, in the fourth month, in the fifth day of the month. . . .

The phrase "the thirtieth year" is ambiguous in that it does not say what time period is being measured. Targum Jonathan to Ezekiel includes the following additional language to explain that what is meant is the 30th year dated from the recovery of the book of the Torah in the Jerusalem Temple—or, rather, as the targumist indicates, in the Temple *court*:[43]

והוה מסוף בתלתין שנין לזמן דאשכח חלקיה כהנא רבא ספרא דאוריתא בבית מקדשא בעזרתא תחות אולמא

It was the thirtieth year, *from the time that Hilkiah the high priest found the book of Torah in the Temple, in the court* (azarta) *under the entrance*. . . .[44]

Similarly, Ezek 43:7–8 provides:

(7) וְלֹא יְטַמְּאוּ עוֹד בֵּית יִשְׂרָאֵל שֵׁם קָדְשִׁי
(8) בְּתִתָּם סִפָּם אֶת סִפִּי וּמְזוּזָתָם אֵצֶל מְזוּזָתִי וְהַקִּיר בֵּינִי וּבֵינֵיהֶם

And the house of Israel shall not profane my holy name any more. . . . In their setting of their threshold by my thresholds, and their post by my posts, and only the wall between me and them.

Targum Jonathan renders that passage as follows:

(7) ולא יסאבון עוד בית ישראל שמא דקודשי
(8) במתנבון ספיהון כקביל ספי בית מקדשי ובנינהון בסטר עזרתי וכותל בית מקדשי בין מימרי וביניהון

(7) . . . and the Children of Israel shall no longer defile My holy name . . .
(8) by placing their threshold beside the threshold of My *Holy Temple*, and *their buildings* beside My <u>Temple Court</u> (*azrati*), with only a wall of *My Holy Temple* between *My Memra* and them. . . .[45]

(4) *Midrashic exegesis*: In the last and largest category describing the way in which the word *azarta* is used in the targums—which includes four occurrences of the word—*azarta* appears as part of newly added text that either alters the biblical text altogether or performs an exegetical (midrashic) interpretive function. Thus, for example, 1 Sam 3:3–4 recounts the following narrative:

(3) וּשְׁמוּאֵל שֹׁכֵב בְּהֵיכַל יְהוָה אֲשֶׁר־שָׁם אֲרוֹן אֱלֹהִים
(4) וַיִּקְרָא יְהוָה אֶל שְׁמוּאֵל וַיֹּאמֶר הִנֵּנִי

---

43. See 2 Kgs 22:3–9.
44. Levey, *Targum of Ezekiel*, p. 20.
45. Ibid., p. 116.

(A)nd Samuel was lying down to sleep in the Temple of the Lord, where the ark of God was, and the Lord called, "Samuel"; and he answered, "Here I am."

Targum Jonathan renders that verse as follows:

(3) ושמואל שכיב בעזרת ליואי וקלא אשתמע מהיכלא דיי דתמן ארונא דיי
(4) וקרא יי לשמואל ואמר האנא

(3) (A)nd Samuel was sleeping *in the court* (*azarat*) *of the Levites. And a voice was heard from* the Temple of the Lord where the ark of the Lord was.
(4) And the Lord called to Samuel. And he said: "Here I am."[46]

As in Chronicles, this addition of language that includes the word *azarta* seems designed to rewrite an earlier text that creates the impression that someone was doing something impermissible. Here, the plain meaning of the biblical text depicts Samuel behaving in a (rabbinically?) untoward way—sleeping in the most holy of places, a place where one ought not enter, much less sleep, especially if one is not a priest. The targum adds language to suggest that he was not sleeping in that prohibited place; rather, while the voice emanated from there, Samuel was sleeping in the court of the Levites, a spot where he was allowed to be.

The Aramaic word for "court" used by the targumist to correct Samuel's infraction is not the more common *darta* but, rather, it is *azarta*. Other uses of the word *azarta* in the targums that appear as midrashic overlays to the biblical text include Targum Isa 10:32, Targum to Song 4:11, and the Second Targum Esth 1:2.

Examining the targumic translations of the Biblical Hebrew word *azarah* as well as the appearances of the related Aramaic words *azarta* and *darta* in the targumim yields the following findings. What was happening in Jewish Literary Aramaic during a period that is contemporaneous with Mishnaic Hebrew seems to parallel what was going on in both late biblical sources and in the Mishnah and Talmud. We observe the following three results:

1. The word *darta* in Jewish Literary Aramaic parallels the word *hatzer* in Classical Biblical Hebrew (meaning any kind of "court," both sacred and nonsacred).
2. The word *azarta* as used by the targumists appears to be the direct counterpart for the word *azarah* in Mishnaic Hebrew (meaning Temple court exclusively).
3. The word *azarta* is almost always used (six out of eight times) as part of additional language added by the targumist in something other than direct translation, often as an explanatory or midrashic move[47]

---

46. Harrington and Saldarini, *Targum Jonathan of the Former Prophets*, p. 108.
47. This phenomenon provides an interesting parallel to the appearance of *azarah* (in place of as well as in addition to *hatzer*) in two verses in 2 Chronicles (4:9; 6:13) that have no parallel in the books of Kings.

(this is unlike the word *darta*, which is used frequently in the targums as a direct translation of the word "court" in the Bible).

This examination of the way the biblical term *azarah* is translated by the targumists and of their use of the corresponding Aramaic word *azarta* supports the lateness attributed to the Hebrew word *azarah*. More interestingly, when the targumists, as text readers, behave not as translators but as midrashists (in a fashion that is similar to rabbinic practice or the innerbiblical interpretation characteristic of the book of Chronicles), they mostly use the term *azarta*. Otherwise they use the word *darta*. This suggests not only that the word *azarah/azarta* itself is late but also that the targumists were influenced by the rabbinic phenomenon exhibited in Mishnaic Hebrew. In other words, when the targumists were "speaking" in their own (contemporary) tongues, the language they used was that of the rabbis. As in the case of the rabbis, for the targumists there developed a special term of art for the sacred Temple court.

Summary of Findings

What has been demonstrated is that in Classical Biblical Hebrew the word *hatzer* is used for all types of courts—secular, private courts as well as sacred courts of the Temple. The word *azarah* does not appear at all in early biblical literature.

In the linguistically transitional book of Ezekiel, where *hatzer* is used repeatedly to refer to the Temple court, the word *azarah* begins to be used in connection with the Temple but with the meaning "ledge of the altar." This unique use of the word is echoed in the targumists' use of the similarly unique word *msamta* in translation. Used in Ezekiel to describe the outer perimeter or small area around the altar, this might be a precursor to the meaning that the word took on later—a larger enclosure defining the main area within the Temple. Indeed, there is an interesting parallel between Ezek 46:21–22, which twice mentions the "four corners of the court (*hatzer*)" (ארבעת מקצועי החצר) and two of the appearances of the word *azarah* in Ezekiel, 43:20 and 45:19, which both mention "the four corners of the *azarah*" (ארבע פנות העזרה). At the very least, there does seem to be a possible semantic connection between this use of the term in Ezekiel and the later use of the word *azarah* in Chronicles. This may indicate a gradual development in the use of that word within Late Biblical Hebrew itself, from the time of Ezekiel (the exilic period) to the postexilic period of Late Biblical Hebrew in the book of Chronicles.

In 2 Chronicles, both *hatzer* and *azarah* are used to refer to the Temple court. This usage of the word *azarah*, which appear in verses that are newly added, having no parallels in the earlier books of the Bible, foreshadows the ubiquitous technical use of *azarah* that will appear in Mishnaic Hebrew.

In Mishnaic Hebrew and throughout rabbinic literature, there is a clear dichotomy between the functions of these two words. *Hatzer* is only used for a regular court, and *azarah* is a technical term that is only used to describe the Temple court. A parallel use of the word *azarta* in the Aramaic targums seems to track the technical use of the word *azarah* in Mishnaic Hebrew, both in substance and in form. Indeed, one thing this study documents is a likely linguistic, as well as substantive, link between targumic and rabbinic material. In their use of the term *azarah*, some targumists not only perform midrashic exegesis, in the pattern of the rabbis, but when doing so they use the same term of art used by the rabbis.

Conclusion

The special nature of the term *azarah* can be expressed by the following linguistic features: The generic words for courtyard—*hatzer* (Hebrew) and *darta* (Aramaic)—are always explicated by another term, as in the phrase "court of the Tabernacle" (*hatzer hamishkan*), or "court of the Tent of Meeting" (*hatzer ohel moed*). By contrast, the term *azarah* is sufficient, in and of itself, to communicate the meaning of Temple court in Mishnaic Hebrew. While it might be necessary to indicate which Temple court is intended (priests' court versus Israelite court, or small court versus large court), there is no need to say anything beyond *azarah* to signify that what is intended is the court of the Temple; there is no need to say *ezrat beit hamikdash*.[48] This point can be illustrated best by the one exception to the rule—the Targum to 2 Chr 6:13:

2 Chronicles 6:13

כִּי־עָשָׂה שְׁלֹמֹה כִּיּוֹר נְחֹשֶׁת וַיִּתְּנֵהוּ בְּתוֹךְ הָעֲזָרָה

For Solomon had made a bronze scaffold and had set it in the midst of the <u>court</u> (*azarah*).

Targum to 2 Chronicles 6:13

ארום עבד שלמה כיורא דנחשא ויהביה <u>במצע דרתא בעזרת קודשא</u>

For Solomon had made the bronze platform and had placed it in the middle of the <u>courtyard, in the sacred enclosure</u>.

Where the biblical text simply says *azarah*, meaning Temple court, Targum Chronicles uses the phrase *darta b'azrat kudsha*. In other words, the targumist uses the Aramaic word *darta* for *azarah*, as in 2 Chr 4:9, but adds *b'azrat kudsha* ("in the holy *azarah*"), resulting in the seemingly redundant phrase "courtyard within the sacred *azarah*." Like the other generic term for court, *hatzer*, the word *darta* does need further explication of course. What is interesting is that the added phrase use the word *azarta* and that it does so in a way that the word *azarta* itself also requires further specification as the holy *azarah*—suggesting that there might be another kind. Why use the word *darta* at all if the word *azarta* is being used? Even more interesting is

---

48. This can also be said of the Aramaic term *azarta*, as opposed to *darta*.

the question triggered here as to whether *azarta* (and *azarah*?) were also, at one point, generic words for (any kind of) court.

The extra language in the Targum to 2 Chr 6:13—*darta* ("court") and *qudsha* ("holy") surrounding the word *azarta*—provides information that is taken for granted as the meaning of the term *azarah* in contemporary usage in rabbinic literature. The meaning was not "courtyard" (as in *hatzer* or *darta*). Rather, the word signifies a bounded space of a particular type, that of sacred space. Rather than seeing the targumic phrase as filled with redundancies, it can be regarded as providing what came to be the precise meaning of *azarah* when used by itself.

Azarah as a term of art that designates a particular kind of sacred space plays an active role in the rabbinic creation of a unique legal phenomenon possessing unique attributes, powers, and "rules of nature."[49] That the rabbis attribute a spatial sanctity to the *azarah* can be seen in the Mishnah.[50] This imagined space is the locus of intersection of the human and divine domains and, as such, it plays a central role in the rabbinic world view. *Azarah* as a term of art is part of the overall rabbinic project of constructing sacred and juridical spaces in the wake of the Second Temple's destruction.

49. The rabbis used the laws of the *mishkan* and particularly of the biblical *hatzer* of the *mishkan* as a basis for the laws peculiar to the *azarah*.

50. See *m. Zebahim* 14:4–8, *Kelim* 1:6–9, *Bikkurim* 1:8–9, and *Middot* 2:6. This sanctity implicates laws governing sacrificing, eating sacrifices, and entrance to various parts of the Temple area and undergoes refinement in later talmudic law.

Bibliography

Alexander, P. S. "How Did the Rabbis Learn Hebrew?" Pp. 71–89 in *Hebrew Study from Ezra to Ben Yehuda*. Edited by W. Horbury. Edinburgh: T. & T. Clark, 1999.

———. "Targum, Targumim." Pp. 320–31 in vol. 6 of *Anchor Bible Dictionary*. Edited by D. N. Freedman. New York: Doubleday, 1992.

Bar Asher, M. "Mishnaic Hebrew: An Introductory Survey." *Hebrew Studies* 40 (1999) 115–51.

Chilton, B. D. *The Isaiah Targum*. Aramaic Bible 11. Wilmington, DE: Michael Glazier, 1987.

Davies, G. I. "The Presence of God in the Second Temple and Rabbinic Doctrine." Pp. 32–36 in *Templum Amicitae*. Edited by W. Horbury. Sheffield: JSOT Press, 1991.

Driver, G. R. "Hebrew Poetic Diction." Pp. 26–39 in *Congress Volume*. Supplements to Vetus Testamentum 1. Leiden: Brill, 1953.

Endres, J.; W. Millar; and J. B. Burns, eds. *Chronicles and Its Synoptic Parallels in Samuel, Kings, and Related Biblical Texts*. Collegeville, MN: Liturgical Press, 1998.

Flesher, P. V. M. "The History of Aramaic in Judaism," Pp. 85–95 in vol. 1 of *Encyclopedia of Judaism*. Edited by J. Neusner, A. J. Avery-Peck, and W. S. Green. 2nd ed. Leiden: Brill, 2007.

azarah in *Biblical, Tannaitic, and Targumic Literature*

―――. "Pentateuchal Targums as Midrash." Pp. 630–45 in vol. 2 of *Encyclopedia of Midrash*. Edited by J. Neusner and A. J. Avery-Peck. Leiden: Brill, 2005.
Greenfield, J. C. "Review of Wagner." *JBL* 8 (1966) 232–34.
Harrington, D. J., and A. J. Saldarini. *Targum Jonathan of the Former Prophets*. Aramaic Bible 10. Wilmington: Michael Glazer, 1987.
Hurvitz, A. *Bechanim Leshoniim Lezihui Mizmorim Meucharim Besefer Tehilim*. Ph.D. dissertation. Hebrew University of Jerusalem, 1967.
―――. *Bein Lashon Lelashon* [The Transition Period in Biblical Hebrew: A Study in Postexilic Hebrew and Its Implications for the Dating of Psalms]. Jerusalem: Mossad Bialik, 1972.
―――. "Continuity and Innovation in Biblical Hebrew: The Case of 'Semantic Change' in Post-Exilic Writings." Pp. 1–10 in *Studies in Ancient Hebrew Semantics*. Abr-Nahrain Supplement 4. Louvain: Peeters, 1995.
―――. "The Evidence of Language in Dating the Priestly Code." *Revue Biblique* 81 (1974) 24–56.
―――. "*Hamikra Vetoldot Yisrael*, '*Chiasmus Diachroni*' *Be-Ivrit Hamikrait*." Pp. 247–55 in *Studies in Bible and Jewish History Dedicated to the Memory of Jacob Liver*. Edited by B. Uffenheimer. Tel Aviv: Tel Aviv University Press, 1971.
―――. "*Leshono Vezmano shel Mizmor 151 Miqumran*." *Eretz-Israel* 8 (Sukenik Volume; 1967) 82–87.
Japhet, S. "*Hilufei Shorshei Hapoel Betextim Hamakbilim Besefer Divrei Hayamim*." *Leshonénu* 31 (1966–67) 165–79, 261–79.
Jastrow, M. *A Dictionary of the Targumim, the Talmud Bavli and Yerushalmi, and the Midrashic Literature*. New York: Putnam, 1903.
Klawans, J. *Purity, Sacrifice and the Temple*. Oxford: Oxford University Press, 2006.
Kutscher, E. Y. *A History of the Hebrew Language*. Edited by R. Kutscher. Jerusalem: Magnes / Leiden: Brill, 1982.
―――. "The Present State of Research into Mishnaic Hebrew (Especially Lexicography) and Its Tasks." Pp. 3–28 in vol. 1 of *Archive of the New Dictionary of Rabbinical Literature*. Ramat Gan, 1972. [Hebrew; English abstract, pp. iii–xxvii]
―――. "Some Problems of the Lexicography of Mishnaic Hebrew and Its Comparison with Biblical Hebrew." Pp. 28–82 in vol. 1 of *Archive of the New Dictionary of Rabbinical Literature*. Ramat Gan, 1972. [Hebrew; English abstract, pp. iii–xxvii]
Levey, S. H. *The Targum of Ezekiel*. Aramaic Bible 13. Wilmington, DE: Michael Glazier, 1987.
Maier, J. "The Architectural History of the Temple in Jerusalem in Light of the Temple Scroll." Pp. 23–62 in *Temple Scroll Studies*. Edited by G. J. Brooke. Journal for the Study of the Pseudepigrapha Supplement 7. Sheffield: Sheffield Academic Press, 1989.
Maori, Y. "The Aramaic Targumim and Rabbinic Exegesis." Pp. 1–12 in *Proceedings of the Ninth World Congress of Jewish Studies*. Edited by M. Goshen-Gottstein and D. Assaf. Jerusalem: Magnes, 1988. [Hebrew]
McIvor, J. S. *The Targum of Chronicles*. Aramaic Bible 19. Collegeville, MN: Liturgical Press, 1994.
Orlinsky, H. M. "*Haser* in the Old Testament." *Journal of the American Oriental Society* 59 (1939) 22–37.
Polzin, R. *Late Biblical Hebrew: Toward an Historical Typology of Biblical Hebrew Prose*. Harvard Semitic Monograph 12. Missoula, MT: Scholars Press, 1976.

Rabin, C. "Israeli Research on Biblical Hebrew Linguistics." *Immanuel* 14 (1982) 26–33.
Rooker, M. F. "The Diachronic Study of Biblical Hebrew." *JNSL* 14 (1988) 199–214.
Saenz-Badillos, A. *A History of the Hebrew Language*. Cambridge: Cambridge University Press, 1993.
Safrai, S. "Were Women Segregated in the Ancient Synagogue?" *Jerusalem Perspective* 52 (1997) 24–36.
Samely, A. "Is Jewish Literary Aramaic Rabbinic Hebrew? A Reflection on Midrashic and Targumic Rewording of Scripture," *JJS* 45 (1994) 92–100.
Segal, M. M. "Mishnaic Hebrew and Its Relation to Biblical Hebrew and to Aramaic." *JQR* 20 (1908) 647–737.
Smith, J. Z. *To Take Place*. Chicago: University of Chicago Press, 1987.
Vermes, G. *The Complete Dead Sea Scrolls in English*. London: Penguin, 2004. For *editio princeps*, see *Les 'Petites Grottes' de Qumrân*. Edited by M. Baillet, J. T. Milik, and R. de Vaux. DJD 3.
Waldman, N. M. *The Recent Study of Hebrew: A Survey of the Literature with Selected Bibliography*. Cincinnati: Hebrew Union College, 1989.

The Adverb אוּלַי ("Perhaps") in the Piety and Prophecy of the Hebrew Bible and Early Versions

WILLIAM READER

The following study examines the usage of the adverb אוּלַי ("perhaps, maybe") in the Hebrew Bible and then traces the way that the early versions (Greek Septuagint, Aramaic Targums, and Syriac Peshitta) handle the word. While at first glance the term may seem inconsequential, the study points to some important theological ideas conveyed by it in biblical piety and prophecy. Then the study explores colorations that the term, when translated, took on in early versions of the Bible and related postbiblical literature. The results of the investigation confirm not only long-noted characteristic features of individual early translations but also the connections or relationships between the various versions that have been proposed by modern scholarship. Finally, the study points to a "theological afterlife" of the adverb that can be observed in postbiblical texts.

In a review of Aramaic dialects, Michael Sokoloff recently observed that lexicographers and philologians generally produce articles on unusual words—*hapax legomena*, odd forms, quadriliterals, or difficult terms—while more pedestrian words typically receive little attention.[1] The dearth of scholarly treatments devoted to the Hebrew adverb אוּלַי appears to corroborate Sokoloff's observation. The standard lexica offer meager data on אוּלַי, and journal articles on the word are virtually nonexistent.[2] Scholarly neglect of

---

1. M. Sokoloff in a lecture series on first-millennium Aramaic given at Duke University, July 13–14, 2004, as part of the NEH Summer Seminar on Aramaic in Postbiblical Judaism and Early Christianity.
2. For example, BDB 19 offers but 13 lines; Koehler and Baumgartner, *Hebräisches und Aramäisches Lexikon*, p. 21 only 7 lines; and the massive Botterweck and Ringgren, *Theologisches Wörterbuch* has no entry whatsoever on אוּלַי. Though skimpy, the best lexicographical treatment to date is in Jenni and Westermann, *Theologisches Handwörterbuch*,

127

what on first glance might appear to be an innocuous lexeme is understandable but unfortunate, because—as this study intends to show—in biblical usage this adverb carries some noteworthy theological implications.

I. אוּלַי in the Hebrew Bible

The modal adverb אוּלַי appears 44 times in the TaNaK (see table 1 below, pp. 144–45). Etymologically it is usually explained as a compound of אוֹ ("or") and [a dissimulated] לֹא ("not") or לוּ ("if").[3] It is not etymology, however, but usage that is determinative for its sense in the Bible. Depending on context it may express possibility, hope, doubt, apprehension, fear, or occasionally condition. But at their core, what is common to all of these meanings is the element of *uncertainty*.[4] This is the sense that the adverb connotes in all cases. Further, the speech pattern with אוּלַי almost always exhibits a two-part structure:

   a. the first part is ordinarily comprised of directive speech (imperative, jussive, cohortative), though in a few instances it may be represented instead by narrative (indicative)
   b. the second part begins with אוּלַי and expresses an uncertainty regarding what the first part urges, describes, or implies

In addition, it should be noted that the adverb can be applied to verbs denoting something in the past, in the present, or in the future. The following examples illustrate these observations.

Past

In Egypt after Joseph had hosted his brothers, who were unaware of his identity, he dismissed them with full sacks containing also the money they had paid for the purchased goods. When they later discovered their payment money in the contents of the sacks and were unsettled by the suspicions that could arise from this, Jacob told them to return to Egypt (Gen 43:12):

   a. Carry back with you the money that was returned in the top of your sacks;
   b. *perhaps* (אוּלַי) it was an oversight.

In Uz, Job's sons used to hold family parties in one another's homes with eating and drinking. When the festivities were over (Job 1:5):

---

vol. 1, cols. 79–81. A notable exception to this lack is Livnat, "אוּלַי from Biblical to Modern Hebrew," which provides an astute review of the word usage in both Biblical and Modern Hebrew.

3. See Jenni and Westermann, col. 79.

4. See Livnat, "אוּלַי from Biblical to Modern Hebrew," p. 81. Here it is worth noting that the counterpart to the אוּלַי-saying in the first half of the book of Jonah (1:6) is the parallel and virtually synonymous מִי־יוֹדֵעַ ("who knows?") in the second half (Jonah 3:9).

a. Job would ... would offer burnt offerings, one for each of them, for Job said,
b. "*Perhaps* (אוּלַי) my children have sinned, and cursed God in their hearts."

Present

Using the deception of worn-out clothing and rotten provisions, the Gibeonites attempted to make a nonaggression pact with Joshua's Israelites (Josh 9:7):

a. We have come from a far country, so now make a treaty with us.

But the Israelites respond:

b. *Perhaps* (אוּלַי) you live among us; how then can we make a treaty with you?

The third poem of Lamentations urges that one should await salvation from the Lord (Lam 3:27–29):

It is good for a man
    that he bear a yoke in his youth.
a. Let him sit alone in silence
    for the Lord has laid it upon him,
Let him put his mouth in the dust;
b. *perhaps* (אוּלַי) there is hope.

Future

When Saul was about to abandon the search for his family's lost donkeys, his servant said to him (1 Sam 9:6):

a. There is a man of God in this town. ... Whatever he says always comes true. Let us go there now;
b. *perhaps* (אוּלַי) he will tell us what way to take.

In a severe drought, King Ahab said to Obadiah (1 Kgs 18:5):

a. Go through the land to all the springs of water and to all the wadis;
b. *perhaps* (אוּלַי) we may find grass to keep the horses and mules alive, and not lose our animals.

Many similar two-part אוּלַי-sayings can be found, for example, on the lips of Sarah (Gen 16:2), Jacob (Gen 27:12; 32:21), Balak, king of Moab (Num 22:6, 11), a widow from Tekoa (2 Sam 14:15), the servants of Ben-Hadad of Damascus (1 Kgs 20:21), or the enemies of Jeremiah (Jer 20:10). It is unnecessary, however, to cite them all here verbatim. The examples quoted are sufficient to make the literary structure of the אוּלַי-sayings clear. But it should be pointed out that most biblical examples of אוּלַי refer not to the past or present but to the future. The cases mentioned above deal by and large with mundane matters. However, what makes the word אוּלַי particularly interesting is its usage in the language of popular piety and in the oracles of prophets. Therefore, with the everyday idiom in mind we turn our attention now to those אוּלַי-sayings that reflect a pious religious sentiment.

Circumspect Piety

In a variety of situations we find biblical characters uttering the conventional two-part אוּלַי-saying in which the human proposal of the first part of the saying is qualified by the "perhaps" of the divine disposal in the second part of the saying. Note the following examples:

At the land distribution, Caleb said to Joshua (Josh 14:12):

> a. Give me this hill country of which the Lord spoke on that day; for you heard on that day how the Anakim were there, with great fortified cities;
> b. *perhaps* (אוּלַי) the Lord will be with me, and I shall drive them out, as the Lord said.

In a skirmish with Philistines, Jonathan said to his armor-bearer (1 Sam 14:6):

> a. Come, let us go over to the garrison of these uncircumcised;
> b. *perhaps* (אוּלַי) the Lord will act for us; for nothing can hinder the Lord from saving by many or by few.

When Shimei was heaping verbal abuse on David, and David's bodyguard Abishai wanted to slit his throat to shut him up, David said (2 Sam 16:12):

> a. Let him alone and let him curse; for the Lord has bidden him;
> b. *perhaps* (אוּלַי) the Lord will look on my distress, and repay me with good for this cursing of me today.

During the siege of Jerusalem, King Zedekiah sent a message to Jeremiah via the priests Pashur and Zephaniah, whom he commissioned as follows (Jer 21:2):

> a. Inquire of the Lord on our behalf, for King Nebuchadrezzar of Babylon is making war against us;
> b. *perhaps* (אוּלַי) the Lord will act for our sake in accordance with all His wonders and will make him withdraw from us.

In all these examples the two-part אוּלַי-saying is used to acknowledge that success of the proposed human action depends in the final analysis on the favor and concurrence of God. This formulaic expression of Hebrew piety is so ingrained in the language that the biblical authors could also readily put it in the mouths of non-Israelites outside the land of promise.

In Moab, for example, after offering up generous sacrifices, Balaam, the (Syrian?) "incantation man," said to Balak, the Moabite king (Num 23:3):

   a. Stay here beside your burnt offerings while I go aside.
   b. *Perhaps* (אוּלַי) the Lord will come to meet me. Whatever he shows me I will tell you.

Subsequently, when Balak did not obtain the curse against Israel that he wanted, he said to Balaam (Num 23:27):

   a. Come now, I will take you to another place.
   b. *Perhaps* (אוּלַי) it will please God that you may curse them for me from there.

In their own territory even the Philistines can be presented using the deferential אוּלַי. When the Ark of the Covenant that they had captured brought them nothing but trouble, their priests and diviners advised them to return it to Israel, saying (1 Sam 6:3, 5):

   a. If you send away the ark of the God of Israel, do not send it empty, but by all means return him a guilt offering. . . . So you must make images of your tumors and images of your mice that ravage the land, and give glory to the God of Israel.
   b. *Perhaps* (אוּלַי) then he will lighten his hand on you and your gods and your land.

Out on the open sea when a storm threatens to swamp the ship on which Jonah is fleeing God's call, the captain said to him (Jonah 1:6):

   a. Get up, call on your god!
   b. *Perhaps* (אוּלַי) the god will take notice of us so that we do not perish.

In all these instances the speakers utter the אוּלַי as a circumspect expression of their dependence upon God's favor. It is as though they would appear presumptuous if they voiced only their own purpose or plan. Hence, to their own agenda they append the אוּלַי-formula, which recognizes that the outcome lies in God's hands. It shows they hope that God will approve of and grant their intent. The sense of this formula, therefore, closely parallels the substance of the double condition once formulated by David: "If it seems good to you, and the Lord our God concurs, let us . . ." (1 Chr 13:2).[5] The pious אוּלַי-formula, therefore, while not the same in form, certainly comes very close in function to the popular Muslim phrase *inshallah* ("if God

---

5. The Hebrew of this passage (. . . אִם־עֲלֵיכֶם טוֹב וּמִן־יְהוָה אֱלֹהֵינוּ) is difficult, and many have posited a text corruption; see Rudolph, *Chronikbücher*, p. 110. Nonetheless, the sense appears clear: "if to you [it seems] good and [it stems] from the Lord our God . . . ," i.e., ". . . and the Lord is in agreement. . . ."

wills"). One could of course just as easily compare it to the similar *Deo volente* ("God willing")–formula once common in the Christian world, though nowadays in the increasingly secularized West one rarely hears this phrase anymore.[6]

The Oracles of the Prophets

It has long been recognized that the classical prophets appropriated traditional speech patterns and conventional idioms from their culture and then retooled them in the service of their own message, so it should come as no surprise that in formulating their oracles they also took over and made use of the formulaic two-part אוּלַי-saying that was familiar both from ordinary colloquial speech and from the language of popular piety.[7] But ever creative, the prophets used this literary form in at least three new ways not evidenced hitherto in Israel's tradition.

Prophetic Ridicule

The book of Jeremiah (51:8) provides us with an instructive example of the prophetic use of an אוּלַי-saying. The authorship and date of the anti-Babylonian oracles at the end of the book of Jeremiah (chaps. 50–51) are difficult to determine with certitude. These oracles either anticipate the imminent fall of Babylon or gloat over its unfolding demise. This puts us in the year 539 B.C.E. or right before. Also, the oracles are at odds with the pro-Babylonian stance of the prophet recorded in the central part of his book (Jeremiah 27–29) and with the notion that Nebuchadnezzar is the "servant" of Yhwh (Jer 25:9; 27:6). It is difficult to reconcile these late exilic prophecies with the long life of the prophet Jeremiah, who was born a century earlier, around 640 B.C.E. (see Jer 1:2, 6–7), and whose career extended from the 13th year of Josiah's reign (627 B.C.E., see Jer 1:2) to the collapse of Jerusalem, the assassination of Gedaliah, and the Judean migration to Egypt—that is, until around 580 B.C.E. (see Jeremiah 41–43). Hence, the material at issue, at least in part, is generally viewed as stemming from a late exilic voice (contemporary with Deutero-Isaiah) which was later incorporated into Jeremiah's

---

6. This pious Latin phrase, an ablative absolute with conditional sense ("[if] God [be] willing"), derives from the corresponding New Testament Greek genitive absolute τοῦ θεοῦ θέλοντος (Acts 18:21). This and similar formulaic expressions were part of the Greek speech patterns of Christianized Jews from the very outset: see Paul's ἐάν ὁ κύριος θελήσῃ = "if the Lord wills" (1 Cor 4:19) and ἐάν ὁ κύριος ἐπιτρέψῃ = "if the Lord permits" (1 Cor 16:7; also Heb 6:3). Indeed, the New Testament letter of James argues that no plans should be formulated without this utterance (Jas 4:15). While it cannot be argued that the Christian usage of this and similar phrases stems from the אוּלַי-formula, it certainly did proceed from the same pious sentiment reflected in that formula.

7. See Westermann, *Grundformen prophetischer Rede*, pp. 64–150; Wolff, *Amos' geistige Heimat*, pp. 5–36; Clements, *Prophecy and Tradition*, pp. 24–92.

אוּלַי in the Hebrew Bible and Early Versions 133

oracles against the foreign nations (Jeremiah 46–49 [+ 50–51]) by the final, postexilic editors of the book of Jeremiah.[8]

In the subsection that urges people to flee from Babylon because it has collapsed (Jer 51:6–10), we find a standard אוּלַי-saying (Jer 51:8):

Suddenly Babylon has fallen and is shattered:
a. Wail for her! Bring balm for her wound!
b. Perhaps (אוּלַי) she may be healed.

In this passage there is disagreement among the commentators about the number of voices speaking within the whole oracle and about how modern editors might indicate and distinguish these voices with various kinds of punctuation signs. If one construes the speaker of the אוּלַי-saying (lines a + b) to be the Babylonians, as some commentators do, then the saying would express their hope, albeit desperate, that maybe some medicine could be applied to cure the mortally ill patient.[9] If, however, one does not posit a change of speaker in Jer 51:6–8—as seems more likely—then the sense of the אוּלַי-saying is quite the opposite.[10] If it is the prophet's own voice here, then the tone is snide and gloating. The אוּלַי is pure sarcasm: the prophet makes fun of the Babylonians' illusory hope; the patient is doomed.

This interpretation is certainly in line with Second Isaiah's taunt song against Babylon (Isaiah 47), which mocks the hubris and imagined security of that regime and predicts its downfall. Among the many resources for domination that Babylon had counted on were included the Mesopotamian "sciences" of sorcery, magic, astrology, enchantments, divinations, incantations, charms, and the like. In his oracle, the exilic prophet derides these arts with an אוּלַי-saying that can only be understood as a caustic sneer (Isa 47:12):

a. Stand fast in your enchantments and your many sorceries
   with which you have labored from your youth;
b. *perhaps* (אוּלַי) you may be able to succeed,
   perhaps (אוּלַי) you may inspire terror.

The double "perhaps" is clearly derisive: any hope is totally groundless. The conventional formula serves an unconventional function. It is uttered in scorn and ridicules the magicians' illusory, ineffective practices.

---

8. See the discussions in Rudolph, *Jeremia*, pp. 297–99; Carroll, *Jeremiah*, pp. 66–69, 814–17, 841–44; Holladay, *Jeremiah 26–52*, pp. 7–8, 401–15.

9. So Weiser, *Der Prophet Jeremiah*, p. 433; Volz, *Der Prophet Jeremia*, p. 427; and possibly Holladay, *Jeremiah*, pp. 396, 422.

10. Of course the shift from second-person-plural verbs in Jer 51:8 to first-person-plural verbs in Jer 51:9 does seem to suggest a change in speakers, but even on this point the commentaries do not agree. Moreover, there is no consensus about who the "we" are—anguished Babylonians? attending physicians? resident aliens? deportees from Judah? In any case, a resolution of the identity of the "we" in 51:9 does not automatically solve the question of the speaker in 51:8.

The ground for the sarcastic use of the אוּלַי-saying by these late exilic prophets may have been prepared by the story about the ninth-century prophet Elijah's confrontation with the Baal prophets recounted in the book of Kings (1 Kgs 18:17–40), a book that appeared shortly before the redacted books of Jeremiah and Second Isaiah.[11] The famous contest between Elijah and the prophets of Baal was to be decided by the outcome of their respective sacrifices. The contestants agreed that both would prepare a similar bull sacrifice, laid out upon wood, and then invoke the name of their deity; and they further agreed that whichever of the two sacrifices should be ignited by fire from heaven would determine whether it was Baal or YHWH who was really God. The Baal prophets performed their ritual first. For hours they invoked Baal, danced around their altar, lacerated themselves with knives, and worked themselves into a frenzy. But all in vain (1 Kgs 18:27):

> When it was noon Elijah mocked at them, and he said:
> a. Call in a loud voice, for he is a god;
>   either he is meditating,
>   or he is doing his "business"
>   or he is on a trip;
> b. *perhaps* (אוּלַי) he is asleep and needs to be awakened.

The two-part character of the typical אוּלַי-saying is not as rigorously maintained here as in most other examples. Between (a) the directive speech and (b) the qualifying *perhaps* clause, there are three separate phrases that each lampoon the deity (namely, כִּי־דֶרֶךְ לוֹ / כִּי־שִׂיג לוֹ / כִּי שִׂיחַ). Though the explanations and renditions of these words vary widely, going back as far as the Septuagint and Targum Jonathan, a long catalogue of interpreters have construed one, two, or all three of these phrases before the *perhaps* as euphemisms for defecating: musing [on the toilet], taking care of business [of bodily functions], on a trip [to the privy].[12] So understood, these phrases constitute a scathing ridicule of the naïve anthropomorphic conceptions in the Baal mythology. The imagery in the following אוּלַי clause may be less crude, but its scorn is no less biting. The anthropomorphic notion that the great god

---

11. The book of Kings was "published" after King Jehoiachin's release from Babylonian confinement and his later death (see 2 Kgs 25:27–30)—that is, sometime after 560 B.C.E. The historical appendices in the books of First Isaiah and Jeremiah were both copied out of the book of Kings (2 Kgs 18:13–20:19 = Isaiah 36–39 and 2 Kgs 24:18–25:21, 27–30 = Jer 52:1–27, 31–34), and presumably Second Isaiah was appended to the final redaction of First Isaiah. In other words, the editors of Jeremiah and Deutero-Isaiah were familiar with the book of Kings. Further, given the fact that the oracles in Jeremiah 51 and Isaiah 47 both anticipate the imminent collapse of Babylon, they are probably best dated during Cyrus's march to power (547–539 B.C.E.). Hence, it seems safe to assume that those who formulated the אוּלַי-sayings in Jer 51:8 and Isa 47:12 were also familiar with the report about Elijah at Carmel (1 Kgs 18:17–40).

12. See among modern commentators Burney, *Book of Kings*, p. 224; Montgomery, *Kings*, p. 302; Fohrer, *Elia*, pp. 16–17; Gray, *I and II Kings*, pp. 388, 397–99.

Baal needs to sleep or might be napping is denigratingly funny. One need only compare Homer's story that Zeus, overwhelmed by sleep—through the wiles of Hera and Hypnos—and thus "neutralized," is unable to come to the aid of his favorites, the Trojan heroes (*Iliad* 14:231–15:34); or Homer's tale about Aphrodite and Ares trapped *in flagrante* by Hephaestus's snare while sleeping in his bed, with the result that the other gods can come and jeer at them (*Odyssey* 8:266–366). Such burlesque comedy contrasts sharply with the view that "the Guardian of Israel will neither slumber nor sleep" (Ps 121:4).

Prophetic Urgency

From the satirical we turn to the serious. Another way that the prophets employed the traditional אוּלַי-saying was to underscore with it the gravity of their summons to moral reform. And just as a tale about Elijah may have provided a precedent for the אוּלַי of disdain, so also a story about Moses may have set the stage for the אוּלַי with an earnest tone. The case in point is the infamous incident of the golden calf (Exodus 32). While Moses was receiving the tablets of the covenant on the summit of Sinai, at the foot of the mountain Aaron presided over the fabrication of the metal image that became the focus for the idolatry and the impetus for an orgy. Upon his return Moses was outraged at the scene: he ordered the Levites to slaughter the ringleaders without quarter (Exod 32:30).

And on the next day Moses said to the people,
a. "You have sinned a great sin. But now let me go up to the Lord;
b. *perhaps* (אוּלַי) I can make atonement for your sin."[13]

Here the אוּלַי underscores how grave the matter is and how precarious the people's future has become. There is absolutely no certainty that the people will weather this crisis unscathed or intact. In the ensuing dialogue all the lines beat the same drum: God himself declares, "Alas, this people has sinned a great sin" (Exod 32:31). Moses offers his own life in place of theirs, "If you will only forgive their sin—but if not, blot *me* out of the book you have written" (Exod 32:32). God does not accept this substitution: "Whoever has sinned against me I will blot out of my book. . . . When the day comes for punishment, I will punish their sin" (Exod 32:33–34). The passage concludes

---

13. All modern translations and commentaries uniformly understand the Hebrew אעלה here as an imperfect indicative and render it as a future: "I will go up." However, given the conventional form of the אוּלַי-sayings, namely with *directive* speech in the first part, it seems to me required that we take the form as a *cohortative*: "Let me go up." To be sure, ordinarily the characteristic of the cohortative form is the lengthened *ā* (הָ) affixed to the first-person singular; however, there are a number of instances with weak third radical ה-verbs where the הָ (with *qametz*) changes into the obtuse הֶ (with *segol*) while still remaining a functional cohortative (see GKC p. 130/§48.3c–d), and it seems cogent to regard this verb in Exod 32:30 as yet another such example.

with the report: "Then the Lord sent a plague on the people" (Exod 32:35). The אוּלַי thus anticipates that there will be no mitigating arguments to sway the Judge. There is a great irony in the story; even as Moses is receiving the Law on top of the mountain, at the bottom the people are breaking its very first two commandments: "You shall have no other gods before me" and "You shall not make for yourself any idol or image" (Exod 20:3–4; see 32:4, 8). The psalmist's reflection on Exodus 32 puts it this way (Ps 106:20):

> They exchanged their glory
> for the image of a bull that eats grass.

Moses' אוּלַי-saying to the people and his intercessory prayer to God both point to the "iffiness" (note the twofold אִם in Exod 32:32) of the people's prospects in view of their apostasy and idolatry. At the establishment of the covenant, what could be more serious?

It is fair to ask whether this Exodus tradition could have prepared the way for the classical prophets' use of אוּלַי-sayings in their earnest summons to repentance. Though scholars do not agree on the pentateuchal source behind the Exod 32:30–35 pericope, nonetheless over the last century a consensus among critical scholars has emerged that the final formulation of Exodus 32 was related in some way to Jeroboam's (ca. 922–901 B.C.E.) setting up the bull-cult in Bethel and Dan (1 Kgs 12:25–33).[14] That is to say, it is certainly in order to assume that this Exodus tradition, if not the text, was familiar to Amos when he preached in the northern kingdom (ca. 750 B.C.E.). And oracles of Amos clearly allude to the bull-cult at Bethel (Amos 3:14; 4:4; 5:5–6). In any case, Amos is the first of the classical prophets to employ an אוּלַי-saying in his oracles, and in an earnest vein.

The saying at issue is an exhortation (Amos 5:14–15) in the middle section of the book (Amos 3–6), which comprises a collection of sayings directed at the northern kingdom of Israel. The אוּלַי-saying is found within a loosely connected series of laments, threats, accusations, warnings, and judgment sayings (Amos 5:14–15):

> Seek good and not evil
> that you may live.
> [Only] so will the Lord, ⟨the God of hosts,⟩ be with you
> as you assert.[15]
> a. Hate evil and love good
> and establish justice at the gate.

---

14. The passage is attributed, for example, on the one hand to the northern Elohist source by Hyatt, *Exodus*, p. 300; and Eissfeldt, *Hexateuch-Synopse*, p. 155; on the other hand it is traced to the southern Yahwist source by Noth, *Exodus*, pp. 243, 246; and Childs, *Exodus*, pp. 558–61. The consensus concerning Jeroboam can be found, for example, in Noth, *Exodus*, pp. 243–52; Hyatt, *Exodus*, pp. 300–312; Childs, *Exodus*, pp. 557–72.

15. The phrase "God of hosts" (אֱלֹהֵי־צְבָאוֹת) in both verses disturbs the *qinah* meter and is in all likelihood a late gloss (see Amos 4:13 with 5:8 and 9:6). Otherwise the oracle presents no textual problems.

b. *Perhaps* (אוּלַי) the Lord, ⟨the God of hosts,⟩ will show mercy to the remnant of Joseph.

The form of the oracle is instructive. The juxtaposition of admonition and contingent consequences in both 5:14a/b and 5:15a/b mirrors a conventional wisdom pattern (see Prov 19:20a/b; 24:21/22; 25:9/10). Verses 14 and 15 could each stand alone as independent sayings, but the two are linked together by the chiasmus of good/evil and evil/good and by the explanation of the "good" with the concrete requirement of "justice at the gate" that connects the two sentences through a kind of climactic parallelism. The poetic form is also noteworthy. Each of the four lines is in the *qinah* meter—that 3 + 2 rhythm characteristic of the dirge (see קִינָה Amos 5:1). The lament form suggests that the prophet anticipated a negative response from the listeners and consequently a sad outcome.

The oracle combats the false notion arising out of a dubious national or cultic piety that one does not need to seek the Lord (Amos 5:4, 6) because—according to the slogan of ancient election faith—the Lord is already "with them" (Amos 5:14; Gen 26:24; 28:15; 46:4; Num 23:21; Deut 31:8; Isa 8:10; Mic 3:10; Ps 46:8, 12). Yet the nation must seek the Lord (Amos 5:6) and it must do this by eschewing evil, pursuing good, and enacting justice in the courts (Amos 5:7, 10, 12, 24). Such conduct constitutes genuine repentance which is the absolute prerequisite for God's mercy. However, even real repentance cannot force the grace of God or allow the nation to lay claim to divine forgiveness. The Lord is no national god. He is not obliged to Israel because of cultic or legal arrangements. Amos's אוּלַי-saying characterizes God's mercy and help as that for which one may hope but that which is beyond all human control. In this oracle the parallelism between "[only] so" (וִיהִי־כֵן) and "perhaps" (אוּלַי) is significant. The אוּלַי in 5:15 forestalls any tit-for-tat understanding of the כֵּן in 5:14, as though God's favor could be a mechanical response to human moral efforts—a popular notion in the ancient world.[16] God will be merciful to whom he will be merciful (Exod 33:19). It remains alone with him if he shows grace or not. The recipient has no guarantee; humans cannot presume upon God. The prophetic *perhaps* preserves the total sovereignty of God and shows that Amos is concerned with radical submission to God and not with securing national existence.

The southern prophet Zephaniah (ca. 630 B.C.E.) is best known for his elaboration of the "Day of the Lord" motif (see Zeph 1:7–10, 14–18; 2:2–3; 3:8–11, 16–18), a concept that first appeared in the prophetic tradition with

---

16. The notion that religion is really about humans giving to the gods what the gods want and then of course getting in return from the gods what humans want was widespread in antiquity. Plato has Socrates label such self-interested religion an ἐμπορικὴ τέχνη, namely, a "business deal" or "barter arrangement" (Plato, *Euthyphro* 14d–e). Satan's famous question, "Does Job fear God for no reason?" [i.e., without expecting some payback] (Job 1:9) also presupposes the same self-interested reciprocity principle as the essence of religion.

Amos (Amos 5:18–20). The nationalistic notion that the Day of the Lord would mean "light" and "brightness" Amos combated with the imagery of "darkness" and "gloom" (Amos 5:18, 20) and with the frightening metaphors of escaping a lion only to meet a bear, or seeking safety at home only to be bitten there by a snake (Amos 5:19). Zephaniah took over the imagery of darkness and gloom (Zeph 1:15) but expanded the description with a plethora of other elements. That day will involve the sacrifice (Zeph 1:7, 8) and punishment (Zeph 1:8, 9) of royalty, elites, frauds, greedy traders, the complacent and self-assured (Zeph 1:8–12). It will mean bitterness and war, anguish and distress, ruin and devastation, bloodbath and fire, thorough termination and consuming wrath (Zeph 1:14–18; 3:8).

Moreover, Zephaniah proclaimed that the Day of the Lord was *near* and *imminent* (Zeph 1:7, 14). This gave added urgency to the concept. It could no longer be awaited with joyous expectation as was the case in Amos's time (Amos 5:18–20). For Zephaniah that day would lay bare the chasm between self-interested humanity and God, whose patience had run its course. That day would reveal the inescapable consequences of divine wrath. In the face of this coming day, the prophet uses an אוּלַי-saying to express the only possible appropriate stance one can take (Zeph 2:2–3):

> Before there comes upon you the fierce anger of the Lord,
>   before there comes upon you the day of the Lord's wrath.
> a. Seek the Lord, all you humble of the land who do his commands;
>   seek righteousness, seek humility;
> b. *perhaps* (אוּלַי) you may be hidden on the day of the Lord's wrath.

This אוּלַי-saying is the climax of the long series of threats and warnings directed at Judah. In the face of this coming divine judgment, the only real option for the hearers is a turn-around repentance. A threefold "quest" is enjoined: seek the Lord, seek righteousness, seek humility. This is the non-negotiable presupposition for restoring a life-giving connection with God. Like Amos, Zephaniah knows that such repentance will not automatically secure salvation. The *perhaps* saying is sober. It is in the same tradition as Amos. Like Moses' אוּלַי-saying in Exodus 32, it makes clear that God's favor remains beyond human manipulation. The אוּלַי-saying preserves the divine sovereignty. Human sin can rupture the covenant bond with God, but repentance cannot reattach it. God alone can do that. The saying recognizes that the sinner can only throw himself on the mercy of the Lord, do what is right, and hope that *maybe* he will be gracious.

Divine Worry

Lastly, the prophetic corpus contains a third category of אוּלַי statements but a kind without any discernable biblical precedent. Namely, we find three instances of the אוּלַי-formula spoken by God himself in directives to his prophets. The prophets in question are Jeremiah and Ezekiel, namely, those who stood closest to Israel's watershed events surrounding the catastrophe of 587 B.C.E.: the collapse of Jerusalem, the destruction of the Temple, the termination of the monarchy, and the deportation from the land.

On the occasion of Jehoiakim's ascent to the throne (609 B.C.E.) the Lord commissioned Jeremiah to preach his now famous Temple sermon (Jer 26:2–3):

   a. Stand in the court of the Lord's house, and speak to all the cities of Judah that come to worship in the house of the Lord; speak to them all the words that I command you; do not hold back a word.
   b. *Perhaps* (אוּלַי) they will listen, all of them, and will turn from their evil way, that I may change my mind about the disaster that I intend to bring on them because of their evil doings.

The sermon was constructed around the multivalent term "place" (מָקוֹם) which can variously mean "temple," "city," or "land" (Jer 7:3, 6, 7, 12, 14, 20) all of which are in jeopardy. He warned his listeners, "Do not trust in the deceptive slogan 'the temple of the Lord'" (Jer 7:4, 8). The worshipers' thrice-repeated chant will not bring them security. The Temple is not some talisman that can ward off evil (Jer 7:8, 10).

Instead Jeremiah challenges them to moral reform: "Amend your ways" (Jer 7:3). What he means by this is spelled out with a detailed list of specifics that sounds like the Decalogue (Jer 7:9) and a summary of Mosaic Law and prophetic ethics (Jer 7:6, 9; 26:4–5). To continue unrepentant on the present course will lead to the same fate that Shiloh suffered (Jer 7:12–14; 26:6, 9) and that befell the northern kingdom (Jer 7:15). The sermon he delivered must have made a deep impression because two separate accounts of it and its aftermath are included in the prophet's book (Jeremiah 7 and 26). Because of it he was accused of treason and put on trial for his life (Jer 26:7–23). Though he was acquitted (Jer 26:24), he was nonetheless barred from the Temple and forbidden to preach there anymore (Jer 36:5).

Putting the two-part אוּלַי formulation in God's "mouth" suggests that, (a) while he commands the sermon and its specifics, he is (b) uncertain about how it will be received, but nonetheless for the sake of his people he hopes for the best. To imply that God is uncertain or unknowing and that he entertains various possibilities regarding the outcome of the Temple sermon is a bold anthropopathism that evokes the idea of God's anguish for his people. Precedent for the notion that God could be anguished because of his people was set by Hosea, who had to experience in his unhappy marriage something analogous to the pain of God (see esp. Hosea 1–3). This אוּלַי-saying in Jeremiah implies a similar or at least related idea.

Four years into the reign of Jehoiakim (Jer 36:1) we find a kind of repeat performance. This is year 605 B.C.E. and no doubt in the wake of the decisive Babylonian victory over Egypt at the battle of Carchemish. This word came to Jeremiah from the Lord (Jer 36:2–3):

a. Take a scroll and write on it all the words that I have spoken to you against Israel and Judah and all the nations, from the day I spoke to you, from the days of Josiah until today.
b. *Perhaps* (אוּלַי) when the house of Judah hears of all the disasters that I intend to do to them, all of them may turn from their evil ways, so that I may forgive their sin.

In the *perhaps* clause the mention of Judah "hearing" anticipates the immediately ensuing report that Jeremiah summoned Baruch, his secretary, who wrote on a scroll at Jeremiah's dictation all the words of the Lord that he had spoken to him. Then Jeremiah ordered Baruch, saying (Jer 36:5–7):

I am prevented from entering the house of the Lord; so
a. you go yourself, and on a fast day in the hearing of the people in the Lord's house you shall read the words of the Lord from the scroll that you have written at my dictation. You shall read them also in the hearing of all the people of Judah who come up from their towns.
b. *Perhaps* (אוּלַי) their plea will come before the Lord, and all of them will turn from their evil ways, for great is the anger and wrath that the Lord has pronounced against this people.

The judgment is approaching; the situation is getting more urgent. God will give it another try—yet another Temple sermon—this time by proxy and incomparably longer. Since the scroll contains a summary of Jeremiah's oracles from the time of his call (22 years earlier; see Jer 1:2) up to the present, it is clearly an extensive document. The second אוּלַי-saying from Jeremiah to Baruch is a paraphrased repetition of the אוּלַי-saying the prophet had just received from God. There is nothing analogous to this repetition anywhere else in the biblical registry of אוּלַי-sayings; it intimates the longing of God that *maybe*, just *maybe*, his word this time will not fall on deaf ears. But there remains uncertainty.

The public reading came on a fast day the following year (Jer 36:9). The scroll must have made an enormous impression because three successive out-loud readings are reported: first publicly in the Temple, then in cloture in the palace, and then finally privately in the king's winter house (Jer 36:9–26). The first reading brought Baruch a governmental summons, the second reading prompted the confiscation of the scroll and the warning that Baruch and Jeremiah had better go into hiding, and at the third reading the scroll was burned column for column by a disdainful Jehoiakim. Hence one will have to say that the tentative hope expressed in God's אוּלַי-saying did not materialize. Or should one rather say that the doubt inherent in the אוּלַי turned out to have been warranted?

The final biblical example of God employing an אוּלַי-saying appears in connection with the siege of Jerusalem (588/587 B.C.E.). It is part of a text recounting one of Ezekiel's prophetic symbolic acts: namely, his act depicting the Jerusalemites' going into exile (Ezek 12:1–16). The Hebrew Bible contains some 30 accounts of symbolic acts performed by the prophets. Diverse and often bizarre in nature, they range from Ahijah's tearing his cloak into 12 pieces (1 Kgs 11:29–31) to Isaiah's going naked in Jerusalem (Isa 20:1–6) to Jeremiah's shattering a pot (Jer 19:1–2, 10–11). As varied as they are, from a form-critical perspective the reports stereotypically exhibit three essential characteristic elements: (1) a divine command to the prophet to perform the symbolic act, (2) a report about the prophet doing the act, and (3) an interpretation of what the symbolic act means.[17] These three elements show up clearly in the literary structure in the account of Ezekiel's enactment of the deportation: the command (Ezek 12:1–6), the performance report (Ezek 12:7), and the interpretation (Ezek 12:8–14[15]).

Despite this apparent clarity, however, the text poses difficulties. Compared with all other biblical accounts of symbolic acts, including those in Ezekiel, the text is unduly long and contains a number of internal tensions and inconsistencies. According to modern critical scholarship these seem best explained as deriving from an overlay of accretion. The "basic account" (Ezek 12:1–4, 6–9, 11) belongs to the situation *during the siege*. Ezekiel, who was part of the contingent of Judeans brought to Babylon in the first phase of the exile (598 B.C.E.), performs his "deportation act" before the Judean exiles in Babylon who harbored the illusory hope that Jerusalem would withstand the siege, and the exiles would return home soon. The act was intended to show, however, that Jerusalem would soon collapse and that there would be a new wave of Judean exiles coming to add to their number in Babylon. The "editorial additions" to this text (Ezek 12:5, 10, 12–14[15]) stem from a later time, which had knowledge of the breach of the city walls and the *outcome of the siege*. The additional material is clearly formulated in light of reports about the fate of Zedekiah (see 2 Kgs 25:4–7; Jer 39:4–7; 52:7–11).[18]

From the outset the אוּלַי-saying in question was part of the "basic" account of the symbolic deportation act. It was employed as part of God's command to the prophet, and so we will examine it in that light: in other words, we should read it as spoken *during the siege* before the military outcome was known. God's command to the prophet reads as follows (Ezek 12:1–4a, 6a, c):

> Son of man, you are living in the midst of a rebellious house, who have eyes to see but do not see, who have ears to hear but do not hear; for they are a rebellious house.
> a. Therefore, son of man, prepare for yourself an exile's baggage, and go into exile by day in their sight; you shall go like an exile from your place to another place in their sight.
> b. *Perhaps* (אוּלַי) they will understand, though they are a rebellious house.

17. See Fohrer, *Die symbolischen Handlungen der Propheten*, pp. 17–19, 95–98.
18. Despite many objections to this literary-critical analysis (see, e.g., Greenberg, *Ezekiel 1–20*, pp. 207–21), this still remains the most cogent explanation for the tensions in the text; see Fohrer, *Ezechiel*, pp. 63–65; Zimmerli, *Ezechiel 1–24*, pp. 254–69; idem, *Ezechiel*, pp. 53–55; Wevers, *Ezekiel*, pp. 80–83.

a. You shall bring out your baggage by day in their sight, as baggage for exile; and you shall go out yourself at evening in their sight, as those do who go into exile. . . . In their sight you shall lift the baggage on your shoulder, and carry it out in the dusk; . . . for I have made you a sign for the house of Israel.

From a literary standpoint this אוּלַי clause is different from all the other examples in that it is placed not at the end (a/b), but in the middle of the directive speech (a/b/a). This variation in form does not, however, affect substance or function. Other features are more interesting. The act itself, performed apparently without words (Ezek 12:7), was ambiguous. The exiles who observed it could understand it two ways: on the one hand they could take it as symbolizing their own yearned-for, imminent repatriation, with each carrying a few important belongings from Babylon with him or her. On the other hand the exiles could interpret it as symbolic of the soon-to-be-defeated Jerusalemites who would be force marched into exile, taking with them only the barest essentials that they could carry on their backs—just as Ezekiel and his audience themselves had done a decade earlier.[19] Inasmuch as the exiles hoped for the former, an interpretation was necessary (Ezek 12:8–9, 11) that would disabuse them of their false expectations: Jerusalem would fall and the survivors would be deported.

In its context God's אוּלַי-saying thus contains a paradox. On the one hand both the command to do the symbolic act and the explanation of the act show God as being *certain* about the outcome of the siege of Jerusalem. On the other hand the אוּלַי clause presents God as being *uncertain* regarding how the Babylonian exiles would understand and respond to the import of the prophet's act. Four times in the text God calls the exiles a "rebellious house" (Ezek 12:2a, 2b, 3, 9), including in the אוּלַי-saying itself (Ezek 12:3). So it might be better to say here that the אוּלַי expresses more doubt than hope.

To summarize, the use of אוּלַי in God's own speech suggests a remarkable anthropopathic conception of God that ought not go unnoticed. That God can be moved by "higher" emotions such as compassion or wrath is found often enough in the Hebrew Bible; but "lesser" emotions? A speech pattern that suggests God could worry or fret, that God might suffer uneasiness, apprehension, or even frustration—such a way of talking could imply an even more human or less elevated picture than is commonly thought in connection with the transcendent Creator who established a covenant with Israel. The אוּלַי language in divine speech should remind the reader that in the last analysis all talk about God is analogical in nature.

---

19. Gripping depictions of just such circumstances can be seen in ancient Egyptian and Assyrian art portraying captives and refugees from war. See Pritchard, *Ancient Near East in Pictures*, pls. 10, 311, 357, 358, 365, 366.

II. The Translation of אוּלַי in the Early Versions (Septuagint, Targums, Peshitta)

After the review of אוּלַי-sayings in the Hebrew Bible the second part of this study will examine how the adverb is handled in its early translations. Table 1 provides a schematic overview of the data to be analyzed. The first column lists the אוּלַי passages of the Hebrew text according to the order of their occurrence in the canonical Masoretic Text. The sequence of the versions in the subsequent columns is roughly according to considerations of language and chronology. The Greek LXX (third to second centuries B.C.E.) is followed by the Aramaic targums: Targum Onqelos (first or early second century C.E.) and the closely related Targum Jonathan (second to third centuries C.E.?); the Samaritan Targum (second or third century C.E.); Targum Neofiti (second or third century C.E.); Targum Pseudo-Jonathan (fourth to fifth centuries C.E.?); the Syriac Peshitta (second to third centuries C.E.); the last column repeats the LXX in order to facilitate an easy comparison with the Peshitta, in a few books of which it seems to have exercised some influence (see the words in bold font). The two passages from the *Ketubim* (Job 1:5 and Lam 3:29) noted in the Pseudo-Jonathan column are bracketed to indicate that they are not part of Pseudo-Jonathan; these late (medieval?) targums are noted here simply to avoid having to create a separate column for them.

By using the אוּלַי-sayings as a test case, this study tries to discern translation policies characteristic of each individual version. Further, by comparing the translation patterns observable within each version and by comparing how the different versions render selected passages, the study tries to understand the possible relationships between the versions. While the analysis cannot establish inter-targumic relationships, it can help to shape our thinking about the possibilities. The whole analysis is based upon the data presented in table 1. The reader, therefore, is encouraged to refer to it regularly.

The Septuagint

Together the postexilic dispersion of the Jews and the post-Alexander Hellenization of the Near East set the stage for the translation of the Hebrew Bible into Greek in the third century B.C.E.[20] This translation, known since at least the second century C.E. by the name *Septuagint* (LXX), is the first and oldest rendering of an entire corpus of Semitic literature into a European language—an unprecedented event and of enormous consequence for European civilization.[21] The LXX of course also had long-term effects on developments

---

20. The Göttingen and Cambridge editions of the LXX with their extensive critical apparatus were not available for this study. The discussion is therefore based upon Rahlfs, *Septuaginta*.

21. The oldest attested use of the term *Septuagint* as title for the translation seems to be that of Justin Martyr (ca. 160 C.E.), who calls it the "Translation of the Seventy [οἱ

Table 1: אוּלַי in Translation

MT	LXX	Onqelos/Jonathan	Samaritan Targum	Targum Neofiti	Pseudo-Jonathan	Peshitta	LXX
Gen 16:2	ἵνα	מא אם	מאן	מה דלמה ד–	מאים	ܕܠܡܐ	ἵνα
Gen 18:24	ἐάν	מא אם	מאן	מה דילמה ד–	מאים	ܐܢ	ἐάν
Gen 18:28	ἐάν	מא אם	מאן	מה דלמה	מאין	ܐܢ	ἐάν
Gen 18:29	ἐάν	מא אם	מאן	מה דילמה ד–	מאים	ܐܢ	ἐάν
Gen 18:30	ἐάν	מא אם	מאן	מה דילמה אם	מאים	ܐܢ	ἐάν
Gen 18:31	ἐάν	מא אם	מאן	מה דילמה ד–	מאים	ܐܢ	ἐάν
Gen 18:32	ἐάν	מא אם	מאן	מה דילמה	מאים	ܐܢ	ἐάν
Gen 24:5	μήποτε	מא אם	מאן	מה דלמה	מאים	ܕܠܡܐ	μήποτε
Gen 24:39	μήποτε	מא אם	מאן	מה דלמה ד–	מאים	ܕܠܡܐ	μήποτε
Gen 27:12	μήποτε	מא אם	מאן	מה דלמה ד–	מאים	ܕܠܡܐ	μήποτε
Gen 32:21	ἴσως	מא אם	מאן	מה דלמה ד–	הלואי	ܕܠܡܐ	ἴσως
Gen 43:12	μήποτε	דלמא	לוי	דלמה	דילמא	ܕܠܡܐ	μήποτε
Exod 32:30	ἵνα	מא אם	מאן	דלמה די	הלואי	⅄	ἵνα
Num 22:6	ἐάν	מא אם	מאן	מה דלמה ד–	לוואי	ܕܠܡܐ	ἐάν
Num 22:11	εἰ ἄρα	מא אם	מאן	[מה דלמה ד–]	לואי	ܕܠܡܐ	εἰ ἄρα
Num 23:3	εἰ	מא אם	מאן	מה דלמא	דילמא	⅄	εἰ
Num 23:27	εἰ	מא אם	מאן	מה דלמה ד–	דילמא	ܕܠܡܐ	εἰ
Josh 9:7	ὅρα μή	דלמא				ܐܢ	ὅρα μή
Josh 14:12	ἐάν	מא אם				ܕܠܡܐ	ἐάν
1 Sam 6:5	ὅπως	מא אם				⅄	ὅπως
1 Sam 9:6	ὅπως	דלמא				⅄	ὅπως
1 Sam 14:6	εἴ τι	מא אם				⅄	εἴ τι
2 Sam 14:15	εἴ πως	מא אם				ܕܠܡܐ	εἴ πως
2 Sam 16:12	εἴ πως	מא אם				⅄	εἴ πως
1 Kgs 18:5	ἐάν πως	מא אם				⅄	ἐάν πως
1 Kgs 18:27	μήποτε (2×)	דלמא (2×)				ܕܠܡܐ (4×)	μήποτε (2×)
1 Kgs 20:31	εἴ πως	מא אם				⅄	εἴ πως
2 Kgs 19:4	εἴ πως	מא אם				⅄	εἴ πως
Isa 37:4	—	מא אם				ܕܠܡܐ	—
Isa 47:12c	εἰ	מא אם				⅄	εἰ
Isa 47:12d	—	מא אם				⅄	—
Jer 20:10	εἰ	מא אם				ܕܠܡܐ	εἰ

אוּלַי in the Hebrew Bible and Early Versions

Table 1: אוּלַי in Translation

MT	LXX	Onqelos/ Jonathan	Samaritan Targum	Targum Neofiti	Pseudo-Jonathan	Peshitta	LXX
Jer 21:2	εἰ	מא אם				ܐܢ	εἰ
Jer 26:3	ἴσως	מא אם				ܐܢ	ἴσως
Jer 36:3	ἴσως	מא אם				ܐܢ	ἴσως
Jer 36:7	ἴσως	מא אם				ܐܢ	ἴσως
Jer 51:8	εἴ πως	מא אן				ܐܢ	εἴ πως
Ezek 12:3	ὅπως	מא אן				ܐܢ	ὅπως
Hos 8:7	ἐάν δε	מא אן				ܒܕܠܡܐ-	ἐάν δε
Amos 5:15	ὅπως	מא אן				ܟܒܪ	ὅπως
Jonah 1:6	ὅπως	מא אן				ܟܒܪ	ὅπως
Zeph 2:3	ὅπως	מא אן				ܟܒܪ	ὅπως
Job 1:5	μήποτε				[מאים]	ܕܠܡܐ	μήποτε
Lam 3:29	εἰ ἄρα				[מאים]	ܒܕܠܡܐ-	εἰ ἄρα

in both Judaism and Christianity. Any endeavor, therefore, to understand the translation strategies and policies requires no justification.

In the case of the אוּלַי-sayings, the first thing that strikes the reader is the great variety of renditions within the Septuagint. A quick look at the LXX column shows 7 different variations of the conditional participle εἰ ("if") alone:

εἰ [by itself]   (if)
εἰ ἄρα   (if indeed)
εἴ πως   (if somehow)
εἴ τι   (if in some way)
ἐάν [= εἰ + ἄν]   (if)
ἐάν δε   (if then)
ἐάν πως   (if somehow)

These translation choices clearly want to reflect the basic sense of uncertainty or "iffyness" inherent in the Hebrew אוּלַי. In all there is a total of 23 occurrences of some form of εἰ; taken together these comprise more than half of the 44 biblical occurrences of אוּלַי. The logic behind the translations with a form of μη also seems clear:

ἑβδομήκοντα]" (*Dialogue with Trypho* 124:3; 68:7; 137:3—this of course is a reference to the now famous legend of origin recounted in the *Letter of Aristeas* 301–11). In the West this Greek was then rendered into Latin literally; see Augustine's comment: *interpretes . . . septuaginta duo . . . quorum interpretatio ut Septuaginta vocetur iam obtinuit consuetudo* ("seventy-two translators . . . whose translation it has now become traditional to call the Septuagint"; *City of God* 18:42).

μήποτε (lest, whether perhaps)
ὅρα μή (take heed lest)

These (8) renderings with μή apparently want to connote a sense of apprehension about unwanted circumstances. These too we may regard as genuine attempts at a faithful rendering of the original sense. Of all the Septuagint choices, however, the Greek word that most aptly renders the אוּלַי is, hands down, the adverb ἴσως ("perhaps, maybe"), and one wonders why it was not used more often (only 4 times).[22]

In contrast to the above choices, it is difficult to construe as legitimate sense-translations the remaining cases, which use final conjunctions:

ἵνα (in order that) Gen 16:2; Exod 32:30
ὅπως (in order that) 1 Sam 6:5; 9:6; Ezek 12:3; Amos 5:15; Jonah 1:6; Zeph 2:3

These instances seem instead to be deliberate attempts to evade or alter the plain sense of the Hebrew. All these cases resemble an interpretive technique which in the targums Michael L. Klein calls "converse translation," whereby the translator for midrashic or theological reasons renders the source language precisely opposite its originally intended meaning.[23] In these last named passages the *uncertainty* is removed and replaced with avowed *purpose*.

In the case of the prophets the LXX translator obviously wants to disambiguate the incentive to repent. He has Amos say, "Hate the evil and love the good, and establish justice in the gates, *in order that* [not "*it may be that*"] the Lord God Almighty will be gracious to the remnant of Joseph" (Amos 5:15). Israel's righteousness will elicit God's grace. The Septuagint's Zephaniah says, "Enact justice and seek righteousness, and respond to these *in order that* [not "*perhaps*"] you may be hidden on the day of the Lord's wrath" (Zeph 2:3). By doing what is right one can surely avoid divine wrath. In the case of Ezekiel the translator is uneasy with an uncertainty coming from the mouth of God, so he rephrases the divine command to make it more definite: "And you, son of man, make for yourself an exile's baggage in front of them in daylight; go into exile from your place to another place in their sight *in order that* [not "*it may be that*"] they see, because they are an obstinate people" (Ezek 12:3). No suggesting a lack of certainty on God's part!

In the other instances as well, the rendering of אוּלַי with a final conjunction removes the uncertainty from the saying. In the case of Moses, for example, the Greek translation enhances his sway with God: Moses says, "You have sinned a great sin. I will go up to the Lord *in order that* [not "*it may be*

---

22. Formed from the adjective ἴσος ("equal, alike"), this adverb at its root (ἰσ-) connotes a perceived balance among potentialities or possible outcomes of the verb it modifies. Hence, the sense "perhaps" or "maybe."
23. See Klein, "Converse Translation," pp. 515–37; idem, *Genizah*, vol. 1, p. xxxi; Alexander, "Jewish Aramaic Translations," p. 228.

that"] I can make atonement for your sin" (Exod 32:30). Instead of doubt, Moses shows confidence. However, using a final conjunction for אוּלַי sometimes requires additional modifications in the sentence to avoid unwanted consequences. In the case of Sarah, for example, translating the Hebrew adverb with a Greek conjunction could have put her in a less complimentary light: Sarah said to Abram: "See, the Lord has restrained me from bearing children; go, therefore, into my slave-girl *in order that you beget* [not "*it may be that I shall obtain*"] children by her" (Gen 16:2). Without also changing the verb from first to second person (אִבָּנֶה > τεκνοποιήσῃς) Sarah's words could suggest an attempt on her part to thwart an intention of God. Also in the remaining passages with ὅπως for אוּלַי (1 Sam 6:5; 9:6; Jonah 1:6) one can discern a midrashic or theological rationale for the translator's choice of a final conjunction.

Such observations about interpretive translation are not new. Already the Greek version by Aquila (second century C.E.) shows an awareness and implicit critique of the translation choices of the LXX.[24] While the complete translation of Aquila has unfortunately been lost, many scattered scraps do remain, and among these are two אוּלַי passages worth noting. The LXX translations of אוּלַי with ἵνα in Gen 16:2 and μήποτε in Job 1:5 were both rendered by Aquila with εἴ πως ("if somehow").[25] This is certainly more accurate and of course in keeping with the general literalness of his translation.

In summary, within the LXX the great range and inconsistency of translations of אוּלַי are no doubt due in part to the large number of different translators who worked on the various individual books over many decades. Each translator operated with different principles ranging from verbatim literal to freely idiomatic. Even within individual אוּלַי passages one finds inconsistencies. For example, in the duplicate passages of 2 Kgs 19:4 and Isa 37:4 the LXX translated the אוּלַי in the former with εἴ πως but completely omitted it in the latter. Or even more striking, the double אוּלַי in Isa 47:12 is rendered in the LXX with a single εἰ, and a single אוּלַי in 1 Kgs 18:27 is rendered by the LXX with a double μήποτε.

In cases of words with obvious theological substance or import the LXX exhibits a general tendency to represent Hebrew words consistently with the same Greek equivalent—a phenomenon that is sometimes called "verbal linkage" or "stereotyping."[26] However, with "ordinary" or "innocuous" vocabulary this principle does not seem to have been as operative. In any case it is clear that the LXX never underwent any sort of homogenizing editorial revision that sought to make all the language consistent or uniform. Furthermore, the cautious idiom of Hebrew piety and the nuanced oracles of robust prophecy often lose their acuity in the Septuagint Greek.

---

24. For an overview of Aquila's work, see Jellico, *Septuagint and Modern Study*, pp. 76–83; Fernández Marcos, *Septuagint in Context*, pp. 109–22.
25. See Reider and Turner, *Index to Aquila*, pp. 66, 263.
26. See Tov, "The Septuagint," pp. 171–76.

The Targums

The Hebrew Scriptures were translated into a number of Aramaic dialects. In Judaism these translations were called *targum*[s]. The meaning of the Aramaic word תרגום includes both "translation" and "interpretation."[27] It can denote a very literal, word-for-word translation as well as a more expansive, midrash-like rendering of the original Hebrew text. The boundary between translation and interpretation is not easily defined; targum and midrash occupy in some sense overlapping segments of the same continuum.

The slow but persistent penetration of Aramaic into Israel is evidenced — at least for the upper classes — as early as the eighth century B.C.E. (see 2 Kgs 18:26). With the establishment of Imperial Aramaic as the administrative language of the Babylonian and Persian Empires, it gradually permeated wider circles of Israel's whole population. This development continued for centuries with the result that in Palestine of the Roman period while Hebrew was still in use, it lived in a kind of symbiotic relationship with Aramaic which had became the principle spoken and written language. This situation set the stage for and made natural the emergence of targums.

The general scholarly consensus is that the pentateuchal targums probably originated primarily in connection with synagogue worship. In the Second Temple period the constituent ingredients of the synagogue service typically included congregational prayer, the recital of psalm-like praises, the reading of lessons from Scripture, and an expository homily. These readings were naturally done from the original Hebrew. Over time it became a necessity also to render the lessons into the Aramaic vernacular for synagogue attendees with insufficient knowledge of Hebrew so that they could become better instructed in the Law and the Prophets.

Exactly when the Aramaic targums became an integral part of liturgical practice is uncertain, but the practice was certainly established by the second century C.E. The Mishnah provides important details on how the translation into Aramaic was to be carried out. The interpreter (מתרגמן) was required to be distinct from the reader. At the reading of the Pentateuch each individual verse was to be put into Aramaic immediately following its reading in Hebrew. For the Prophet-lectionary up to three verses could be read out loud before being translated (*m. Meg.* 4:4). The Aramaic targums had to be given orally; written texts were not allowed for this purpose.

The rabbis offered several reasons for this liturgical practice. The worshipers should be able to distinguish clearly between the sacred Scripture and the interpretive translation (*b. Meg.* 32a). It was also argued that the

---

27. See Sokoloff, *Jewish Palestinian Aramaic*, p. 1231; Bacher, *Exegetische Terminologie der jüdischen Traditionsliteratur*, part 1, pp. 204–6; part 2, pp. 242–45. The quadriliteral root (*trgm*) behind the verb (תרגם) and nouns (תרגום and מתרגמן) suggests that the term is a loanword out of a non-Semitic language. Origins have been posited from Indo-European possibly via Hittite; see Rabin, "Hittite Words in Hebrew," pp. 134–36.

written revelation should be presented from writing while the oral tradition should be conveyed by word of mouth (*y. Meg.* 4.1 [74d]). This meant that the *meturgeman* had to practice reciting the targum prior to the actual service. The third-century rabbinic advice both in Palestine and Babylon was to review the weekly Torah portion "twice from the biblical text and once from the targum" [שנים מקרא ואחד תרגום] (*b. Ber.* 8a–b).[28] This suggests that by early Amoraic times the targums had achieved a relatively fixed written form.

The question of exactly when the oral targums began to be recorded in a written text is difficult to answer. The oldest attested targum texts stem from Qumran: a targum of Leviticus (4QtgLev = 4Q156) and a targum of Job (4QtgJob = 4Q157; 11QtgJob = 11Q10). These might be dated as early as the second century B.C.E. but certainly no later than the Roman destruction of Qumran in 68 C.E. Rabbinic literature also mentions a targum of Job known to Gamaliel I [ca. 25–50 C.E.] and Gamaliel II [90–110 C.E.] (*t. Shabb.* 13.2; *b. Shabb.* 115a; *y. Shabb.* 16.1 [15c]; *Sopherim* 5; 15). Whether this is the same targum text as that at Qumran is uncertain. Nonetheless, it is clear that some targum texts were in existence already in the first century C.E. However, inasmuch as Job belongs to the *Ketubim* (which were not part of the regular synagogue lectionary cycle) a liturgical setting in the synagogue (as בית־תפלה) does not seem to account for the whole phenomenon of targums. No doubt one needs also to consider a didactic setting in the synagogue (as בית־מדרש) as part of the context for the genesis of targums.

Whatever their *Sitz im Leben*, there emerged a number of targums reflecting different regional traditions, various Aramaic dialects, and divergent translation policies. Every targum has its own "personality" traits. An examination of how each targum handles the biblical אוּלַי passages sheds light on some characteristic earmarks of each text.

Targum Onqelos and Targum Jonathan

While the character of Onqelos (on the *Torah*) and Jonathan (on the *Nebiim*)[29] are not identical, they are quite similar, though the latter tends to be more aggadic and expansive. Nevertheless, the two are consistent enough to be treated here together. Both exhibit a unified, stable textual tradition, and both are vocalized with the supralinear Babylonian pointing system. While their origins may well have been in Israel, their final form was clearly achieved in Babylonia, where they were regarded as having authoritative or "official" status. Indeed, the Babylonian Talmud refers to Onqelos as "our targum" (*b. Qidd.* 49a), and quotations from Jonathan are sometimes introduced by the phrase "were it not for the targum of this verse we should not know what it means" (*b. Ber.* 28b; *b. Meg.* 3a; *b. Moed Qatan* 28b; *b. Sanh.* 94b).

---

28. In Palestine this dictum was attributed to Yehoshua ben Levi (ca. 250 C.E.?) and Ammi (ca. 300 C.E.?), and in Babylonia to Huna bar Yehuda (ca. 290 C.E.?), see *b. Ber.* 8a–b.

29. The definitive critical edition is that of Sperber, ed., *The Bible in Aramaic.*

In stark contrast to the LXX, the way the Hebrew adverb אוּלַי is rendered in these targums is indicative of their general tendency to use consistent translation equivalents—what is sometimes called "verbal linkage" or "stereotyped" translations. A glance at table 1 shows that, in the Pentateuch, with one exception (Gen 43:12), אוּלַי was uniformly rendered with the Aramaic phrase מָא אִם ("what if?"). This one exception with דִּלְמָא is probably due to an old, widespread oral tradition for Gen 43:12 that resisted change. This explanation is suggested by the observation that this same word (דלמא) also appears here in the Neofiti and Pseudo-Jonathan targums as well as in the Peshitta. In Jonathan the verbal linkage is not quite as uniform: 22 cases have מָא אִם (once with the variant מָאִים, Isa 47:12), but there are 3 passages with a rendering of דלמא (Josh 9:7; 1 Sam 9:6; 1 Kgs 18:27). The מא אם–formula is thus clearly the preferred rendering of אוּלַי. Otherwise in both Onqelos and Jonathan the lexeme דלמא (always pointed with a *ḥireq* in the first syllable) is used almost exclusively to render the Hebrew conjunction פֶּן ("lest, that not"; see, e.g., Gen 3:3, 22; 11:4; 19:15, 17, 19; 26:7, 9; 31:24, 29, 31; 32:12, and 100 more examples). For Targum Jonathan's 3 departures from the מא אם preference there is no obvious explanation, but these three cases do show that any final editing in Jonathan with an eye to verbal linkage was not thoroughgoing.

The only example from the Jonathan Targum worthy here of a separate note is the instance of Elijah's mockery of the Baal worshipers (TJ 1 Kgs 18:27) because here one can see a development also paralleled in the LXX and Peshitta—namely, a single "perhaps" in the source text becoming a multiple "perhaps" in the target text:

Masoretic Text

When it was noon Elijah mocked at them	וַיְהִי בַצָּהֳרַיִם וַיְהַתֵּל בָּהֶם אֵלִיָּהוּ
and said, "Call in a loud voice!	וַיֹּאמֶר קִרְאוּ בְקוֹל־גָּדוֹל
Surely he is a god;	כִּי־אֱלֹהִים הוּא
either he is meditating,	כִּי שִׂיחַ
or he has wandered away,	וְכִי־שִׂיג לוֹ
or he is on a journey;	וְכִי־דֶרֶךְ לוֹ
perhaps he is asleep and he will wake up."	אוּלַי יָשֵׁן הוּא וְיִקָץ

Targum Jonathan

And at noontime Elijah laughed at them	והוה בעדן טיהרא וחייך בהון אליה
and said, "Cry in a loud voice!	ואמר קרו בקל רב
For you say he's a god.	ארי אתון אמרין דהלא הוא
Perhaps he is involved in a conversation,	דלמא שועי ליה
or he is relieving himself,	או אשתדפא אשתדיף [ליה]
or he is on a trip,	או אורח הות ליה
or *perhaps* he is asleep and will wake up."	או דלמא דמוך הוא ויתער

The sarcastic Hebrew taunt, "Surely (כִּי־) he is a god," is changed in the Aramaic to a declarative "for you say (ארי אתון אמרין) he is a god" in order to eliminate any possible misunderstanding. The single אוּלַי that culminates the series of jeers in Hebrew has become in Aramaic a double דלמא, opening and closing the series like a set of brackets. The four elements in the series virtually invited this development. The double μήποτε in the LXX rendering is in a way analogous, and the fourfold דלמא in the Peshitta's translation brought the tendency to full fruition. Beyond this, the targumic tradition of Onqelos and Jonathan exhibits little that is distinctive in the reception, rendering, or reuse of the biblical "perhaps."

Samaritan Targum

Abraham Tal, one of the leading experts on the Samaritan Targum,[30] dates the emergence of the written fixation of the older Samaritan oral-translation tradition to the mid-third century C.E.[31] Only eight (late) manuscripts survive to attest to the text of the Samaritan Targum, the oldest of these having been copied in the twelfth century. Of these manuscripts only one is complete; the rest are fragmentary. Three of the manuscripts reflect the oldest form of the Samaritan language, which resembles Jewish targumic Aramaic, in particular that of the Targum Onqelos. The other manuscripts are closer to the later language of Jewish midrashim and the Palestinian Talmud.[32]

In contrast to the Palestinian Targum, the translation of which is often characterized by expanded renderings and midrashic augmentations, a general earmark of the Samaritan Targum is its extreme literalness. The predominant principle seems to have been word-for-word translation: ordinarily the Samaritan Targum has only one Aramaic word for each Hebrew word of the biblical text.[33] In this regard the Samaritan translators fell under the critique of the first axiom, but not the second, in the famous dictum of Rabbi Yehuda ben Elai (ca. 150 C.E.):

המתרגם פסוק כצורתו הרי זה בדאי והמוסיף הרי זה מגדף

The one translating a verse according to its form [i.e., literally] is a liar, the one adding [to it] is a blasphemer.[34]

As a consequence of this deliberate and consistent literalness not much theological yield comes of an analysis of the how the Samaritan Targum handles the אוּלַי passages in the Pentateuch. The main point to stress here is that just like Targum Onqelos (as a review of table 1 shows), the Samaritan Targum also systematically rendered the Hebrew אוּלַי with the term מאן (a contraction of מא אין, literally: "what if?"). The only exception to this verbal

---

30. The most-recent modern critical edition of the Samaritan Targum (transcribed into Hebrew characters) is provided by Tal, *Samaritan Targum of the Pentateuch*.

31. See idem, "Samaritan Targum," pp. 189–90; earlier scholars had dated the text to the fourth century C.E.; see Gaster, "Samaritans," p. 196.

32. See Tal, "The Samaritan Targum," pp. 191–92.

33. See Lowy, *Samaritan Bible Exegesis*, pp. 300–304; Tal, "Samaritan Targum," pp. 200–202.

34. *T. Meg.* 3.41; also cited in *b. Qidd.* 49a. See Zuckermandel, *Tosephta*, p. 228.

linkage is the translation with לוי ("O that") in Gen 43:12. However, it was pointed out above that the old targumic translation of this particular verse appears to have been so fixed in the oral tradition that the traditional rendering trumped any vocabulary the targumists might otherwise have opted for. The divergent Samaritan choice here also seems to reflect the distinctive character of Gen 43:12.

Targum Neofiti

The way Targum Neofiti[35] handles the אוּלַי passages is striking. Here too, in contrast with the LXX, as in the other targums there is systematic, stereotyped, verbal linkage, but a different solution is employed than in the previous targums. In Neofiti all 17 Pentateuch occurrences of אוּלַי are rendered with some variant of the phrase מה דילמה די ("perhaps"). Sokoloff calls this phrase a conjunction (though he identifies דילמה by itself as an adverb ["perhaps"] and מה alone as an interrogative ["how?"]).[36] Etymologically viewed, the word ד[י]למה is a compound of מה + ל + די.[37] In Neofiti the adverb exhibits two different spelling variations. The first syllable is sometimes written as דיל- and sometimes as דל-. In the former case the vowel is clearly a *ḥireq* written *plene*; however, in the latter case the vowel is ambiguous: it could be taken as a *ḥireq* written defectively or as a *pathaḥ*.[38] In the second syllable the terminal *â* vowel can be written with a final א- or final ה-. These variations are indiscriminate and have no bearing on the meaning, as is obvious from the fact that they can even occur within the same passage (see Gen 18:24–32). This simply reflects the absence of any standardized orthography.[39] Whether the conjunction די/-ד follows דילמה or not also makes no difference in meaning (see Gen 18:24, 29, 31 with 18:28, 32; and see Gen 24:5 with 24:39).

The two exceptions without the interrogative מה are easily explained. In Exod 32:30 the entire clause, "*perhaps* I can make atonement for your sins,"

---

35. This study is based upon the *editio princeps*: A. Díez Macho, *Neophyti 1*. English translations superior to those in Díez Macho are provided by M. McNamara in the series The Aramaic Bible, vols. 1A, 2, 3, 4, and 5A.

36. Sokoloff, *Jewish Palestinian Aramaic*, pp. 293, 150–51. See Golomb (*Grammar of Neofiti*, pp. 34–35), who labels the phrase מה דילמא די- a conditional conjunction ("what if?").

37. The components are evident from earlier Biblical Aramaic (see לְמָה ["lest," literally: "for what reason?, why should . . . ?"], Ezra 4:22 = דִּי־לְמָה ["lest, so that . . . not"], Ezra 7:23). This Aramaic corresponds to the later Hebrew usage of לָמָּה as a conjunction ("in order that not," literally: "for what reason?, why?"; see Qoh 5:5; 7:16, 17; Neh 6:3); even closer to the Aramaic is the Hebrew שַׁלָּמָה (Song 1:7). This Hebrew use of לָמָּה is analogous to the Hebrew פֶּן ("lest"); see *HALOT* 2:523, *sub verbum* מה, D. 3.

38. Cairo Genizah fragments of the Palestinian Targums that survive with Tiberian pointing contain passages in which the first syllable of דלמא shows a *pathaḥ*: דַלְמָא (Gen 15:1; 32:21); see Klein, *Genizah*, 1:29, line 4; p. 67, line 11; vol. 2, MS H, pl. 100, line 4; MS C, pl. 13, line 11.

39. Orthographic chaos is an earmark of the Neofiti codex; see Golomb, *Grammar of Targum Neofiti*, pp. 15–22.

was omitted in the Neofiti manuscript because of a *homoioteleuton*; a later hand corrected the omission by adding the missing words in the margin.[40] Hence, the absence of מה derives from the corrector, not from the scribe of the manuscript. More interestingly, the other exception, in Gen 43:12 (where דלמה stands alone without a preceding מה), appears to derive from an old popular rendition that had become so familiar, so widely used, and so indelibly fixed in the oral tradition that later written targums apparently felt constrained to retain the solitary דלמה even though it did not correspond to their otherwise prevalent idiom. Note how in this same verse Onqelos and Pseudo-Jonathan have דלמה and the Peshitta ܕܠܡܐ. All these otherwise divergent versions have here retained the same word, even though it deviates from their vocabulary of first choice. The Samaritan Targum too seems to reflect the fact that this verse had a popular traditional translation that the targumist's rendering was unable to supplant. As was noted above, here alone it renders אוּלַי with the interjection לוי ("oh that") instead of with its otherwise stereotypical translation (מאן, "what if?").

An analysis of how Targum Neofiti handles the 17 אוּלַי passages in the Pentateuch shows that in all cases the translation policy was to provide a literal rendition of the Hebrew; fidelity to the source text appears paramount. There are only a few instances where the translator departs from a strictly literal rendition. These are cases in which the targumist's reverential language puts God at a greater remove than is inherent in the Hebrew. For example, whereas in the original of Num 23:3 Balaam says, "perhaps the Lord will come to meet me," in the Neofiti translation he says, "Perhaps *the Word of* (מימריה ד-) the Lord will come to meet me." Similarly, whereas in the original Hebrew of Num 23:27 Balak says, "perhaps it will be right in the eyes of God," the targum puts these words in his mouth, "perhaps *there may be good pleasure before the Lord* (יהווי רעווה מן קדם ייי)." This translation avoids the anthropomorphic description of God having eyes. Such reverential language that preserves distance between humanity and divinity and that de-anthropomorphizes metaphorical expressions for God is, in general, characteristic of the targums, though not always consistent.[41] In any case this altered language is not prompted by the Hebrew אוּלַי, nor does it reveal anything about how the targum may have understood theological nuances of that term.

While this overview may seem to yield meager results, there is more to be said. In addition to these 17 passages that render the Hebrew אוּלַי with [מה] דלמה [-ד], the Neofiti codex has again as many occurrences of דלמה without any corresponding אוּלַי in the Hebrew Vorlage (see Gen 6:3; 15:1; 16:5; 18:21; 30:3; 31:22; 32:3; 44:18–19; 50:15; Lev 24:12; 26:41; Deut 6:4).[42] A perusal of

---

40. See Díez Macho, *Neophyti 1*, vol. 2: *Exodo*, pp. 216–17, 507.

41. See McNamara, *Testament and Targum*, pp. 93–97; Alexander, "Jewish Aramaic Translations," p. 226; Sperber, *Bible in Aramaic*, 4b:37; Klein, "Translations of Anthropomorphisms and Anthropopathisms," pp. 162–77.

42. See Kaufman and Sokoloff, *Key-Word-in-Context Concordance to Targum Neofiti*, p. 411.

these passages is instructive. In 2 cases the Aramaic renders a different Hebrew word: behind דלמה in TN Gen 50:15 stands the Hebrew לוּ ("perchance") and in TN Lev 26:41 the Hebrew אוֹ ("if perchance").[43] In another 2 cases Neofiti in brief interpretive insertions repeats the words of Gen 16:2, "*perhaps* I will have children through her"—either Sarah repeats herself (TN Gen 16:5), or Rachel uses her same words (TN Gen 30:3).[44]

Two further passages are of special interest here because they, like passages in the Hebrew prophets, link the term "perhaps" (דלמה) with the idea of repentance (תתובה). Both involve short paraphrastic explanations of a point in the Hebrew text.

Within the quasi-mythological tale about the "sons of God" having sexual relations with the "daughters of men" and producing as offspring the giants and heroes of old (Gen 6:1–4) there is the dictum of the Lord, "My spirit shall not abide in mortals forever, for they are flesh; their days shall be one hundred twenty years" (Gen 6:3). The targum renders this verse in part as follows (TN Gen 6:3b):

> Behold I have put my spirit in the sons of men because they are flesh and their works are evil. Behold I have given [them] the span of one hundred twenty years [hoping that] *perhaps* (דלמה) they might do repentance (תתובה), but they have not done so.[45]

This brief midrashic expansion explains that the longevity was meant as an opportunity for repentance. The *perhaps* shows God's longing for the best, though the hope was vain. Similar language appears in the story about God announcing the fate of Sodom and Gomorrah to Abraham (Gen 18:17–33). In that narrative God says, "I must go down and see whether they have done altogether according to the outcry that has come to me; and if not, I will know" (Gen 18:21). Though clumsy, Neofiti's paraphrase of this passage uses the "perhaps" in a way similar to Gen 6:3—this time, however, not from the divine, but from the human perspective (TN Gen 18:21).

> I will now be revealed, and I will see if according to the complaint that has ascended before me they have performed the destruction. [If so] they are worthy of total destruction. And if they seek to do *repentance* (תתובה) and if they hope in their souls that *perhaps* (דלמה) their evil works are not manifest before me—behold they are before me, as if I did not know.[46]

---

43. See GKC p. 475/§150i.
44. This interpolation is also preserved in the Fragment Targum but without the דלמא. See Klein, *Fragment*, 1:57; 2:13. The reiteration of דלמה may take its cue from the Hebrew reiterations of אוּלי in Gen 24:5, 39; Num 22:6, 11; and Jer 36:3, 7.
45. See Díez Macho, *Neophyti 1*, vol. 1: *Genesis*, pp. 33, 511. The passage is preserved in the Fragment Targums, but without דלמה, see Klein, *Fragment-Targums*, 1:48; 2:10.
46. See Díez Macho, *Neophyti 1*, vol. 1: *Genesis*, pp. 101, 540–41. The passage is very difficult; see various solutions outlined in McNamara, *Genesis*, p. 105 n. 19. This דלמה passage is also found in the Fragment Targums; see Klein, *Fragment-Targums*, 1:52; 2:14.

אוּלַי in the Hebrew Bible and Early Versions

In this passage the human "perhaps" seems to signal the insincerity of the Sodomites' repentance. The language anticipates Abraham's failed efforts to negotiate clemency for Sodom on the basis of a small minority of righteous inhabitants; recall that for his part Abraham would open each new bargaining position with the word "perhaps" (Gen 18:24–32).

In many ways, however, Neofiti's most interesting non-אוּלַי occurrences of דלמה are those found in lengthy midrashic insertions in an otherwise fairly literal translation, in order to explain some point in the original text that apparently had given rise to questions. The following examples make this clear.

Subsequent to the accounts of Abraham rescuing Lot and his family from a band of marauders (Gen 14:1–16) and then being blessed by Melchizedek (Gen 14:17–24), the Hebrew text continues with the seemingly inconsequential remark, "After these things the word of the Lord came to Abram in a vision, 'Do not be afraid, Abraham, I am your shield; your reward shall be great'" (Gen 15:1). Targum Neofiti renders this verse with the following lengthy explanation (the extrabiblical expansion is put in italics, as will be the case in all targumic citations):

> After these things, *after all the kingdoms of the earth had gathered together and had drawn up battle-lines against Abram and had fallen before him, and he had killed four kings from among them and had turned back nine camps, Abram thought in his heart and said: Woe is me now!* Perhaps (דלמה) *I have received the reward of the precepts in this world and there is no portion for me in the world to come. Or* perhaps (דילמא ד-) *the brothers or relatives of those killed, who fell before me, will go and be in their fortresses and in their cities and many legions will become allied with them and they will come against me and kill me. Or* perhaps (דילמא ד-) *there were a few meritorious deeds in my hand the first time they fell before me and they stood in my favor; and* perhaps (דלמה ד-) *no meritorious deed will be found in my hand the second time and the Name of the heavens will be profaned in me. For this reason there was a word of prophecy from before* the Lord upon Abram *the just* saying: "Do not fear, Abram," *for although many legions are allied and come against you to kill [you], my Memra will be* a shield for you *and it will be a shield for you in this world. And although I delivered up your enemies before you in this world, the reward of your good works is prepared for you before me in the world to come.*[47]

In this expansive midrashic insertion, the four *perhaps* clauses serve to explain exactly what things Abraham had been afraid of.

After the story of the covenant between Laban and Jacob (Gen 31:43–32:1) and before the narrative of Jacob sending messengers ahead to Esau (Gen 32:4–22) the biblical text says, "Jacob went on his way and the angels of God

---

47. See Díez Macho, *Neophyti 1*, vol. 1: *Genesis*, pp. 17, 530–31. This whole pericope is also preserved with quite similar wording (and Tiberian pointing) in a fragment from the Cairo Genizah; see Klein, *Genizah*, 1:28–29. The passage is also preserved in the Fragment Targums with the threefold דלמה; see idem, *Fragment*, 1:50; 2:12.

met him; and when Jacob saw them he said, 'This is God's army (מַחֲנֶה)!' So he called that place *Maḥanaim* (מַחֲנָיִם = twofold army? two armies?)" (Gen 32:2–3). Theoretically, instead of a dual, the consonantal text could also be pointed as a plural (מַחֲנִים = "armies," as in Num 13:19), though the plural does more often have the form מחנות (see Gen 32:8, 11; Num 2:17, 32; 10:2, 5, 6, 25; 1 Sam 17:4; Zech 14:14; 1 Chr 9:18; 2 Chr 31:2). The Masoretic pointing of the toponym as a dual (see Song 7:1), not a plural, has puzzled exegetes across the ages, and it occasioned in the Neofiti Targum the following explanatory insertion (TN Gen 32:2–3):

> And Jacob went on his journey and angels (messengers) *from before the Lord* overtook him. And Jacob said when he saw them: *"Perhaps* (דלמא) *they are messengers from Laban, my mother's brother, who has returned to pursue after me, or* (או) *armies of messengers of Esau my brother who comes to meet me, or* (או) *armies of angels (messengers) from before the Lord come to deliver me from the hands of both of them."* Because of this he called the name of that place *Maḥanaim*.[48]

In this expansion of the text, the "perhaps" followed by the double "or" wants to provide an etiology of the place-name. Unfortunately, from the unvocalized targum it is unclear whether the named options intend to explain a dual (hostile human armies versus protective angel armies?) or a plural (enemies behind, enemies ahead, and God's angels at the side?).

A related example appears in the book of Deuteronomy in the famous passage of the *Shema*, where Moses instructs the Israelites thus: "Hear, O Israel: The Lord is our God, the Lord alone (יהוה אֱלֹהֵינוּ יהוה אֶחָד). You shall love the Lord your God with all your heart, and with all your soul, and with all your might" (Deut 6:4–5). This centerpiece of Jewish identity is rendered in the Neofiti Targum with the following midrashic expansion:

> When the appointed time of our father Jacob arrived *to be gathered in peace from the midst of the world*, he gathered the twelve tribes and made them stand *around his bed of gold. Our father Jacob answered and said to them: From Abraham, my father's father, arose the blemished Ishmael and all the sons of Keturah, and from Isaac, my father, arose the blemished Esau, my brother. Perhaps* (דלמה) *you worship the idols which Abraham's father worshipped, or perhaps* (דלמה) *you worship the idols which Laban, my mother's brother, worshipped? Or do you worship the God of Jacob your father? The twelve tribes of Jacob answered together with a perfect heart and said:* Listen *to us,* Israel *our father:* The Lord our God is one Lord; *may his name be blessed for ever and ever.* And *you shall love the teaching of the Law of* the Lord with all *your heart* and all *your* soul and all *your wealth.*[49]

---

48. See Díez Macho, *Neophyti 1*, vol. 1: *Genesis*, pp. 213, 586. This passage is also preserved in the Fragment Targums with a threefold דלמא; see Klein, *Fragment-Targums*, 1:58–59; 2:22.

49. See Díez Macho, *Neophyti 1*, vol. 5: *Deuteronomio*, pp. 71, 469. This midrashic insertion is also preserved in the Fragment Targums with the double דלמא; see Klein, *Fragment-Targums*, 1:213; 2:171.

This expansive insertion in the Neofiti text wants to address the longstanding debate about how the Hebrew אֶחָד in Deut 6:4 should be understood. For example, does this "one" refer to the *singleness*, the *indivisible unity* of the Lord? Or to the *incomparability* of the Lord (see 2 Sam 7:22), *unrivaled* by any other god (see Isa 43:11; 44:6; 45:18)? Or to the *uniqueness* of the Lord in Israel's exclusive relationship with him (see Zech 14:9)? Or as an ordinal number to the *primacy* of the Lord, who ranks *first?*[50]

While these various interpretations are not mutually exclusive, in this Neofiti expansion Jacob's two דלמה sentences point to Terah's idolatry in southern Mesopotamia and to Laban's idolatry in northern Mesopotamia as options counterposed to the worship of the God of Jacob. The worship (פלח) of idols (טעוות, literally, "errors") stands in contrast to the worship (פלח) of the God of Jacob (אלהיה דיעקב) so that for the targumist, whatever else, the Hebrew אחד implies *monolatry* for Israel. The Lord is the "one and only"; he "alone" is to be worshiped. The targum concretizes this undivided worship with its expanded "translation": "You shall love *the teaching of the Law of* (אולפן אורייתה) the Lord" (Deut 6:5). Israel's monolatry requires Torah instruction! Finally and notably, this interpretive expansion does not trace the *Shema* back to Moses, but retrojects it all the way back to the sons of Jacob— possibly with the idea that more antiquity means more weightiness.

Lastly, there is an interesting example of the lexeme דלמה in the Holiness Code. At issue is the case of the man [boy?] from a mixed marriage (Egyptian father, Danite mother) who in a fight with an Israelite cursed the divine Name (Lev 24:10–16). The text says they brought him to Moses, "and they put him in custody (ויניחהו במשמר), until the decision of the Lord should be made clear to them" (Lev 24:12). In order to explain further the rationale for the custody, the Neofiti text inserts before this line an extended discussion about determinative legal principles:

> This was one of the four legal cases that came up before Moses, and he decided them in the understanding from above. In two of them Moses was quick and in two of them Moses was slow. In the former and in the latter he said: "I did not hear [him]." In [the judgment of] impure persons who were not able to observe the Passover and in the judgment of the daughters of Zelophehad Moses was quick, because their cases were civil cases. [In the judgment] of him who gathering wood (see Num 15:32–36) desecrated the Sabbath willfully, and [in the judgment] of the blasphemer who expressed his holy Name with blasphemies, Moses was slow, because their cases were capital cases, and in order to teach the judges who would rise up after Moses to be quick in civil cases and slow in capital cases, so that those would not kill quickly [even] one deserving according to the law to be killed, — *perhaps* (ד- דילמה) acquittal might be found for him from another angle in the trial.[51] They ought not be ashamed to say, "We did not hear [him]," since

---

50. For an overview of the exegetical options, see Weinfeld, *Deuteronomy 1–11*, pp. 330–38; Nelson, *Deuteronomy*, pp. 89–91; Driver, *Deuteronomy*, pp. 89–91.

51. To translate the דילמה with "lest" (as do Díez Macho, *Neophyti 1*, vol. 3: *Levitico*, p. 401; and McNamara, *Deuteronomy*, p. 97) misses the point. "Lest" is a conjunction

Moses their master said, "I did not hear [him]." And they guarded him in prison until it is declared to them from before the Lord by which judgment they should put him to death.⁵²

In this long midrashic expansion, the whole point of the incarceration and delayed judgment is brought out by the term "perhaps" (דילמה): it is wise not to hasten to judgment, but to wait and explore every possibility that *perhaps, just maybe*, some mitigating circumstance might be found that could preclude the death penalty.

In these last three examples cited above, the lexeme דילמה has the function of presenting *options* that may be rejected or acted upon. The fourfold דילמא in Targum Neofiti Gen 44:18–19 has a similar function.⁵³ This targumic use of דילמא as a means for presenting options has no real biblical precedent unless one counts the story where Abraham negotiates with God over the fate of Sodom by beginning each new bargaining position with the word אוּלַי (Gen 18:24–32).

Targum Pseudo-Jonathan

Of all the extant targums, Pseudo-Jonathan⁵⁴ is the most expansive, containing an amalgam of materials from different eras and various sources, including both material paralleled in other targums as well as material without analogy anywhere else in the targumic corpus. It is recognizably a composite text, or as some might say, a "compote," containing three basic ingredients: (1) those words that actually *translate* Scripture stand in proximity to the renderings in Targum Onqelos; (2) a sizable number of the midrashic *expansions* (some 500+ examples) have parallel counterparts in the Palestinian Targums (Neofiti, Cairo Genizah fragments, and the Fragment Targum); (3) and finally there is a much larger number (some 1,500+ passages) of expansions that are unique to Pseudo-Jonathan. Much of this unique material exhibits priestly reflections and concerns. Both from the standpoints of language (Late Aramaic dialect) and source-critical considerations (extensive

---

ordinarily following an expression of fearing. The term should rather be taken adverbially in a positive sense, "perhaps." The sense here is analogous to that in an earlier Neofiti expansion where the shepherds of Laban waited by their well for three days, "hoping that perhaps (דלמה דהיא) it would brim up" (TN Gen 31:22).

52. This whole midrashic insertion is preserved in the Fragment Targums but without the דילמה line; see Klein, *Fragment-Targums*, 1:188; 2:63–64.

53. See Díez Macho, *Neophyti 1*, vol. 1: *Genesis*, pp. 292–97; 620–21. Portions of a similar version of this long midrashic interpolation in the Palestinian Targum are preserved in the Fragment Targums, but without any occurrences of דלמא; see Klein, *Fragment-Targums*, 1:64; 2:28–29. The passage is also preserved in fragments from the Cairo Genizah but unfortunately there are lacunae in the lines that might have contained דלמא; see Klein, *Genizah*, 1:138–43.

54. The definitive critical edition is: Clarke et al., *Targum Pseudo-Jonathan of the Pentateuch*.

expansions and late historical allusions) this distinctive material appears to constitute the youngest stratum in Pseudo-Jonathan.[55]

For over a century now there has been a lively debate concerning the date of composition of this targum.[56] It is clear that in its present form it cannot be older than its youngest source. Part of the debate has revolved around the questions of whether Pseudo-Jonathan contains anti-Islamic references or exhibits dependency on late rabbinic writings.[57] Further, there is the corollary question of whether such alleged allusions or dependencies are constituent elements in the unique PJ material or whether they merely represent later accreted scribal glosses or interpolations. While a scholarly consensus has not yet been reached on the date of composition, the current state of research seems to be settling on a date of composition in the pre-Islamic period, probably in the fourth or fifth century C.E.[58]

These general characterizations of Pseudo-Jonathan as a *mixtum compositum* are borne out by a review of how the targum handles the אוּלַי passages in the Pentateuch. A glance at table 1 shows that Pseudo-Jonathan used 3 different words to render the Hebrew אוּלַי: in 10 occurrences the Aramaic מאים ("perhaps," literally: "what if?") does the job (PJ Gen 16:2; 18:24, 28 [מאין is but a spelling variant], 29, 30, 31, 32; 24:5, 39; 27:12); in 4 instances we find some form of the interjection לואי ("oh that!" PJ Gen 32:21; Exod 32:30; Num 22:6, 11); and in 3 cases we have דילמא ("perhaps" PJ Gen 43:12; Num 23:3, 27).[59] No stereotyped translations here!

Rather, we can see clearly the composite nature of this targum: מאים is a contraction of the earlier Onqelos rendition with מא אם (see also מאן in the Samaritan Targum); דילמא represents the Palestinian rendition (see מה דילמה די in Neofiti); and לואי is indigenous to Pseudo-Jonathan. The pattern of אוּלַי

---

55. See Kaufman, "Dating the Language of the Palestinian Targums"; Flesher, "Late Jewish Literary Aramaic and the Sources of Targum Pseudo-Jonathan."

56. See, for example: York, "Dating of Targumic Literature"; Splansky, *Targum Pseudo-Jonathan*; Hayward, "Date of Targum Pseudo-Jonathan"; Shinan, "Dating Targum Pseudo-Jonathan"; Kaufman, "Dating the Language of the Palestinian Targums."

57. For example, attention has been focused on the figure of Ishmael as an alleged code for Islam (e.g., PJ Gen 21:15; 22:1; 25:8, 11; 35:22) and on the names Kadijah, Aisha, and Fatima, the wives and daughter of Mohammed (PJ Gen 21:21). See Ohana, "La polémique judéo-islamique"; Hayward, "Anti-Islamic Polemic." Others have argued that PJ reflects use of *Pirke Rabbi Eliezer* and of both *Tanhumas* (eighth- or ninth-century works); see Maher, *Targum Pseudo-Jonathan: Genesis*, pp. 11–12; Alexander, "Jewish Aramaic Translations," pp. 219–20.

58. See Cook, *Rewriting the Bible*; Mortensen, *Targum Pseudo-Jonathan: A Document for Priests*, now revised and published as *Priesthood in Targum Pseudo-Jonathan*; idem, "Pseudo-Jonathan and Economics for Priests"; Flesher, "Literary Legacy of the Priests?"

59. The orthographic variants הלואי/לוואי/לואי have no difference in meaning. This term and its Palestinian Aramaic counterpart לווי is cognate with the Hebrew לו. Pseudo-Jonathan's spelling with terminal אי- appears to have been influenced by the orthography common in the Babylonian Talmud (אלואי); see Sokoloff, *Jewish Palestinian Aramaic*, p. 278.

translations suggests that the compiler-redactor of Pseudo-Jonathan, who was editing or rewriting his Palestinian source with the help of Onqelos as a control text, ran out of steam a little over halfway through Genesis (somewhere between Genesis 27 and 32). His "successor-redactor" then either let the דילמא of his Palestinian source stand or replaced it with לואי.

However, this successor too apparently ran out of steam when he reached Numbers 22, because internally there is no cogent explanation why the rendition of the 4 similar אוּלַי passages in the Balaam narrative should suddenly shift right in the middle from לואי (Num 22:6, 11) to דילמא (Num 23:3, 27). In general the Pseudo-Jonathan compilers/redactors may have wanted to steer away from דילמא because that was otherwise (as in Onqelos) their word of choice for rendering the Hebrew conjunction פֶּן ("lest"; see PJ Gen 3:3; 19:15, 17, 19; 24:6, 7, 9; 31:24, 31; 32:12; 38:11, 23; 42:4, plus 40 more examples).

On the whole, Pseudo-Jonathan translated all the אוּלַי passages in the Pentateuch quite literally, but there is one interesting passage where the targumist offers a uniquely creative expansion prompted precisely by the אוּלַי. It is the famous account of Abraham's negotiation with God over the fate of Sodom based on the premise that it would be unjust for God to punish the righteous with the wicked. Abraham's bargaining tries to determine how few righteous could outweigh the mass of the wicked. The Pseudo-Jonathan Targum of this text reads as follows (PJ Gen 18:24–32):

> What if (מאים) there are fifty innocent people within the city *who pray before you, ten for each city of the five cities of Sodom, Gomorrah, Admah, Zeboiim, and Zoar? Will your anger* wipe [them] out and not forgive the place for the sake *of the merits* of the fifty innocent people who are in it? *It would be a profanation* for you to do such a thing, to kill the innocent with the guilty, so that the innocent would be as the guilty; *that would be a profanation* for you. *Is it possible that he who* judges the whole earth should not do justice?"
>
> And the Lord said, "If in Sodom I find fifty innocent people within the city *who pray before me,* I will forgive the whole place for their sake."
>
> Abraham replied and said, *"I beseech, by (your) mercy!* Behold, I have begun to speak *before the Lord,* I who am *like* dust and ashes. What if (מאין) five of the fifty innocent are lacking? Will you destroy the whole city because of five *who are lacking in Zoar?"*
>
> He said, "I will not destroy if I find forty-five there."
>
> He spoke again *before* him and said, "What if (מאים) forty are found there, *ten for each of the four cities? As for Zoar, whose guilt is light, forgive it, for the sake of your mercy."*
>
> He said, "I will not make *an end* for the sake of the merits of forty."
>
> He said, "Let not the anger of the Master *of all the worlds, the Lord,* be enkindled, and I will speak. What if (מאים) thirty, *who pray* are found there, *ten for each of the three cities? As for Zeboiim and Zoar, forgive them for the sake of your mercy."*
>
> He said, "I will not make *an end* if I find thirty there."
>
> He said, *"I beseech, by (your) mercy!* Behold, I have begun to speak *before the Master of all the worlds, the Lord.* What if (מאים) twenty *who pray* are

found, *ten for each of the two cities? As for the (other) three, forgive them for the sake of your mercy."*
And he said, "I will not destroy for the sake of *the merits of* twenty."
He said, *"I beseech by the mercy before you,* let not the anger of the Master *of all the worlds,* the Lord, be enkindled, and I will speak this last time. What if (מאים) ten are found there, *and they and I beseech mercy for the whole place will you forgive them?*
And he said, "I will not destroy for the sake of *the merits of* ten."

In order to provide a rationale for the numbers in the suppositions introduced by Abraham's "what if?" or "perhaps" clauses, the targumist makes use of an old biblical tradition of a southern Salt Sea pentapolis: Sodom, Gomorrah, Admah, Zeboiim, and Zoar (see Gen 14:2, 8). This tradition holds that the first four cities were destroyed by fire from heaven (Gen 19:24; Deut 29:22; Hos 11:8) while Zoar, the smallest, was preserved (Gen 19:20–22) because the sins of its citizens were minimal (see *b. Shab.* 10b).[60] The targumist's argument corresponds to the midrashic reflection that each city might present a *minyan* of ten righteous who pray to the Lord (*Genesis Rabbah* to Gen 49:13).

Finally, one more feature of דילמא usage in Pseudo-Jonathan requires comment. In addition to the appearances of דילמא, which represent either אוּלַי ("perhaps" 3×) or פֶּן ("lest" [following a cohortative or a verb of fearing] 58×), in the Hebrew Vorlage there are 10 more cases where דילמא occurs in the sense of "lest" but with a word other than פֶּן or with no corresponding word in the original Hebrew, but there is nothing particularly noteworthy about these cases (PJ Gen 27:11; 37:13; 45:24; Exod 29:37; 33:1; Lev 11:43; Deut 7:17; 17:16; 20:8; 22:8). What does draw our attention, however, are the 14 occurrences of דילמא as the lead word in a sentence with the sense of "perhaps" and signaling a negative possibility or an objectionable interpretation. These are all found in targumic expansions without any correspondence in the Hebrew text. They deserve our consideration.

Three of these expansions have parallels in the Neofiti Targum (see TN and PJ Gen 15:1; 31:22; Deut 6:4). Since they have been handled above in connection with Neofiti, they will not be discussed here, though they do show some interesting differences. The remaining דילמא expansions, however, are listed below so that their common coloration or flavor will be apparent. Again, the words with no counterpart in Hebrew are printed in italics:

1. After Eve and Adam ate from the forbidden fruit (PJ Gen 3:11):

   He [God] said, "Who told you that you were naked? Have you *perhaps* (דילמא) eaten of *the fruit of* the tree from which I commanded you not to eat?"

---

60. The name Zoar (צוער) derives from the verb צער, which means "be small, insignificant." Despite the claim that the city of Zoar had survived destruction, there were also traditions that spoke of all 5 cities' being destroyed (see, e.g., Wis 10:6–7; Josephus, *Jewish War* 4.8.4 §§482–85).

2. After the first fratricide (PJ Gen 4:9):

The Lord said to Cain, "Where is your brother Abel?" He said, "I do not know. Amos I, *perhaps* (דילמא), my brother's keeper?"

3. The narrative of the *Aqedah* is introduced by a lengthy expansion recounting an argument between Ishmael and Isaac about each's legitimacy (PJ Gen 22:1):

After these events, *after Isaac and Ishmael had quarreled, Ishmael said, "It is right that I should be my father's heir, since I am his first-born son." But Isaac said, "It is right that I should be my father's heir, because I am the son of Sarah, his wife, while you are the son of Hagar, my mother's maidservant." Ishmael answered and said, "I am more worthy than you, because I was circumcised at the age of thirteen. And if I had wished to refuse, I would not have handed myself over to be circumcised. But you were circumcised at the age of eight days. If you had been aware,* <u>perhaps</u> (דילמא) *you would not have handed yourself over to be circumcised." Isaac answered and said, "Behold, today I am thirty-seven years old, and if the Holy One, blessed be He, were to require all my members I would not refuse."*

4. After the death of Rachel at the birth of Benjamin comes the following expansion (PJ Gen 35:22):

While Israel dwelt in that land, Reuben went and *disarranged the couch of Bilhah, his father's concubine, which had been arranged opposite the couch of Leah, his mother: and it was reckoned to him as if he had lain with her.* When Israel heard [this] he was distressed, and he said, "Woe! <u>Perhaps</u> (דילמא) *an unworthy person has gone forth from me, as Ishmael went forth from Abraham and Esau went forth from my father."* The Holy Spirit replied and said thus to him, "Fear not, for they are all righteous, and there is no unworthy person among them."

5. After Moses' consecration of Aaron and his sons (PJ Lev 8:15):

He [Moses] purified the altar of *every suspicion of violence and robbery. For Moses thought to himself:* "<u>Perhaps</u> (דילמא) *the officers of the children of Israel have taken the offering of separation from their brothers by force, and offered it for the work of the tabernacle. Or* <u>perhaps</u> (דילמא) *someone has been found among the children of Israel who had not intended to bring [anything] for the work of the tabernacle, but, having heard the voice of the public crier, was afraid and brought [something] against his will."* Therefore [Moses] purified it with the blood of the bull.

6. At the inauguration of Aaron's priesthood (PJ Lev 9:23):

But when the offerings had been made and the Shekinah was not revealed Aaron was bewildered, and he said to Moses, "<u>Perhaps</u> (דילמא) the Memra of the Lord was not pleased with the works of my hands." Then Moses and Aaron went into the tent of meeting *and prayed for the people of the house of Israel.*

7. After the catalogue of blessings and before the catalogue of curses in Deuteronomy, the following expansion is inserted (PJ Deut 28:15):

When Moses, the prophet, began to say these following words of reproof, the land was shaken, the heavens trembled, the sun and the moon darkened, and the stars suppressed their light. The patriarchs shouted from their graves, while all the creatures were silent, and the trees did not move their branches. The patriarchs answered and said: "Woe to our children when they sin and bring these curses upon them! How will they be able to endure them? <u>Perhaps</u> (דילמא) destruction shall work against them, and our merit will not be a protection for them and [perhaps] no man shall arise who will pray on their behalf?" A celestial voice fell from the heavens on high and said thus: "Do not fear, patriarchs, for even if the merit of all the generations shall cease, your merit shall not cease and the covenant that I established with you shall not be annulled, but it shall protect them."

Of these 7 expansions containing דילמא, the term in Gen 3:11 is paralleled in the Neofiti Targum with the word דלא ("perhaps"). In Gen 4:9, דילמא could be viewed as a simple editorial insertion by the targumist to add a touch of color. But the remaining 5 expansions (PJ Gen 22:1; 35:22; Lev 8:15; 9:23; Deut 28:15) are all lengthy and all exhibit the same use of דילמא introducing a negative option or objectionable interpretation. The linguistic uniformity of the דילמא idiom suggests that these various expansions do not stem from multiple hands or sources, but more likely go back to a single common origin. For this targumic usage the "perhaps" (אוּלַי) passages of Scripture do not offer a real precedent. On the other hand, דילמא is often used in this way as a mode of expression in the Palestinian Talmud.[61]

No other known targum contains these interpolated דילמא expansions. It is hard to decide with certainty whether they were (a) drawn from an older pentateuchal targum, be it complete or fragmentary, that until now has not yet come to light, or whether they were (b) composed by the author[s] of Pseudo-Jonathan.[62] The former seems far less likely than the latter if for no

---

61. See for instance the following typical examples:

> (Villagers once came to R. Pinhas b. Yair . . .) "They said to him, 'Our spring does not supply us with enough [water to irrigate our crops, which are drying up].' He said to them, 'Perhaps (דילמא) you are not tithing them?' They said to him, 'Pledge to us [that if we tithe our crops properly, the spring will supply us with enough water].' He pledged to them, and it [the spring] supplied them with enough [water]." (y. Demai 22a)

Or similarly:

> R. Simeon b. Laqish guarded his fig trees in the (garden called) Barbarit. Thieves came, robbed the fruit, and crept away by night. Finally he caught sight of them. He said to them: "May those people [= you] be under the ban!" They, however, responded and said: "May that man [= you] be under the ban!" But then he worried about his soul; for he said to himself: "They [only] owe me money [for the stolen figs]. Perhaps (דילמא) their souls [have been unjustly put under the ban]?" So he went out and ran after them and said to them: "Free me from [your] ban." They answered him, "Free us [first] from [your] ban, then we'll also free you from [our] ban." From this one can conclude that whoever puts someone under a ban which he ought not to have pronounced and nevertheless did, that ban is still a [valid] ban. (y. MQ 81d)

62. The דילמא expansions are found, after all, in Genesis, Leviticus, and Deuteronomy.

other reason than that the disappearance of an entire targum containing such interpretive substance is very difficult to explain. In any case current scholarship on Pseudo-Jonathan inclines toward the position that this distinctive material derives directly from the author[s] of Pseudo-Jonathan, who composed this work in the fourth or fifth century.[63]

The Peshitta

The Peshitta is the translation of the Bible into Syriac, an eastern dialect of Aramaic that employs its own script.[64] A debate has been carried on now for well over a century about the possible relationship between this Syriac translation and the Aramaic targums.[65] *Relationship* is an imprecise term that may, but does not necessarily, imply dependency. To clarify matters Piet Dirksen has drawn distinctions among "three levels of relationship: (1) that of language, (2) that of exegetical tradition, and (3) that of literary dependency."[66] With regard to possible connections between the Peshitta and the targums (or the LXX for that matter), our observations in this study will confine themselves primarily to the level of language.

A review of table 1 above discloses that for its translation of the Hebrew adverb אוּלַי the Syriac translators of the Peshitta employed five different terms: ܟܐ (7×), ܕܠܡܐ (9×), ܠ (17×), ܟܒܪ (12×), and ܒܠܚܘܕ-ܕ (2×). These terms are distributed randomly across the canonical books. Any attempt to see them allocated according to some system—be it canonical, chronological, semeiological, or other—is an unconvincing artificial construct. Four of the terms used in the Peshitta are standard Aramaic words, appearing in Syriac and other Aramaic dialects, and the remaining term is a Greek loanword (see table 2).

From the variety of choices and from the indiscriminate distribution of these Syriac translation terms, an obvious difference for the Peshitta emerges when compared with all of the targums: in stark contrast to the Aramaic translations, it is clear that the Peshitta does not have nor did it strive to achieve any consistent translation equivalencies; that is to say, there is no verbal linkage for the adverb אוּלַי. This observation alone makes it hard to conclude that the Peshitta translators made use of any targum (be it as *Vorlage* or as

---

63. See the literature cited in nn. 57 and 58 above.
64. The definitive critical edition is nearing completion in the series The Old Testament in Syriac according to the Peshitta Version (Leiden: Brill, Peshitta Institute of Leiden University, 1972–).
The term *Peshitta* (the feminine form of the passive participle of the verb ܦܫܛ [*pešaṭ*], "stretch out, extend") presupposes with it the noun ܡܦܩܬܐ ("translation"). The name has elicited several interpretations: (1) "(the translation) in common use," *vulgata*; (2) the "plain [i.e., 'noneloquent' or 'nonparaphrastic'] (translation)"; (3) the "simple" [i.e., "monolingual" text, as opposed to the multilingual text of Origen's *Hexapla*]; see Dirksen, "Old Testament Peshitta," p. 256.
65. See Flesher, *Targum and Peshitta*.
66. Dirksen, "Basic Questions," p. 4.

Table 2: אוּלַי in the Peshitta

Syriac		Equivalent			
ܐܢ	if	Aramaic	אן	אין	if
ܕܠܡܐ	perhaps, perchance, lest	Aramaic	דלמה	דילמה	perhaps, lest
ܟܒܪ	perhaps, perchance	Aramaic	כבר		already
ܒܓܠܠ ܕ	because of, by reason of	Aramaic	מטול		because of
ܛܟ	perhaps	Greek	τάχα		perhaps, probably, possibly

control text for double-checking) when they rendered the Bible into Syriac. In this respect the Peshitta resembles more the LXX with its wide range of choices (εἰ +, μή +, ἴσως, ἵα, and ὅπως), though none of the Peshitta choices is as far off the mark as the Greek final conjunctions. From the vocabulary spread, it would appear that many hands were at work in the translation project, perhaps with each book being a product of separate translators.

One could conceivably posit that the Syriac translators consulted the LXX. A comparison of the Peshitta with the LXX in table 1 (see esp. the terms in bold font) shows some evidence that might suggest this. The most striking is the consistent correspondence between the Syriac use of ܕܠܡܐ and the Greek use of μήποτε (Gen 24:5, 39; 27:12; 43:12; 1 Kgs 18:27; Job 1:5). Especially interesting here is 1 Kg 18:27, where the MT only has the adverb once, but both the LXX and Peshitta have it multiple times. At first glance a correspondence between the occurrences of the Syriac ܐܢ and the Greek ἐάν (Gen 18:24, 28, 29, 30, 31, 32) might also seem noteworthy, but this is not as significant as it appears because the multiple occurrences are all in a single passage so that the apparent verbal linkage is undercut by the other example of ܐܢ in Josh 9:7, where the counterpart in the LXX is ὅρα μή. By contrast, in the cases of ܟܒܪ and ܛܟ both Syriac terms have as random LXX counterparts the same wide range of Greek terms.[67] This fact seems to militate against any LXX influence.

Finally, it is noteworthy here that for the most frequently used Syriac translation term, namely ܛܟ (17×), there is not a single corresponding cognate τάχα in the LXX list of translation choices for אוּלַי. Indeed, outside of the book of Wisdom (13:6; 14:19) the word τάχα is completely absent from the LXX. In summary, the most that one could possibly argue from all of these data is that the Peshitta translators may well have been influenced by the LXX in a few biblical books, namely Genesis, Kings, and possibly Jonah. But beyond that, this word analysis provides little that could confirm or corroborate any LXX influence on the Peshitta translation.

---

67. See εἰ (Num 23:3, 27; Isa 47:12; Jer 20:10; 21:2); εἴ πως (2 Sam 14:15; 16:12; Jer 51:8; 1 Kg 20:31; 2 Kg 19:4); ἵνα (Gen 16:2; Exod 32:30); ἴσως (Gen 32:21; Jer 26:3; 36:3, 7); ὅπως (1 Sam 6:5; 9:6; Ezek 12:3; Amos 5:15; Jonah 1:6; Zeph 2:3).

Given the relatively literal translation technique of the Peshitta, there is little to single out in the "perhaps" passages for special comment. The one interesting exception is the passage in Elijah's contest with the devotees of Baal (1 Kgs 18:27) because here the Syriac translators multiplied the single אוּלַי of the Hebrew *Vorlage* into a quadruple ܕܠܡܐ in the Syriac text:

Hebrew
When it was noon Elijah mocked at them   וַיְהִי בַצָּהֳרַיִם וַיְהַתֵּל בָּהֶם אֵלִיָּהוּ
and said, "Call in a loud voice!   וַיֹּאמֶר קִרְאוּ בְקוֹל־גָּדוֹל
Surely he is a god;   כִּי־אֱלֹהִים הוּא
either he is meditating,   כִּי שִׂיחַ
or he has wandered away,   וְכִי־שִׂיג לוֹ
or he is on a journey;   וְכִי־דֶרֶךְ לוֹ
perhaps he is asleep and he will wake up."   אוּלַי יָשֵׁן הוּא וְיִקָץ

Syriac
And when it was midday he ridiculed them
and he said, "Call in a loud voice
because he is a god.
Perhaps he is steeped in meditation;
or *perhaps* he is inspecting some matter;
or *perhaps* he is on a journey;
or *perhaps* he is sleeping and needs to be awakened."

The tendency to replicate and multiply the "perhaps" in this passage was visible already in the LXX and in Targum Jonathan (both doubled the word), but here the Syriac translators go all the way and quadruple the word, thus increasing Elijah's scorn.

These brief observations about the Peshitta rendering of אוּלַי into Syriac suggest that in at least these cases of "perhaps" the Syriac translated directly from the Hebrew without direct influence in word choice or style from any known targum. Furthermore, in most cases beyond the book of Genesis, there is little evidence of any influence coming from the LXX either.

Conclusion

In the Classical Hebrew of the Bible, the adverb אוּלַי very often appears as part of a conventional, two-part oral or literary form in which the first part comprises directive (imperative, jussive, cohortative) speech, and the second part is introduced by a "perhaps" that qualifies the directive language in the first part. This fixed idiom appears frequently in the rhetoric of Israelite piety and prophetic oracles as a means to express caution or urgency. From a lexicographical perspective, the early versions of the Bible usually, but not always, captured the general sense of the adverb, though their success at this was sometimes spotty. However, from a literary standpoint the translators do

אוּלַי in the Hebrew Bible and Early Versions 167

not seem to have felt the conventionality of the stereotypical two-part saying, nor did they always adequately convey the religious circumspection or theological nuance inherent in such sayings.

The study shows that the Aramaic targums differ in several important ways from the LXX and the Peshitta. It is an earmark of the early Aramaic translations that they strive for a single verbal linkage, that is, a consistent terminological equivalency from source language to target language. With that in mind we can observe that Pseudo-Jonathan's renderings of אוּלַי exhibit influence on the one hand from Onqelos (or the earlier proto-Onqelos) and on the other hand influence from Targum Neofiti (or another similar Palestinian targum). That is to say, this lexical study corroborates the mixed character of Pseudo-Jonathan. But at the same time the study also makes clear that the influence from these sources was not even throughout. Table 1 shows that in Pseudo-Jonathan the rendering of אוּלַי at the beginning of the Pentateuch (Genesis 1–27) was influenced by [proto-?]Onqelos, but then for the word choice in the rest of the Pentateuch (Genesis 32 to Numbers 23) it was the Palestinian Targum that had the primary influence.

By contrast the LXX and the Peshitta both exhibit a wide range of translation choices for אוּלַי with little regard for verbal linkage or how the term was translated elsewhere in the canon. Yet these two versions are also differentiated from one another by the fact that the LXX took far more liberty with its renderings than did the Peshitta. It has been shown that the LXX could at times render the אוּלַי in ways quite at odds with its original sense, namely, when it used the final or purpose conjunctions ἵνα and ὅπως to produce "converse translations." For its part the Peshitta, even with its five different word choices, never strayed far from the sense of the original Hebrew.

From this study another feature also emerges that sets the LXX and Peshitta apart from the Aramaic versions. The LXX and Peshitta usually render the Hebrew (be it literally or idiomatically) without extraneous words, whereas the Aramaic targums are frequently and characteristically marked by intermittent, paraphrastic expansions or textual augmentations—what Paul Flesher has aptly called "hidden midrash."[68]

Further, in both the Palestinian Targums and in the unique Pseudo-Jonathan expansions, the word of preference to express "perhaps" was the term דילמא, which in the earlier [proto-]Onqelos Targum was used instead to render the Hebrew conjunction פֶּן ("lest"). So in the study of this one word we can observe a small example of the semantic shift of a lexeme within the Aramaic dialects.

The study has also shown that in the targums there are instances where it is precisely the Hebrew word אוּלַי that elicits an interpretive or aggadic expansion. Furthermore, a number of targumic expansions make use of an

---

68. See Flesher, "Pentateuchal Targums as Midrash," esp. pp. 2–10.

Aramaic "perhaps," not to qualify directive speech (as in the Bible), but (as in the rabbinic literature) to present a range of options for consideration or rejection—be they legal, psychological, or theological.

Finally, the results of this study do not lend support to the proposition that the Syriac translators made use of a targum (either as Vorlage or as a control text) when they produced the Peshitta.

Bibliography

Alexander, P. S. "Jewish Aramaic Translations of Hebrew Scripture." Pp. 217–53 in *Mikra: Text, Translation, Reading and Interpretation of the Hebrew Bible in Ancient Judaism and Early Christianity*. Compendia Rerum Iudaicarum ad Novum Testamentum 2/1. Edited by M. J. Mulder and H. Sysling. Philadelphia: Fortress, 1988.

Bacher, W. *Die exegetische Terminologie der jüdischen Traditionsliteratur*. 2 parts. Darmstadt: Wissenschaftliche Buchgesellschaft, 1965.

Botterweck, G. J., and H. Ringgren. *Theologisches Wörterbuch zum Alten Testament*. Stuttgart: Kohlhammer, 1973–2000 (10 vols.).

Burney, C. F. *Notes on the Hebrew Text of the Book of Kings*. Oxford: Clarendon, 1903.

Carroll, R. P. *The Book of Jeremiah*. Old Testament Library. Philadelphia: Westminster, 1986.

Childs, B. *The Book of Exodus*. Old Testament Library. Philadelphia: Westminster, 1975.

Clarke, E. G.; W. E. Aufrecht; J. C. Hurd; and F. Spitzer. *Targum Pseudo-Jonathan of the Pentateuch: Text and Concordance*. Hoboken, NJ: Ktav, 1984.

Clements, R. E. *Prophecy and Tradition*. Atlanta: John Knox, 1975.

Cook, E. M. *Rewriting the Bible: Text and Language of the Pseudo-Jonathan Targum*. Ph.D. dissertation. University of California, 1986.

Díez Macho, A. *Neophyti 1: Targum Palestinensa ms. de la Biblioteca Vaticana*. 6 vols. Madrid: Consejo Superior de Investigaciones Cientificas, 1968–79.

Dirksen, P. "The Old Testament Peshitta." Pp. 255–97 in *Mikra: Text, Translation, Reading and Interpretation of the Hebrew Bible in Ancient Judaism and Early Christianity*. Edited by M. J. Mulder and H. Sysling. Compendia Rerum Iudaicarum ad Novum Testamentum 2/1. Philadelphia: Fortress, 1988.

———. "Targum and Peshitta: Some Basic Questions." Pp. 3–13 in *Targum Studies*, vol. 2: *Targum and Peshitta*. Edited by P. V. M. Flesher. South Florida Studies in the History of Judaism 165. Atlanta: Scholars Press, 1998.

Driver, S. R. *A Critical and Exegetical Commentary on Deuteronomy*. International Critical Commentary. 3rd ed. Edinburgh: T. & T. Clark, 1951.

Eissfeldt, O. *Hexateuch-Synopse*. Darmstadt: Wissenschaftliche Buchgesellschaft, 1973.

Fernández Marcos, N. *The Septuagint in Context: Introduction to the Greek Versions of the Bible*. Leiden: Brill, 2001.

Flesher, P. V. M. "Late Jewish Literary Aramaic and the Sources of Targum Pseudo-Jonathan." Unpublished paper delivered at the 2003 conference of the European Association of Biblical Studies.

———. "The Literary Legacy of the Priests? The Pentateuchal Targums of Israel in the Social and Linguistic Context." Pp. 467–508 in *The Ancient Synagogue from Its*

Origins until 200 CE: Papers Presented at an International Conference at Lund University, October 14–17, 2001. Edited by B. Olsson and M. Zetterholm. Stockholm: Almqvist & Wiksell, 2003.

———. "Pentateuchal Targums as Midrash." Pp. 630–46 in vol. 2 of The Encyclopedia of Midrash. Edited by J. Neusner and A. Avery-Peck. Leiden: Brill, 2005.

———, ed. Targum Studies, vol. 2: Targum and Peshitta. South Florida Studies in the History of Judaism 165. Atlanta: Scholars Press, 1998.

Fohrer, G. Elia. Abhandlung zur Theologie des Alten und Neuen Testaments 53. Zurich: Zwingli, 1968.

———. Ezechiel. Handbuch zum Alten Testament. Tübingen: Mohr/Siebeck, 1955.

———. Die symbolischen Handlungen der Propheten. Abhandlung zur Theologie des Alten und Neuen Testaments. 2nd ed. Zurich: Zwingli, 1968.

Gaster, T. H. "Samaritans." Pp. 190–97 in vol. 4 of The Interpreter's Dictionary of the Bible. Edited by G. A. Buttrick. 4 vols. Nashville: Abingdon, 1962.

Golomb, D. H. A Grammar of Targum Neofiti. Harvard Semitic Monographs 34. Chico, CA: Scholars Press, 1985.

Gray, J. I and II Kings. Old Testament Library. Philadelphia: Westminster, 1976.

Greenberg, M. Ezekiel 1–20. Anchor Bible 22. Garden City, NJ: Doubleday, 1986.

Hayward, R. "The Date of Targum Pseudo-Jonathan: Some Comments." JJS 40 (1989) 7–30.

———. "Targum Pseudo-Jonathan and Anti-Islamic Polemic." Journal of Semitic Studies 34 (1989) 77–93.

Holladay, W. L. Jeremiah 2: A Commentary on the Book of the Prophet Jeremiah, Chapters 26–52. Hermeneia. Minneapolis: Fortress, 1989.

Hyatt, J. P. Exodus. New Century Bible. London: Oliphants, 1971.

Jellico, S. The Septuagint and Modern Study. Oxford: Clarendon, 1968.

Jenni, E., and C. Westermann. Theologisches Handwörterbuch zum Alten Testament. 2 vols. Munich: Chr. Kaiser, 1971–76.

Kaufman, S. A. "Dating the Language of the Palestinian Targums and Their Use in the Study of First Century CE Texts." Pp. 118–41 in The Aramaic Bible: Targums in Their Historical Context. Edited by M. McNamara and D. R. G. Beattie. Sheffield: Sheffield Academic Press, 1994.

———, and M. Sokoloff. A Key-Word-in-Context Concordance to Targum Neofiti. Baltimore: Johns Hopkins University Press, 1993.

Klein, M. L. "Converse Translation: A Targumic Technique." Biblica 57 (1976) 515–37.

———. The Fragment-Targums of the Pentateuch. 2 vols. Rome: Pontifical Biblical Institute, 1980.

———. Genizah Manuscripts of Palestinian Targums to the Pentateuch. 2 vols. Cincinnati: Hebrew Union College Press, 1986.

———. "The Translations of Anthropomorphisms and Anthropopathisms in the Targumim." Pp. 162–77 in Congress Volume: Vienna, 1980. Vetus Testamentum Supplement 32. Leiden: Brill, 1981.

Koehler, L., and W. Baumgartner. Hebräisches und Aramäisches Lexikon zum Alten Testament. 4 vols. Leiden: Brill, 1967–90.

Livnat, Z. "אוּלַי from Biblical to Modern Hebrew: A Semantic-Textual Approach." Hebrew Studies 42 (2001) 81–104.

Lowy, S. The Principles of Samaritan Bible Exegesis. Leiden: Brill, 1977.

Maher, M. *Targum Pseudo-Jonathan: Genesis.* Aramaic Bible 1B. Collegeville, MN.: Liturgical Press, 1992.

McNamara, M. *Targum Neofiti 1: Deuteronomy,* Aramaic Bible 5A. Collegeville, MN: Liturgical Press, 1997.

———. *Targum Neofiti 1: Genesis.* Aramaic Bible 1A. Collegeville, MN: Liturgical Press, 1992.

———. *Testament and Targum.* Grand Rapids, MI: Eerdmans, 1972.

———, and E. G. Clarke. *Targum Neofiti 1: Numbers. Targum Pseudo-Jonathan: Numbers.* Aramaic Bible 4. Collegeville, MN: Liturgical Press 1995.

———; R. Hayward; and M. Maher. *Targum Neofiti 1: Exodus. Targum Pseudo-Jonathan: Exodus.* Aramaic Bible 2. Collegeville, MN: Liturgical Press, 1994.

———, and M. Maher. *Targum Neofiti 1: Leviticus. Targum Pseudo-Jonathan: Leviticus.* Aramaic Bible 3. Collegeville, MN: Liturgical Press, 1994.

Montgomery, J. A. *The Book of Kings.* International Critical Commentary. Edinburgh: T. & T. Clark, 1960.

Mortensen, B. P. *The Priesthood in Targum Pseudo-Jonathan: Renewing the Profession.* 2 vols. Studies in the Aramaic Interpretation of Scripture 4. Leiden: Brill, 2006.

———. "Pseudo-Jonathan and Economics for Priests." *Journal for the Study of the Pseudepigrapha* 20 (1999) 39–71.

———. *Targum Pseudo-Jonathan: A Document for Priests.* Ph.D. dissertation. Northwestern University, 1994. [See now Mortensen, *Priesthood.*]

Nelson, R. D. *Deuteronomy: A Commentary.* Old Testament Library. Louisville, KY: Westminster John Knox, 2002.

Noth, M. *Exodus.* Old Testament Library. Philadelphia: Westminster, 1962.

Ohana, M. "La polémique judéo-islamique et l'image d'Ismaël dans Targum Pseudo-Jonathan et dans Pirke de Rabbi Eliezer." *Augustinium* 15 (1975) 367–87.

Payne Smith, J. *A Compendious Syriac Dictionary.* Oxford: Clarendon, 1903. Reprinted Winona Lake, IN: Eisenbrauns, 1998.

Pritchard, J. B. *The Ancient Near East in Pictures relating to the Old Testament.* Princeton: Princeton University Press, 1969.

Rabin, C. "Hittite Words in Hebrew." *Orientalia* 32 (1963) 113–39.

Rahlfs, A., ed. *Septuaginta.* 2 vols. 6th ed. Stuttgart: Privilegierte Württembergische Bibelanstalt, 1935.

Reider, J., and N. Turner. *An Index to Aquila.* Leiden: Brill, 1966.

Rudolph, W. *Chronikbücher.* Handbuch zum Alten Testament 21. Tübingen: Mohr/Siebeck, 1955.

———. *Jeremia.* Handbuch zum Alten Testament 12. Tübingen: Mohr/Siebeck, 1968.

Shinan, A. "Dating Targum Pseudo-Jonathan: Some More Comments." *JJS* 41 (1990) 57–61.

Sokoloff, M. *A Dictionary of Jewish Palestinian Aramaic.* 2nd ed. Ramat Gan: Bar-Ilan University Press, 2002.

Sperber, A., ed. *The Bible in Aramaic: Based on Old Manuscripts and Printed Texts.* 5 vols. Leiden: Brill, 1959–73.

Splansky, D. M. *Targum Pseudo-Jonathan: Its Relationship to Other Targumim, Use of Midrashim and Date.* Ph.D. dissertation. Hebrew Union College, 1981.

Tal, A. *The Samaritan Targum of the Pentateuch.* 3. vols. Tel Aviv: Tel Aviv University Press, 1980–83.

———. "The Samaritan Targum of the Pentateuch." Pp. 189–216 in *Mikra: Text, Translation, Reading and Interpretation of the Hebrew Bible in Ancient Judaism and Early Christianity*. Compendia Rerum Iudaicarum ad Novum Testamentum 2/1. Edited by M. J. Mulder and H. Sysling. Philadelphia: Fortress, 1988.
Tov, E. "The Septuagint." Pp. 161–88 in *Mikra: Text, Translation, Reading and Interpretation of the Hebrew Bible in Ancient Judaism and Early Christianity*. Compendia Rerum Iudaicarum ad Novum Testamentum 2/1. Edited by M. J. Mulder and H. Sysling. Philadelphia: Fortress, 1988.
Volz, P. *Der Prophet Jeremia*. Leipzig: Deichert, 1922.
Weinfeld, M. *Deuteronomy 1–11*. Anchor Bible 5. New York: Doubleday, 1991.
Wevers, J. W. *Ezekiel*. New Century Bible. Grand Rapids: Eerdmans, 1982.
Weiser, A. *Der Prophet Jeremiah*. Das Alte Testament Deutsch 21. Göttingen: Vandenhoeck & Ruprecht, 1960.
Westermann, C. *Grundformen prophetischer Rede*. Beiträge zur evangelischen Theologie 31. Munich: Chr. Kaiser, 1978.
Wolff, H. W. *Amos' geistige Heimat*. Wissenschaftliche Monographien zum Alten und Neuen Testament 18. Neukirchen-Vluyn: Neukirchener Verlag, 1964.
York, A. D. "The Dating of Targumic Literature." *JSJ* 5 (1974) 49–62.
Zimmerli, W. *Ezechiel*. Biblische Studien 62. Neukirchen-Vluyn: Neukirchener Verlag, 1972.
———. *Ezechiel 1–24*. Biblisher Kommentar, Altes Testament 13/1. Neukirchen-Vluyn: Neukirchener Verlag, 1969.
Zuckermandel, M. S. *Tosephta*. Jerusalem: Wahrmann, 1970.

Translating the Hebrew Particle כי אם into Aramaic and English:
An Exploration through the Targums and the Peshitta

BLANE W. CONKLIN

In general, the particles of a language—the function words such as conjunctions, prepositions, and articles—are at the same time the smallest, most often used, and least studied words. Without carrying heavy semantic freight, these words manage to be the most important, most versatile, and hardest to define.

This is a beginning study of the Aramaic translations of a particular Hebrew particle combination, כי אם. This combination occurs some 157 times in the Hebrew Bible. In about one-quarter of these (38), the two particles, כי and אם, function independently within the conventional modes for the respective particles. In the remaining three-quarters, they function together as a single compound particle. This particle combination was chosen for this study for several reasons. First, the function of the compound particle cannot be derived intuitively from its constituent elements. Second, there is no direct cognate in Aramaic, so the Aramaic translators could not "get off the hook" easily thereby. Third, there are some difficult cases in the interpretation of the Hebrew texts. Fourth, there appears to be room for improvement in the modern scholarly treatment of the Hebrew particle. These all make כי אם an interesting case to explore how the Peshitta and targum translators addressed these challenges.

Given the difficulties already inherent in the interpretation of כי אם, a definitive and exhaustive treatment of the Hebrew particle might be a prerequisite to any study of the Aramaic translations of it, yet no such study has been published. The reference grammars and lexicons offer an adequate starting framework, but it is necessary to examine each Hebrew passage to evaluate the function of the particle in each context. A summary of this analysis appears

173

in the second column of table 1. Nevertheless, a full study of כי אם in Hebrew remains a *desideratum*.

Table 1 identifies three main categories. First, as noted above, the two particles may function independently, to mean "for if" or "that if," for example. In the table, these are identified by the label *Independent*. The majority of occurrences find the two particles functioning together as a compound particle. Within this group of compound particles, there is a slight semantic distinction—a distinction, it should be noted, that is necessary in English, but may not have been felt so strongly in Hebrew. The second and third categories come under the heading *Compound*. A clause containing a question or a negative statement may be followed by a כי אם clause that limits the preceding clause. This usage requires a translation in English of "until," "unless," or "except." This second category is identified in the table with the label *Compound-Limiting*. Third, the כי אם clause may offer a contrast to the preceding clause, requiring an adversative translation in English: "but," or "however." This is identified in the table as *Compound-Contrasting*.

In general, the analysis of the syntax of כי אם represented below agrees with that found in the standard reference works, with one exception. There is no justification for an asseverative function of this compound particle, "surely, indeed." Most of the contexts in which this asseverative function is alleged are oath contexts. These texts will be addressed in the final section of the paper. In the two central sections of this paper, following the table, the character and tendencies of the targums and the Peshitta will be discussed in turn.

In addition to the syntax of the Hebrew instances of כי אם, the table lists the various translations of the particle in the targums and the Peshitta. The abbreviations used in the table for the pentateuchal targums are: O—Targum Onqelos; PJ—Targum Pseudo-Jonathan; N—Targum Neofiti; G—Fragments of Palestinian Targums found in the Cairo Genizah (= Genizah); F—Fragmentary Targums.[1] Passages in which the text of the Hebrew is in question include the notation (*text*) after the syntactic label.

Tendencies in the Targums

The targums are generally quite mechanical in their translation of Hebrew כי אם. On the one hand, when the particles function independently, each particle is usually represented by a corresponding particle in Aramaic. Hebrew כי is consistently translated, here and elsewhere, regardless of its function, by the presentative particle ארי (outside Onqelos and Jonathan, it is often spelled ארום, and in Neofiti, once each, ארו, ארון, and אלום). In a few rare cases, this single particle ארי is used alone in translating the Hebrew combination, whether the Hebrew syntax is Independent or Compound. Hebrew אם is represented by the same conditional particle in Aramaic, variously spelled אם, אן, or אין. On the other hand, when כי אם functions as a [*text continues on p. 181*]

---

1. For primary text editions, see the bibliography.

Translating the Hebrew Particle כי אם

Table 1: The Syntax of Hebrew כי אם; Aramaic Translations

כי אם	Hebrew Syntax (according to Conklin)	Targums		Peshitta
Gen 15:4	Compound-Contrasting	O:	אלהין	ܐܠܐ
		PJ:	אלהין	
		N:	ארום אלהן	
		G:	ארום אילאהן	
Gen 28:17	Compound-Limiting	O:	אלהין	ܐܠܐ ܐܢ
		PJ:	ארום אלהן	
		N:	ארום (marg: אילהן)	
		G:	אלאהן	
		F:	ארום אילהין	
Gen 32:27	Compound-Limiting	O:	אלהין	ܐܠܐ ܐܢ
		PJ:	אלהין	
		N:	ארום אלהן	
		G:	ארום אילאהן	
Gen 32:29	Compound-Contrasting	O:	אלהין	ܐܠܐ
		PJ:	אילהין	
		N:	ארום אלהנן	
		G:	ארום אלאהין	
Gen 35:10	Compound-Contrasting	O:	אלהין	ܐܠܐ
		PJ:	אילהין	
		N:	ארום אלהן	
		G:	ארום אלאהין	
Gen 39:6	Compound-Limiting	O:	אלהין	ܐܠܐ ܐܢ
		PJ:	אלהין	
		N:	ארום אלהן	
		G:	ברם אלאהן	
Gen 39:9	Compound-Limiting	O:	אלהין	ܐܠܐ ܐܢ
		PJ:	אלהין	
		N:	ארום אלהן	
		G:	ברם אלאהן	
Gen 40:14	Independent	O:	אלהין	ܐܠܐ
		PJ:	אלהין	
		N:	ארום אן	
		G:	ארום אלאהן	
Gen 42:15	Compound-Limiting	O:	אלהין	ܐܠܐ ܐܢ
		PJ:	אלהין	
		N:	ארום אלהן	
Gen 47:18	Independent	O:	אלהין	ܡܛܠ ܕ-
		PJ:	ארום אין	
		N:	ארום אלהן	
Exod 8:17	Independent	O:	ארי אם	ܐܢ
		PJ:	ארום אין	
		N:	ארום אן	
Exod 9:2	Independent	O:	ארי אם	ܐܢ
		PJ:	ארום אין	
		N:	ארי	

Table 1: The Syntax of Hebrew כי אם; Aramaic Translations (cont.)

כי אם	Hebrew Syntax (according to Conklin)		Targums	Peshitta
Exod 10:4	Independent	O: PJ: N:	ארי אם ארום אין ארום אן	אלא
Exod 12:9	Compound-Contrasting	O: PJ: N: G:	אלהין אלהין ארום אלהן ארום אלאהן	אלא
Exod 22:22	Independent	O: PJ: N:	ארי אם ארום אין ארום	אלא
Exod 23:22	Independent	O: PJ: N:	ארי אם ארום אין ארום אן	אלא
Lev 21:2	Compound-Limiting	O: PJ: N:	אלהין אלהין ארום אלהן	אלא אן
Lev 21:14	Compound-Contrasting	O: PJ: N:	אלהין אילהן ארו אלהן	אלא
Lev 22:6	Compound-Limiting	O: PJ: N:	אלהין אלהין אין ארום אלהן	אלא אן
Num 10:30	Compound-Contrasting	O: PJ: N:	אלהין אלהין ארום אלהן	אלא
Num 14:30	Compound-Limiting	O: PJ: N:	אלהין ארום אילהין אלהן	אלא אן
Num 24:22	Compound-Contrasting or Independent?	O: PJ: N: F:	ארי אם ארום אין ארום אן ארום אין	אן
Num 26:33	Compound-Contrasting	O: PJ: N:	אלהין אלהין ארום אלהן	אלא
Num 26:65	Compound-Limiting	O: PJ: N:	אלהין אלהין ארום אלהן	אלא אן
Num 35:33	Compound-Limiting	O: PJ: N:	אלהין אלהין ארום אלהין	אלא אן
Deut 7:5	Compound-Contrasting	O: PJ: N:	ארי אם ארום אין ארום אלהן	אלא אן
Deut 10:12	Compound-Limiting	O: PJ: N:	אלהין אלהן ארום אלהן	אלא

Table 1: The Syntax of Hebrew כי אם; Aramaic Translations (cont.)

כי אם	Hebrew Syntax (according to Conklin)	Targums	Peshitta
Deut 11:22	Independent	O: ארי אם PJ: ארי אין N: ארום אן	אלא
Deut 12:5	Compound-Contrasting	O: אלהין PJ: אלהין N: ארום אלהן	אלא
Deut 12:14	Compound-Contrasting	O: אלהין PJ: אלהן N: ארום אלהן	אלא אן
Deut 12:18	Compound-Contrasting	O: אלהין PJ: אלהן N: ארום אלהן	אלא
Deut 16:6	Compound-Contrasting	O: אלהין PJ: אילהין N: אלהן	אלא
Josh 14:4	Compound-Limiting	אלהין	אלא אן
Josh 17:3	Compound-Contrasting	אלהין	אלא
Josh 23:8	Compound-Contrasting	אלהין (variant: ארי)	אלא
Josh 23:12	Independent	ארי אם	דאן
Judg 15:7	Independent	אלהין קד	∅
1 Sam 2:15	Compound-Contrasting	אלהין	אלא
1 Sam 8:19	Compound-Contrasting?	אלהין	אלא
1 Sam 14:39	Independent	ארי אלו	דאן
1 Sam 20:9	Independent	ארי אם	מטל דאן
1 Sam 21:5	Compound-Contrasting	אלהין	אלא
1 Sam 21:6	Compound-Contrasting (text)	בקשטא	∅
1 Sam 21:7	Compound-Limiting	אלהין	אלא אן
1 Sam 25:34	Independent	אלהין (variant: אם)	אן (var: אלא)
1 Sam 26:10	Independent	אלהין	אלא אן
1 Sam 30:17	Compound-Limiting	אלהין	אלא (var: אלא אן)
1 Sam 30:22	Compound-Limiting	אלהין	אלא
2 Sam 3:13	Compound-Limiting	אלהין	אלא אן
2 Sam 3:35	Independent	אלהין	אן
2 Sam 5:6	Compound-Contrasting	אלהין	אלא אן
2 Sam 12:3	Compound-Limiting	אלהין	אלא אן (var: אלא)
2 Sam 13:33	Compound-Contrasting (text)	אלהין	מטל ד–
2 Sam 15:21	Independent (text)	אלהין	אלא

Table 1: The Syntax of Hebrew כי אם; Aramaic Translations (cont.)

כי אם	Hebrew Syntax (according to Conklin)	Targums	Peshitta
2 Sam 18:3	Independent	ארי אם	אן
2 Sam 19:29	Compound-Limiting	אלהין	∅
2 Sam 21:2	Compound-Contrasting	אלהין	אלא
1 Kgs 8:19	Compound-Contrasting	אלהין	אלא אן
1 Kgs 17:1	Compound-Limiting	אלהין קד	אלא אן גד
1 Kgs 17:12	Compound-Limiting	אלהין	אלא אן
1 Kgs 18:18	Compound-Contrasting	אלהין	אלא
1 Kgs 20:6	Compound-Contrasting or Independent?	אלהין	∅
1 Kgs 21:15	Compound-Contrasting (text)	אלהין (variant: ארי)	rewritten
1 Kgs 22:8	Compound-Contrasting	אלהין	אלא
1 Kgs 22:18	Compound-Contrasting	אלהין	אלא
1 Kgs 22:31	Compound-Contrasting	אלהין	אלא
2 Kgs 4:2	Compound-Limiting	אלהין	אלא אן
2 Kgs 4:24	Compound-Limiting	אלהין קד	אלא אן
2 Kgs 5:15	Compound-Limiting	אלהין	אלא אן
2 Kgs 5:17	Compound-Contrasting	אלהין	אלא אן
2 Kgs 5:20	Independent	אלהין	אלא
2 Kgs 7:10	Compound-Contrasting	אלהין	אלא אן
2 Kgs 9:35	Compound-Limiting	אלהין	אלא אן
2 Kgs 10:23	Compound-Contrasting	אלהין	אלא אן
2 Kgs 13:7	Compound-Limiting	אלהין	אלא אן
2 Kgs 14:6	Compound-Contrasting	אלהין	אלא
2 Kgs 17:36	Compound-Contrasting	אלהין	אלא
2 Kgs 17:39	Compound-Contrasting	אלהין	אלא
2 Kgs 17:40	Compound-Contrasting	אלהין	אלא
2 Kgs 19:18	Compound-Contrasting	אלהין	אלא
2 Kgs 23:9	Compound-Contrasting	אלהין	אלא אן
2 Kgs 23:23	Compound-Contrasting	אלהין	אלא אן
Isa 10:22	Independent	ארי אם	הא
Isa 33:21	Compound-Contrasting	אלהין	מט-ד
Isa 37:19	Compound-Contrasting	אלהין	אלא
Isa 42:19	Compound-Limiting	rewritten	אלא (var: אין)
Isa 55:10	Compound-Contrasting	אלהין	אלא

Table 1: The Syntax of Hebrew כי אם; Aramaic Translations (cont.)

כי אם	*Hebrew Syntax (according to Conklin)*	*Targums*	*Peshitta*
Isa 55:11	Compound-Contrasting	אלהין	ܐܠܐ ܐܢ
Isa 59:2	Compound-Contrasting	אלהין	ܐܠܐ
Isa 65:6	Compound-Limiting?	אלהין	ܥܕܡܐ ܕ-
Isa 65:18	Compound-Contrasting	אלהין	ܐܠܐ
Jer 2:22	Independent	ארי אם	ܘܐܢ
Jer 3:10	Compound-Contrasting	אלהין	ܐܠܐ ܐܢ
Jer 7:5	Independent	ארי אם	ܐܢ
Jer 7:23	Compound-Contrasting	אלהין	ܐܠܐ
Jer 7:32	Compound-Contrasting	אלהין	ܐܠܐ ܐܢ
Jer 9:23	Compound-Contrasting	אלהין	ܐܠܐ
Jer 16:15	Compound-Contrasting	אלהין	ܐܠܐ
Jer 19:6	Compound-Contrasting	אלהין	ܐܠܐ ܐܢ
Jer 20:3	Compound-Contrasting	אלהין	ܐܠܐ
Jer 22:4	Independent	ארי אם	ܘܐܢ
Jer 22:17	Compound-Limiting	אלהין	ܐܠܐ
Jer 22:24	Independent	ארי אם	ܐܢ
Jer 23:8	Compound-Contrasting	אלהין	ܐܠܐ
Jer 26:15	Independent	ארי אם	ܕܐܢ
Jer 31:30	Compound-Contrasting	אלהין	ܐܠܐ
Jer 37:10	Independent	ארי אם	ܩܠܠ ܕܝܢ
Jer 38:4	Compound-Contrasting	אלהין	ܐܠܐ ܐܢ
Jer 38:6	Compound-Contrasting	אלהין	ܐܠܐ ܐܢ
Jer 39:12	Compound-Contrasting (text)	אלהין	∅
Jer 44:14	Compound-Limiting? (text)	אלהין	ܐܠܐ ܐܢ
Jer 51:14	Independent	אלהין	ܕ-
Ezek 12:23	Compound-Contrasting	אלהין	ܐܠܐ
Ezek 33:11	Compound-Contrasting	אלהין	ܐܠܐ
Ezek 36:22	Compound-Contrasting	אלהין	ܐܠܐ
Ezek 44:10	Compound-Contrasting	אלהין	ܘܐܦܠܐ
Ezek 44:22	Compound-Contrasting	אלהין	ܐܠܐ ܐܢ
Ezek 44:25	Compound-Limiting	אלהין	ܐܠܐ ܐܢ
Hos 9:12	Independent	ארי אם	ܐܦܢ
Amos 3:7	Compound-Limiting	אלהין	ܐܠܐ ܐܢ
Amos 5:22	Independent	ארי אם	ܐܦܢ
Amos 8:11	Compound-Contrasting	אלהין	ܐܠܐ
Mic 6:8	Compound-Limiting	אלהין	ܕ-

Table 1: The Syntax of Hebrew כי אם; Aramaic Translations (cont.)

כי אם	Hebrew Syntax (according to Conklin)	Targums		Peshitta
Zech 4:6	Compound-Contrasting	אלהין		ܐܠܐ ܐܢ
Ps 1:2	Compound-Contrasting	אלהין		ܐܠܐ
Ps 1:4	Compound-Contrasting	אלהין		ܐܠܐ
Job 42:8	Compound-Contrasting	ארום אלהן		∅
Prov 2:3	Independent	ארום אימא		∅
Prov 18:2	Compound-Contrasting	אלא		ܡܛܠ ܕ-
Prov 19:19	Independent (text)	rewritten		rewritten
Prov 23:17	Compound-Contrasting	אלא		ܐܠܐ
Prov 23:18	Independent (text)	-מטול ד		ܕ-
Ruth 3:12	Independent (text)	ארום		∅
Ruth 3:18	Compound-Limiting	אילהין		ܒܠܚܘܕ ܕ-
Qoh 3:12	Compound-Limiting	ארום אילהין		ܐܠܐ
Qoh 4:10	Independent	ארום אילהין אין		ܕܐܢ
Qoh 5:10	Compound-Limiting	אין אל		ܐܠܐ ܐܢ
Qoh 8:15	Compound-Limiting	ארום אילהין		ܐܠܐ
Qoh 11:8	Independent	ארום אין		ܗܘ ܕ- ܓܝܪ
Lam 3:32	Independent	ארום אלהין		ܐܠܐ
Lam 5:22	Independent	ארום אלהין		ܡܛܠ ܕ-
Esth 2:14	Compound-Limiting	1 ארום אילהין 2 אלא אין 3 ארום אלהן		ܐܠܐ ܐܢ
Esth 2:15	Compound-Limiting	1 ארום אילהין 2 אלא 3 ארום אלהן		ܐܠܐ
Esth 4:14	Independent	1 ארום אם 2 אלא אם 3 ארום אם		ܐܢ
Esth 5:12	Compound-Limiting	1 ארום אילהין 2 אלא 3 אלהן		ܐܠܐ ܐܢ
Dan 10:21	Compound-Limiting	N/A		ܐܠܐ ܐܢ
Neh 2:2	Compound-Limiting	N/A		ܐܠܐ ܐܢ
Neh 2:12	Compound-Limiting	N/A		ܐܠܐ ܐܢ
1 Chr 2:34	Compound-Contrasting	אלאהן		ܐܠܐ ܐܢ (var: ܐܠܐ)
1 Chr 15:2	Compound-Limiting	אילהן		∅
1 Chr 23:22	Compound-Contrasting	אלהן		ܐܠܐ

Table 1: The Syntax of Hebrew כי אם; Aramaic Translations (cont.)

כי אם	Hebrew Syntax (according to Conklin)	Targums	Peshitta
2 Chr 2:5	Compound-Limiting	אלאהן	∅
2 Chr 18:17	Compound-Contrasting	ארום אלהן	ܐܠܐ ܐܢ
2 Chr 18:30	Compound-Contrasting	ארום אלהן	ܐܠܐ
2 Chr 21:17	Compound-Limiting	אלהן	ܐܠܐ ܐܢ
2 Chr 23:6	Compound-Limiting	אלהן	ܐܠܐ
2 Chr 25:8	Independent	ארום אין	ܒܓܠ-ܕ

Table 2: Treatment of כי אם in the Targums

	Onqelos	Ps. Jonathan	Neofiti	Genizah	Fragmentary	Prophets	Writings
Independent	A – 6/7 B – 2	A – 7/8 B – 1	A – 5/6 C – 1 D – 2	C – 1	A – 0/1	A – 12 B – 6/7 D – 2	A – 3 C – 2 D – 5
Compound-Limiting	B – 11	B – 8 C – 2 D – 1	B – 1 C – 9 D – 1	B – 1 C – 1 D – 2	C – 1	B – 18 D – 3	B – 6 C – 4 D – 1
Compound-Contrasting	A – 1/2 B – 11	A – 1/2 B – 11	A – 0/1 B – 1 C – 11	C – 4	A – 0/1	B – 49/50 D – 1	B – 4 C – 3 D – 2

compound particle, the targums typically use the particle אלהין, which outside Onqelos and Jonathan can be spelled in half a dozen different ways. The word אלהין carries the same adversative-exceptive functions as the compound particle כי אם in Hebrew. In addition, the Palestinian Targums—but never targums Onqelos and Jonathan—contain another combination, ארום אלהין, which appears to be a bit redundant. There are a dozen or so additional cases in which some other formulation is used, such as ד-, אלהין כד, והן, אלהין אין, מטול, and the even more redundant ארום אילהין אין.

In order to organize the presentation of the targum data efficiently and to remove the factor of variant spellings from the equation, I use the following notation system (A through D) in table 2:

A = presentative particle + conditional particle: e.g., ארום אין, ארי אם, etc.
B = the particle אלהין and its variants
C = presentative particle + אלהין: e.g., ארום אלהן
D = any other formulation

Table 2 displays the number of times any given translation choice listed above is used in the various targums, according to the syntax of the Hebrew particle combination. The slashed numbers (e.g., 6/7) take into account the instances where doubt was expressed above with regard to the syntax (e.g., Num 24:22).

If the Aramaic translators analyzed the Hebrew syntax just as we have proposed above, and if they chose the simplest means of translating the particle, two results would occur: First, the Independent syntax should be represented by two independent particles in Aramaic, indicated in table 2 by the letter A. Second, the Compound syntax, regardless of the semantic subdivision between Limiting and Contrasting, should be represented by the particle אלהין, indicated by the letter B. The letters C and D would be unnecessary in this hypothetical reconstruction. Based on these presuppositions, the following observations about what actually occurs should be made.

Targums Onqelos, Pseudo-Jonathan, and Jonathan broadly correspond to this theoretical sketch. A is prominent in Independent syntax, and B is prominent in Compound syntax. Exceptions to these tendencies are most conspicuous when B occurs in the Independent row, and when A occurs in either of the Compound rows. Most, if not all, of these deviations from the expected distribution can be explained by textual difficulties or by the difficult nature of the passage itself. These passages will be studied in detail in the final section of this paper. In Onqelos, there are only 3 or 4 exceptions out of 32 texts. That is, in only 3 or 4 texts did the translator of TO analyze the syntax differently from my analysis in table 1. But TO was perfectly consistent in translating כי אם once the choice between Independent and Compound syntax was made; ארי אם and אלהין are used without exception, respectively. In Pseudo-Jonathan, there are only 2 or 3 texts out of 32 where the translator analyzed the syntax differently from my analysis in table 1. For translating Compound syntax, PJ departs from אלהין only 3 times. In Jonathan, out of 92 texts, there are only 7 or 8 where the translator analyzed the syntax differently from table 1. There are only 6 texts in which the translator did not translate with either ארי אם for Independent syntax or אלהין for Compound.

The use of C, a rather redundant ארום אלהן, is almost exclusively limited to Targum Neofiti, the Genizah fragments, and the Fragmentary Targums—in all of which it is the preferred alternative over B for Compound syntax. This is also true for the Targums of the Writings. In Neofiti, there are a handful of exceptions (anywhere from 1 to 5 out of 32, depending on what the translator was thinking, which is not always easy to determine)—a handful of places where the translator analyzed the syntax differently from table 1. In only 5 texts, TN departed from the use of either ארי אם or ארום אלהן for Independent and Compound syntax, respectively. In the Genizah fragments, there is only 1 exception out of 9, but 3 instances where CG did not translate Compound syntax with ארום אלהין. In the Fragmentary Targums, there may be 1 exception to our syntactic analysis in the 2 texts in our corpus.

These targums (TN, CG, and FT) are representative of Jewish Palestinian Aramaic, as distinct from the Jewish Literary Aramaic (TO, TJ) and Late Jewish Literary Aramaic (PJ). This literary distinction, in conjunction with

Table 3: Treatment of כי אם in the Peshitta

	ܐܠܐ	ܐܠܐ ܐܢ
Compound-Limiting	9/46 – 20%	30/46 – 66%
Compound-Contrasting	45/72 – 63%	18/72 – 25%

the distribution of the data we have presented, suggests that the compound particle ארום אלהין, one of the translations of the Compound syntax of כי אם, is a Palestinian phenomenon.

In keeping with the varied and sketchy nature of the Writings Targums, there is little uniformity there in the translation of כי אם. Nearly anything can be used anywhere. What can be said is that *B* is never used for Independent syntax (and we should not expect it to be), and *A* is never used for Compound syntax (and we should not expect it to be).

Regardless of the targum and its tendencies (with the exception of the Genizah fragments), there is a clear distinction in the translations between those we have labeled *Independent* and those we have labeled *Compound*, and there is very little distinction between the two semantic subdivisions of Compound syntax.

Tendencies in the Peshitta

The notation system used above for the targums is not amenable to the Peshitta. A different approach is needed to describe the Peshitta's handling of the Hebrew particle כי אם. For passages in which the Hebrew particles are Independent, the translators did not use one standard translation but employed a number of different formulations that represent both elements of the Hebrew expression, such as ܡܛܠ ܕܗ, ܐܪ ܕܗ, ܕܐܪ, ܐܡܪ, and so on.

For the passages where the Hebrew particle is Compound, the Peshitta uses two different but similar translations: the particle ܐܠܐ and the compound particle ܐܠܐ ܐܢ. Both of these particles have the same possible functions as Hebrew כי אם, an adversative, "but, however," and an exceptive, "unless, except." Both of these are used in both subdivisions of the Compound syntax, Limiting and Contrasting, but unlike the targums, there is a trend seen in their distribution. Out of 157 occurrences of כי אם in the Hebrew Bible listed above, 46 are labeled Compound-Limiting, 72 are labeled Compound-Contrasting. Table 3 shows how many of these in the Peshitta are translated by ܐܠܐ and how many by ܐܠܐ ܐܢ.

We are presented in table 3 with a trend that does not exist in the targums, a trend that reflects the semantic distinction we have noted in the instances of כי אם that exhibit Compound syntax. The Hebrew Compound-Limiting texts (translated in English by "unless" or "except") are translated ܐܠܐ ܐܢ by more than a three-to-one margin, while the Compound-Contrasting texts (translated in English by "but" or "however") are translated ܐܠܐ by a five-to-two margin.

Though the two particles in Syriac are often apparently interchangeable, the trend here strongly suggests that the translators of the Peshitta also recognized the semantic distinction in the Compound syntax and used different translations to try and reflect that distinction. If we look at the breakdown in the Peshitta a little closer, the numbers suggest that the translators of the Pentateuch took greater care or were more aware of the semantic distinction than the translators of the other portions of the Bible. In the Pentateuch of the Peshitta, Compound-Contrasting and Compound-Limiting instances of כי אם are translated ܐܠܐ and ܐܠܐ ܐܢ, respectively, 91% of the time (21/23). In the Prophets, the percentage drops to 58% (42/72), while in the Writings it drops further to 52% (12/23). Further study needs to be done to determine whether this state of affairs reflects an artificial assignment of semantic distinction for ܐܠܐ and ܐܠܐ ܐܢ by the translators of the Pentateuch that was subsequently lost or ignored, or whether it was a real semantic distinction that was naturally lost in the evolution of the language at later stages.

Exceptions to Tendencies

Most of the exceptions to the tendencies described in the two previous sections can be explained due to textual or interpretive difficulties of the Hebrew text, difficulties that have also challenged modern scholars. Several such deviations appear in passages where modern analysts have alleged an asseverative function for the compound particle כי אם. Such a solution to these Hebrew passages has enjoyed such a long life because it works; that is, it helps make sense of the passages. But the very nature of an alleged asseverative meaning, "indeed" or "surely," makes it easy to apply in a broad manner, because such a meaning adds so little to the sentence. It is therefore hard to disprove an asseverative meaning, because it is so weak and free of content, while the plausibility of any particular particle meaning "surely" is easy to assert if the proof is merely translational plausibility. However, there are simply no certain examples of an asseverative כי אם in Classical Hebrew.[2] The most important suggestions to the contrary are discussed below.

Textual problems underlie several passages where the Aramaic translations constitute exceptions to the general observations made above. This is

---

2. A telling example comes from the *Dictionary of Classical Hebrew*, where a Qumran text supposedly contains an instance of כי אם with an asseverative meaning: כיא אם לכה המלחמה, "surely the battle is yours!" in 1QM 11:1. There are two parallel phrases that are positive and that clearly influence this interpretation, כיא לכה המלחמה (line 2) and then לכה המלחמה (line 4), respectively. However, the compound particle in line 1 *begins* the first preserved line on the column. There are at least one or two complete lines missing from the end of col. 10, and the last preserved line of col. 10 is barely restorable, so we simply cannot say what preceded the כיא אם in 11:1. We therefore should certainly not give this compound particle a meaning that is never attested elsewhere. It is just as plausible to imagine that a negative clause preceded this on the bottom of col. 10, that perhaps a pessimistic or antagonistic statement is made, and that 11:1 asserts to the contrary, "Rather, the battle is yours [O Lord]!"

particularly true where the אם is omitted in some of the Hebrew manuscripts. The Masoretic notation "one of eight words written not read" is applied to three of these: 2 Sam 13:33 and 15:21, and Jer 39:12. One that is not given this designation by the Masoretes but where the אם is missing in a few manuscripts is 1 Sam 21:6.

וַיַּעַן דָּוִד אֶת־הַכֹּהֵן וַיֹּאמֶר לוֹ כִּי אִם־אִשָּׁה עֲצֻרָה־לָנוּ

In 1 Sam 21:6, a few Hebrew manuscripts do not have an אם after the כי. The textual discrepancy may be accounted for by the fact that the text as it stands is difficult, because the clause headed by כי אם is at the beginning of the speech. In v. 5 the priest says that David and his men may eat of the holy bread if they have abstained from contact with women. Most translators of David's answer opt for the asseverative meaning, "surely women have been kept from us!" Targum Jonathan also follows this course, translating בקשטא, "in truth." It should be noted that this is the only instance in which one of the ancient Aramaic translations attempts to translate the compound particle with an asseverative expression; the modern proclivity to this option has slim ancient support.[3] The Peshitta simply avoids representing the particles at all and cuts straight to the content of David's answer. But an adversative meaning could be possible here, as seen in the LXX's ἀλλά, especially if David was offended by the question posed to him, and his extended answer suggests that this could be the case, "but women *have* been kept from us!"

If the אם is not to be read, then the כי אם can still have an adversative function here. In fact, it is possible to see how a slight misunderstanding of the verb עצר could have led a scribe to insert an אם. The meaning of the verb עצר is "to restrain or hold back." In later Hebrew it develops the nuance "to retain (e.g., strength)." If a scribe thought that the text had David saying, "women have been retained for us," when certainly this was not what was intended, a scribe could have inserted an אם after the כי אם, transforming the statement into a negative oath, "but if women have been retained for us [may I be cursed]," meaning, "women certainly have not been retained for us."

Difficult interpretive questions account for other deviations from the expected tendencies. The remaining examples illustrate this.

Gen 40:14

Hebrew כִּי אִם־זְכַרְתַּנִי אִתְּךָ כַּאֲשֶׁר יִיטַב לָךְ וְעָשִׂיתָ־נָּא עִמָּדִי חָסֶד

But if you remember me when it goes well for you, then do me a kindness . . .

Onqelos אלהין תדכרינני עמך

But you (must) remember me . . .

Peshitta אלא אתדכרני לי

But remember me . . .

---

3. Neither the Septuagint nor the Vulgate, for that matter, supports an asseverative interpretation of the compound particle כי אם.

The context preceding this verse contains Joseph's interpretation of the butler's dream. In this verse Joseph asks the butler to remember him when he returns to Pharaoh. The Aramaic translations treat כי אם as compound and transform the Hebrew's perfective verb, זכרתני, into an imperfective (Onqelos) and an imperative (Peshitta), respectively. This approach, reflected in many modern translations as well, fails to deal with the fact that the Hebrew verb is perfective, and only by recognizing that the sentence is a conditional one can the future reference of the perfective verb make sense. If the text is properly recognized as a conditional sentence, then the syntax of כי אם can only be analyzed as Independent. Failure to recognize this compels interpreters to treat the כי אם as a Compound-Contrasting particle.

Gen 47:18

Hebrew לֹא־נְכַחֵד מֵאֲדֹנִי כִּי אִם־תַּם הַכֶּסֶף וּמִקְנֵה הַבְּהֵמָה אֶל־אֲדֹנִי לֹא נִשְׁאַר לִפְנֵי אֲדֹנִי בִּלְתִּי אִם־גְּוִיָּתֵנוּ וְאַדְמָתֵנוּ

We will not hide from my lord (the fact) that if the silver and the livestock (belong) to my lord, (then) there is nothing left for my lord except our bodies and our land.

Onqelos לא נכסי מן רבוני אלהין שלים כספא

We will not hide from my lord (אלהין) the silver is gone.

Peshitta ܠܐ ܡܟܣܝܢܢ ܡܢ ܡܪܢ ܡܛܠ ܕܓܡܪ ܟܣܦܐ

We will/cannot hide from our lord, because all the silver is gone.

Onqelos awkwardly translates כי אם by אלהין, although neither the adversative nor exceptive functions make sense here. The Peshitta simply ignores the conditional particle, and makes a causal clause out of it with ܡܛܠ ܕ-. This makes sense of the passage, but the Hebrew can be taken at face value. It is necessary to analyze the כי אם here as two independent particles. The כי is the object complement of the verb "to hide," "to hide *that*," and what follows is a full conditional sentence, as rendered above.

Judg 15:7

Hebrew וַיֹּאמֶר לָהֶם שִׁמְשׁוֹן אִם־תַּעֲשׂוּן כָּזֹאת כִּי אִם־נִקַּמְתִּי בָכֶם וְאַחַר אֶחְדָּל׃

And Samson said to them, "If you do this, then if I am avenged of you, then I will cease."

Jonathan אלהין כד אתפרע מנכון ובתר כין אתמנע

When I am avenged of you, then I will cease.

Peshitta ܐܢ ܬܥܒܕܘܢ ܗܕܐ ܡܢܟܘܢ ܗܕܐ ܐܬܦܪܥ ܐܠܐ ܐܢܐ

Even if you do this, I will be avenged of you, then I will cease.

Both Aramaic translations transform the Hebrew perfective verb, נקמתי, into a more manageable verbal form. Targum Jonathan uses an imperfective, and though it rather mechanically translates כי אם by the standard אלהין, it adds the particle כד, "when," to make sense of the passage. The Peshitta does not translate the compound particle but changes the perfective to a participle, which is not marked for time and thus can be adapted for the desired future tense. This Hebrew passage is commonly translated in English, "If you do this, *surely* I will be avenged over you and then I will cease," translating כי אם as an asseverative particle and transforming the perfective נקמתי into a future tense, similar to the Aramaic translations.

The use of the suffix-conjugation, or the perfective, is attested particularly in the prophetic genre with reference to future actions, commonly called the "prophetic perfect," but in regular prose, the use of the perfect to denote a purely future action is very rare. Is this an instance of this phenomenon? Certainly the action denoted by this verb must have a future reference, because Samson has not yet avenged what remains a future act of provocation. However, the Hebrew's use of the perfective verb is more intelligible here if the אם is understood as the conditional particle marking the protasis of a full conditional clause followed by the apodosis: "If (or when) I have avenged myself over you, (only) then will I cease." The alternation between the perfective and the imperfective, for the protasis and apodosis, respectively, illustrates well the aspectual nature of the Hebrew verbal system. If a certain action, represented by the perfective verb, is done in its entirety, then the apodosis will follow, and any verb aspect/tense can be used in the apodosis. In this text and in 2 Kgs 5:20 and Jer 51:14 below, the alternation between perfective and imperfective verbs is incomprehensible if the כי אם is seen as a compound particle with an asseverative meaning, but as full conditional sentences they make better sense.

In Judg 15:7, we actually have a conditional sentence within a conditional sentence. The larger sentence is, "if you do this, (then) X." In this larger sentence, the כי is functioning to mark the apodosis, and this apodosis in turn consists of a full conditional sentence marked by אם.

The final four examples are oaths. This is an ideal breeding ground for the alleged asseverative function of כי אם. The syntax of these texts is difficult, and in each the scholarly approach has been to interpret the כי אם as a compound particle with an asseverative function, because such a function, "surely, indeed," seems to make sense of the passages. But this solution is too easy, and it begs the question of the existence of this function in the first place. Though the Aramaic translations struggle with the difficulties as well, none of them supports the asseverative option. The particles in these texts are better analyzed as functioning independently. The אם belongs to either a conditional clause or another clause that expresses contingency in some other way. The כי clause belongs to the oath formula. It is beyond the scope of this paper to argue the point in detail here, but I contend that the כי is the object complement of the verb of swearing that is often elided, "[I swear] that. . . ."[4] In fact, the verb remains unelided in the final example, Jer 51:14.

---

4. See my 2005 University of Chicago dissertation, *Oath Formulae*, chap. 4, for a defense of this function of כי in oaths, and chap. 5, for the alleged function of כי־אם in oaths.

1 Sam 26:10

Hebrew חַי־יְהוָה כִּי אִם־יְהוָה יִגְּפֶנּוּ אוֹ־יוֹמוֹ יָבוֹא וָמֵת אוֹ בַמִּלְחָמָה יֵרֵד וְנִסְפָּה
(By) the life of the Lord, [I swear] that either the Lord will strike him, or his day will come and he will die, or he will go down into battle and be wiped out.

Jonathan אלהין מן קדם יי יתמחי
... אלהין he will be struck by the Lord ...

Peshitta ܐܠܐ ܐ‍ܪ ܢܬܡܚܐ ܡܢ ܡܪܝܐ
... ܐܠܐ ܐ‍ܪ the Lord will strike him ...

In 1 Sam 26:10, the predominant understanding of the passage is that David is sure that God will kill Saul somehow, "surely Yahweh will strike him," though he refuses to be the instrument to inflict such a sentence on the "Lord's anointed." However, another understanding of the כי אם is possible, an understanding that avoids the dubious asseverative function for the compound particle and makes better sense of the options that David outlines. The two particles function independently, the כי is the object clause marker of the elided verb שבע, and the אם here functions as the first term of a list of alternatives, followed by the two occurrences of או, "or." This sequence is attested elsewhere (Lev 15:23), and the sense of the passage is much better (as v. 11 helps make clear): "(By) the life of Yahweh [I swear] that either the Lord will strike him, or . . . ." The Aramaic translators must have struggled with the awkward Hebrew text as well and resolved simply to translate the particle as if it was compound—the safest alternative available to them.

2 Sam 15:21

Hebrew חַי־יְהוָה וְחֵי אֲדֹנִי הַמֶּלֶךְ כִּי אִם־בִּמְקוֹם אֲשֶׁר יִהְיֶה־שָּׁם ׀ אֲדֹנִי הַמֶּלֶךְ
אִם־לְמָוֶת אִם־לְחַיִּים כִּי־שָׁם יִהְיֶה עַבְדֶּךָ׃
(By) the life of the Lord, and (by) the life of my lord the king, [I swear] that אם in the place where my lord the king is, whether for death or for life, your servant will be there.

Jonathan אלהין באתרא
... אלהין in the place ...

Peshitta ܐܠܐ ܒܐܬܪܐ
... ܐܠܐ in the place ...

The text is difficult, and the אם is lacking in some Hebrew manuscripts. If the first אם here is indeed legitimate, it could be functioning in concert with the two instances of אם that follow, which express two alternatives. The Aramaic translators, sensing the difficulties, translate the particle combination conventionally, if not comprehensibly. That is to say, אלהין and אלא are the most generic ways to translate כי אם in Targum Jonathan and the Peshitta, respectively, but the possible meanings of those translations ("but" or "except") do not work here.

2 Kgs 5:20

Hebrew חַי־יְהוָה כִּי־אִם־רַצְתִּי אַחֲרָיו וְלָקַחְתִּי מֵאִתּוֹ מְאוּמָה׃
(By) the life of the Lord, [I swear] that if I run after him, (then) I will get something from him.

Jonathan אלהין ארהוט בתרוהי ואסב מניה
אלהין ... I will run after him, and I will get (something) from him.

Peshitta ܐܠܐ ܐܪܗܛ ܒܬܪܗ ܘܐܣܒ ܡܢܗ ܡܕܡ
ܐܠܐ ... I will run after him, and I will get something from him.

The use of the verbal forms mirrors the forms in Judg 15:7. Here the first verb is perfective, and the second is imperfective. Therefore, the understanding of these passages as conditional sentences—with כי and אם functioning independently—makes better sense than viewing the כי אם combination here as a compound asseverative particle, "surely." The Aramaic translations transform the perfective to an imperfective and clumsily translate the כי אם in the conventional way for a compound particle.

Jer 51:14

Hebrew נִשְׁבַּע יְהוָה צְבָאוֹת בְּנַפְשׁוֹ כִּי אִם־מִלֵּאתִיךְ אָדָם כַּיֶּלֶק וְעָנוּ עָלַיִךְ הֵידָד׃
The Lord of Armies swears by his life that, "If I fill you (with) men like locusts, then they will chant a war cry over you."

Jonathan אלהין אמליניך
אלהין ... I will fill you ...

Peshitta ܕܐܡܠܝܟܝ
... that I will fill you ...

In this text the כי marks the object of the verb שבע. Here again, like Judg 15:7 and 2 Kgs 5:20, the first verb after the אם is perfective, and the verb in the apodosis is imperfective. Targum Jonathan goes with אלהין, while the Peshitta ignores the conditional particle and simply translates the כי with d-. As in the previous examples, the failure to recognize a full conditional sentence here—and subsequently, failure to recognize that the syntax of the כי־אם combination is Independent—leads interpreters to become creative in dealing with the juxtaposition of כי and אם.

This section has demonstrated that many of the exceptions to the expected tendencies in translating כי אם in the targums and the Peshitta are due to difficulties in interpreting the Hebrew text or problems in the Hebrew text itself. By highlighting these difficulties and the exceptions they instigate, the tendencies presented in the preceding two sections appear all the more impressive.

Conclusion

This study has provided some measure of quantification for the notion often expressed that the targums are more mechanical, word-for-word translations, while the Peshitta is more idiomatic. Each of the targums typically selects one standard way of treating the כי אם particles when it is exhibiting Independent syntax, and another when it is exhibiting Compound syntax, but there is no distinction made between the semantic nuances of examples with Compound syntax. By contrast, the Peshitta deals with the 39 passages in which the particles exhibit Independent syntax in 13 different ways, and when the particles exhibit Compound syntax, the translation shows a tendency to reflect the semantic distinction with a translational distinction. Significantly, the exceptions to the expected tendencies in both the targums and the Peshitta can usually be explained by textual or interpretive difficulties in the Hebrew text.

An examination of the Aramaic translations of Hebrew has also opened up an opportunity to reexamine modern notions of some finer syntactic points in Hebrew. The Aramaic translations are by no means prescriptive, but they provide a window on different ways to think about the Hebrew. The Aramaic translations, for example, provide no support for the alleged asseverative function of the compound particle כי אם, and a renewed look at the passages in question confirms that this is indeed a phantom category.

No doubt more can be done (not only on this particular topic but also on others) by way of improving our grasp of particle morpho-syntax in the Semitic languages. These interrelated questions in particular, which are beyond the reach of this paper, need more attention: When, why, and how was the targumic particle אלהין formed? What is the derivation of the other similar particles encountered here and elsewhere in Aramaic, ארי, אלא, אלו, להן, and so on? The conventional explanation, for example, that אלא is a contraction of אן and לא needs further scrutiny.

Bibliography

The Bible in Syriac. United Bible Societies' corrected reprint of the S. Lee 1826 edition. New York: United Bible Societies, 1987.

Conklin, B. W. *Oath Formulae in Classical Hebrew and Other Semitic Languages*. Ph.D. dissertation. The University of Chicago, 2005.

Díez Macho, A., ed. *Neophyti I: Targum Palestinense Ms de la Biblioteca vaticana*. 6 vols. Barcelona: Consejo Superior de Investigaciones Cientificas, 1968–79.

Klein, M. L. *The Fragment-Targums of the Pentateuch: According to their Extant Sources*. Analecta Biblica 76. 2 vols. Rome: Pontifical Biblical Institute, 1980.

———. *Genizah Manuscripts of Palestinian Targum to the Pentateuch*. 2 vols. Cincinnati: Hebrew Union College, 1986.

Peshitta: The Old Testament in Syria. Edited on behalf of the International Organization for the Study of the Old Testament by the Peshitta Institute, Leiden. In 5 parts. Leiden: Brill, 1966–.

Sperber, A. *The Bible in Aramaic: Based on Old Manuscripts and Printed Texts*. 5 vols. Leiden: Brill, 1959–73. [Repr. 1993]

Recasting:
Making an Old Text New

The Use of the First Person in the *Genesis Apocryphon*

STEPHEN A. REED

One of the curious features of the *Genesis Apocryphon* is its use of the first person. While this has been noted by scholars, it has not been analyzed consistently throughout the preserved portions, and the significance of this feature has not been explained. New readings of previously unpublished columns and the use of new technology have provided further evidence concerning this issue. In this paper I will analyze the use of the first person in the *Genesis Apocryphon* and explain how this feature is used.

Nickelsburg has devoted the most attention to the use of the first person in the book. He notes that "the first person singular narrative voice is a striking feature of the scroll's version of the story of Noah's birth," which is also used in the Abram story.[1] He concludes a two-page discussion of this feature by saying, "In any case, further work needs to be done on the use of first person narration, its characteristics, the forms in which it occurs, its relationships to other types of 'rewritten Bible' and the broader phenomenon of pseudepigraphy, and its possible parallels in contemporary non-Israelite literature."[2] Here he lays out many issues that need further reflection.

Description of the Use of First Person in the Genesis Apocryphon

While only parts of the scroll have been preserved, and the early columns are very deteriorated, in the portions that remain the scroll tells stories related

---

Author's note: I am appreciative of having been able to participate in the National Endowment for the Humanities Summer Seminar for College and University Teachers on the theme of Aramaic in Postbiblical Judaism and Early Christianity at Duke University, June 14–July 23, 2004. I learned much from Eric Meyers, Paul Flesher and Lucas Van Rompay and became interested in this topic on the *Genesis Apocryphon* while reading the work under the direction of Eric Meyers and Paul Flesher. Seminar members provided helpful suggestions in response to my initial report of this paper to the group.

1. Nickelsburg, "Patriarchs Who Worry about Their Wives," p. 157.
2. Ibid.

to Lamech, Noah, and Abram. The scroll follows the order of the stories in Genesis. For the Lamech and Noah materials, there is considerable material not found in the biblical text that parallels stories in *Jubilees* and *Enoch*. In the Abram materials, the episodes follow the biblical story rather closely from Gen 12:20 to 15:4. One of the best ways of noting how the first person is used in this scroll is to compare these texts with parallel ones in Genesis, *Jubilees*, and *Enoch*. Since the Abram material is the best preserved, I will give the most attention to this material in this study.

The *Genesis Apocryphon* has been described as a "rewritten Bible" by Vermes and others.[3] In the Masoretic Text of Genesis there is an anonymous, third-person narrator of the events. Direct speech is used in dialogues in which the speakers within the stories refer to themselves in the first person. The author of the *Genesis Apocryphon* continues to report direct speech in which individuals refer to themselves in the first person. More direct speech is added and speeches are expanded. Beyond this, there is a shift from the third- to the first-person narrator in the stories. Lamech, Noah, and Abram are the three certain narrators.

Direct Speech by Various Characters within Stories

In addition to Lamech, Noah, and Abram speaking in the first person, other characters also speak in the first person in reported dialogue. In direct speech, the following speak in the first person: Lamech, 2:3–7; Bitenosh, 2:9–11, 13–18; Methuselah, 2:24–26; Enoch, 5:9, 20; Sarai, 19:18, 20:9–10; Lot, 20:22–23; Hirqanos, 20:24–26; Pharaoh, 20:26–28; king of Sodom, 22:18; Abram, 19:17–18, 19–21; 22:20–24, 32–34; God, 11:15–12:1; 15:23? 21:8–10, 12–14; 22:27–32.[4] One could also include prayers that are addressed to God by Abram: 19:7–8, 20:12–16, 22:32–34. By contrast, some instances of quoted speech do not explicitly refer to the self as I (Melchizedek, 22:16–17; God, 22:34ff.). There are also reports of prayers and indirect speech without quotations of precisely what is said.

Narrators: Lamech, Noah, Abram

Many of the Genesis stories are retold by changing the third-person reports of Genesis to first-person reports by each story's key figures. This first person is usually "I," although occasionally "we" appears. Avigad and Yadin noted this already in their edition: "the narrative in the scroll is in large part couched in the first person."[5]

Not only is the story told by a narrator in the first person but the narrator changes throughout the book from Lamech (to Enoch?) to Noah to Abram.

---

3. Vermes, "Life of Abraham(2)," *Scripture and Tradition*, p. 126; Evans, "The Genesis Apocryphon and the Rewritten Bible."
4. This list starts with col. 2 and is based on the readings found in Fitzmyer, *Genesis Apocryphon of Qumran*, pp. 69–111.
5. Avigad and Yadin, *Genesis Apocryphon*, p. 38.

Initially when the first fragments of this document were published, Trever named the document the Lamech Scroll because he was able to read "I, Lamech" in one fragment that was detached from the scroll.[6] After the scroll was unrolled it was found that there were other narrators throughout the text who spoke in the first person. Recent publications supplement the deteriorated columns at the manuscript's beginning and provide further narratives that have Lamech and Noah speaking in the first person.[7] The *Genesis Apocryphon* contains stories in which Lamech, Noah, and Abram each in his turn tells about certain events. As Fitzmyer observed, "it presents each of the patriarchs telling his own story."[8]

Markers of Shift of Speaker/Narrator within Direct Discourse

Since so many different speakers can be "I" within direct discourse, the author must assist the reader to know who is speaking at any particular time. Because there are no quotation marks in Hebrew, as Walsh notes, the author must clarify who is speaking if a text is to be clear.[9] Walsh states that usually speech is introduced by "and he said."[10] Often the author of the *Genesis Apocryphon* helps the reader by using a speech report, usually with a personal name or a personal pronoun in which the antecedent is clear.

What complicates this further is that the reader must distinguish between the narrative "I" who tells the story in certain sections and the "I" used in direct discourse by many people and God throughout the scroll. As an example, note the translation of 19:17b–21a by Fitzmyer.[11]

> That night I awoke from my sleep and said to Sarai, my wife, "I have had a dream; [and] I [am] frightened [by] this dream." She said to me, "Tell me your dream that I may know (it)." So I began to tell her this dream [and made it known] to [her, and (also) the meaning of this] dream, (and) s[aid], "[   ] who will seek to kill me and to spare you. But this is all the favor [that you must do for me]: In what[ever place we shall be, say] about me, 'He is my brother.' Then I shall live by your protection, and my life will be saved because of you. [And they will s]eek to take you away from me and to kill me."

In English, double and single quotation marks help clarify the speaker/narrative transitions. The story is told by the narrator "I" (Abram) in which he quotes direct speech "I" of himself and quotes direct speech "I" by Sarah. Abram then returns to the narrative "I" and then quotes direct speech "I" of himself and then quotes direct speech for Sarah to say in which she uses the first person "my" to refer to her husband, Abram. Then he returns to the

---

6. Trever, "Identification of the Aramaic Fourth Scroll from ʿAin Feshka," p. 9.
7. Greenfield and Qimron, "Genesis Apocryphon Column XII"; Morgenstern, Qimron, and Sivan, "Hitherto Unpublished Columns."
8. Fitzmyer, *Genesis Apocryphon of Qumran*, p. 16.
9. Walsh, *Style and Structure*, pp. 124–25.
10. Ibid., p. 124.
11. Fitzmyer, *The Genesis Apocryphon of Qumran*, p. 99.

narrative "I." The combination of direct speech in the first person and narration in the first person makes the text difficult to follow at such places.

Another way the narrator helps the reader is with the use of paragraph divisions in the text. Lange and Fröhlich have studied the *vacats* of the *Genesis Apocryphon* as a means to determine the structure of the text.[12] Lange suggests that, "While the small *vacats* (about 1–2 cm) indicate subunits, the large ones mark main units."[13] Fröhlich identifies subunits as narrative, monologue, and dialogue and shows that a *vacat* frequently proceeds the shift to these forms. This does not mean that each speaker gets a new paragraph, as in English, but it does help the reader. In the text discussed above (1QapGen 19:17b–21a), a *vacat* appears before this unit but not within it.

Markers of Identity of Narrators

Since there is a shift of narrators throughout the scroll, the author of the scroll assists the reader to know when transitions to new narrators are made and sometimes reminds the reader of the narrator's identity at a specific point of time.

Headings

Clear transitions between the major sections from Lamech to Noah to Abram are missing in the fragments that remain. A newly deciphered fragment of the scroll, however, may help us understand how such transitions were made. New technology used by Gregory Bearman and Bruce Zuckerman allowed them to read three words on a fragment of the scroll. Steiner has deciphered these words as "the book of the words of Noah."[14] This heading follows a *vacat* near the end of col. 5 and is situated between "I, Lamech," 5:26 and "I, Noah" in 6:6. Steiner contends that "the author or compiler of the *Genesis Apocryphon* viewed the latter not as a book but as a collection of books."[15] Steiner notes the following quote from Avigad and Yadin and wonders if this is what they meant: "The work is evidently a literary unit in style and structure, though for the reasons referred to above, it may perhaps be divisible into books—a Book of Lamech, a Book of Enoch, a Book of Noah, a Book of Abraham."[16]

The new title helps us to note the transition from the Words of Lamech to the Words of Noah, but we are not certain where the other transitions took place. Perhaps each of the sections of the *Genesis Apocryphon* was clearly marked with such a heading when a transition to a new speaker took place. The writer does seem interested in alerting the reader to a new speaker. Direct quotations of speakers other than the narrators are clearly identified (at least when the text is preserved).

12. Lange, "1QGenAp XIX 10–XX 32"; Fröhlich, "Narrative Exegesis," pp. 89–93.
13. Lange, "1QGenAp XIX 10–XX 32," p. 193 n. 14.
14. Steiner, "The Heading of the *Book of the Words of Noah*," p. 69.
15. Ibid.
16. Avigad and Yadin, *Genesis Apocryphon*, p. 38.

"I" with Personal Name

Another way in which the narrator helps the reader identify the speaker within sections is by the use of the independent pronoun "I" followed by a personal name. One has "I, Lamech," 2:3, 2:19, 5:26; "I, Enoch," 5:1; "I, Noah," 6:6, 6:23, 11:1?, 11:9?, 11:11?, 15:21?; "I, Abram" 19:14, 20:10, 20:10–11, 20:33, 21:15.[17] There is only one case, with "I, Enoch," in which this formula is used for someone who is not the narrator of a section. This is a marker that can be used to distinguish the narrative "I" from the "I" of direct speech embedded within the narrative.

Muraoka has noted, "The most frequent use of the pers. pron. in our scroll is what one may designate 'self-conscious story-teller's "I."'"[18] As he indicates, it is only used for the first-person singular and is followed by the personal name and either precedes or follows the predicative verb.[19] He suggested, "Very probably the usage under consideration originated in the official style of the Imperial Aramaic used in inscriptions, letters, documents, etc."[20] However, while this might explain the origin, it does not explain its function in the *Genesis Apocryphon*.

While the independent pronoun followed by the name is not used consistently throughout the scroll, one can make some observations. Since the *Genesis Apocryphon* has a different narrator throughout the preserved fragments, this formula is useful to identify the speaker at a particular time. Furthermore there are reports of direct speech of others who speak in the first person. This formula helps clarify whether the narrator is narrating events or speaking at particular points. The formula is used in 1QapGen 20:10 and 20:10–11 in the midst of dialogue in which several people speak in the first person.

Sometimes the independent pronoun followed by the personal name introduces a new section or part of the story. This may also be associated with a *vacat* that introduces a new paragraph. In 19:14, "I, Abram" (after a *vacat*) introduces Abram's report of a dream that he has after traveling to Egypt. In 20:33 (after a *vacat*), "I, Abram" tells about how he leaves Egypt and returns home. In 21:5, "I, Abram" (after a *vacat*) follows a long speech of God in the first person and this introduces Abram's compliance of obeying the instruction of God to walk around the promised land.

This formula is not unique to this document but is used in other first-person Aramaic documents as well. It appears in Ezra at the beginning of official documents to indicate the authority of a ruler making a particular decree (Ezra 6:12, "I, Darius"; Ezra 7:21, "I, Artaxerxes"). In Daniel 4, it is

---

17. The questionable instances are based on reconstructions made in the newly published columns found in Morgenstern, Qimron, and Sivan, "Hitherto Unpublished Columns."
18. Muraoka, "Notes on the Aramaic of the Genesis Apocryphon," p. 8.
19. Ibid., pp. 8–9.
20. Ibid., p. 9.

used three times ("I, [King] Nebuchadnezzar," Dan 4:1, 15, 31 Aramaic; 4:4, 18, 34 English) in parts of this story that are told in the first person by Nebuchadnezzar. It often marks a major division in the story: introducing a report of a dream (Dan 4:1), following a report of the dream (Dan 4:15), and prior to a prayer of praise (Dan 4:31). Daniel 4 is understood as a public epistle that begins and ends with a first-person account by Nebuchadnezzar. This first-person account has a third-person report of events in the middle of the chapter (Dan 4:16–30 Aramaic; 4:19–33 English). In Daniel 7, "I, Daniel" appears twice (Dan 7:15, 28). In Dan 7:15, this follows the report of the dream he had. Dan 7:28 comes at the end of the story, concluding a chapter that marks the shift from the third-person narrator in the first six chapters of the book (Daniel 1–6) to the first-person narrator in the final half of the book (Daniel 7–12).

There are further usages in Hebrew of the expression "I, Daniel" throughout the rest of the book (Dan 8:1, 15, 27; 9:2; 10:2, 7; 12:5). Similarly, following a third-person introduction in Tob 1:1–2, the first three chapters of Tobit are in the first person and begin with "I, Tobit" (Tob 1:3 in Greek; not preserved in Aramaic fragments of Tobit). While in the Aramaic fragments of Tobit preserved at Qumran only one example of "I, Azar[iah]" is found in 5:13, presumably the formula was used in 1:3 as well. The formula "I, Ahiqar" is used several times in the first-person narrative account of *Ahiqar*. While the above examples are primarily from Aramaic documents, the formula does not seem to be restricted to Aramaic.

The examples found in Ezra indicate the use of the formula "I, *personal name*" to give authority for official speech, as Muraoka suggests. The other examples in Daniel, Tobit, and *Ahiqar*, however, are closer to the *Genesis Apocryphon* and function to introduce first-person accounts of narration as well as direct speech. The formula may introduce a new section of the narrative or indicate a shift of speaker. Instead of calling this a "self-conscious formula" as Muraoka does, I consider it to be more of a "self-introduction" or "self-identification" formula. Whereas third-person narration generally remains anonymous, the identity of the narrator can be made explicit by the use of this formula in first-person narration.

Consistency of First-Person Narration throughout the Scroll

Bernstein has pointed out the third-person anomalies found in each of the three sections of the text. He says that "All three of the extant sections of the Apocryphon employ both first and third person narration."[21] While there are some anomalies, they are not as prevalent as Bernstein suggests. In some cases there may be narration of events in which the patriarch is not personally involved as a participant, but the same narrator still could be speaking.

---

21. Bernstein, "Pseudepigraphy in the Qumran Scrolls," p. 16.

In the better-preserved Abram material, the author has used the first-person forms consistently for about three columns, from col. 19 to 21:22, and then the text shifts entirely to the third person at 21:23–22:34. In the earlier Lamech and Noah materials, there are some cases in which Lamech and Noah are referred to in the third person. However, some of these anomalies might disappear if we had the full text, because if another first-person speaker were talking he or she might refer to Lamech and Noah in the third person. Because of the fragmentary nature of these early columns of the *Genesis Apocryphon*, it is sometimes difficult to know precisely who the "I" is.

In the extant Lamech material, the author seems to be consistent in having Lamech speaking in the first person, with only one instance of Lamech in the third-person singular. In 1QapGen 5:25, one finds "to Lamech, his son," while the following verse again has "I, Lamech." Bernstein says that "the portions of the Lamech segment where he is off-stage, as it were, while the action focuses on his father Enoch and grandfather Methuselah are narrated by an unnamed narrator."[22] The "I, Enoch" (1QapGen 5:1) may be in direct speech since, in the story, Methuselah has been directed to go and visit Enoch, so the report makes sense. It is true, however, that usually the expression "I, personal name" is used by the narrator.

There might have been a book of Enoch here. It is possible that Abram reads to the Egyptians from the book of the words of Enoch (1QapGen 19:25). The reading here is not certain, but Fitzmyer thinks it is likely.[23] Nickelsburg notes that "Noah recounts his own story" (1QapGen 6:2, 6; 7:7; 10:13, 15; 12:3, 8, 10, 13, 15–17, 19).[24] Bernstein quotes Steiner that "the Words of Noah cannot be viewed as Noah's testament" since "there are no second person addresses to Noah's sons, and the recently published columns confirm that assertion."[25] In cols. 6–7, Noah consistently speaks in the first person even when speaking about his birth. Line 8:1 is very fragmentary, and the editors translate "his wife after."[26] If this refers to Noah, it would be an anomaly, but it is difficult to be certain about this. Morgenstern, Qimron, and Sivan have "to Noah at night" in 1QapGen 10:2, but the letters are not certain.[27]

In col. 12 there are no problems. Bernstein thinks that the "he" in "he apportioned to Japhet and to his sons" (1QapGen 16:12) must be Noah. The text here is not that certain, however. 1QapGen 17:15 does seem to have "the portion that his father Noah apportioned to him and gave to him."[28] This is the most problematic text. As for Bernstein's suggestion that there is only one

---

22. Ibid.
23. Fitzmyer, *The Genesis Apocryphon of Qumran*, p. 191.
24. Nickelsburg, "Patriarchs Who Worry about Their Wives," p. 156.
25. Bernstein, "Noah and the Flood at Qumran," p. 207 n. 18.
26. Morgenstern, Qimron, and Sivan, "Hitherto Unpublished Columns," p. 45.
27. Ibid.
28. Ibid., p. 53.

clear reference to Noah in the first person in this section (1QapGen 16:7), this section is largely a geographical description of lands given to his children, so it may be possible that this is the issue here.[29]

In the preserved material about Abraham, the author consistently has the first-account report from 1QapGen 19–21:21 and then shifts entirely to a third-account report in 1QapGen 21:23–22:34. Fitzmyer noted that when one reaches the story of Genesis 14–15 (1QapGen 21:23–22:26) the author shifts to the more biblical third-person report. Fitzmyer reports some proposed explanations that are not too convincing.[30] Since the earlier events of Genesis 14 refer to events that took place some 13 years earlier, it is perhaps not surprising that no claim is made for Abram to speak in the first person here. When one reaches Abram's own time, however, the story continues in the third person. This continues until the end of the book that has been preserved. It is curious that the translation of this material follows the biblical story more closely than earlier sections.

The anomalies in the use of the third person at times for the first-person narrators need explanation. The fragmentary nature of the Lamech and Noah materials make it difficult to come to firm conclusions about these sections. In the Abram materials, however, there is a clear shift from first-person to third-person narrative. This means that first-person accounts seem to be embedded within or are placed beside some other third-person accounts. Still, for the most part, the extensive first-person reports are more prominent than the third-person narrative accounts.

Ways in Which First Person Shapes the Materials

The episodes of the Abram story in the *Genesis Apocryphon* follow the sequence found in the Bible. The following table shows the Genesis texts with corresponding sections of the *Genesis Apocryphon*.

Event	Genesis	Genesis Apocryphon
Going down to Egypt	12:10–20	19:10–20:32
Return to Bethel and separation from Lot	13:1–12	20:33–21:7
Promise to Abram from God concerning the promised land	13:14–18	21:8–22
Lot's captivity and rescue by Abram	14:1–24	21:23–22:26
God's promise to Abram related to a son	15:1–4	22:27–34 (end of text)

Each section is dealt with in different ways. The *Genesis Apocryphon* significantly expands its version of "going down to Egypt" (Gen 12:10–20), while

---

29. Bernstein, "Noah and the Flood at Qumran," p. 228 n. 75.
30. Fitzmyer, *The Genesis Apocryphon of Qumran*, p. 229.

the story of the return to Bethel and separation from Lot (Gen 13:1–12) is summarized more briefly than the biblical text. The *Apocryphon* likewise expands God's promise to Abram concerning promised land (Gen 13:14–18). One finds the first-person report from 1QapGen 19:10–21:22, but then the text shifts to the third-person report in the rest of the scroll.

In order to understand how the author of the *Genesis Apocryphon* uses the first-person narrative, we must look in some detail at particular passages in the *Genesis Apocryphon*. Two texts featuring first-person narrative repay more indepth investigation: the story of going down to Egypt in 1QapGen 19:10–20:32, and the promise to Abram from God concerning promised land in 1QapGen 21:8–22.

Rewriting of Genesis 12:12–20

Nickelsburg notes that the story of Gen 12:10–20 has been expanded "nine times its original size, from approximately 520 characters in the Hebrew Bible to approximately 4,450 in 1QapGen."[31] He notes the many additional narrative details that have reshaped the text. I would like to highlight the changes related to the first person.

Fröhlich makes some helpful comments about what she calls the different types of rhetoric used within the *Genesis Apocryphon*, including narrative, monologue, and dialogue.[32] By "monologue," she means "the reflection of one of the characters of the narrative in the form of a monologue."[33] She has a helpful list of the different sections of the *Genesis Apocryphon* and shows how these correspond to paragraph divisions of the text.[34]

The following chart shows the differences between the Masoretic Text and the *Genesis Apocryphon*. I have attempted to show correspondences between the texts and note particularly the use of narrative and direct speech. The expansions of the *Genesis Apocryphon* can clearly be noted since there are no parallels in the Masoretic Text at this point. The distinction that Fröhlich makes between monologue and dialogue does not seem very helpful because it is difficult to distinguish between a self-report of events and reflection about events. If these are "monologues," they are often very short. In my description, I distinguish between "self-report" for first-person report and "report" for the third-person report. The first term is used to indicate Abram's reports of events in which he is personally involved, and the second term is used for events in which his personal involvement is not certain. In such reports, the narrator's identity is less clear. The inclusion of *vacat* in the chart indicates divisions in the text and whether the *vacat* precedes or follows the text section.

31. Nickelsburg, "Patriarchs Who Worry about Their Wives," p. 147.
32. Fröhlich, "Narrative Exegesis," p. 94.
33. Ibid.
34. Ibid., pp. 89–94.

MT of Genesis 12:10–20	Genesis Apocryphon 19:10–20:32
Third-person narration of going to Egypt, 10–11a	Self-report of going to Egypt—*vacat*, 19:10–13
First-person speech of Abram reflecting concern about being killed because of Sarai, 11b–13	Self-report of dream of Abram (introduced by I, Abram) *vacat*, 19:14–17
	Dialogue between Sarah and Abram (quotes dialogue: Abram, Sarai, Abram) *vacat*, 19:17–21
	Report of Sarai's response to this, 19:21–23
	Self-report of 5 years later about Abram's meeting with three Egyptians—(missing text) description of Sarai's beauty—speech of Egyptians?), 19:23–20:8
Third-person narration of Sarai's being taken, prosperity of Abram, and affliction of Pharaoh, 14–17	Report of Pharaoh's taking Sarai and attempt to kill him, 20:8–9
	Report of Sarai speaking: "He is my brother," 20:10; "I, Abram" used
	Self-report of sorrow; "I, Abram" used, 20:10–11
	Self-report of prayer to God, *vacat*, 20:12–16
	Report of affliction of Pharaoh and that no sexual relations took place for two years, 20:16–18
	Report of Pharaoh's seeking help from plague—no success, 20:18–21
	Lot's speech in response to report of request from Hirkenosh, *vacat*, 20:21–23
	Hirkenosh's speech to Pharaoh concerning Lot's response, *vacat*, 20:24–26
First-person speech of Pharaoh to Abram rebuking him for saying, "She is my sister," telling him to leave, 18–19	First-person speech of Pharaoh to Abram asking why he said, "She is my sister," when she was wife, 20:26–27
Third-person report of Pharaoh's dismissal of Sarai and Abram, 20	(Continuation of speech) instruction to go, 20:27–28
	(Continuation of speech) request that Abram pray for house so could be rid of evil spirit, 20:28

Self-report of prayer and laying on of hands and result of cure 20:28–29

Report of king's swearing an oath that he had not touched her (missing text could allow for direct speech), 20:30

Self-report of Sarai's being brought, and gifts given to her and Hagar, and given guide to lead them out of Egypt, 20:30–32, *vacat*

The Masoretic Text contains only a third-person report of the events. Within this report, two direct quotations use first-person direct speech. The first is by Abram, who speaks to his wife Sarai (Gen 12:11b–13), and the second is by the pharaoh who addresses Abram (Gen 12:19).

It is interesting to compare *Jub.* 13:11–15, which is another retelling of this story. The story is actually shorter than the Masoretic Text, and no direct speech is used at all. The only interest the author seems to have is to add some chronological details to the story, such as, staying in Egypt for five years before Pharaoh takes Sarai, and that Sarai is with Pharaoh for two years. These added details are shared by *Jubilees* and the *Genesis Apocryphon*. Beyond this, however, there is little resemblance between the two rewritten accounts.

In the *Genesis Apocryphon*, the whole text is reported by the first-person Abram 1QapGen (19:14–20:32). While the *Genesis Apocryphon* contains all of the details from Gen 12:10–20, there are many additional details. Some of the expansions to the story relate in various ways to the first-person form. First of all, there is more direct speech not only from Abram and Pharaoh but from Sarai, Lot, Hirkenosh, and probably the three Egyptians as well. Sometimes the speeches are brief, but at other times there is brief dialogue between characters.

Bernstein distinguishes between "internal" and "external" pseudepigrapha.[35] "Internal pseudepigrapha" is a phrase that refers to the insertions of first-person speech within particular works. The term "external pseudepigrapha" means that the whole text is attributed to or connected with a particular speaker. One has both types of pseudepigrapha here. On "internal pseudepigrapha," Bernstein makes the comment, "The retelling and expansion of the biblical story is accomplished more easily, and the narrative rendered more vivid, through the creation and insertion of speeches into the mouths of characters."[36]

Bernstein thinks that "internal pseudepigrapha" is not "authoritative" but is "convenient pseudepigrapha," which does not make a claim to the authority of the person speaking but simply is used as a means of retelling the story

---

35. Bernstein, "Pseudepigraphy in the Qumran Scrolls," p. 7.
36. Ibid., p. 10.

in a new way. While this may be partly correct, a first-person account can be viewed by the reader as having a certain authority that a third-person account cannot have. Savran suggests that "from the standpoint of objectivity such speech is considered far more reliable by the reader because it is free of the kind of narrative interference or bias that inevitably accompanies indirect speech or summary."[37] In reality, of course, the narrator is in control of the dialogue. Furthermore, Bernstein correctly observes that the writer of the *Genesis Apocryphon* is not trying to promote a particular revelation or *halakic* understanding, which some might claim when they attribute a document to Enoch or Moses.

Direct speech and more details of actions of characters allow for further character development. The characters are quite undeveloped in the biblical account. Nickelsburg has pointed out that there is a certain psychologizing interest in the *Genesis Apocryphon*. There is interest "in the character's emotions and expression of these emotions."[38] Abram is frightened after his dream (1QapGen 19:18) and cries when Sarai is taken (1QapGen 20:10, 12, 16). Sarai cries and is frightened as well when Abram warns her of problems in Egypt (1QapGen 19:21, 23). Sarai is more developed as a character in that she has a short dialogue with her husband and protects her husband when the pharaoh is ready to kill him. The poem in honor of her beauty (and her wisdom) highlights her importance in the story. When the pharaoh hears about her beauty, he desires her. Two new characters are introduced in the story: Lot and Hirkenosh, who function as intermediaries between Abram and Pharaoh.

As a first-person account, it reflects, as Nickelsburg says, "the husband's point of view and focuses on his expressed anxiety" about his wife.[39] One expects that a first-person account will provide further personal details about events. Some of the additional details of the story fit this perspective: a dream warning him about the future, a discussion with his wife about the matter, his grieving about his wife and crying, his prayer to God for help for himself, his prayer for the pharaoh, and the report of the king swearing an oath to him. These details are consistent with a first-person account of the events.

One problem, however, of the shift to the first person is that eyewitnesses can usually only know of events in which they are personally involved. When one finds a report of events in which the narrator is not personally involved, it is hard to know whether one should designate this a first- or third-person narrative. Sometimes a third-person narrator can speak about events that no human being could possibly know. This is referred to as the omniscience of the narrator.[40] There are examples of reports in this story that do not involve Abram personally. There is a report about the affliction of Pharaoh and the

---

37. Savran, *Telling and Retelling*, p. 77.
38. Nickelsburg, "Patriarchs Who Worry about Their Wives," p. 148.
39. Ibid., p. 152.
40. Gunn and Fewel, *Narrative in the Hebrew Bible*, pp. 52–53.

fact that no sexual relations took place in two years (1QapGen 20:16–18). This is followed by the report of Pharaoh's seeking help concerning the plague with no success (1QapGen 20:18–21). Although the earlier dream provides Abram with some knowledge of the future, no explanation is given about how he knows what is happening in the court and even the bedroom of Pharaoh.

There has probably been some influence from the parallel passage of the danger to the ancestress in Gen 20:1–28, where the king is Abimelech of Gerar rather than Pharaoh. There, a dream comes to Abimelech in Gen 20:3, which may parallel a dream of the Pharaoh in 1QapGen 20:22. Similarly, a dream comes to Abram in 1QapGen 19:14–17. Abraham's prayer for the healing of Abimelech in Gen 20:7, 17 seems to be paralleled by Abram praying for the pharaoh in 1QapGen 20:28. Fitzmyer points out that many later traditions have both Sarai and Abram praying for help.[41]

Additions may be made in various places in the texts, but some types of expansion seem very popular and appear in manuscripts copied by scribes, as well as literary refashionings of texts. Some of these are already used within biblical texts. We have already mentioned the use of direct speech rather than simply reported speech. Not only can an author use direct speech by the characters but he or she may expand speeches that are already found in texts. Details from parallel texts may be used to clarify other texts.

Beyond this, one may note silences in the biblical text that beg for explanation. A brief detail, such as the mention of the Egyptians' noting the beauty of Sarai and praising her beauty to the pharaoh (Gen 12:14–15), becomes an opportunity for a delightful meeting of Abram with three Egyptians and their subsequent lengthy praise of Sarai's beauty. Fitzmyer comments, "Here it has all the characteristics of an insertion that is not really an essential part of the story."[42] The insertion makes the story more interesting to the reader. Nickelsburg has pointed out what he thinks is an eroticizing interest of the writer.[43] This too could serve to make the story more entertaining for the reader. The praise of Sarai here may seem to be overdone, but the poem does carry along the story and enhances it.

It could be argued that the changes to the story come less from the use of first person than from the content of the additions. Still the added details and portions must find a place within the text. Where and how are insertions made to a previously existing text? Fröhlich has suggested three different rhetorical forms used by authors: narrative, dialogue, monologue.[44] How and in what ways do authors explain things to the reader? Often, a monologue in direct speech can be used for this. A separate narrator does not need to be used if characters take up the narration.

---

41. Fitzmyer, *The Genesis Apocryphon of Qumran*, p. 201.
42. Ibid., p. 197.
43. Nickelsburg, "Patriarchs Who Worry about Their Wives," p. 148.
44. Fröhlich, "Narrative Exegesis," p. 94.

In addition to the influences from parallel stories in Genesis, the *Genesis Apocryphon* is likewise shaped like a court tale in Daniel. Nickelsburg has noted that "the author is recasting the biblical patriarch in the mold of Daniel."[45] There is a dream that is interpreted by Abram. There is a court contest to heal Pharaoh, but only Abram can do this. Abram even reads the book of *Enoch* to them and instructs them. A beautiful Jewish woman becomes an object of beauty to the men of the story. Sarah might be compared with Susanna or Esther, but Abram is still the dominant character. Lange reads the story as a wisdom tale.[46]

Rewriting of Genesis 13:14–18

The narrator of the *Genesis Apocryphon* uses a short report of divine speech to Abram with a short response by Abram (Gen 13:14–18) and expands it by providing additional details (1QapGen 21:8–22). This speech is set within a dream and is divided into two parts, each followed by a compliance by Abram to the instructions given by God. At the end Abram invites three men over for lunch, an episode that anticipates their role in the next story. The following chart helps show the differences.

Third-person narrative (Genesis 13:14–18)	*First-person narrative* (Genesis Apocryphon 21:8–22)
Third-person report of speech of the LORD to Abram, 13:14–17	Self-report of night vision with speech of God, *vacat* 21:8–10
• *Command*: look in all directions at land, 13:14–15	• *Command*: Go up to Ramath-Hazor and look at land, 21:8–10
	Self-report of compliance by Abram, 21:10–12
• *Promise* of giving land, 13:16	Direct speech of God to Abram, 21:12–14, *vacat*
• *Command*: walk around land, 13:17	
	• *Promise* + *command*
Third-person report of Abram's response, 13:18	Self-report of compliance by Abram, 21:15–22, *vacat*, introduced by "I, Abram"
• Moving tent and building an altar	• Traveling around land and building an altar; inviting 3 for a meal

The narrator of the *Genesis Apocryphon* gives more details than are found in the Masoretic Text. While the Masoretic Text focuses on the words of the divine speech with the aspect of promise, 1QapGen focuses on the obedience of Abram in carrying out the commands of the deity. Abram must travel to the highest mountain around if he is going to see the land. The report of

---

45. Nickelsburg, "Patriarchs Who Worry about Their Wives," p. 149.
46. Lange, "1QGenAp XIX10–XX32."

Abram's moving his tent in the Masoretic Text (Gen 13:18) seems an inadequate response to the deity's instructions that he should walk about the land, especially in light of 1QapGen, where Abram walks all around the land. The vagueness in the Masoretic Text is clarified in terms of the boundaries of land.

Jub. 13:19–21 follows the Masoretic Text closely here. It retains the first-person speech of God but without the compliance that is found in the *Genesis Apocryphon*. Fitzmyer has noted that the directions given to Moses vary in each tradition: Gen 13:14 presents the order of God's instructions as north, south, east, west: *Jub.* 13:9 organizes them as north, south, west, east; and the *Genesis Apocryphon* designates them east, west, south, north.[47]

Is there anything personal that the first-person narrator records about himself here that would not be possible for a third-person narrator? Fitzmyer says, "Abram acts out the part of the owner-lord; he surveys it all with a circular glance; he tours it all on foot."[48] There is a certain realism here that makes more sense than the MT. If someone offers you some land, it is unimaginable that you would not want to look it over and walk around it. Fitzmyer further observes that "walking around the land is a symbolic way of taking possession of it."[49] Furthermore, since the vision is given at night, Abram must wait until the next morning to see the land. In this sense, Abram's response seems quite reasonable. Of course, what is unimaginable is the extent and size of this allotment. How can one see that far? How can one walk that far? This seems quite unrealistic.

Abram says nothing in this encounter with God. It is hard to get any sense of what he is thinking other than that he must obey God when he speaks to him, without question or response. There is little that is personal between Abram and God. Of course, Abram had seen God in a dream initially. The second speech that comes from God arrives with no introduction. The personal notes come at the end when Abram indicates that he came home safely and found everyone of his household also safe. Following the building of an altar and the offering of praise to God, Abram invited three men—Mamre, Arnem, and Eshcol—over for a meal, a bond that foreshadows their role in the next story, when they join Abram in war.

Attention to Abram's compliance at this point parallels the actions of Moses in Deuteronomy 32 and 34 related to the land. In Deut 32:48–52 God instructs Moses to look at the land before he dies. This is followed by the testament of Moses in Deut 33:1–29. The compliance of Moses then appears in Deut 34:1–3, where Moses climbs up Mount Nebo and looks out at the land. Moses does not see as much as Abram does on his looking out from Ramoth Hazor. In Deut 34:4, there is a repetition of the promise as a divine speech.

---

47. Fitzmyer, *Genesis Apocryphon of Qumran*, p. 221.
48. Ibid.
49. Ibid., p. 224.

While there is little character development here in the *Apocryphon*, it provides a more satisfactory account of Abram's compliance to God's commands. Abram here serves as a model of obedience. The text also highlights the geographical boundaries of the promised land. What is left rather vague in the Hebrew texts of both the Masoretic Text and *Jubilees* is expanded here. Even God's instructions are clearer, because he tells Moses to go up to Ramoth Hazor to look around the land. This is the highest place near Abram's dwelling that could provide a good vantage point for surveying the land.[50]

Questions of Genre and "First Person"

The question of the genre of the *Genesis Apocryphon* relates to more than the question of the "first-person" character of the book, but our interest here is in asking how and in what ways the "first-person" character of the book can help us better understand the genre of the book.

Sources for Book

An important initial question is whether the first-person character of the book arose from the sources used by the author of the *Genesis Apocryphon* or whether the shift from third to first person was made by this author. Complicating this question is that the sources available seem to vary throughout the book.

The earlier sections of the text relating to Lamech (cols. 1–5) refer to stories that clearly are not part of the Masoretic Text, since Scripture contains only three relevant verses, which appear in a genealogical list of Cain's descendants. The story in the *Genesis Apocryphon* about Lamech's concern about the patrimony of his son Noah and his seeking insight from Enoch via his father, Methuselah, that the child is not a child of one of the Watchers has a close parallel in *1 Enoch* 105–6. One interesting difference between the two accounts is that, in the book of *Enoch*, the first-person narrator is Enoch while in the *Genesis Apocryphon* the first-person narrator is Lamech. The "I" of the book of *Enoch* is essential to provide authority for the contents of the book including eschatological information that Enoch reveals to the people. Having Lamech as the first-person narrator seems more appropriate for narrating this story as a concerned father. In the book of *Enoch*, Enoch can know about what is happening to Lamech because it is revealed to him, while Lamech must seek wisdom from Enoch by asking him for help.

In the Noah and Abram materials, there are parallels to both Genesis and *Jubilees*. Neither the Masoretic Text nor *Jubilees* was written with the first-person singular for the main characters. Once one reaches the Abram materials in the *Apocryphon*, there is considerable interaction with the biblical stories, and here one has more of a rewritten Bible. Toward the end of the Abram materials, the text becomes closer and closer to the Masoretic Text

---

50. Ibid., p. 220.

and is more like a free targum with some additions. At this point, one also returns to the third-person report, as in the Hebrew Bible.

Many scholars, such as Fitzmyer, argue that the *Genesis Apocryphon* was dependent on *Jubilees* and *1 Enoch*.[51] Concerning the use of the first person, the best antecedent here would be *1 Enoch*, although one can see that even this usage is shifted from Enoch to Lamech in the *Genesis Apocryphon*. Thus the most obvious sources for the text cannot adequately explain the use of the first person in the *Genesis Apocryphon*. It seems more likely that the author of the *Genesis Apocryphon* revised the sources in order to produce at least three first-person narratives.

Translation

Since *Enoch* was written in Aramaic, in cases of close parallels between the *Genesis Apocryphon* and *Enoch*, the author of the *Genesis Apocryphon* may have simply edited or revised an Aramaic text. Since *Jubilees* was written in Hebrew, use of it would have involved a translation into Aramaic. Similarly the biblical text of Genesis had to be translated into Aramaic. It is certainly possible that Aramaic translations of Genesis may have been available in either oral or written forms. The Hebrew biblical text used was probably from a Palestinian form of the text, possibly already fuller than the MT Babylonian form.

In an article entitled "The Textual Affinities of the Biblical Citations in the *Genesis Apocryphon*," VanderKam argues that the *Genesis Apocryphon* seems to be using a Palestinian text very similar to the one used by the author of *Jubilees*.[52] According to Cross's theory of local texts, this text was the basis of the later Samaritan Pentateuch. While there are many features of this text, it is characterized by "orthographic corrections and harmonizations with parallel texts elsewhere found in the Pentateuch."[53]

Fitzmyer has compared the translational technique of the *Genesis Apocryphon* to the classical targums.[54] Sometimes the *Genesis Apocryphon* does present a word-for-word translation of the Hebrew text of Genesis. Fitzmyer concludes, however, by saying that "it is evident that the *Genesis Apocryphon*, though a literal translation of the Hebrew text in places or in isolated phrases, is more frequently a paraphrase of the biblical text."[55]

Rewritten Bible

A group of texts called "Reworked Pentateuch"—4Q158, 4Q364–367—are known as word-for-word translations of passages of the Pentateuch with small additions, harmonizing of parallel texts, and rearranging of materials. It is

---

51. Fitzmyer, *Genesis Apocryphon of Qumran*, pp. 20–21.
52. VanderKam, "The Textual Affinities of the Biblical Citations," p. 47.
53. VanderKam and Flint, *The Meaning of the Dead Sea Scrolls*, p. 143.
54. Fitzmyer, *Genesis Apocryphon of Qumran*, pp. 38–45.
55. Ibid., p. 43.

difficult to know if such texts should be considered scribal copying of biblical texts along the lines of the Palestinian text or a "Rewritten Bible."[56] The issue of shift to the first person, however, does not seem to be central in most instances except for some occasional additional first-person speeches. There may be an inserted dialogue between Rebecca and Isaac in 4Q364 3 ii as reported by Bernstein.[57]

Vermes in his classic work *Scripture and Tradition*, classifies the *Genesis Apocryphon* as a rewritten Bible and provides many details in which midrashic tendencies similar to those found in this book appear in later texts.[58] He sees the *Genesis Apocryphon* as one of the earliest and purest forms of this genre.[59] He argues that the writer of this document does not have a desire "to graft upon the biblical story doctrines sometimes foreign to them."[60] Instead, "The author of GA does indeed try, by every means at his disposal, to make the biblical story more attractive, more real, more edifying, and above all more intelligible."[61] Vermes later says, "His technique is simple and he exercises no scholarly learning, no exegetical virtuosity, no play on words."[62] While Vermes intends this to be understood as praise, one might wonder if it is an accurate assessment. Vermes does not comment much on the first-person usage in the book, but it is this first-person usage that in part contributes to the very characteristics that Vermes finds so charming in the book.

Alexander discusses four case studies as he examines components of the rewritten Bible genre: *Jubilees, Genesis Apocryphon*, Josephus's *Jewish Antiquities*, and Pseudo-Philo's *Liber Antiquitatum Biblicarum*.[63] *Jubilees* is understood to have been revealed to Moses by the angel of the presence, and this setting is reinforced throughout the text. Alexander notes that "the narrative is regularly punctuated by first-person interventions by the angel, and passages in the second-person addressed by the angel to Moses."[64] In this case the "I" indicates revelation and would establish the authority of the text. In contrast to this, Alexander says that since the *Genesis Apocryphon* is in Aramaic it allows for "greater distinctness from the biblical text, and avoids the risk of confusing it with Scripture. It is probable that the *Genesis Apocryphon*, unlike Jubilees, made no exalted claims to divine inspiration."[65] Although Alexander notes the use of the first person in the *Genesis Apocryphon*, he does not comment on any significance of this.

---

56. VanderKam and Flint, *The Meaning of the Dead Sea Scrolls*, pp. 210–11.
57. Bernstein, "Pseudepigraphy in the Qumran Scrolls," p. 11.
58. Vermes, *Scripture and Tradition*, pp. 96–126.
59. Ibid., p. 124.
60. Ibid., pp. 124–25.
61. Ibid., p. 125.
62. Ibid., p. 126.
63. Alexander, "Retelling the Old Testament," pp. 99–121.
64. Ibid., p. 100.
65. Ibid., p. 104.

Pseudepigrapha

Nickelsburg sees more significance in the use of the first person. He observes, "This suggests that the scroll presented itself as a collection of extracts from a Book of Lamech, A Book of Noah, and Abram."[66] Later he says, "Thus, the events in Genesis are presented to the reader in a new form, recited by the central characters in various sections of its narrative."[67] He is convinced that this form is related to the dependency on the book of *Jubilees*. While the book of *Jubilees* does not present the main characters speaking in the first-person singular, it uses the "first-person plural," which "founds its authority on the claim that it was dictated to Moses by 'us angels of the presence.'"[68] He sees the movement in this way: "the anonymous text of Genesis, believed to be Mosaic in Hellenistic times, is recast into the explicitly Mosaic narrative of Jubilees, ascribed more basically to the angels of the presence."[69] He suggests, then, "On the one hand the Apocryphon moves away from the angelic revelation of Jubilees (which provides authority for its halakah); on the other hand, it provides reliability for its narrative by placing it on the lips of the characters themselves."[70] While this is an interesting idea, one wonders if the *Genesis Apocryphon* does not shift authority away from Moses to the individual patriarchs as well. While it removes the anonymity of Genesis, it does so in a way quite different from the book of *Jubilees*.

Nickelsburg points out other texts that use first-person-singular narrative: Aramaic Levi texts, 4Q537 Jacob, 4Q538 Judah, and 4Q215 Naphtali. *4 Maccabees* is a first-person wisdom text. The *Prayer of Manasseh* is a first-person prayer. Others include 4Q439 Last Words of Joseph, 4Q542 Last Words of Kohath, 4Q543–48 Visions of Amram, 4Q213–14 Aramaic Levi, and 4Q540–41 Apocryphon of Levi[a–b?]. The testamentary genre uses the "first-person form" but such a form is not restricted to testaments, as Nickelsburg notes. The first-person narrator also appears in such works as Tobit and *1 Enoch*, which he suggests are influenced by the testamentary genre.[71] The testaments of Tobit use the first person in 4:1–20 and 14:3–11.

Bernstein has a helpful article on different types of *pseudepigraphy*.[72] He uses the term to mean "composing texts or portions of texts which are placed into the mouths of ancient figures."[73] Bernstein characterizes the *pseudepigraphy* of the *Genesis Apocryphon* as an example of "convenient pseudepigraphy" instead of "authoritative pseudepigraphy" or "decorative pseudepigraphy." He suggests:[74]

66. Nickelsburg, "Patriarchs Who Worry about Their Wives," p. 156.
67. Ibid.
68. Ibid., p. 157.
69. Ibid.
70. Ibid.
71. Ibid.
72. Bernstein, "Pseudepigraphy in the Qumran Scrolls."
73. Ibid., p. 3.
74. Ibid., p. 10

The goal of convenient pseudepigraphy is, in this case, obvious. The retelling and expansion of the biblical story is accomplished more easily, and the narrative rendered more vivid, through the creation and insertion of speeches into the mouths of characters. At an early stage of biblical exegesis, before the development of the commentary form, rewriting offered one of the few literary options for interpretation.

The first person can be used in a number of genres and literary forms. It appears in direct discourse in narrative, testaments, memoirs and autobiographical reports, apocalypses, wisdom instructions, farewell discourses, didactic addresses to students, prayers, and vision or dream reports. Many of these genres exist within the Bible. During the Hellenistic period, many texts were "attributed to figures appearing in the Old Testament (Adam, Enoch, Abraham, Moses, etc.)"[75] which became known as Old Testament Pseudepigrapha. The first person was commonly used in such pseudepigrapha. The use of the first person in the *Genesis Apocryphon* belongs to this larger movement. Such pseudepigrapha may be written in Hebrew or Aramaic, but a number of Aramaic Qumran documents share this feature.

Conclusion

The surviving fragments and columns of the *Genesis Apocryphon* contain rewritten stories of Lamech, Noah, and Abram that follow the biblical story but add many embellishments. One of the interesting changes made in this rewritten Bible is the use of the first-person narrative accounts of each of the major characters: Lamech, Noah, and Abram. Not only this, but there is additional direct speech within the stories in which other speakers also use the first person.

Since there is a shift from first-person narrator throughout the scroll and the first person is used in direct speech within the narratives, the composer of the *Genesis Apocryphon* had to use a variety of means to indicate shifts from one speaker to another. Clear identification of speakers is necessary when there are shifts. Small and larger divisions in the text are indicated with the use of the *vacat*. At least one heading, "Book of Noah," seems now evident, and there may have been other ones throughout the text. The use of "I" with personal name appears sporadically throughout the text, sometimes to indicate new sections of the narrative and sometimes to help identify the narrator or speaker.

In the better-preserved Abram materials, the first-person narrative from Abram is found in 1QapGen 19–21:22, and then the third person is used in 1QapGen 21:23–22:34. There are some anomalies of the use of third-person narrative in the earlier materials related to Lamech and Noah that are much more fragmentary. The meaning of these anomalies is not certain.

75. Collins, "Apocrypha and Pseudepigrapha," p. 35.

In this essay, attention has been given to describing how this shaping of the stories has taken place. While some overall comments have been made, special attention has been given to two units that are rewritten: versions of Gen 12:10–20 and 13:14–20. These two examples show how the author of the *Genesis Apocryphon* has rewritten the biblical text. One of the methods that he uses is the first-person narrative voice, which adds credence to additional inserted materials. The first-person narrative allows the stories to be more personal, and sometimes the feelings of Abram are indicated, such as his concern about his wife and his prayer on her behalf. Abram's abilities as interpreter of dreams and exorcist are emphasized in the story of going down to Egypt in 1QapGen 19:10–20:32. In the promise to Abram from God concerning the promised land in 1QapGen 21:8–22, Abram faithfully follows the specific commands given by God. The narrative attempts to personalize the stories and to make them more entertaining. Sometimes questions raised by the Hebrew text are clarified by additional details.

In terms of the genre of the book and the use of the "first person," it is helpful to consider the book a translation, a rewritten Bible, and a pseudepigraphic work. There are no clear antecedents in any known sources that use the "first-person narrative" in precisely the same way, even though there are helpful parallels in the books of *Jubilees* and *1 Enoch*. While there is more direct speech from the three speakers of the *Genesis Apocryphon* than one finds in the Hebrew Bible, *Jubilees*, or *1 Enoch*, there are no long speeches or spoken revelations.

As Bernstein has shown, pseudepigraphy is a widespread phenomenon found in many texts written during Hellenistic times. His three categories of "authoritative," "convenient," and "decorative" pseudepigraphy are helpful. The use of the first-person narrative in the *Genesis Apocryphon* does not seem to be purely "authoritative," in the sense that some narratives are. Still, the category "convenient" seems to fall short of the *Genesis Apocryphon* as well. Abram as a character is developed more than in the biblical text, and he becomes a faithful model of appropriate behavior. He not only is the recipient of divine promises but responds appropriately to those promises. The *Genesis Apocryphon* provides another example of a pseudepigraphic work that is also an Aramaic paraphrase of a biblical text and is also a rewritten Bible.

I hope that this essay has provided some progress in addressing the issues that Nickelsburg raised concerning the first-person narrative of the book. This analysis needs to be applied to each literary unit of the book. A similar analysis would need to be done with other pseudepigraphic texts so that parallels could be drawn more carefully.

Bibliography

Alexander, P. "Retelling the Old Testament." Pp. 99–121 in *It Is Written—Scripture Citing Scripture: Essays in Honour of Barnabus, Lindars*. Edited by D. A. Carson and H. G. M. Williamson. Cambridge: Cambridge University Press, 1988.

Avigad, N., and Y. Yadin. *A Genesis Apocryphon: A Scroll from the Wilderness of Judaea: Description and Contents of the Scroll, Facsimiles, Transcription, and Translation of Columns II, XIX–XXII*. Jerusalem: Magnes and Heikhal Ha-Sefer, 1956.

Bernstein, M. J. "Noah and the Flood at Qumran." Pp. 199–231 in *The Provo International Conference on the Dead Sea Scrolls: Technological Innovations, New Texts and Reformulated Issues*. Edited by D. W. Parry and E. Ulrich. STDJ 30. Leiden: Brill, 1999.

———. "Pseudepigraphy in the Qumran Scrolls: Categories and Functions." Pp. 1–26 in *Pseudepigraphical Perspectives—The Apocrypha and Pseudepigrapha in Light of the Dead Sea Scrolls: Proceedings of the International Symposium of the Orion Center for the Study of the Dead Sea Scrolls and Associated Literature, 12–14 January, 1997*. Edited by E. G. Chazon and M. E. Stone. Leiden: Brill, 1999.

Collins, J. "Apocrypha and Pseudepigrapha." Pp. 35–39 in vol. 1 of *Encyclopedia of the Dead Sea Scrolls*. Edited by Lawrence Schiffman and James C. VanderKam. New York: Oxford University Press, 2000.

Evans, C. A. "The Genesis Apocryphon and the Rewritten Bible." *Revue de Qumran* 13 (1988) 153–65.

Fitzmyer, J. A. *The Genesis Apocryphon of Qumran Cave I (1Q20): A Commentary*. 3rd ed. Biblica et Orientalia 18/B. Rome: Pontifical Biblical Institute, 2004.

Fröhlich, I. "'Narrative Exegesis' in the Dead Sea Scrolls." Pp. 81–99 in *Biblical Perspectives—Early Use and Interpretation of the Bible in Light of the Dead Sea Scrolls: Proceedings of the First International Symposium of the Orion Center for the Study of the Dead Sea Scrolls and Associated Literature, 12–14 May 1996*. Edited by M. Stone and E. Chazon. Leiden: Brill, 1998.

Greenfield, J. C., and E. Qimron. "The Genesis Apocryphon Column XII." *Abr-Nahrain* Supplement 3 (1992) 70–77.

Gunn, D., and D. N. Fewell. *Narrative in the Hebrew Bible*. New York: Oxford University Press, 1993.

Lange, A. "1QGenAp XIX 10–XX 32 as Paradigm of the Wisdom Didactive Narrative." Pp. 191–204 in *Qumranstudien: Vorträge und Beiträge der Teilnehmer des Qumranseminars auf dem internationalen Treffen der Society of biblical Literature, Münster, 25.–26. Juli 1993*. Edited by H.-J. Fabry et al. Göttingen: Vandenhoeck & Ruprecht, 1996.

Morgenstern, M.; E. Qimron; and D. Sivan. "The Hitherto Unpublished Columns of the Genesis Apocryphon." *Abr-Nahrain* 33 (1995) 30–54.

Muraoka, T. "Notes on the Aramaic of the Genesis Apocryphon." *Revue de Qumran* 8 (1972–75) 7–51.

Nickelsburg, G. W. E. "Patriarchs Who Worry about Their Wives: A Haggadic Tendency in the Genesis Apocryphon." Pp. 137–58 in *Biblical Perspectives—Early Use and Interpretation of the Bible in the Light of the Dead Sea Scrolls: Proceedings of the First International Symposium of the Orion Center for the Study of the Dead Sea Scrolls and Associated Literature, 12–14 May, 1996*. Edited by M. E. Stone and E. G. Chazon. Leiden: Brill, 1998.

Savran, G. *Telling and Retelling: Quotation in Biblical Narrative.* Indiana Studies in Biblical Literature. Bloomington: Indiana University Press, 1988.
Steiner, R. "The Heading of the *Book of the Words of Noah* on a Fragment of the Genesis Apocryphon." *Dead Sea Discoveries* 2 (1995) 66–71.
Trever, J. C. "Identification of the Aramaic Fourth Scroll from ʿAin Feshka." *Bulletin of the American Schools of Oriental Research* 115 (1949) 8–10.
VanderKam, J. "The Textual Affinities of the Biblical Citations in the *Genesis Apocryphon*." *JBL* 97 (1978) 45–55.
———, and P. Flint. *The Meaning of the Dead Sea Scrolls: Their Significance for Understanding the Bible, Judaism, Jesus, and Christianity.* San Francisco: HarperSanFrancisco, 2002.
Vermes, G. *Scripture and Tradition in Judaism: Haggadic Studies.* Leiden: Brill, 1961.
Walsh, J. *Style and Structure in Biblical Hebrew Narrative.* Collegeville, MN: Liturgical Press, 2001.

Syntactic Double Translation in the *Targumim*

Michael Carasik

It is by now a commonplace to speak of "double" translation in the Aramaic targums of the Hebrew Bible. In its simplest form, this involves "the rendition of a single verb or noun by a translational doublet."[1] In fact, the phenomenon is broader than the translation of single words. Michael Klein has focused on one important aspect of the larger phenomenon. He notes that many biblical phrases and longer passages are duplicated or even triplicated, in comparable but not identical language. "The targumim, in many of these cases, equalize the varying texts by translating one of them in conformity with the other—or, less frequently, by altering both versions in a mutually complementary fashion."[2] But double translation is not restricted to this process of equalization. More often, as Martin McNamara points out, "The point in the double rendering may have been the targumist's desire to bring out the wealth of the [Hebrew text]."[3] One example appears at the very beginning of Targum Neofiti, where the Hebrew word בראשית of Gen 1:1 is translated "From the beginning with wisdom"—that is, once literally and again understanding the word in a midrashic sense based on Prov 8:22.[4]

This essay will focus on an aspect of targumic double translation that has not yet been recognized.[5] I call this particular technique "syntactic double translation." The basis behind this technique is the recognition, found already in Tannaitic literature, that some verses in the Hebrew Bible can be grammatically parsed in more than one way. In such cases, the targum sometimes

---

1. Klein, "Associative and Complementary Translation," p. 138*.
2. Ibid., p. 134*. In fact, the biblical text itself is often the result of the phenomenon that Klein describes. See Talmon, "Synonymous Readings"; idem, "Textual Study."
3. McNamara, *Neofiti 1: Genesis*, p. 30.
4. Ibid., p. 52. For the Proverbs link, see Rashi's commentary, ad loc.
5. Grossfeld (*Neofiti I: Genesis*, p. xxxiii) includes "Clarification of difficult Hebrew syntax or lexicography" as #13 in his list of 22 causes of "syntactic expansion"; but see his comment to Gen 49:6–7, cited below.

translates in accordance with *both* possibilities. In what follows, I will describe this phenomenon and speculate on its implications by looking at a series of biblical passages and their targumic renderings.

Song of Songs 2:12

Let us begin by considering syntactic double translation through the lens of the phenomenon to which Cyrus Gordon gave the name *Janus parallelism*.[6] What Gordon meant by the term is that a word seems to carry one meaning if read with what precedes it and a different meaning when read with what follows it. It is a "Janus" word in that it means something different when it faces backward than it does when it faces forward. Gordon's example, which has become the classic one, is Song 2:12:

הַנִּצָּנִים נִרְאוּ בָאָרֶץ   עֵת הַזָּמִיר הִגִּיעַ   וְקוֹל הַתּוֹר נִשְׁמַע בְּאַרְצֵנוּ׃

The middle word of the middle phrase of this line, זמיר, can mean either "pruning" or "singing."[7] We have, then, "the time of זמיר has arrived," with no clue but context as to what it means. Having read "the blossoms appear in the land," the reader is thinking along botanical lines and takes זמיר at first to mean "pruning." But when one continues by reading "and the voice of the turtledove is heard in our land," with its reference to birdsong, one retroactively rereads זמיר as singing. Both meanings serve a function in the line and in the poem from which it is taken, and both were undoubtedly intended by the author of the poem.[8]

Psalms 93:1

In the previous example, it is meaning only, not syntax, that alters. Syntactically, it is clear that the phrase is to be interpreted as "the time of *zamir* has come," and the only question is what זמיר means. But there are other cases where it is not the meaning, but the syntax, that is potentially two-faced. Ps 93:1 provides an example:[9]

---

6. The term was originally coined in Gordon, "New Directions," p. 59. He subsequently (at the suggestion of Paul Friedrich) sharpened the term by calling it *Asymmetric Janus Parallelism* (Gordon, "Asymmetric Janus parallelism," 80* and 81* n. 4; Song 2:12 is discussed here as well). But the shorter phrase continues to be more commonly used. My thanks to Theodore A. Perry for pointing out to me the connection between Janus parallelism and double syntactic translation, and for bibliographical assistance.

7. According to *HALOT*, זמר I and II, the two meanings come from two different original Proto-Semitic roots, "singing" from *zmr* and "pruning" from *zbr*.

8. Edward Greenstein of Tel Aviv University, at the conference "Remembering H. L. Ginsberg" in New York City on April 28, 2004, proclaimed "Greenstein's law": "If a word can mean A or it can mean B, it means both until proven otherwise."

9. I have added an upper and a lower set of brackets to the verse to demonstrate the two different ways in which the phrase can be parsed. I first learned this example in a class taught by Stephen Geller at Brandeis University. Geller refers to this phenomenon as an

יְ-הֹ֭ ¹⁰ מָלָךְ֮ גֵּא֪וּת לָ֫בֵ֥שׁ לָבֵ֣שׁ יְ֭-הֹ [עֹ֣ז] הִתְאַזָּ֑ר אַף־תִּכּ֥וֹן תֵּ֝בֵ֗ל בַּל־תִּמּֽוֹט׃

The LORD has become king, He has donned majesty . . . the very world is made firm, never to totter.

It is the phrase לבש י-ה עז התאזר that causes the difficulty here. The standard usage of the verb לבש in the Qal is that it demands an accusative of the garment that is put on, as at the beginning of the verse: "He has donned majesty." The natural way to continue reading, then, is לבש י-ה עז, "The Lord has donned might." The Masoretic punctuation marks here, however, mark י-ה with a disjunctive accent, and group עז, "might," together with התאזר, the verb that follows it: "With might has He girded Himself." Though the word עז appears only once, we read it twice, first as the end of one phrase and again as the beginning of the next. Here, unlike our first example, the meaning of the word stays the same, but it is *syntactically* reread, again with the result that the verse packs two meanings where only one seems to be written. Again, it is likely that this is a deliberate effect.

This kind of effect is the bane of translators. The NJPSV translates our phrase, following the Masoretic punctuation marks, as follows: "the LORD is robed, He is girded with strength," ignoring the usual use of לבש and eliminating the first of the possible readings of the verse.[11] The KJV is just slightly more successful: "the LORD is clothed with strength, wherewith he hath girded himself." Here עז is translated twice, once as one would naturally interpret it at first reading, syntactically related to what precedes it ("the LORD is clothed with strength"), and again a second time, as a relative pronoun, following the Masoretic accents ("wherewith he hath girded himself").

Exodus 17:9

A passage from the Mekhilta de Rabbi Ishmael, the Tannaitic midrash to Exodus, recognizes explicitly that there are five verses in the Pentateuch that are syntactically "undecided" in this fashion.[12] Here, for example, is Exod 17:9:

וַיֹּ֨אמֶר מֹשֶׁ֤ה אֶל־יְהוֹשֻׁ֙עַ֙ [בְּחַר־לָ֣נוּ אֲנָשִׁ֔ים וְצֵ֖א הִלָּחֵ֣ם בַּעֲמָלֵ֑ק] מָחָ֗ר אָנֹכִ֤י נִצָּב֙ עַל־רֹ֣אשׁ הַגִּבְעָ֔ה וּמַטֵּ֥ה הָאֱלֹהִ֖ים בְּיָדִֽי׃

---

example of "X-Y-X," since the Y term makes sense in either direction, but the three terms together do not.

10. For religious reasons, I will transcribe the Tetragrammaton euphemistically in this article.

11. *Tanakh: The Holy Scriptures* (Philadelphia: Jewish Publication Society, 1985). This is the "new" JPS version in relation to an older translation published by the same organization in 1917.

12. *Mekhilta de-Rabbi Ishmael* Amalek 1, to Exod 17:9 (Horovitz-Rabin ed. p. 179, Lauterbach ed. 2:142–43). The five are Gen 4:7, 49:6–7; Exod 17:9, 25:34 (= 37:20); and Deut 31:16. They are listed as well in *b. Yoma* 52b.

If we forget about the Masoretic markings on the verse (which were of course not in existence at the time the rabbinic passage was formulated), this can be translated in either one of two ways:

1. Pick us some men and go out to fight Amalek tomorrow. I will stand on top of the hill. . . .
2. Pick us some men and go out to fight Amalek. Tomorrow I will stand on top of the hill. . . .[13]

And here is how Onqelos translates it:

בחר לנא גברין ופוק אגיח קרבא בעמלק מחר אנא קאים על ריש רמתא

Lacking punctuation, this translation exactly mimics the Hebrew verse. "Tomorrow" is located precisely in between "Amalek" and "I" and can be read with either of them or both, as one chooses. Unlike the English translators of Ps 93:1, the Aramaic translator of Exod 17:9 was able to preserve the indecisiveness inherent in the original Hebrew.

Qohelet 10:6

But this approach is not always possible. When it is not, the only way to preserve the undecidability of a particular syntactic construction is by translating it twice, as the King James translators did with Ps 93:1. The Targum to Qohelet does in fact use this method, as the following example from Qoh 10:6 will show:

נִתַּן הַסֶּ֫כֶל ׀ בַּמְּרוֹמִ֥ים רַבִּ֖ים ׀ וַעֲשִׁירִ֑ים בַּשֵּׁ֖פֶל יֵשֵֽׁבוּ׃

This verse has been identified by modern biblical scholars as one in which the accent marks do not fit the most natural reading of the text.[14] The NJPSV nevertheless translates in accordance with them: "Folly was placed on lofty heights, while rich men sat in low estate." But this translation ignores the grammatical incompatibility of בַּמְרוֹמִים, which has the definite article, and רַבִּים, which does not.[15] Perhaps for this reason, the NEB implicitly transposes the *etnachta*, the major pause in the verse, from רבים back to במרומים. It

---

13. Note that the Masoretic accents accord with translation 2, which (with its apparent suggestion that Joshua should fight today while Moses will not act until tomorrow) makes slightly less sense. I have suggested elsewhere that the Masoretic accents are sometimes intended to push the reader in the direction of a more difficult reading with the intent not to contradict the simpler reading (which readers can easily find on their own) but to add to it. See my "Exegetical Implications," p. 165.

14. See the discussion in Seow, *Ecclesiastes*, pp. 314–15; Breuer, "Dissonance," pp. 207–8; Kogut, *Correlations*, pp. 198–99.

15. Against this, Kogut (ibid., p. 198) points to הגוים רבים in Ezek 39:27, where the punctuation is not in question, to show that the punctuators might well have considered this syntax possible in Biblical Hebrew. Note also Qoh 3:19, where both the sense and the cantillation marks suggest that מקרה (twice) is a construct form, though spelled with the *seghol* of the absolute form.

translates, "the fool given high office, but the great and the rich in humble posts." The English translators felt constrained to select one or the other of the two possible syntactic alternatives, but the Aramaic translator did *not* feel such a constraint:

יהב ית אדום רשיעיא ושטיא למחוי במזלא ומשמיש באצלחותא מן שמי מרומא וחילותוי גיוותנין וסגאין ועמא בית ישראל משתעבדין תחותוי בגלותא ומן סגיאות חוביהון עתירי נכסין דיבהון מתמסכנין ובמכיכותא יתבין ביני עמיא

The Lord enabled the wicked and the foolish Edom to enjoy good luck and to enjoy prosperity from the highest heavens [מן שמי מרומא] and his armies are proud and numerous [גיוותנין וסגאין] while the people of the household of Israel are enslaved under him in exile. Because of the multitude of their sins [סגיאות חוביהון], those rich [עתירי] in property become poor and dwell in a lowly state among the nations.[16]

This, of course, is not a literal translation of the Hebrew or anything close to one. Alexander Sperber has characterized the Targum of Qohelet as falling under a translation category that he describes as "Translation and Midrash completely fused together."[17] Nonetheless, despite this fusion, the targumic "leave-no-word-behind" translation policy is still clearly in effect.[18] For example, the Hebrew במרומים appears in the targum as "from the highest heavens [מן שמי מרומא]," and עשירים appears in the phrase "those rich [עתירי] in property." But the word in between them, רבים, is translated (by its standard Aramaic cognate, סגיאין) twice: once in the first part of the translation, along with the translation of במרומים ("his armies are proud and numerous [גיוותנין וסגאין]"), and again in the second part of the translation, with עשירים ("because of the multitude of their sins [סגיאות חוביהון]"). The word רבים is not merely "not left behind"; it is "not left behind" from *either* of the two possible ways it could be read in the verse. Because of the expansive nature of this targum, the option taken by Onqelos in Exod 17:9, leaving the word to be parsed either way as the reader chooses, was not possible. But unlike the English translators, the Aramaic translator has not felt compelled to choose one version of the Hebrew syntax and ignore the other. By translating twice, he provides the reader with both.[19]

Ruth 4:5

In the Targum of Ruth, where the expansions to the text are more easily separated from the straightforward translation than in the Targum of Qohelet,

16. Knobel, *Targum Qohelet*, p. 48.
17. Sperber, *Bible in Aramaic*, vol. 4a, v.
18. This again is a well-known phenomenon; see method #30 in Luzzatto, *Philoxenus*, p. 21, where it is attributed to the need not to surprise listeners to an oral translation, who could follow closely enough to realize if a Hebrew word were left untranslated.
19. The same phenomenon can be found elsewhere in the Targum to Qohelet. See my "Exegetical Implications," pp. 152–54 on Qoh 6:10; pp. 158–59 on 9:17; pp. 161–62 on 10:11; and pp. 162–63 on 11:3.

there is just one verse, Ruth 4:5, that is syntactically difficult, and here too the targum offers a syntactic double translation.[20] The Hebrew text reads:

וַיֹּאמֶר בֹּעַז בְּיוֹם־קְנוֹתְךָ הַשָּׂדֶה [מִיַּד נָעֳמִי] [וּמֵאֵת רוּת הַמּוֹאֲבִיָּה] אֵשֶׁת־הַמֵּת קָנִיתִי [קָנִיתָה] לְהָקִים שֵׁם־הַמֵּת עַל־נַחֲלָתוֹ:

The phrases מיד נעמי and ומאת רות המואביה seem to belong together in the first part of the verse, and this is how the NJPSV translates it: "When you acquire the property from Naomi and from Ruth the Moabite, you must also acquire the wife of the deceased." But the *etnachta*, the Masoretic equivalent in this verse of the English comma, falls not after "Ruth the Moabite" but after "Naomi," and that is how the KJV translates it: "What day thou buyest the field of the hand of Naomi, thou must buy it also of Ruth the Moabitess, the wife of the dead."[21] Here too, the targum manages to translate the verse *both* ways:

ואמר בועז ביום זבינתך ית חקלא מן ידא דנעמי ומן ידא דרות מואביתא איתת מיתא חייב את למפרוק ובעי ליבמא יתה ולמסבה לאנתו מן בגלל לאקמא שום מיתא על אחסנתיה

On the day that you buy the field from the hand of Naomi and from the hand of Ruth the Moabite, wife of the deceased, you are obliged to redeem and required to act as her brother-in-law and to marry her in order to raise up the name of the deceased upon his inheritance.[22]

The phrase "Ruth the Moabite, wife of the deceased" is parsed (against the later Masoretic reading) with "from the hand of Naomi"—to the extent that "the hand of" Ruth is added to it. Then the entire phrase is reread as part of the second half of the verse and translated again in the new syntax, albeit this time represented merely by the pronoun "her" (יתה).

Genesis 49:6–7

So far we have seen the technique of double syntactic translation only in the Writings, the *targumim* of which are late and notoriously expansive. But

---

20. Philip Alexander describes the Targum to Qohelet as "periphrastic" (Alexander, "Targum," col. 328a) but notes that the Targum to Ruth, though moderately expansive, "alternates blocks of aggadic material . . . with passages of more or less literal translation" (col. 327b). Similarly, Sperber characterized Targum Ruth's approach to including additional material as "*Quellen-Scheidung* [that is, separation of sources] still possible" (Sperber, *Bible in Aramaic*, vol. 4a, v).

21. For a full discussion of the difficulty of this phrase in the Hebrew text, see Sasson, *Ruth*, pp. 120–22. Note that in this case, unlike our example from Qohelet, it is the KJV that is faithful to the Masoretic Text and the NJPSV that silently revises it, despite the latter's claim (on its title page) to be translating "the traditional Hebrew text."

22. Beattie, *Tg. Ruth*, p. 30. He gives a different version of the Aramaic text in "Preliminary Edition," p. 279, from what is cited here, but the differences do not materially affect our conclusions.

Gen 49:6–7 provides an example from Targum Onqelos. We begin with the Hebrew text.

6 בְּסֹדָם אַל־תָּבֹא נַפְשִׁי בִּקְהָלָם אַל־תֵּחַד כְּבֹדִי
כִּי בְאַפָּם הָרְגוּ אִישׁ וּבִרְצֹנָם עִקְּרוּ־שׁוֹר׃
7 אָרוּר אַפָּם כִּי עָז וְעֶבְרָתָם כִּי קָשָׁתָה
אֲחַלְּקֵם בְּיַעֲקֹב וַאֲפִיצֵם בְּיִשְׂרָאֵל׃

In the NJPSV translation:

> Let not my person be included in their council,
> Let not my being be counted in their assembly.
> For when angry they slay men,
> And when pleased they maim oxen.
> Cursed be their anger so fierce,
> And their wrath so relentless.
> I will divide them in Jacob,
> Scatter them in Israel.

There is not any immediately evident difficulty in the Hebrew of this verse, as in the earlier examples we have seen. But it is one of the examples listed in the Mekilta as a grammatically undecidable passage. The issue turns on whether the adjective ארור, which begins v. 7, is to be read with the following word, אפם ("cursed be their anger"), or with the word that precedes it at the end of v. 6, שור ("they maim cursed oxen"). The latter reading (as explained by Rashi in his comment to the same listing of passages at *b. Yoma* 52b) would suggest that the ox that Simeon and Levi maimed was that of Shechem, "cursed" because he was a descendant of Canaan, who was cursed in Gen 9:25 because his father, Ham, saw *his* father, Noah, naked. And indeed the Aramaic of Targum Onqelos provides *both* possibilities:

. . . ארי ברוגזיהון קטלו קטול וברעותהון תרעו שׁוור סנאה ליט רוגזיהון ארי תקיף
וחמתהין ארי קשיא

[I]n their fury *they executed a great slaughter*, and at their whim *they razed the wall of the enemy*. Cursed be their fury for it is fierce; and their anger for it is extreme.[23]

Verse 7 begins by translating ארור "cursed," in a straightforward rendering of the Hebrew of that verse: "Cursed be their anger so fierce." But ארור has already been translated at the end of v. 6 as סנאה, "the enemy," with שׁוור connected to it in a construct chain: "they razed the wall of the enemy" (reading Hebrew שור ארור as a unit).[24] The translator reads through the *siluq* at the end of v. 6 to include the first word of v. 7; then he returns to the first

---

23. Grossfeld, *Onkelos: Genesis*, p. 158.
24. Luzzatto (*Philoxenus*, p. 21), in discussing the 30th of the 32 methods used (according to him) by Onqelos, points out that שׁוור, "wall," reflects Hebrew שׁור, "ox," even though it does not accurately translate it. But he does not specifically note the phenomenon of syntactic double translation.

word of v. 7 as if it were indeed the beginning of a sentence, and continues normally. Note that Pseudo-Jonathan offers a double translation based on the same syntactic rereading, but with different language:

ארום ברוגזיהון קטלו מלכא ושולטניה וברעותהון <u>שור בעלי דבביהון</u> (ז) אמר יעקב <u>לוט</u> הוה כרכא דשכם כד עלון לנוה למחרבה ברוגיהון דתקיף וחמתהון על יוסף ארום קשיא

"For in their anger they killed *the king and his ruler*, and at their whim *they demolished the wall of their enemies*." Jacob said, "Cursed *was the city of Shechem when they went into it to destroy it in* their anger that was fierce; and (cursed was) their wrath *against Joseph*, for it was cruel."[25]

Rather than שוור סנאה, we have שור בעלי דבביהון, a different phrase for "the wall of their enemies." This still understands the Hebrew ארור at the beginning of v. 7 to represent Shechem and his fellows, and for the same reason; again, the translator returns to ארור as if it were indeed the beginning of v. 7 rather than the end of v. 6, going so far as to add a superfluous אמר יעקב ("Jacob said") before it.[26]

Nahum 1:8

I have focused exclusively on the most dramatic kind of syntactic rereading, that which shifts a word or phrase from one half of the verse to the other or even from one verse to another. But syntactic rereading of a more general kind is no doubt responsible for a great many of the double translations found throughout all the targum. An example appears in Targum Jonathan to the Prophets. We begin with the Hebrew text.

וּבְשֶׁטֶף עֹבֵר כָּלָה יַעֲשֶׂה מְקוֹמָהּ וְאֹיְבָיו יְרַדֶּף־חֹשֶׁךְ׃

And with a sweeping flood He makes an end of her place,
And chases His enemies into darkness. (NJPSV)

David Toshio Tsumura has pointed to the word מקומה in this verse as another that is capable of being read as a Janus parallelism.[27] The word מקומה can be read as the Masoretes have pointed it, with its feminine-singular suffix referring (evidently) to Nineveh, or (as the Septuagint apparently read it) as some form of the word קמים, "those who rise up in enmity," paralleling

---

25. Maher, *Pseudo-Jonathan: Genesis*, p. 158. Neofiti is essentially equivalent to Pseudo-Jonathan here. Grossfeld (*Neofiti I: Genesis*, p. 292) notes בעלי דבביהון and סנאה merely as "an explanatory addition."

26. I note here Paul Flesher's observation that "whenever [Neofiti] and [ms. V in Klein, *Fragment Targums*] share an expansion in the special sections [Genesis 49, Numbers 21 and 22–24, Deuteronomy 32–33] that does not appear in [Pseudo-Jonathan], PJ tends to have a different expansion for that verse. . . . PJ may have once had the expansions but later replaced them with other material" (Flesher, "Translation and Exegetical Augmentation," pp. 66–67).

27. See the full discussion in Tsumura, "Janus Parallelism in Nah 1:8."

איביו ("his enemies") of the second half of the verse. Here is how Targum Jonathan renders this verse:

וברגיו חמין ובחימא תקיפא גמירא יעביד עם עממיא דקמו ואחריבו ית בית מקדשא

The English translators of this targum render it as follows: "But in fierce anger and in great wrath he shall make an end of the nations which rose up and utterly destroyed the Sanctuary," and they note: "MT *mqwmh* has been rendered both as the noun meaning 'place' (and hence 'Sanctuary' . . .), and as a part of the verb *qwm*, which in the *Hithpolel* means 'rise in opposition.'"[28] In fact, the Hebrew phrase כלה יעשה מקומה has been reread so that מקומה is first the object of God's destruction (as it is the object in the original Hebrew), then the *subject* exercising destruction, and a third time again the object of destruction by the enemies, the Sanctuary.

Qoheleth 9:10

As the previous example makes clear, an expansive translation may in fact be based nonetheless on a close syntactic rereading of the Hebrew text. Our next example demonstrates such a case with an additional feature: the fact that a syntactic rereading has taken place may not be obvious without an awareness of rabbinic midrash. This is the case with Qoh 9:10:

כֹּל אֲשֶׁר תִּמְצָא יָדְךָ [לַעֲשׂוֹת בְּכֹחֲךָ] עֲשֵׂה

Seow explains the syntactic problem: "The Masoretic punctuation suggests that [בכחך] is to be read with the infinitive [לעשות]: 'Whatever your hand finds to do with strength, do!' We should, however, follow [several manuscripts, the Syriac text, and the Vulgate] in taking [בכחך] with the imperative [עשה]: 'Whatever your hand finds to do, do with strength!' The point is that one should wholeheartedly do whatever one is able to do."[29] The standard rabbinic exegesis of this verse reads in accordance with the Masoretic cantillation, giving to the word בכחך the particular meaning "while you are alive."[30] The following example from *Deuteronomy Rabbah* (Margoliot) 2:27 makes this clear:[31]

זש״ה כל אשר תמצא ידך לעשות בכחך עשה כל מה שאתה יכול לעשות מצוה עד שכחך עליך עשה למה משאדם בטל מן העולם בטלה מחשבתו כל מה שאתה יכול לחטוף מצות עד שאתה בחיים וכן עשה

This is what Scripture says, "All that your hand finds to do בכחך, do" (Qoh 9:10). All you are able to do in the way of commandments while your strength

---

28. Cathcart and Gordon, *Targum Jonathan of the Former Prophets*, pp. 132–33 and n. 25.
29. See the discussion in Seow, *Ecclesiastes*, p. 302.
30. See my "Exegetical Implications," pp. 157–58.
31. Similar interpretations are found in *Qoh. Rab.* 9:10, *Midrash Zuta Qoh.* 9:8, *Pirke Rabbati* 3:3, and *Otzar Hamidrashim Yelammedenu* 4.

is still upon you, do. Why? Once a person is nullified from the world, his intentions are nullified. As much of commandments as you can grab, you *should* grab while you are still in life, and do them.

The assumption here, as in the other texts that follow this interpretation, is that "whatever your hand finds to do" refers to your ability to perform God's commandments. More significantly for our question, however, is that they all interpret the word בכחך, "with your strength," as meaning "while you are alive." This explanation, of course, is based on the rest of the Qohelet verse: "For there is no action, no reasoning, no learning, no wisdom in Sheol, where you are going" (NJPSV). The Masoretic punctuation seems to be another example of the Janus phenomenon, aimed at pushing the reader (who may be assumed to have naturally read the verse as does Seow, "do them with all your might") to reinterpret the verse in accordance with the midrashic understanding.

Reading the Targum to Qohelet through this lens, we see that it is not merely expansive in a general way but that part of the expansion results from specifically translating the Hebrew verse in accordance with both of its possible punctuations: "Whatever *charity* your hand finds to do *for the needy* do it with all your strength [בכל חילך], for *after the death* [ארום בתר מותא] *a man has* neither work nor reckoning nor knowledge or wisdom in the grave where you are going *and nothing will help you but good deeds and charity alone*."[32] "Do it with all your strength" clearly translates בכחך עשה as a phrase, in accordance with Seow's suggestion. "A man has neither work nor reckoning" and so forth just as clearly translates the second half of the Hebrew verse. Without an awareness of the midrashic reading of this verse, the phrase "after the death" would simply seem to be an awkward addition, making "in the grave where you are going" into a redundancy. But a reader who is tuned in to the midrashic reading of the verse can recognize "after the death" as based on a *second* translation of the Hebrew word בכחך, now recontextualized (in accordance with the Masoretic punctuation) to read as the second word of the phrase לעשות בכחך, "to do while you are in strength," that is, "alive." The phenomenon of double syntactic translation permits the targumist to read the biblical verse both in accordance with the most natural reading and in accordance with the traditional understanding.

Deuteronomy 31:16

To be sure, there are cases where it is not clear whether an expansion is indeed based on a close reading and syntactic double translation or whether it is motivated solely by other factors. A case in point is another of the five verses cited in the Mekhilta as being undecidable, Deut 31:16:

---

32. Knobel, *Tg. Qohelet*, p. 45.

וַיֹּאמֶר יְ־הֹוָה אֶל־מֹשֶׁה [הִנְּךָ שֹׁכֵב עִם־אֲבֹתֶיךָ] וְקָם֩ הָעָם הַזֶּה וְזָנָה | אַחֲרֵי | אֱלֹהֵי נֵכַר־הָאָרֶץ אֲשֶׁר הוּא בָא־שָׁמָּה בְּקִרְבּוֹ וַעֲזָבַנִי וְהֵפֵר אֶת־בְּרִיתִי אֲשֶׁר כָּרַתִּי אִתּוֹ:

The straightforward reading of the verse is provided by the King James translation:

> And the LORD said unto Moses, Behold, thou shalt sleep with thy fathers; and this people will rise up, and go a whoring after the gods of the strangers of the land.

Here the semicolon after "fathers" corresponds to the *etnachta* under the word אבתיך in the Masoretic Text, and the second half of the verse begins with the word וקם, "will rise up." The other alternative is to move the Masoretic pause forward one word and interpret the verse as if it read הנך שוכב עם אבתיך וקם, "Behold, thou shalt sleep with thy fathers and shall rise up."

There are two serious difficulties with this reading: first, the verb וקם is third person, not second person, as the English translation of the rereading makes it seem; second, moving the verb to the first half of the verse leaves the phrase "this people" without a plausible interpretation, since a separate clause begins immediately after it. The reason that rabbinic tradition declared this verse undecidable was undoubtedly to provide a reference within the Pentateuch to the resurrection of the dead. According to *m. Sanh.* 10:1, anyone who maintains that there is no reference to resurrection in the Torah "has no share" in the World to Come.

Now let us read Deut 31:16 as translated by Targum Pseudo-Jonathan:

ואמר ייי למשה הא אנת שכיב בעפרא עם אבהתך ונשמתך תהוי גניזא בגניז חיי עלמא עם אבהתך ויקום רשיעי עמא הדיך ויטעון בתר טעוות עממיא ארעא דהינון עללין תמן ביניהון וישבקון דחלתי וישנון ית גזרית עימהון

> Then the Lord said to Moses: "Behold, you are about to lie in the dust with your fathers; *and your soul shall be deposited in the treasury of eternal life with your fathers*. Then *the wicked ones* of this people <u>shall arise</u> and shall stray after the idols of the nations."[33]

There is certainly no reference to resurrection of the *body* here, nor does even Moses' *soul* "rise" again. But the inserted assurance to Moses that his soul will be "deposited in the treasury of eternal life with your fathers" would seem, nonetheless, in light of rabbinic tradition, to be a second reflex of the verb וקם in the original Hebrew of the verse, reread together with אבתיך of the first half of the verse as a reference to a continuation of life beyond physical death.[34] At least Moses' soul, if not his body, "will rise" after death to some transcendent form of ongoing existence. If this reading is correct, then

---

33. Clarke, *Pseudo-Jonathan: Deuteronomy*, p. 87.

34. I refer to this as a "second" reflex because it is conceptually secondary to the literal "shall arise," which follows in its proper place and is thus second in consecutive order of reading.

here too we find the targum translating a verse twice, in accordance with two different possible syntactic readings of the original Hebrew. Moshe Goshen-Gottstein observes, "[O]ne can only wonder to what extent it makes sense to treat Targum Studies as a sub-area of Bible Studies in general, but not as a sub-area of Rabbinic Studies."[35]

Exodus 22:12

It might be possible to conclude that such double translations are the result of a combination of two earlier translation variants. Note the following example of translation variants in Targum Neofiti, described by Moshe Bernstein:

> Exodus 22:12 reads ואם טרף יטרף יבאהו עד הטרפה לא ישלם ("If it be totally torn apart, let him bring it as a witness; he shall not pay for the torn animal"). Neofiti: ואין מטרפה יטרף ייתון סהדין קטילא לא ישלם ("If it is totally torn apart, let them bring witnesses; the torn one he shall not pay"); Margin I: מתקטלה יתקטל יתיה (= יתי) ליה מן אברוי שהד ("[if it is] indeed killed let him bring one of its limbs as a proof"). Both of these translate the Masoretic Text, although there is an interesting exegetical dispute regarding the nature of the proof which is required to exempt the bailee from payment. Is the torn piece of the animal sufficient proof, or are human witnesses demanded? But Margin II reads חיובא (= היווא) דתבירא ולא ישלם ימטינ[יה] עד גושמת ("let him bring him to the body of the torn animal and he shall not pay"). This version seems to read עד הטרפה, a reading, incidentally, which is found also in midrashic halakhic literature.[36]

And here is Pseudo-Jonathan's rendering of the same verse:

אין איתברא יתבר מן חיות ברא מייתי ליה סהדין או ימטייניה עד גופת דתביר לא ישלים

If it was torn *by a wild beast*, he shall bring him *witnesses, or he shall bring him to the body of* (the animal) that was torn; he shall not make restitution.[37]

"He brings witnesses" reads the Hebrew text with the Masoretic vowels and punctuation; "let him bring him to the body of the torn animal" rereads עֵד as עַד and reads across the Masoretic break between the two words.

Given the variants in the margins of Neofiti, it is possible to argue that Pseudo-Jonathan (or its predecessor) had only a single translation here and that the other translation was added secondarily. This model would conceivably also explain the example we saw in Ruth 4:5. Philip Alexander notes, too, that "[Pseudo-Jonathan] regularly has doublets in which one element corresponds to [*Onqelos*], while the other appears to represent a Palestinian

---

35. Goshen-Gottstein, "Recent Developments," p. 8.
36. Bernstein, "Aramaic Targumim," p. 151; n. 34 there provides the rabbinic citation, pointing to the view of R. Yonatan in *Mekilta de-Rabbi Ishmael*, Neziqin 16 (Horowitz-Rabin ed. p. 305, Lauterbach ed. 3:125–26). See also Kogut, *Correlations*, p. 132 n. 26.
37. Maher, *Pseudo-Jonathan: Exodus*, p. 226.

Targum."[38] It has been observed elsewhere that the text of Targum Jonathan, too, "is not free from later additions; from this cause arise the double translations of which the Targum contains several."[39] But we have found the phenomenon of double syntactic translation even in Targum Onqelos. I would add that all the examples given here were found without an exhaustive search.[40] There may well be many more.

Conclusion

Since this phenomenon is so easily found in such a wide range of *targumim* (the various Targums to the Torah as well as those to the Prophets and the Writings), my suggestion is that in most cases this is *not*, in fact, an additive phenomenon created inadvertently, either by the accumulation of translational doublets from various sources or as an artifact of simultaneous interpretation in a synagogue setting.[41] Rather, the translators were "actuated by a desire to preserve the indeterminability of the text."[42] Even after postmodernism, it is natural for a twenty-first-century reader to think of a text as having a single, fixed meaning, intended by its author. This, after all, is how most of us ourselves write most of the time. But it is just as natural for a Jewish reader to look at the originally unpointed text of the Hebrew Bible and see it as deliberately open to multiple intended meanings. As we have noted in our discussion of Exod 17:9, it is sometimes possible to translate in a way that leaves the multiple possibilities open.[43] More often, the shift to a new language demands that the translator choose a single one of the possible options. But the Jewish translators of the Bible into Aramaic sometimes refused to make this choice.

I have referred above to the targumists' "leave-no-word-behind" translation policy. Speaking of the targumists as a group (though they cover a fairly

---

38. Alexander, "Targum," p. 322b, citing as examples Gen 3:5, 4:13, 8:11, 27:29; Exod 1:19; Lev 16:4; Num 26:9; and Deut 5:3.

39. "Targum," *Catholic Encyclopedia* (1913), http://www.newadvent.org/cathen/14454b.htm.

40. I approached the problem experimentally in three ways: (1) by making a close reading of the targum and biblical text of Qohelet and of Ruth; (2) by examining the five verses cited in rabbinic literature as "undecidable"; and (3) by examining some verses that biblical scholars have explained as containing Janus parallelism. The intent was to mimic an archaeologist's use of various test trenches by quickly probing the biblical text from three different angles.

41. The role such interpretation played in the creation of the *targumim* is still in dispute and cannot be resolved here; compare the opinion of Shinan, "Live Translation," p. 47 ("the text's oral provenance is evident") with that of van der Kooij, "Origin and Purpose," p. 213 (whose examination of three passages does "not support the idea that the Bible translations as written versions originated in a liturgical or synagogal setting").

42. I made this suggestion previously with regard to the unusual punctuation of some of the verses in the Masoretic Text of Qohelet; see my "Exegetical Implications," p. 165.

43. This seems to be the case as well in another of the Mekilta's undecidable verses, Targum Onqelos to Exod 25:33 (= 37:20).

wide range both temporally and geographically), it seems to have been their intent to preserve as much as possible of the "extra" information provided in the biblical text alongside a straightforward, univocal reading. I believe that the phenomenon of double syntactic translation is not an artifact of mindless compilation of variants but a bold attempt to make the *targumim* convey what the translators saw as the richness of an intentionally manifold revelation.

Bibliography

Alexander, P. S. "Targum, Targumim." Cols. 321b–331b in vol. 6 of *Anchor Bible Dictionary.* Edited by D. N. Freedman et al. New York: Doubleday, 1992.

Beattie, D. R. G. "The Targum of Ruth: A Preliminary Edition." Pp. 231–90 in *Targum and Scripture: Studies in Aramaic Translations and Interpretation in Memory of Ernest G. Clarke.* Edited by P. V. M. Flesher. Leiden: Brill, 2002.

———. *The Targum of Ruth.* Aramaic Bible 19. Collegeville, MN: Liturgical Press, 1994.

Bernstein, M. "The Aramaic Targumim: The Many Faces of the Jewish Biblical Experience." Pp. 133–65 in *Jewish Ways of Reading the Bible.* Edited by G. J. Brooke. Oxford: Oxford University Press on behalf of the University of Manchester, 2000.

Breuer, Y. "מחלוקת ניקוד וטעמים בחלוקת פסוקים" ["Dissonance between Masoretic Accentuation and Vocalization in Verse Division of the Biblical Text"]. Pp. 191–242 in ספר היובל לרב מרדכי ברויאר [*Rabbi Mordechai Breuer Festschrift*]. Jerusalem: Academon, 1992.

Carasik, M. "Exegetical Implications of the Masoretic Cantillation Marks in Ecclesiastes." *Hebrew Studies* 42 (2001) 145–65.

Cathcart, K., and R. P. Gordon. *The Targum Jonathan of the Former Prophets.* Aramaic Bible 10. Collegeville, MN: Liturgical Press, 1999.

Clarke, E. G., with S. Magder. *Targum Pseudo-Jonathan: Deuteronomy.* Aramaic Bible 5B. Collegeville, MN: Liturgical Press, 1998.

Flesher, P. V. "Translation and Exegetical Augmentation in the Targums to the Pentateuch." Pp. 29–85 in *Judaic and Christian Interpretation of Texts: Contents and Contexts.* Edited by J. Neusner and E. S. Frerichs. New Perspectives on Ancient Judaism 3. Lanham, MD: University Press of America, 1987.

Gordon, C. H. "Asymmetric Janus Parallelism." *Eretz-Israel* 16 (Orlinsky Volume; 1982) 80*–81*.

———. "New Directions." *Bulletin of the American Society of Papyrologists* 15 (1978) 59–66.

Goshen-Gottstein, M. H. "Targum-Studies: An Overview of Recent Developments." *Textus* 16 (1991) 1–11.

Grossfeld, B. *Targum Neofiti I: An Exegetical Commentary to Genesis.* New York: Sepher-Hermon, 2000.

———. *The Targum Onkelos to Genesis.* Aramaic Bible 6. Wilmington, DE: Michael Glazier, 1988.

Klein, M. L. "Associative and Complementary Translation in the Targumim." *Eretz-Israel* 16 (Orlinsky Volume; 1982) 134*–140*.

Knobel, P. S. *The Targum of Qohelet*. Aramaic Bible 15. Collegeville, MN: Liturgical Press, 1991.

Kogut, S. המקרא בין טעמים לפרשנות [*Correlations between Biblical Accentuation and Traditional Jewish Exegesis: Linguistic and Contextual Studies*]. Jerusalem: Magnes, 1996.

Kooij, A. van der. "The Origin and Purpose of Bible Translations in Ancient Judaism: Some Comments." *Archiv für Religionsgeschichte* 1 (1999) 204–14.

Luzzatto, S. D. *Philoxenus* [אוהב גר]. Krakow: Joseph Fischer, 1895.

Maher, M. *Targum Pseudo-Jonathan: Genesis*. Aramaic Bible 1B. Collegeville, MN: Liturgical Press, 1992.

———. *Targum Pseudo-Jonathan: Exodus*. Aramaic Bible 2. Collegeville, MN: Liturgical Press, 1994.

McNamara, M. *Targum Neofiti 1: Genesis*. Aramaic Bible 1A. Collegeville, MN: Liturgical Press, 1992.

Sasson, J. M. *Ruth: A New Translation with a Philological Commentary and a Formalist-Folklorist Interpretation*. Biblical Seminar. Sheffield: JSOT Press, 1989.

Seow, Choon-Leong. *Ecclesiastes: A New Translation with Introduction and Commentary*. Anchor Bible 18C. New York: Doubleday, 1997.

Shinan, A. "Live Translation: On the Nature of the Aramaic Targums to the Pentateuch." *Prooftexts* 3 (1983) 41–49.

Sperber, A. *The Bible in Aramaic*. 5 vols. Leiden: Brill, 1959–73.

Talmon, S. "Synonymous Readings in the Textual Traditions of the O.T." *Scripta Hierosolymitana* 8 (1961) 335–83.

———. "The Textual Study of the Bible: A New Outlook." Pp. 321–400 in *Qumran and the History of the Biblical Text*. Edited by F. M. Cross and S. Talmon. Cambridge: Harvard University Press, 1975.

Tsumura, D. T. "Janus Parallelism in Nah 1:8." *JBL* 102 (1983) 109–11.

The Fish Grows Bigger: Angelic Insertions in Targums Neofiti and Pseudo-Jonathan

DAVID L. EVERSON

From antiquity to the present, angels have been the subject of much curiosity and speculation. Great efforts have been made by the academic and the religious to understand better the character, function, and perception of angels. The targumist is no exception to such efforts. Unfortunately, though considerable work has been done in the fields of biblical, pseudepigraphic, and rabbinic angelologies, comparatively little has been done with respect to targums.[1] Nonetheless, a few have explored targumic angelology, as a matter of either primary or secondary focus.[2]

In order to understand any topic of theology within the targums, such as angelology, it is important to distinguish the targumic theology from the biblical. As Moshe Bernstein has noted, it is "very easy, if we are not careful, to confuse the theology of the underlying biblical original with that of the targum."[3] A convenient means of distinguishing targumic and biblical theologies is to examine Aramaic insertions and/or expansions. When the targum makes a decided break from the biblical text, by means of adding material for which there is no Hebrew counterpart, there is a greater likelihood that the translation reflects the theology of the targum. Furthermore, this means of

---

Author's note: I would like to thank Duke University for hosting the NEH Seminar: Aramaic in Postbiblical Judaism and Early Christianity. Professors Eric Meyers, Lucas Van Rompay, and Paul V. M. Flesher were excellent scholars and wonderful hosts.

1. Azuelos, *Angelology*; Gruenthaner, "Demonology"; Olyan, *Thousand Thousands*; Davidson, *Angels at Qumran*; Flusser, "Resurrection and Angels"; Schäfer, *Rivalitäta zwischen Engeln und Menschen*; Rubio, *La angelología*; Urbach, *Sages*, pp. 135–83; Shapiro, *Rabbinic Angelology*.

2. Shinan, *Aggadah*; idem, "Live Translation"; idem, "Angelology"; idem, *Embroidered Targum*; Kasher, "Angelology"; Vermes, "Archangel Sariel"; Glazov, "Ps. 51:17."

3. Bernstein, "Aramaic Versions of Deuteronomy 32," p. 29.

theological distinction may also be used when comparing one targum to another. When a given targum deviates from its *Vorlage* (or for our purposes, one estimated to be quite similar), there is the same likelihood of theological exposure.

In light of these factors, every insertion of מלאך within Targum Neofiti (TN) and Targum Pseudo-Jonathan (PJ) has been examined (i.e., passages where מלאך occurs in the Aramaic text but is absent from the Hebrew). For the sake of succinctness, the remaining Palestinian Targums (i.e., the Fragmentary Targums and the Geniza fragments) have been excluded from the present discussion. Similarly, Onqelos has been excluded as a result of the paucity and nature its angelic insertions.[4] Thus, what follows is an evaluation of the insertions of מלאך as found in TN and PJ. In total, there are 56 verses where one or both of the targums have inserted מלאך into the translation. The results break down as one might expect. There are 21 instances of angelic insertions within TN and 50 instances within PJ.[5]

It will be argued that, in comparison with TN, the use of angels in PJ is invariably more embellished and is consistent with the angelological perspective of later rabbinic literatures. The angels of PJ are of a higher status and greater ability than those of TN, often to a fantastic or miraculous degree. This will be demonstrated through the following categories: (1) titles or descriptions assigned to angels, (2) the numbering of angels, (3) the angelic role with regard to revelation, (4) the naming of angels, and (5) the divine status of angels.

Titles or Descriptions

Never in the targums does one find a clear description of angelic hierarchy. Though a few of the usual suspects are present, the archangels of *1 Enoch* or those of Tobit are never listed as such. Nonetheless, there are various groups of angels for which numerous descriptions or titles are given in both TN and PJ. Table 1 should serve to illustrate the various attestations.

The column entitled "common attestations" refers to passages where both TN and PJ have the indicated title. Conversely, the "unique" columns refer to passages where either TN or PJ has the indicated title, always to the exclusion of the other. One notices immediately that, though PJ has nearly double the attestations of TN, the variety of titles remains comparable. Commonly

---

4. Of the 5 insertions, 3 use מלאך as a standard translation for Beer-lahoi-roi (Gen 16:14, 24:62, 25:11), and the remaining 2 resolve an anthropomorphic difficulty present within the biblical text (Gen 32:31[30]; Exod 4:24).

5. TN: Gen 3:5; 18:1–2; 22:10; 30:22; 32:3, 25–26, 29, 31; 33:10; 37:15; Exod 4:24–26; 33:22–23; Lev 22:27; Deut 32:3; 33:2–3. PJ: Gen 1:26; 3:5, 6, 22; 4:1; 6:20; 11:7, 8; 18:2, 10, 15–16, 20, 22; 19:26; 22:10, 19; 27:25; 31:24; 32:3, 10, 25, 26, 29, 31; 35:7; 37:15; Exod 4:24, 25–26; 5:2; 12:12, 13, 23, 42; 15:2; 20:23; 26:28; 33:23; Num 15:40; 24:3; 25:8, 12; 26:46; Deut 9:19; 10:14; 32:8; 33:2; 34:5–6.

Table 1: Descriptions or Titles of Angels

Title or Description	Common Attest.	Unique TN Attest.	Unique PJ Attest.
כיתי מלאכיה	Exod 33:23	Exod 33:22	
מלאך חבלא			Exod 4:25, 26
מלאך מותא		Exod 4:26	Gen 3:6; Exod 12:13
(מלאכא) מחבלא		Exod 4: 25, 26	Exod 12:12, 23, 42; Deut 9:19
מלאכי מרומא	Gen 22:10	Gen 18:1	Gen 22:19
(מלאכיא) משבחייא	Gen 32:26		
מלאכיא משמשין	Exod 33:23		Gen 3:22; Exod 20:23; Num 15:40; Deut 10:14
מלאכין קדישין	Gen 32:3; Deut 33:2	Deut 33:3	
מלאכא דשירותא		Deut 32:3	Gen 18:2, 29; Deut 34:6
רברבי עממין			Deut 32:8
שרף וגדוד		Gen 30:22	

attested throughout TN and PJ, we find "praising angels," "attending angels" (of both the שמש and the שירות type), "holy angels," "hosts of angels," "destroying angels," "angels on high," and, finally, "the angel of death."

TN has one unique attestation of entitled angels, whereas PJ has two. In Gen 30:22, TN mentions four keys that are held by God but are available to no angels, neither "Seraf" nor "troop." For whatever reason, PJ disregards the sizable expansion of TN and simply mimics the text of Onqelos. It may be that TN seeks to deny any angelic jurisdiction within these respective spheres and/ or seek to preclude any cause for angelic invocation in circumstances of this sort. It is probably for this reason that PJ has not included this familiar tradition in its translation of Gen 30:22. This is confirmed by Deut 28:12 of PJ, where the "four keys" tradition has been included. However, so as not to diminish angelic jurisdiction, "angel" and "Seraf" have been replaced with "official" (טיפסרא). In this manner, a limitation is only placed upon human beings.

In Exod 4:25 we find a title unique to PJ:

MT – וַתַּגַּע לְרַגְלָיו
and she threw [it] at his feet

TN – וקרבת לרגלוי דמחבלה
and she placed it before the feet of the destroyer

PJ – ואקריבת ית גזירת מהולתא לריגלוי דמלאך חבלא
and she brought the circumcised foreskin to the feet of the Angel of Destruction

The challenge faced by the translator of this verse is to determine the referent of רַגְלָיו. In the previous verse, both targums render "the Lord" with "the angel (of the Lord)" in order to avoid an anthropomorphism. Thus, the "feet" of this verse belong to that angel. TN, instead of simply repeating מלאכא of the previous verse, further clarifies the angel's identity by informing the reader that he is, in fact, "the destroyer." PJ takes the translation one step further. A noun now replaces the participial form used by TN. Instead of describing or typifying the action of the angel in question, PJ provides a title: "the Angel of Destruction." Notice that the construction of [indefinite מלאך + definite חבלא] is identical to what one finds with "the Angel of Death" (i.e., מלאך מותא). In fact, in the very next verse, TN identifies this destroying angel as "the Angel of Death" (Exod 4:26). PJ, however, continues its use of "the Angel of Destruction." Thus, in deviating from TN's use of מלאך מותא, PJ couples separate titles with different episodes. The Angel of Death is associated with the Garden of Eden and Passover, while the Angel of Destruction is associated with the Bridegroom of Blood.

PJ's unique attestation of "the princes of the nations" in Deut 32:8 bears a remarkable similarity to apocalyptic traditions and Jewish mysticism.

MT—יַצֵּב גְּבֻלֹת עַמִּים לְמִסְפַּר בְּנֵי יִשְׂרָאֵל

PJ—בי היא זימנא רמא פיצתא עם שובעין מלאכיא רברבי עממין דאתגלי עימהון למחמי קרתא ובי היא זימנא אקים תחומי אומיא כסכום מניין שובעין נפשתא דישראל דנחתו למצרים

At that time he cast lots with the seventy angels, the princes of the nations, to whom it is revealed to oversee the city, and at that time he established the borders of the nations according to the sum of the seventy souls of Israel who went down to Egypt.

This passage purports the apocalyptic notion that God has dispatched the 70 angels or princes to help govern the nations. This is attested in a variety of locations within the Apocrypha and Pseudepigrapha.[6] Traditionally, the rabbis harbor a fair amount of skepticism for the guardian angels.[7] However, this passage seems to reflect the apocalypticism that one finds in the Zohar. In fact, the title "princes of the nations" (רברבי עממין) is found repeatedly throughout the Zohar.[8]

Numbering of Angels

In addition to angels being assigned a given title or description, they are also described as occurring in great numbers. Deut 33:2 is a good example.

---

6. For example, in the Hebrew text of the *Testament of the Twelve Patriarchs* (Naphtali 8–9), we find that 70 ministering angels were deployed by God, with Michael at their head, so as to teach the nations their respective languages. The appointment of angels as national guardians is also seen in Sir 17:17 (ἑκάστῳ ἔθνει κατέστησεν ἡγούμενον καὶ μέρις κυρίου Ἰσραηλ ἐστίν).

7. *Exodus Rabbah* 42:1; *Genesis Rabbah* 56:11; *Deuteronomy Rabbah* 1:22.

8. *Zohar* vol B. 14b, 46b; vol C. 4b, 32a, 72b, 265b.

PJ—ואתגלי בקדושא על עמיה בית ישראל ועימיה ריבו ריבוון מלאכין קדישין

He was revealed in holiness to his people, the House of Israel, and with him 10,000 myriads of holy angels.

TN—ואתגלי על טורה דסיני ועימיה ריבוון דמלאכין קדישין

He was revealed on Mt. Sinai and with him myriads of holy angels.

Earlier in this expansion, both TN and PJ recorded the popular midrash of God's "shopping" the Torah around to Rome and to the Ishmaelites.[9] After the others had declined the Torah, Israel accepted it. As a result, God revealed to Israel not only himself but also myriads of angels. PJ simply inserts ריבו into the text to render TN's "myriads of angels" as "10,000 myriads of angels." In this way, PJ vastly increases the number of those present in the heavenly host.

An even greater number of angels is found in the Passover narrative of PJ (Exod 12:12–13). In this passage we learn that the Angel of Death has been assigned to pass over the houses of Israel and spare those who have the blood of the Passover sacrifice on their doorposts. Additionally, 90,000 myriads of destroying angels were sent into Egypt to kill their firstborn sons.[10] That is a grand total of 900,000,000 angels.

Num 26:46 of PJ provides another example.

PJ—ושום ברת אשר סרח דאידברת בשיתין ריבוון מלאכין ואיתעלת לגינתא דעדן בחייהא מן בגלל דבשרת ית יעקב דעד כדון יוסף קיים:

And the name of Asher's daughter was Serah, who was led by 60,000 myriads of angels and brought into the Garden of Eden alive, because she reported to Jacob that Joseph was still alive.

The number of angels in this passage serves as fanfare for the reward given to Serah. The garden, of course, represents heaven. Within rabbinic literature, the Garden of Eden and Gehenna are consistently identified as either the reward or punishment given to individuals in the hereafter.[11] In light of the stationed cherubim of Gen 3:24, it only makes sense that PJ would associate angels with the Garden of Eden. However, in addition to the specified number of 60,000, what is distinctive about this passage is that the angels first lead Serah to the garden and then bring her into the garden. They function as both escort and gatekeeper. The depiction of Serah as one who reveals secret information is found in a related talmudic passage where she reveals to Moses the secret grave of Joseph.[12] However, it is not until a much later period that one finds a midrash similar to our passage. In the satirical/heretical

---

9. See *Exodus Rabbah* 17:2, 27:9; *Leviticus Rabbah* 6:6; *Numbers Rabbah* 14:10.
10. תשעין אלפין ריבוון מלאכין מחבלין.
11. *Genesis Rabbah* 21:9; b. *Shabb.* 152b; *Ruth Rabbah* Prologue.
12. B. *Sotah* 13a.

Alphabet of Ben Sira, as a result of informing Jacob that Joseph is still alive, Serah is listed among those who have been "gathered into the Garden of Eden."[13]

Revelation

This category of development refers to angels as the means and/or source of special revelation. In TN, angels are associated with divine revelation, but they are never the means of that revelation. For example, in order to resolve the anthropomorphic tension of passages such as Gen 32:31 and 33:10, angels become the object of revelation in both TN and PJ. In these passages, the angels are merely visual representatives of the deity that do not impart additional information. Likewise, the expansion of Deut 33:2 found in TN records that, when God revealed the Torah to Israel at Sinai, he was accompanied by myriads of holy angels. Again, instead of being a means of revelation, the angels are simply an accoutrement.

In PJ's expansion of Gen 38:25, Judah has ordered that Tamar be burned to death as punishment for her fornication. Tamar is unable to find the life-saving witnesses (i.e., the signet ring, the cords, and staff), so she cries out to God and swears an oath whereby she dedicates her future offspring to him. Concerned for her welfare, God signals for the angel Michael to come to her assistance. Michael "enlightens" the eyes of Tamar, who is on the brink of destruction, so that she finds the witnesses and is saved. Thus, in PJ, Michael functions as a means through which special information is revealed.

Here is another example. "The seventy angels" make an appearance in Gen 11:7 with regard to the confusion of the languages. In an effort to resolve the tension created by the cohortative forms of the Hebrew text (נֵרְדָה and נָבְלָה), PJ translates these as a reference to the heavenly court. Thus, these angels are revealed with God before the nations and function as the means by which each nation receives its language. Now, the angels are both the object and means of revelation. In this instance, PJ explicitly contradicts a teaching found in the Babylonian Talmud, namely, that angels are ignorant of all languages except Hebrew (with Gabriel possibly knowing Aramaic).[14] The most striking example of angels serving as a source of secret or hidden knowledge is Exod 5:2. In the biblical text of this passage, Pharaoh asks, "Who is the Lord?" PJ understands Pharaoh to be asking, "What is the Lord's name?" PJ's Pharaoh responds that he has searched for His name in the Book of Angels (בספר מלאכייא) but was unable to find it. It is notable that PJ here presents a foreign ruler who, when seeking secret information pertaining to the true God of Israel, turns to a document associated with angels. PJ could have

---

13. *Alphabet of Ben Sira* 18a: סרח בת אשר . . . מבני אדם נכנסו בחיים בגן עדן. See Eisenstein, *Ozar Midrashim*, 1:50a: בעבור שאמרה ליעקב יוסף חי.

14. B. *Sotah* 12b; b. *Shabb.* 33a. See Yahalom, "Angels."

Table 2: Named Angels without the Use of מלאך

Aramaic	English	Verse Location
אוריאל	Uriel	Deut 34:6 (PJ)
אף	Wrath	Deut 9:19 (PJ)
גבריאל	Gabriel	Gen 37:15 (PJ); Exod 24:10 (PJ); Deut 32:9 (PJ); 34:6 (PJ)
זגנזגאל	Zagnazgael	Exod 3:2 (PJ)
חימה	Burning	Deut 9:19 (PJ)
חרון	Indignation	Deut 9:19 (PJ)
יופיאל	Jophiel	Deut 34:6 (PJ)
מיטטרון	Metatron	Gen 5:24 (PJ); Deut 34:6 (PJ)
מיכאל	Michael	Gen 3:25 (PJ); 38:25 (PJ); Exod 24:1 (PJ); Deut 32:9 (PJ); 34:3 (PJ); 34:6 (PJ)
יפהפה	Jephephia	Deut 34:6 (PJ)
משחית	Destruction	Deut 9:19 (PJ)
סמאל	Samael	Gen 3:6 (PJ); 4:1 (PJ)
סטנא	Satan	Gen 22:20 (PJ); Exod 32:1 (PJ); 32:19 (PJ); 32:24 (PJ); Lev 9:2 (PJ); 9:9 (PJ); Num 10:10 (PJ); 29:1 (PJ)
עזאל	Uzziel	Gen 6:4 (PJ)
קצף	Relentlessness	Deut 9:19 (PJ)
שמחזאי	Shamchazai	Gen 6:4 (PJ)
שריאל	Sariel	Gen 32:25 (TN)

something in mind as early as the Book of Watchers (*1 Enoch*) or as late as the Book of the Angel Raziel.

The Naming of Angels

In examining the 56 passages relevant for this paper, I have found that by far the most noticeable difference between TN and PJ would be the naming of angels. Unfortunately, there are a number of instances where a named angel is given without the insertion of מלאך (and consequently outside the scope of this analysis). For the sake of completeness, these are included (and italicized) in table 2.[15]

Looking at this data, we must note the variety and quantity of angelic identities present within PJ. Remarkably, of these numerous references, only *one* belongs to TN. In Gen 32:25, TN alone mentions Sariel. This isolated attestation is a significant parallel to the *War Rule* (1QM) and *1 Enoch*, where Sariel

15. Taken from Shinan, "Angelology," pp. 188–95.

appears as one of the four angels who stand in the Lord's presence.[16] In this passage, TN describes Sariel as the choirmaster who is eager to return to his duties.

It is in this category that PJ demonstrates the greatest departure from TN. As shown above, PJ showed little creativity when it came to creating or incorporating new angelic titles with respect to ranks or groups of angels. Here, however, PJ has assembled a chorus of specified angels. A few notable names should be mentioned. Within rabbinic literature, more than any other angel, Metatron is portrayed in the most dramatic terms. In the Talmud, Metatron's abilities are so fantastic that Elisha b. Abuyah nearly concedes to Gnostic dualism.[17] Metatron, "the Prince of the Universe," is considered to be a powerful angel, who is given preeminent status over the other angels.[18] Notably, however, in these passages Metatron is never identified with Enoch (i.e., there is no reference to Enoch's attaining angelic status and becoming Metatron). However, in later Jewish mystic circles, Enoch and Metatron are equated.[19] This is precisely how Metatron is understood in Gen 5:24 of PJ.

PJ—ופלח חנוך בקושטא קדם ייי והא ליתוהי עם דיירי ארעא ארום איתניגיד וסליק
לרקיעא במימר קדם ייי וקרא שמיה מיטטרון ספרא רבא:

And Enoch worshiped in truth before the Lord, and behold he was no longer with the inhabitants of earth, for he was pulled away and ascended to the firmament by the *memra* before the Lord. And he called his name Metatron, the great scribe.

Another instance of PJ challenging a standard rabbinic position is found in Gen 6:4. In this passage Uzziel and Shamchazai are identified as fallen angels. Initially, in light of dualistic implications, the rabbis rejected the idea of fallen angels and their introduction of evil into the world.[20] In the Mishnah, for example, rather than rebelling against God, the demons (מיזקין) were simply created during the twilight of the first *Erev Shabbat*.[21] Nevertheless, the notion of fallen angels was eventually embraced by the later rabbinic writings.[22] In fact, in his commentary on Num 13:33, Rashi identifies Uzziel and Shamchazai by name as fallen angels. Again, the angelology of PJ corresponds well with later rabbinic texts.

Deut 9:19 of PJ provides a miraculous encounter between Moses and a number of named angels. In the biblical text Moses mentions to Israel how

---

16. *1 Enoch* 9:1; 1QM 9:16. See Vermes, "Archangel Sariel."
17. B. *Hag*. 15a.
18. B. *Sanh*. 94a; See also b. *Hag*. 15a; b. *Sanh*. 38b; b. *AZ* 3b; *Exodus Rabbah* 18:4; *Numbers Rabbah* 12:12; and *Lamentations Rabbah* Prologue 24.
19. *3 Enoch* 4:1–4.
20. Shapiro, *Rabbinic Angelology*, pp. 28–30. Urbach, *Sages*, pp. 167–69.
21. M. *Avot* 5:6.
22. *PRE* 13, 14, 21, 22, 27; *Pseudo-Seder Eliahu Zuta*, p. 49.

he feared the wrath (הָאַף) and burning anger (הַחֵמָה) of the Lord that resulted from the incident of the golden calf. According to PJ, אף and חימה represent two of the five destroying angels that were sent to attack Israel (the other three being קצף, משחית, and חרון). In order to defend Israel, Moses resurrects Abraham, Isaac, and Jacob from the grave to contend with the mercenary angels. For the remaining two, namely "Wrath" and "Burning," Moses prays to God for salvation and is delivered.

The Divine Status of Angels

This category refers to the status of angels before God vis-à-vis the status of humanity. Within rabbinic literature, some rabbis argue that, regardless of righteousness, God's love for humanity is greater than his love for the angels. On a number of occasions, the attending angels approach God to dissuade him from creating human beings, but their concerns are eventually dismissed in favor of humanity's creation.[23] Likewise, based on Ps 91:11 ("he will give his angels charge over you"), R. Judah maintains that man is greater than the angels, for they are sent as guardian servants.[24] Elevating the status of angels, there are rabbis who maintain that it is the destiny of the righteous and/or Israel to become like the angels at the end of days, while others maintain that at that time the righteous will teach the angels the mysteries of heaven.[25]

It is difficult to determine the position of TN with respect to these issues. One possible indicator might be Deut 32:3. In this passage, according to TN, Moses states that it is impossible for the angels to praise God until Israel recites the liturgical phrase "holy, holy, holy" (Isa 6:3). In this way, angelic praise is contingent upon the praise that Israel offers God. For whatever reason, PJ modifies the expansion found in TN so as to exclude this statement made by Moses.

The status of angels in PJ is far more certain. In Num 15:40 of PJ, the Lord implores the people to keep his commandments so that they might be as "holy as the angels." Elsewhere, PJ provides two clear instances of angelification. As mentioned earlier in Gen 5:24, we read that Enoch, having lived a righteous life before the Lord, was drawn up into heaven and became the angel Metatron. Num 25:8 describes the 12 miracles of Phinehas that occurred after he killed the man who had taken a Midianite wife.[26] As a reward for that righteous deed, Phinehas is destined to become an angel, live eternally, and proclaim redemption at the end of days.

---

23. *Genesis Rabbah* 8:5, 10; *b. Sanh.* 38b.
24. *Genesis Rabbah* 78:1.
25. *Y. Shabb.* 6.10, 8d.
26. A similar tradition is found in *Numbers Rabbah* 20:25.

Conclusion

In light of the aforementioned analysis and previous discussion, we may draw the following conclusions. In comparing TN and PJ, one must conclude that the depiction of angels in PJ is consistently more embellished. One must also conclude that such a depiction is consistent with latter rabbinic angelologies. (1) With regard to titles or descriptions given to angels, though the variety of titles remains approximately the same, the number of attestations in PJ is significantly greater. (2) Even though the angels of TN occur in great number, those numbers are vastly increased in PJ. (3) In TN, angels only function as the object or accoutrement of revelation. In PJ, however, they become both the object and means of revelation. (4) Perhaps most dramatically, PJ specifies 16 angelic names that have no counterpart in TN. (5) Though the status of angels is somewhat indeterminate in TN, in PJ angels are portrayed as having a privileged and coveted status vis-à-vis humanity. Finally, in every one of the aforementioned categories, the use of angels in PJ most often corresponds to the later works of rabbinic literature (the Zohar, the *Alphabet of Ben Sira*, Hekhalot literature, Pseudo-Seder Eliahu Zuta, etc.). As we move from a Palestinian Targum, such as TN, to a literary targum, such as PJ, and to later forms of rabbinic literature, we seem to find that the rabbinic theological imagination only increases in boldness and creativity.

Bibliography

Azuelos, Y. *The Angelology of the Aramaic Targums on the Pentateuch*. Ph.D. dissertation. Schechter Institute of Jewish Studies, 2001. [Hebrew]

Bernstein, M. J. "The Aramaic Versions of Deuteronomy 32: A Study in Comparative Targumic Theology." Pp. 29–52 in *Targum and Scripture: Studies in Aramaic Translation and Interpretation in Memory of Ernest G. Clarke*. Edited by P. V. M. Flesher. Leiden: Brill, 2002.

Davidson, M. J. *Angels at Qumran: A Comparative Study of 1 Enoch 1–36, 72–108 and Sectarian Writings from Qumran*. Journal for the Study of the Pseudepigrapha Supplement 11; Sheffield: JSOT Press, 1992.

Eisenstein, J. D. *Ozar Midrashim*. New York: Eisenstein, 1915–18.

Flusser, D. "Resurrection and Angels in Rabbinic Judaism, Early Christianity, and Qumran." Pp. 568–72 in *The Dead Sea Scrolls Fifty Years after Their Discovery: Proceedings of the Jerusalem Congress, July 20–25, 1997*. Edited by L. H. Schiffman, E. Tov, and J. C. VanderKam. Jerusalem: Israel Exploration Society, 2000.

Glazov, G. "The Invocation of Ps. 51:17 in Jewish and Christian Morning Prayer." *JJS* 46 (1995) 167–82.

Gruenthaner, M. J. "The Demonology of the Old Testament." *Catholic Biblical Quarterly* 6 (1944) 6–27.

Kasher, R. "Angelology and the Supernal Worlds in the Aramaic Targums to the Prophets." *JSJ* 28 (1996) 168–91.

Olyan, S. M. *A Thousand Thousands Served Him: Exegesis and the Naming of Angels in Ancient Judaism*. Tübingen: Mohr Siebeck, 1993.
Rubio, C. G. *La angelología en la literatura rabínica y Sefardí*. Barcelona: Ameller, 1977.
Russell, D. S. *The Method and Message of Jewish Apocalyptic, 200 BC–AD 100*. London: SCM, 1964.
Schäfer, P. *Rivalitäta zwischen Engeln und Menschen: Untersuchungen zur rabbinischen Engelvorstellung*. Berlin: de Gruyter, 1975.
Shapiro, M. D. *The Philosophy Implicit in Rabbinic Angelology*. Cincinnati: Hebrew Union College, 1977.
Shinan, A. *The Aggadah in the Aramaic Targums to the Pentateuch*. Jerusalem: Makor, 1979. [Hebrew]
———. "The Angelology of the 'Palestinian' Targums on the Pentateuch." *Sefarad* 43 (1983) 182–98.
———. *The Embroidered Targum: The Aggadah in Targum Pseudo-Jonathan of the Pentateuch*. Jerusalem: Magnes, 1992. [Hebrew]
———. "Live Translation: On the Nature of the Aramaic Targums to the Pentateuch." *Prooftexts* 3 (1983) 41–49.
Stuart, M. "Sketches of Angelology in the Old and New Testament." *Bibliotheca Sacra* 1 (1843) 88–154.
Urbach, E. E. *The Sages: Their Concepts and Beliefs*. Cambridge: Harvard University Press, 2001.
Vermes, G. "The Archangel Sariel: A Targumic Parallel to the Dead Sea Scrolls." Pp. 159–66 in *Christianity, Judaism and Other Greco-Roman Cults*. Edited by Jacob Neusner. Leiden: Brill, 1975.
Yahalom, J. "Angels Do Not Understand Aramaic: On the Literary Use of Jewish Palestinian Aramaic in Late Antiquity." *JJS* 47 (1996) 33–44.

Hapax legomena and the Development of Proto-Onqelos: The Case of Genesis

KYONG-JIN LEE

For over a century, the origin of Targum Onqelos (TO) has been an important issue for those who study the history of interpretation of the Hebrew Bible (HB). Scholars have debated whether TO was authored by Babylonian Jews in the East or Palestinian Jews in the West. Although a significant number of literary and linguistic analyses have favored the Western origin of Onqelos, scholarly opinions still remain divided due to the lack of decisive evidence to settle the debate. Indeed, the earliest evidence of the authorship and status of TO appears in the most important Eastern text, the Babylonian Talmud, while the Palestinian rabbinic literature never mentions TO's translation.[1] It was not until Theodor Nöldeke's groundbreaking work that a strong case was made favoring a Palestinian provenance for TO, with a later Babylonian redressing.

Although his original formulation has undergone frequent revision, Nöldeke argued that the targum that became Onqelos was initially formulated in Palestine, for its main dialect is Western. Later it was taken to Babylonia, where it was recast into the final form that today we call Targum Onqelos. Thus, it is fair to credit Nöldeke with creating the concept that is today commonly known as "proto-Onqelos."[2] By "proto-Onqelos" one refers to the ensemble of elements—linguistic and exegetical—that an examination of the

---

1. B. *Qidd.* 49a refers to Onqelos as "our targum." The traditional attribution of the authorship to Onqelos is based on *b. Meg.* 3a: "R. Yirmeyahu—or some say R. Hiyya b. Abba—also said: The targum of the Pentateuch was composed by Onqelos the proselyte under the guidance of R. Elazar and R. Yehoshua." Modern scholars concur that *y. Meg.* 71c (the parallel passage to the *b. Meg.* 3a) speaks of *Aqilas*, the translator of the Greek version of the Pentateuch (not to be confused with Onqelos).
2. Nöldeke, *Die semitischen Sprachen*, pp. 37–38.

historically documented targumic traditions identifies as being part of the first stage of Onqelos's development.

The notion that an old Palestinian Targum was taken to Babylonia, where it was redacted also helps to explain the language and some of the common exegeses that the Palestinian Targums (PTs) and Targum Pseudo-Jonathan (PJ) share with TO. Targumic scholars such as Paul Flesher have repeatedly observed the shared nature between the PTs and PJ as well as between the PTs and TO. "Palestinian Targums [show] that these targums are often based upon knowledge of Onqelos' rendering.[3] This indicates that far from being unknown in Palestine, a version of Targum Onqelos (i.e., proto-Onqelos) was used as the base, alongside the Hebrew text, in the composition of the Palestinian Targums in Galilee."[4]

This paper will demonstrate that a useful way to explore the relationships among the pentateuchal targumic traditions may be through an examination of *hapax legomena* (hereafter HL) in the biblical text, since such renderings reveal a genetic connection more readily than other contexts. Scholars have long suspected the remarkable similarities among the PTs. However, they have been confronted by the sheer quantity of biblical texts necessary for studying the exact nature of relationships among the targums. In this sense, the HL in the book of Genesis can serve as a quantitative indicator of the degree of shared and distinctive interpretive traditions in handling difficult Hebrew words among the different pentateuchal Targums: Targum Onqelos, Palestinian Targums, and Targum Pseudo-Jonathan.

In the present paper, a synoptic approach to the HL of the targums will explore the interconnection between exegetical layers within given targumic traditions and their variants. Analysis of the extent of the similarities and differences among the Aramaic variants provides critical information to identify proto-Onqelos's interpretive approach from the approaches of the later targums for which it served as the base-text. The Aramaic treatment of the HL serves to distinguish the extent of exegetical makeover that proto-Onqelos (seen by some scholars as the common foundation for the targums) underwent during the redactional stage. One may presume that proto-Onqelos contained a relatively complete rendition of the book of Genesis. Nevertheless, its literal translation evidences difficulties and even lacunae, especially when it came across difficult terms. In a number of instances, when later versions found the rendering of proto-Onqelos unsatisfactory, they offered their own solution.

This study seeks to contribute to the ongoing scholarly debate on the relationship among different targums by unwrapping the exegetical traditions

---

3. See, for instance, Flesher, "Mapping the Synoptic Palestinian Targums"; "Exploring the Sources"; and "Is Targum Onqelos a Palestinian Targum?".

4. Idem, "History of Aramaic in Judaism." p. 93.

that underlie particular targumic passages.⁵ To facilitate this analysis, the study adheres to the idea that TO was composed in two stages.⁶ The first stage was the creation of proto-Onqelos by Jews in Judea. Most scholars today accept the view that TO was initially composed in the West, in the Aramaic dialect found in Judea, even though it exhibits some influence of eastern Aramaic. This base-text probably originated "during the first or early second century C.E."⁷

In the second stage, proto-Onqelos was used to develop new targums in the East and West. In the East, proto-Onqelos was redacted by Babylonian hands, and today is known as TO. The final text is highly unified and characterizes a stable tradition. The official recension must have taken its shape "before the end of the fourth century."⁸ In the West, scholars used proto-Onqelos to develop the PTs. As this study shows, the Palestinian versions often consulted proto-Onqelos, and many times they heartily agreed with its rendering. While some scholars hold that the PTs reached their final form most likely "in the latter half of the second century C.E.," others such as Philip Alexander are more cautious.⁹ He states that the PTs were composed no later than the third or fourth century C.E.¹⁰

During the second phase, Palestinian scholars produced several new targums: Targum Neofiti, two Fragment Targums, and several others that are collectively known as the Cairo Geniza Targum Fragments. This study will use two of these recensions: the Fragmentary Targum (FT) and Targum Neofiti (TN).¹¹ The dialects of both targums have been identified as Jewish Palestinian Aramaic, a Western Aramaic dialect.¹² These two Palestinian recensions typically share a literal translation complemented by inserted interpretive materials of various lengths. The FT distinctively catalogues technical

---

5. For current discussions on dating TO, see Müller-Kessler, "The Earliest Evidence for Targum Onqelos"; Flesher, "Is Targum Onqelos a Palestinian Targum?"; and Cook, "A New Perspective on the Language of Onqelos and Jonathan." On the date of PJ, scholars concur that it is a collection of interpretations deriving from widely different periods; it contains some of the earliest and latest datable sources (as late as the seventh century C.E.). See Hayward, "The Date of Targum Pseudo-Jonathan"; and Shinan, "Dating Targum Pseudo-Jonathan." Dating the Fragment Targums is equally complex because the work encompasses various readings.

6. For recent scholarship that successfully demonstrates proto-Onqelos's origin in Palestine, see Flesher, "Translations of Proto-Onqelos and the Palestinian Targums"; idem, "The Literary Legacy of the Priests?"

7. Idem, "History of Aramaic in Judaism," p. 89.

8. Ibid., p. 93.

9. Ibid., p. 90.

10. See Alexander, "Targum."

11. In this study, the verses drawn from the FT were selected from MS Vatican Ebr. 440, as edited by Michael Klein in his *Fragment-Targums of the Pentateuch.*

12. See, for example, Shinan, "The 'Palestinian' Targums"; Kaufman, "Dating the Language"; and Alexander, "Targum."

terms, *hapax legomena*, and other terms that require lexical and/or morphological explanation. The form of TN's translation characterizes a restrained and sober rendering, clearly in an attempt to preserve the original text's philological character. The translation contains numerous insertions of added material, although Neofiti is not as expansive as PJ. Most important for our study, Neofiti's exposition of the Pentateuch is virtually complete.

PJ was once mistakenly labeled a Palestinian Targum. From a linguistic point of view, its dialect combines various strands of the Aramaic dialect — ranging from Biblical Aramaic through Jewish Palestinian Aramaic to Babylonian Talmudic Aramaic. PJ's reliance on multiple sources is clearly demonstrated not only through elements from proto-Onqelos and midrashic sources but also through its incorporation of the PTs and their language, in addition to "its own distinctive language — its own grammar and its own lexicon."[13]

Hence, despite the intricate redactional phase that each targum underwent, whether in the East or the West, all three targums derive from a common prototype, and later each acquired its individual attributes. Such a development is evident given the remarkable number of instances of identical renderings parallel across all the extant targums — 10 out of the 18 HL found in Genesis.

This study is organized in two parts. The first provides a brief summary of the theoretical aspect of HL, based mainly on two of the few scholarly works that treat the conceptual issues and the historical use of the rare Hebrew terms and forms for exegetical purposes.[14] The essay's second section examines how the HL in the book of Genesis are rendered in the PTs, PJ, and TO. These targums exemplify the Jewish Aramaic translations of Hebrew Scripture in antiquity. Examples of parallel renderings will reveal how the targumists applied their exegetical skills to provide a learned Aramaic translation *and* an interpretation of the Hebrew parent text. This cross-analysis seeks to distinguish between instances of proto-Onqelos and instances of passages that developed at a later stage during redaction using the corpus of absolute HL.

Part I

In biblical studies, *hapax legomenon* is a term commonly understood to mean any word other than a proper name that occurs only once in the canon. This originally Greek term, which literally means "once said," was first used by early Homeric scholars in Alexandria as marginal notes to the Homeric epics for the purpose of classifying terms used only once.[15] Because terms of rare occurrence in the Bible are widely known as posing linguistic and hermeneutic challenges and also as being highly susceptible to scribal errors, they have beckoned the attention of scholars throughout centuries. HL have

---

13. Kaufman, "Dating the Language," p. 124.
14. See Cohen, *Biblical Hapax Legomena*; and Greenspahn, *Hapax Legomena*.
15. Cohen, *Biblical Hapax Legomena*, p. 1.

also been defined in various ways depending on the criteria applied to identify these problematic terms. Thus, the definitions have shifted over the ages according to the biblical scholars' focus of interest.[16]

Terms of rare occurrence were not necessarily the sole recipients of the designation of HL by the Masoretes. Among the marginal annotations made by the Masoretes in the HB, for instance, the ל, which stands for the Aramaic לית meaning "there is none other," appears the most frequently. The letter ל served to indicate unique forms and expressions, presumably to free the extant text from any potential suspicion of scribal error. In other words, it warned scribes that, although it was an unusual morphological or syntactical form or word, it was certainly not a mistake, and it ought to be preserved.

In another instance, the issue of HL, which is seemingly a strictly linguistic matter, lay at the heart of a major theological debate in the Middle Ages. Defenders of Rabbinic Judaism—Saadiah Gaon (882–942 C.E.), among others—used their extensive philological work on the rare biblical words in order to refute sectarian claims of the Karaite movement. Saadiah sought to demonstrate through the incorporation of the rabbinic tradition in his interpretation of HL that the Oral Tradition was indispensable to complement the understanding of the Written Torah.[17] Hence, the definition of HL was broadened to incorporate those terms of difficulty, which indeed occurred more than once and were considered to be important to the polemics of the time. These words were also attested in rabbinic literature.[18]

Several important scholarly works in the twentieth century have attempted to redefine HL. These studies share an emphasis on the functional aspect of HL. They understand HL as "any biblical word whose root occurs in but one context."[19] According to this definition, any Hebrew root that occurs in more than one context as well as proper names are not considered to be HL. This also excludes any root that may recur in the Aramaic portions of the Bible. Absolute HL are words that "are either absolutely new coinages of roots, or which cannot be derived in their formation or in their specific meaning from other occurring stems."[20] It must be further elaborated, however, that following Harold Cohen's conclusions in his authoritative 1977 work, an HL is any word that appears in only one context, no matter how often it recurs, because all the instances present one single context for their interpretation.[21]

So what did targumists do when they encountered a problematic word in the Hebrew *Vorlage*? When Aramaic translators were faced with a difficult term, they might initially have attempted to render the Hebrew original with apparent cognates. One may suspect such methods to be Hebraisms, where

16. Blau, "Hapax Legomena," col. 1318.
17. Ben-Sasson, *Jewish People*, pp. 441–49.
18. Cohen, *Biblical Hapax Legomena*, pp. 2–4.
19. Ibid., p. 7.
20. Casanowicz, "Hapax Legomena," pp. 226–28.
21. Cohen, *Biblical Hapax Legomena*, pp. 6–7.

the translator directly "copied" the Hebrew term into the translations. However, a comprehensive survey reveals that the ancient scholars avoided such a methodological blunder, for most of the words so treated also occur in Aramaic.[22] This was proven when the same words were found in similar context or usage in other rabbinic literature.

When a word could not be immediately identified with biblical or rabbinic usage, ancient scholars resorted to philological devices to provide the connection between Hebrew and Aramaic. One such device was metathesis, incorporated when the translator thought that the rare appearance and the consequential incomprehensibility of the Hebrew term were due to a scribal error and concluded that a reversed order of the Hebrew root letters was the solution to the problem. Additional relationships may be asserted on a similar assumption—not so much an unintended interchange of consonants but the practice of common sets of interchanges. In other words, targumists were aware that phonetically similar consonants interchange in writing. Consequently, some HL were treated in such a way that their roots could be legitimately substituted by an alternate consonant.

It is highly likely that certain targumic variant renderings may have resulted from orthographic confusion (such as ס and שׁ) or similar pronunciation (for example, between ע and א).[23] In fact, the weakening of gutturals and the interchange of sibilants are often attested in extrabiblical literature around the time of the targums—for example, the Dead Sea Scrolls. One must also be aware of the visual similarity of ר and ד, and the consequent interchange by the targumists.[24] Likewise, there are cases in which שׁ and צ are interchanged; also the dentals ט and ת were often regarded as equivalent. Naturally this does not mean that all cases of sibilants should be seen with suspicion but only that, at times, the translators saw the interchange as the solution to the understanding of the problematic term.[25]

When HL were perceived to be totally isolated, because cognate terms or philological ascriptions were irrelevant to a particular case, targumists were compelled to rely on less certain methods. First, context often served as recourse, though with some significant shortcomings by its nature. The attempt to clarify the meaning of a difficult word in light of its context is a crucial methodological step. A semantic elucidation solely based on this resource is, however, inherently subject to error and imprecision. When the context is obvious, this is not a particular problem. Thus, as will be shown in example 7 in part II below, targums unanimously translate דגה in Gen 48:16 as "multiply," although there is no certain etymological proof that corroborates this translation.

22. Greenspahn, *Hapax Legomena*, p. 49.
23. Ibid., pp. 52–53.
24. Ibid.
25. Ibid., pp. 53–54.

An important aspect of this approach is parallelism, when one word or line corresponds with another. If a grammatical construction joins two clauses, drawing the second under the first one, and is equivalent in meaning or expressing a contrasting idea, the understanding of the parallel terms may be greatly helped.[26] Needless to say, the importance of parallelism is greatly appreciated when the establishment of text or of meaning is in doubt.[27]

Second, another potential venue for understanding HL was by appealing to the rabbinic tradition. Because of the Jewish roots of the targumic translations, use of the same vocabulary or interpretive tradition between the larger rabbinic literature and the targums is not surprising.

Third, if neither context nor rabbinic tradition provided an explanation of HL, the targums opted for the so-called "free translation," and Aramaic works abound in such examples, attesting that there was no shortage of literary or hermeneutical ingenuity.[28] This is to say that the Aramaic targums, just like other variant translations, supply meanings and attach elaborate expositions that are often far from the original Hebrew. However, long-standing tradition and its familiarity to the audience at large make such translations and interpretations seem to be suitable to the biblical context. In addition, one must bear in mind that "the variants implicit in the *kětîb* and *qěrê* of HL certainly provide ample opportunities for different interpretations and translations."[29]

Part II

The most difficult HL is one whose isolation is "absolute," that is, when its consonantal tri-root occurs in a single biblical context, and so its meaning cannot be drawn from a recurring instance of the stem in Scripture. According to this criterion, Genesis contains 18 instances of absolute HL. Table 1 is a systematic presentation of the treatment of the absolute HL in four Aramaic versions of Genesis. These are classified by agreement:

A. Complete agreement across all extant versions
B. PJ agreeing with TO, while diverging from the PTs
C. Divergence in every extant version
D. Complete agreement between the PTs and PJ, while TO stands on its own[30]

---

26. See the summary of R. Lowth's influential study on parallelism in Berlin, *Dynamics of Biblical Parallelism*, pp. 1–3.
27. Barr, *Comparative Philology*, p. 277.
28. See Greenspahn, *Hapax Legomena*, pp. 55–60; and Syrén, *Blessings in the Targums*, pp. 16–24.
29. Cohen, *Biblical Hapax Legomena*, p. 23.
30. In the present exegetical discussion, the morphological and syntactical differences between Jewish Palestinian Aramaic and Jewish Babylonian Aramaic are beyond the scope of our analysis. The chart focuses on the convergences and divergences of the semantic aspect of the HL.

Table 1

		HB	TO	PJ	TN	FT
A	Gen 6:14	גפר	קדרום	קדרונין	קדרונין	קדרונין
A	Gen 11:6	יזמו	חשיבו	חשיבו	חשבו	Missing
B	Gen 15:2	משק	בר פרנסא דמשקאה	בר בפרנסת ביתי בדרמשק מסכי למירת יתי	בר ביתי דעל ידוי איתעבד לי נסין בדרמשק ירית יתי	בר ביתי דעל ידוי אתעביד לי ניסין בדמשק
C	Gen 21:16	מטחוי	כמיגר	מן ברה כשיעור מיגד	כמרמי	Missing
C	Gen 24:21	משתאה	שהי בה מסתכל	מסתין	שתי ונסתכל	Missing
A	Gen 24:63	שוח	לצלאה	לצלאה	למצלוייה	Missing
B	Gen 25:30	הלעיטני	אטעמני	אטעים	איכל	Missing
A	Gen 26:20	התעשקו	אתעסיקו	אתעסקו	אתעשקו	Missing
A	Gen 28:12	סלם	סלמא	סולמא	סלם	סולמא
A	Gen 30:37	לוז	לוז	לוז	לוז	Missing
C	Gen 36:24	ימם	גבריא	דארבע ית ערדיא עם אתני ולזמן	Missing	Missing
A	Gen 40:11	אשחט	עצר	עצרית	עצרית	Missing
B	Gen 41:23	צנמות	נצן	נצן	צנימן	Missing
D	Gen 41:43	אברך	אבא למלכא	אבא למלכא ורכיך בשנייא	אבוי דמלכא ורכיך בשנייה	אבוי דמלכא ורכיך בשנייה
A	Gen 43:11	בטנים	בטנין	בוטנין	בוטנין	Missing
A	Gen 47:13	תלה	אשתלהי	אשתלהון	אשתלהון	Missing
A	Gen 48:16	ידגו	וכנוני ימא יסגון בגו בני אנשא על ארעא	והיכמא דכוורי ימא סגי מסתגי במיא	ויסגון בארעא היך דנוניי יסגון במיא	Missing
B	Gen 49:17	שפיפן	חיוי חורמן	לחורמנא	לחיוויא	לחויא

The following examples feature a close examination of seven renderings of HL among the variant versions, identifying early and later exegetical layers that underlie targumic passages. This synoptic analysis seeks to identify proto-Onqelos's contribution by comparing the variants' exegetical texts and uncovering the targumists' methodological criteria.

Example 1: Genesis 15:2

וַיֹּאמֶר אַבְרָם אֲדֹנָי יֱהֹוִה מַה תִּתֶּן לִי וְאָנֹכִי הוֹלֵךְ עֲרִירִי וּבֶן מֶשֶׁק בֵּיתִי הוּא דַּמֶּשֶׂק אֱלִיעֶזֶר

JPS: But Abram said, "O Lord GOD, what can You give me, seeing that I shall die childless, and the one in charge of my household is Dammesek Eliezer!"

ויאמר אברם אדני יהוה מה תתן לי ואנכי הולך ערירי ובן משק ביתי הוא דמשק אליעזר

TO: But Abram said, "O Lord God, what will you give me, seeing that I go childless, and this manager who is in my house is Eliezer of Damascus?"[31]

ואמר אברם ייי אלקים סגין יהבת לי וסגין אית קדמך למיתן לי ברם מה הנייה אית לי דאנא עביר מן עלמא דלא בנין ואליעזר בר פרנסת ביתי דעל ידוי איתעבידו לי ניסין בדרמשק מסכי למירת יתי

PJ: But Abram said, "Lord God, you have given me much, and there is much before you to give me. But what benefit do I have, since I pass from the world childless, and Eliezer, the manager of my house, at whose hands miracles have been performed for me in Damascus, expects to be my heir?"[32]

ואמר אברם בבעו ברחמין מן קדמך ייי סגין יהבת לי וסגין קדמך למיהן לי ואנה אזל מן עלמא בלא בנין ואליעזר בר ביתי דעל ידוי איתעבד לי נסין בדרמשק ירית יתי

TN: And Abraham said: I beseech by the mercies that are before you, O Lord; many things have you given to me, but I am going from this world without sons, and Eliezer the son of my house, by whose hand wonders were worked for me in Damascus, will be my heir.[33]

ואמר אברם בבעו רחמין מן קודמך ה אלהים סגיין בירכן יהבת לי וסגין אית קודמך למיתן לי ברם מה הנייה לי דאנא אזיל מן גו עלמא דלא בנין ואליעזר בר בייתי דעל ידוי איתעבידו לי ניסין בדרמסק הוא סבר בגתמי למירת יתי

FT: And Abraham said: "Lord God, You have given me much; and there is before You more to give to me; however, what benefit do I have since I leave the world childless; and Eliezer, son of my house, through whom You performed miracles for me in Damascus, will subsequently inherit me.[34]

Ancient Aramaic scholars were seemingly uncertain of the meaning of the Hebrew term משק in Gen 15:2. They could infer from the context of the conversation that takes place between the childless Abraham and God that Eliezer was a member of Abraham's household, most likely a slave rather than a kin. Biblical commentators have typically understood ובן משק ביתי הוא דמשק אליעזר as referring to Abraham's servant, "the Damascan." Abraham may have adopted him as a son and, if the Hurrian law of inheritance had been applied, Eliezer would have been Abraham's proper beneficiary.[35] According to von Rad, Israel does not know such a rule of inheritance. But the Nuzi contracts (fifteenth century B.C.E., east of Tigris) attest cases in

---

31. English translations for TO are based on Aberbach and Grossfeld, *Targum Onkelos to Genesis*, based on the text of Sperber.

32. English translations for PJ are based on Maher, *Targum Pseudo-Jonathan: Genesis*.

33. English translations for TN are based on Díez Macho's *Neophyti 1: Targum Palestinense*. Note: Whenever English translations differ from the rest in spite of identical Aramaic renderings, English translations on the given HL have been harmonized across versions for the purpose of this comparative study.

34. English translations for the FT are based on Klein, *Fragment-Targums of the Pentateuch*.

35. Plaut, *Torah*, p. 109.

which childless individuals adopted slaves. The adoptee's duty, in turn, was to give the testator proper burial.[36] Albright proposed that Abraham adopted Eliezer so that he would be able to obtain credit from the local inhabitants. The native-born Eliezer could own property, thus extending Abraham's credit base.[37]

Verse 3 states that this Eliezer was born in Abraham's house: "One born in my house is to be my heir."[38] Where the Hebrew original refers to Eliezer as בן משק ביתי, both FT and TN conspicuously leave out the translation of the Hebrew HL משק. They simply state אליעזר בר ביתי. These targumists attempted to make up for the obvious absence of a word-for-word translation of משק by appending a comment, which is groundless from the biblical standpoint.[39] FT and TN, joined by PJ all concur that this Eliezer is the man through whom God performed miracles on behalf of Abraham in Damascus.

Gen 15:2 is the only occasion on which Abraham's servant Eliezer is mentioned in the Bible. Moreover, nowhere is there mention of God's working wonders for Abraham through the agency of Eliezer or any incident that remotely fits such a description. The only occasion when Abraham was near Damascus was when he launched a rescue campaign for his nephew Lot and pursued the captors as far as Hobah, north of Damascus (Gen 14:15). One may equally wonder whether the biblical author meant the ancient Aramean city of Damascus, given that the HL in question here shares its tripartite root with משק. Had the Hebrew author meant that Eliezer's ancestry was from Damascus, as TO has it, one may wonder at the lack of the gentilic *yod* in הוא דמשק אליעזר. Both PJ and TO insert the Aramaic term פרנסא instead of משק. English translations typically render פרנסא "manager."

PJ's treatment of this verse reflects its typically composite character when it integrates an expansionary comment to the already extant translation of the term. FT and TN here are clearly oblivious of the term פרנסא. Evidence in this example suggests strongly that proto-Onqelos's version was economic, to the degree that it did not even incorporate a proper explication of the difficult term in question. At a later stage, when the PTs and PJ found themselves in the process of composing their respective targum, consulting or basing each

---

36. Von Rad, *Genesis*, pp. 178–79.
37. Albright, *Yahweh and the Gods of Canaan*, pp. 65–66.
38. JPS, 1917.
39. *Genesis Rabbah* 44:9 (trans. by H. Freedman) explains, "AND HE THAT SHALL BE POSSESSOR (BEN MESHEK) OF MY HOUSE, etc. (xv, 2). R. Leazar said in the name of R. Jose b. Zimra: BEN MESHEK BETHI (MY HOUSE) alludes to Lot, whose soul, [said Abraham,] longs (*shokeketh*) to be my heir. IS DAMESEK ELIEZER [E.V. 'ELIEZER OF DAMASCUS']: this means, for whose sake I pursued the kings as far as Damascus and God helped me. R. Simeon b. Lakish said: BEN MESHEK BETHI means 'The son of my household'; IS ELIEZER OF DAMASCUS—i.e., by his assistance I pursued the kings as far as Damascus, and his name was actually Eliezer; for it says, He led forth his trained men, three hundred and eighteen (Gen. xiv, 14), the numerical value of Eliezer being three hundred and eighteen."

largely on proto-Onqelos, they saw that what TO left out needed to be given proper treatment. The PTs, however, failed to fill in the gap. They smoothed out their texts by supplementing the lacuna with an extrabiblical tradition regarding Eliezer, which neglects to explicate the meaning of the HL.

As mentioned above, PJ is a composite text in terms of its language and especially content. It was at a later stage in development when the understanding of פרנסא was possibly imported from the final version of TO, which had been fleshed out in Babylonia. Scholars assert that TO, as known today, may date sometime between the second and fourth centuries C.E.[40] Hence, one may conclude that the expansive addition shared between the PTs and TO's literal rendering of the text gave birth to PJ's understanding of Abraham's competent servant. Proto-Onqelos's rendering of Gen 15:2 not only halted at a plain rendering of the Hebrew text, it also left out the translation of a crucial term in this verse—משק. It was during the recasting process in the East that TO was finally able to solve the enigma by providing the missing piece, פרנסא, for a complete translation of the verse.

Example 2: Genesis 24:21

וְהָאִישׁ מִשְׁתָּאֵה לָהּ מַחֲרִישׁ לָדַעַת הַהִצְלִיחַ יְהוָה דַּרְכּוֹ אִם לֹא

JPS: The man, meanwhile, stood gazing at her, silently wondering whether the LORD had made his errand successful or not.

וגברא שהי בה מסתכל שתיק למדע האצלח יוי אורחיה אם לא

TO: The man gazed at her observing silently to know whether the Lord had made his way successful or not.

וגברא הוה ממתין לה ושתיק למינדע האצלח ייי אורחיה אין לה

PJ: The man was waiting for her and was silent to know whether the Lord had made his way successful or not.

וגבר הוה שתי ומסתכל בה שתק למידע הא אן אצלח ייי אורחה או לא

TN: And the man drank and observed her silently to see whether the Lord had made his way successful or not.

FT: None.

The three extant Aramaic variants exhibit slightly different understandings of the HL משתאה in Gen 24:21. Here the *hithpaʿel* form has clearly undergone metathesis—the ת is interchanged with the immediately following sibilant שׁ. The root of this verb-form is שאה ("to gaze" in *hithpaʿel*), and not שתה ("to drink," which is not attested in *hithpaʿel*). TN, however, offers the Aramaic equivalents of both Hebrew triliteral roots in place of מסתכל-משתאה ("to observe") and שתי ("to drink"). It is highly likely that TN did not know the meaning of this HL. In fact, there is no evidence in antiquity that biblical scholars viewed שאה as being interchangeable in meaning with שעה. Thus

---

40. Flesher, "History of Aramaic in Judaism," p. 93.

it provided the Aramaic equivalent of what it considered to be two equally plausible Hebrew roots. Modern scholars typically understand the rare stem שאה to be a by-form of שעה ("to gaze").[41]

PJ translates משתאה as מתן ("to wait").[42] More often than not, Pseudo-Jonathan engages in elaborate interpretation in addition to a literal translation whenever a hermeneutical source is at reach. In this example, however, PJ is atypically economical in its rendering. TO translates the Hebrew HL שהי, "to gaze" alongside מסתכל, "to observe." One may assume that all three Aramaic renderings were familiar with some interpretive tradition in which the man was watching the girl intensely as he wondered in his heart "whether the Lord had made his journey successful or not."[43] PJ's selection of ממתין indeed embodies all three notions of gazing, plotting, and pondering as depicted in Gen 24:21. By the same token, it eludes a direct translation. Hence, one may conclude that PJ opted in this case for an exegetical summary—unlike its usual hermeneutical expansions.

The Aramaic variants on this verse reflect one of those instances when the Hebrew term is so problematic that even resorting to context does not grant a uniform understanding among translators. All three surviving targumic variants exhibit distinct understandings on the given HL.

In this verse, one suspects the variant versions were not acquainted with each other. Though the term מסתכל is present in both TO and TN, the alternatively pairing words exhibit disagreement. One could conclude that the rendering found in TO does not originate from proto-Onqelos, taking into account its absence across all variants. At the same time, both TO and TN offer two verbs to convey the meaning of the once-occurring term. The term מסתכל found in both Onqelos and Neofiti suggests a high likelihood that proto-Onqelos rendered Hebrew משתאה simply as מסתכל. It was during redaction when an alternative view was added by later targumists.

Example 3: Genesis 24:63

וַיֵּצֵא יִצְחָק לָשׂוּחַ בַּשָּׂדֶה לִפְנוֹת עָרֶב וַיִּשָּׂא עֵינָיו וַיַּרְא וְהִנֵּה גְמַלִּים בָּאִים

JPS: And Isaac went out walking in the field toward evening and, looking up, he saw camels approaching.

ונפק יצחק לצלאה בחקלא למפני רמשא וזקף עינוהי וחזא והא גמליא אתן

TO: And Isaac went out to pray in the field toward evening time, and he raised his eyes, and saw, and behold, camels were coming.

ונפק יצחק לצלאה באנפי ברא לעידוני רמשא וזקף עינוי וחמא והא גמלייא אתיין

PJ: And Isaac went out to pray in the open field at evening time, and he raised his eyes, and saw, and behold, camels were coming.

---

41. See שאה in *HALOT* col. 1368; and שאה in BDB 981.
42. See מתן in Jastrow, *Dictionary*.
43. Evidence for this common exegetical tradition is in *Genesis Rabbah* 60:6, "R. Phinehas said in the name of R. Hanan of Sepphoris: He scrutinized her and looked at her."

ונפק יצחק למצלוייה באפי ברא לעדוני רמשא ונטל עייוני וחמה והא גמלין אתין

TN: And Isaac had gone out to pray in the open field at evening time and he raised his eyes and saw and behold, camels were coming.

FT: None.

The exact meaning of the HL שוח evades biblical scholars to this day. Early translations differ from each other.[44] Accordingly modern Bible commentaries tend to offer varying views on Gen 24:63. The targums, however, exhibit a remarkably uniform understanding of this term. All three targums (Neofiti, Pseudo-Jonathan, and Onqelos) understand שוח to mean "to pray." Moreover, they all restrain themselves from the urge to add any aggadic comments—including PJ. In this case, a direct influence of proto-Onqelos over the extant versions is evident. Scholars agree that the targums adopted the rabbinic view, which traditionally knew Isaac to be the founder of the *Minḥa* prayer. This rabbinic notion itself is grounded in Gen 24:63.[45]

Numerous aggadic traditions are paralleled in the rabbinic literature and the targums. However, the targum and the midrash have different agendas. For instance, TO is known to quote the midrash when it is helpful in explicating the text's simple meaning.[46] The common rendering of שוח across the rabbinic tradition and the witnesses to proto-Onqelos indicates that this particular translation ought to be attributed to an early tradition. In other words, the uniform understanding of this HL in the rabbinic literature as well as the targums strongly indicates that it originated from a common source that was deeply embedded in the Jewish culture; thus, it was of popular knowledge.

Example 4: Genesis 25:30

וַיֹּאמֶר עֵשָׂו אֶל־יַעֲקֹב הַלְעִיטֵנִי נָא מִן־הָאָדֹם הָאָדֹם הַזֶּה כִּי עָיֵף אָנֹכִי עַל־כֵּן קָרָא־שְׁמוֹ אֱדוֹם

JPS: And Esau said to Jacob, "Give me some of that red stuff to gulp down, for I am famished"—which is why he was named Edom.

ואמר עשו ליעקב אטעימני כען מן סמוקא סמקא הדין ארי משלהי אנא על כין קרא שמיה אדום

TO: And Esau said to Jacob, "Now give me to taste of that red dish, for I am exhausted." Therefore, his name was called Edom.

ואמר עשו ליעקב אטעם יתי כדון מן תבשילא סמוקא הדין ארום משלהי אנא בגין כן קרא שמיה אדום

PJ: And Esau said to Jacob, "Give me to taste of that red dish, for I am exhausted." Therefore, his name was called Edom.

---

44. For example, the Septuagint has "in order to gossip" (ἀδολεσχῆσαι); *Vulgate*, "in order to meditate" (*ad meditandum*); Peshitta, "so as to result" (ܠܡܬܠܐ). See שוח in *HALOT* col. 1312.

45. The Babylonian and Palestinian Talmuds as well as the *Mekilta* state that Isaac was the precursor of the afternoon prayer. See n. 41 to this verse in Maher, *Targum Pseudo-Jonathan: Genesis*. See also n. 22 to the same verse in Aberbach and Grossfeld, *Targum Onkelos to Genesis*.

46. See Shinan, "The 'Palestinian' Targums."

ואמר עשו ליעקב איכל יתי כען מן תבשילא סמוקא הדין ארום משלהי אנה בגין כדין קרא שמה אדום

TN: And Esau said to Jacob, "Give me to eat of that red dish for I am exhausted." Because of this his name was called Edom.

FT: None.

The one-time occurrence of לעט is usually translated into English as "to swallow greedily," or "to gulp down," which describes the action of voracious eating—appropriate to convey the sense of urgency in Esau's request.[47] Interestingly, however, both TO and PJ have Esau asking Jacob merely to taste, not to eat from the "red dish." Here the targums' word choice, which tones down Esau's rough and urgent behavior, raises a question. A number of literary sources in Mishnaic Hebrew suggest that the rabbis were not unaware of the forcefulness of the biblical expression. The word טלע is used to express stuffing or forceful feeding of animals in a number of examples: *m. Shabb.* 24:3; *t. BQ* 6.17; *t. Ḥul.* 3.19.[48] Aberbach and Grossfeld suggest that "owing to the absence of a precise Aramaic equivalent of לעט in Jewish-Aramaic sources, TO and PJ employ the ʿaphel of טעם, possibly in the sense of feeding rather than merely giving to taste."[49]

TN supplies איכל for לעט. Due to the lack of a precise Aramaic equivalent, TN seems to have chosen the most basic term to fit the sentence. However, TN also maintained the causative stem from the original Hebrew *hiphʿil* of לעט. Esau asks that he be allowed to eat of the red dish. Thus Neofiti forthrightly conveys the nature of Esau's request, without sorting through the finer nuance of the Hebrew HL. If the ancient Aramaic translators actually understood the meaning of this rare term, as corroborated by the usage attested in Mishnaic Hebrew, this may be an instance when the targumists felt the need to nuance their translation in order best to convey their perception of the Hebrew original.

It is true that a rendering shared only by TO and PJ cannot be proven to derive from proto-Onqelos, because PJ might have gotten it from the final version of TO. Identifying a proto-Onqelos version in this case is even more complicated by TN's variant rendering. The question what the original proto-Onqelos version read like is difficult to guess. In the final form of both TO and PJ, the ʿaphel form of טעם is the main verb in their respective renderings. It is hard to imagine that proto-Onqelos's translation simply left out the verb in the sentence.

---

47. For "to swallow greedily," see BDB 542. For "to gulp down," see von Rad, *Genesis*, p. 261. Skinner, in his classical commentary on Genesis (p. 361 n. 30), notes that לעט refers to "a coarse expression suggesting bestial voracity . . . , used in the feeding of the cattle." Speiser writes in *Genesis*, p. 195 n. 30, "Esau is depicted as an uncouth glutton; he speaks of 'swallowing, gulping down,' instead of eating, or the like."

48. See n. 20 to Genesis 25 in Aberbach and Grossfeld's *Targum Onkelos to Genesis*, p. 152.

49. Ibid., p. 153.

Example 5: Genesis 36:24

וְאֵ֣לֶּה בְנֵֽי־צִבְע֗וֹן וְאַיָּ֤ה וַעֲנָה֙ ה֣וּא עֲנָ֔ה אֲשֶׁ֨ר מָצָ֤א אֶת־הַיֵּמִם֙ בַּמִּדְבָּ֔ר בִּרְעֹת֥וֹ אֶת־הַחֲמֹרִ֖ים לְצִבְע֥וֹן אָבִֽיו׃

JPS: The sons of Zibeon were these: Aiah and Anah—that was the Anah who discovered the hot springs in the wilderness while pasturing the asses of his father Zibeon.

ואלין בני צבעון ואיה וענה הוא ענה דאשכח ית גבריא במדברא כד הוה רעי ית חמריא לצבעון אבוהי

TO: Now these were the sons of Zibeon: Aiah, and Anah—this is Anah who had found the mighty ones in the wilderness, while he was pasturing the asses for his father Zibeon.

ואילין בני צבעון ואיה וענה הוא ענה דארבע ית ערדיא עם אתני ולזמן אשכח ית כודנייתא דינפקו מנהון כד הוה רעי ית חמרייא לצבעון אבוי

PJ: These are sons of Zibeon: Aiah and Anah; that was the Anah who crossed wild asses with she-asses, and in due time found the mules that had come forth from them, while he was pasturing the asses of Zibeon his father.

TN: Missing.

FT: None.

The two surviving targumic variants in this example strongly suggest that TO and PJ were not aware of each other's understanding of the Hebrew HL ימם. Both interpretive traditions attest to the fact that the meaning of ימם was obscure also to the ancient interpreters. In fact, most translators of the Masoretic Text (including the *Vulgate* and *Peshitta*) understand ימם to be "hot springs." Some renderings state "water" because they assume a metathesis from an original מים.

PJ's reading was supported to some extent by rabbinic interpreters when both the *Bavli* and *Yerushalmi* as well as *Genesis Rabbah* concur that ימם signifies "mules."[50] *Genesis Rabbah* 82:14 explains that the rabbis interpreted ימם as "hybrids"—meaning the crossbreed of a horse and an ass. The controversy in this particular midrash sought to come up with the exact meaning of ימם. However, all parties agree that the Hebrew word means "mules."

TO seemingly connects ימם with אמים in Deut 2:10–11: "a large and numerous people, as tall as the Anakim, had formerly inhabited it. Like the Anakim, they are usually reckoned as Rephaim, though the Moabites call them Emim."[51] The Hebrew noun also derived from the same tri-root, אימה, means "terror, dread." Hence, it is understandable that TO would derive גבריא from the Anakim, who were famous for their unusually tall and terrifying stature.[52]

---

50. See *y. Ber.* 12b; *b. Pes.* 54a.
51. Bible quotations, unless otherwise noted, are from the NRSV, 1989.
52. See Deut 1:28, 2:21, 9:2.

In summary, both TO and PJ were uncertain of the meaning of the rare term, thus they resorted to aggadic expositions instead of a direct translation. Both renderings resorted to metathesis. Targumists seemingly were of the opinion that the rare appearance and, accordingly, the incomprehensibility of ימם may owe to a scribal error. Each targumist reached a different conclusion, yet the two concurred that a reversed order of the Hebrew root might be the solution to their puzzle.

Example 6: Genesis 41:43

וַיַּרְכֵּב אֹתוֹ בְּמִרְכֶּבֶת הַמִּשְׁנֶה אֲשֶׁר־לוֹ וַיִּקְרְאוּ לְפָנָיו אַבְרֵךְ וְנָתוֹן אֹתוֹ עַל כָּל־אֶרֶץ מִצְרָיִם

JPS: He had him ride in the chariot of his second-in-command, and they cried before him, "Abrek!" Thus he placed him over all the land of Egypt.

וארכיב יתיה ברתיכא תנייתא דיליה ואכריזו קדמוהי דין אבא למלכא ומני יתיה על כל ארעא דמצרים

TO: He then had him ride in the chariot of his second-in-command, and they proclaimed before him, "This one is father of the king." Thus he appointed him over all the land of Egypt.

וארכיב יתיה ברתיכא תנייתא דלפרעה והוו מקלסין לקדמוי דין אבא דמלכא רב בחכמתא ורכיך בשנייא ומני יתיה סרכן על כל ארעא דמצרים

PJ: He had him ride in Pharaoh's second chariot, and they cried out before him, "This is the father of the king, great in wisdom and tender in years." And he appointed him prince over all the land of Egypt.

וארכב יתיה בארתכא תנינתא דידיה והוון מקלסין קדמוי יחי אבוי דמלכא דרב בחכמתא וזעית בשפר ורכיך בשנייה ומני יתה רב ושליט על כל ארעא דמצרים

TN: And he made him ride in his second chariot and they cried out before him: Long live the father of the king who is great in wisdom although young in beauty and tender in years. And he appointed him master and officer over all the land of Egypt.

והוון מקלסין קודמוי ואמרין יחי אבוי דמלכה דרב בחכמתה ורכיך בשנייה

FT: And they sang praise before him and said: "Long live the father of the king; who is great in wisdom and tender in years."

From the context, the HL אברך is a cry of homage for Joseph. Biblical commentators remain divided as to a sure meaning and etymological derivation for this word. Geza Vermes has suggested that it may originally have been an Egyptian term.[53] The targums treat אברך as a combination of two Hebrew words: אב, "father," and רך, "tender." TN, FT, and PJ highlight the seemingly contrasting qualities that distinguish Joseph: he is young, yet he is exalted above the Pharaoh. Such accolade of Joseph that elucidates the problematic Hebrew term is shared by *Genesis Rabbah* and the Babylonian Talmud.[54] This interpretation seems to derive from Joseph's own explanation of his

---

53. See Vermes, "Haggadah in the Onkelos Targum," p. 162.
54. *Genesis Rabbah* 90:3; *b. BB* 4a.

miraculous change of fate to his brothers: "So it was not you who sent me here, but God; he has made me a *father to Pharaoh*, and lord of all his house and ruler over all the land of Egypt" (Gen 45:8). Given the shared interpretation between the PT and PJ, it is surprising that TO contains only the explanation of אב. It is apparent that the rest of the versions broke אברך in two and gave each its corresponding Hebrew translation. A satisfactory explanation as to why TO did not take the same logical step remains elusive.

Example 7: Genesis 48:16

הַמַּלְאָךְ הַגֹּאֵל אֹתִי מִכָּל רָע יְבָרֵךְ אֶת הַנְּעָרִים וְיִקָּרֵא בָהֶם שְׁמִי וְשֵׁם אֲבֹתַי אַבְרָהָם וְיִצְחָק וְיִדְגּוּ לָרֹב בְּקֶרֶב הָאָרֶץ

JPS: The angel who has redeemed me from all harm—
Bless the lads,
In them may my name be recalled,
And the name of my fathers Abraham and Isaac,
And may they be teeming multitudes upon the earth.

מלאכא דפרק יתי מכל בישז יברין תי עולימיא ויתקרי בהון שמי ושום אבהתי אברהם ויצחק וכנוני ימא יסגון בגו בני אנשא על ארעא

TO: The angel who has redeemed me from all evil, may he bless the boys, and in them may my name be recalled, and the names of my ancestors Abraham and Isaac. And may they multiply like the fish of the sea among mankind on earth.

יהי רעוא קדמך דמלאכא דזמינת לי למפכרק יתי מכל בישא יברך ית טלייא ויתקרי בהון שמי ושום אבהתי אברהם ויצחק והיכמא דכוורי ימא סגי ומסתגי במיא כדין ברך יוסף יתקפון לסגי בגו ארעא

PJ: May it be pleasing before you that the angel whom you assigned to me to redeem me from all evil, bless the boys; and let my name be recalled in them, and the name of my fathers Abraham and Isaac. And as the fish of the sea multiply continually in the water, so may the children of Joseph grow into a multitude on the earth.

מלאכא די פרק יתי מן כל עקא יברך ית טליא ויתקרי בהון שמי ושם אבהתי אברהם ויצחק ויסגון בארעא היך נוניא יסגון במיא

TN: The angel who has redeemed me from all tribulation, may he bless the boys and let my name be called in them and the names of my fathers Abraham and Isaac. And may they multiply in the land like the fish multiply in the waters.

FT: None.

This is a good example of those cases in which targumists resort to context when a term does not appear in contemporary literature or cognate languages. Therefore, even though there is no etymological proof that ידגו is connected to דג "fish," targumic traditions explain this form as being related.[55] The underlying assumption here is that fish are characteristically

---

55. Greenspahn, *Hapax Legomena*, p. 55.

prolific.⁵⁶ Hence Bible translations have traditionally understood ידגו as "multiply." The targumists replace the Hebrew HL with Aramaic verb forms of סגי. They do not simply provide a word-for-word translation, but they paraphrase ידגו, "may they multiply like the fish of the sea." Here TN, PJ, and TO upheld proto-Onqelos's tradition on Gen 48:16, while adhering to the universally recognized and typically explained derivation of the noun דג. This is obviously an instance of a proto-Onqelos rendering.

Conclusion

This study used the *hapax legomena* as a diagnostic tool to examine the exegetical interrelationship among targums of Genesis. To summarize, there are 10 instances when translations of the HL unanimously agree across all the extant versions. In 4 other instances, there is agreement between PJ and TO, while these diverge from the renderings of the PTs. In 3 more instances, there is a divergent rendering in each extant version. In 1 instance, the PTs and PJ agree, while TO stands on its own.

The cross-analysis displayed in table 1 reveals that there is sufficient evidence of a genetic relationship among the pentateuchal targums. In a substantial number of instances the versions reach unanimity with respect to the meaning of a given problematic term: 10 out of 18 cases of absolute HL that exist in Genesis.⁵⁷ In this majority of instances, versions not only match with regard to the translation of a given HL, but they also contain a similar word order in the rest of the verse. These Aramaic versions share more than lexical and morphological choices. A synoptic reading of the four versions shows clearly that shared creativity and ambiguity inherited from a base-text have been preserved by each targum. Furthermore, a verbatim resemblance of entire sentences is quite common among these clauses that originally contained rare Hebrew terms. In cases where there are additions (usually of an interpretive nature), one still observes that the treatments of the given problematic term bear a striking resemblance. The evidence is too strong to suggest that the commonality among the targums in their translation and interpretation of the HL is simply a coincidence.

As noted above, PJ distinguishes itself by being "the most paraphrastic of all the Pentateuchal targums: it is estimated to be about twice the length of the original Hebrew text."⁵⁸ Thus, even among these 10 cases, PJ is interspersed with expansions that are typically absent in other versions. However, apart from such a prominently distinguishing feature, all 10 verses present either an "exact quotation" or a "quotation with minor changes" across the

---

56. This popular etymological understanding of דגה is also found in rabbinic interpretations of Gen 48:17; b. Ber. 20a; b. Sotah 36b; *Genesis Rabbah* 97:3.
57. Gen 6:14, 11:6, 24:63, 26:20, 28:12, 30:37, 40:11, 43:11, 47:13, and 48:16.
58. Alexander, "Jewish Aramaic Translations," p. 219.

variant renderings.⁵⁹ Materials composed in an earlier period were often consulted and used as the starting point for the composition of later texts. This is widely evidenced by the presence of common literary elements across parallel targums. This phenomenon clearly demonstrates that the extant Aramaic versions consulted a common base-text now identified as proto-Onqelos. A common literary source underlies both the Eastern and the Western traditions.

Moreover, in 4 out of these 10 instances, the Aramaic rendering is a cognate of the Hebrew root.⁶⁰ A cursory examination may lead to the conclusion that the agreement among the versions could have derived from transliterating the Hebrew original rather than from proto-Onqelos. In other words, Aramaic terms that derive from a common root with their Hebrew counterpart may be mistaken as instances of Hebraism. However, targumists most likely did not slavishly copy these words from the parent-text for lack of a satisfactory Aramaic translation. They knew better.

One may reject the possibility of Hebraism in the above 4 cases on three bases. First, had the targumists felt incapable of providing proper translation, they most likely would have chosen to engage in interpretation, as they tended to do when they were at a loss, as in Gen 36:24 and 15:2. Second, multiple recurrences of these terms in contemporary rabbinic literature composed in Aramaic confirm that the renderings in question are genuine Aramaic cognates, and thus they were widely used in antiquity.⁶¹ At any rate, the 10 examples that proffer identical renderings of the HL soundly testify that targumists were working from the same original targum. Third, if the passages were independent, they would not all follow the Hebrew parallel.

Only in 4 instances in the present study does PJ disagree with TO: Gen 21:16, 24:21, 36:24, and 41:43. When versions hold differing views on a given HL, PJ consistently shares the translation of TO rather than the translations of the PTs. This seems to indicate that PJ maintained a closer connection to TO than the PTs did. This finding coincides with the observation that "Targum Pseudo-Jonathan was once considered a Palestinian Targum.... But although it contains most of the Proto-PT expansions, its translation draws from—indeed copies almost verbatim—the translation of Targum Onqelos."⁶²

---

59. On clausal parallelism, which analyzes the degree of literary dependence between texts, see Flesher, "Translations of Proto-Onqelos and the Palestinian Targums," pp. 10–23.

60. The 4 instances are עשק in Gen 26:20, סלם in 28:12, לוז in 30:37, and בטן in 43:11. All of the targumic versions produce the same Hebrew tripartite root for the Aramaic equivalent.

61. For example, for אתעשקן, see *Genesis Rabbah* section 8; *Targum to Qohelet* 6:8; *Targum to Proverbs* 7:18. For סלמא, see *Genesis Rabbah* section 68; *y. AZ* 40a. For לוז, see *b. Bek.* 8a; *y. Taan.* 68c; *Genesis Rabbah* section 69. For בטנים, see *t. Sheb.* 5.11; *y. Sheb.* 7.5, 37a; *b. BB* 80b.

62. Flesher, "History of Aramaic in Judaism," p. 90.

Five instances of HL found in the FT indicate that this version was largely based on proto-Onqelos, at least in today's extant verses. A rendering of a HL may originate from proto-Onqelos if it appears in all the extant targum-types. In fact, in each of the 5 instances there is either an exact quotation or a quotation with minor modifications—clear evidence of a shared archaic text.

Furthermore, a cross-analysis between TN and the FT to Genesis suggests that the two texts may share a closer relationship than their Palestinian provenance.[63] One may presume that their authors developed their texts in close contact with each other, albeit each served a particular purpose, especially so in the case of the FT. Their final texts resemble not only each other's knowledge but also each other's lack of knowledge. There are only 5 instances of absolute HL rendered in the FT to Genesis. Remarkably its Palestinian counterpart, TN, agrees with FT's translation in every single instance. Gen 15:2 is particularly interesting in that neither targum is able to provide a rendering for this verse's problematic term משק, while PJ and TO proffer the same translation for this HL.

In fact, 2 verses in the FT—Gen 15:2 and 49:17—reveal a closer resemblance to the rendering of the Palestinian counterpart, namely, TN. This suggests that they are tied to a common source of origin, which scholars commonly designate "proto-Palestinian Targum" (proto-PT).[64] The archaic material derives from proto-Onqelos, yet the relationship between TN and FT develops further through the proto-PT. Moreover, in 4 verses TN proffers its unique interpretation on the HL: Gen 21:16, 24:21, 25:30, and 41:23. These same examples lack counterparts in the FT, and they find no match in either TO or PJ. This finding further supports the notion of the proto-PT as well as the aforementioned scholarly hypothesis that TO grew in isolation from the PT.

In 6 instances, the PTs present a different reading of the Hebrew original than that of TO. These are: Gen 15:2, 21:16, 24:21, 25:30, 41:23, and 41:43. It is interesting to note that here even TO strays from its usual literal translation, an orderly word-for-word rendering faithful to the Hebrew *Vorlage*. Five out of 6 examples proffer interpretation instead of direct translation. These interpretive expansions suggest the possibility that initially proto-Onqelos failed to provide a satisfactory translation.

In 3 verses, each rendering provides a uniquely different understanding of the given term. It may be assumed that the meanings of these particular HL were obscure also to the ancient scholars, thus yielding disputable translations. In these instances, as reflected in example 2, targumists may have resorted to contemporary interpretive traditions, which would have wrestled with the same challenge before them. At any rate, in spite of the overwhelm-

---

63. For a detailed study, see idem, "Translations of Proto-Onqelos and the Palestinian Targums."

64. See idem, "Mapping the Synoptic Palestinian Targums."

ing evidence of inherited tradition across variants, a few cases such as Gen 21:16, 24:21, and 36:24 reveal that there was still some room for interpretive genius for those who followed in the steps of proto-Onqelos.

In this survey, the high percentage of shared exegetical views presented for the HL in Genesis establishes that there is a genetic relationship between proto-Onqelos and later pentateuchal targums. This synoptic study of the targums yields the conclusion that proto-Onqelos was highly revered by later targums, which not only considered the archaic tradition to be a springboard but allowed it to serve as the backbone for both Eastern and Western Aramaic interpretive traditions. The 10 examples show that the interpretive tradition of proto-Onqelos was already highly developed, as is evident in a number of instances of agreement among TO, PJ, and the PTs. Although each version later added characteristics of its own trademark, evidently an inherited tradition was usually the departing point of the exegetical endeavor.

This study's findings support the notion that proto-Onqelos provided a foundation out of which at least 4 different targumic versions developed, thus adding to the already extant exegetical *and* linguistic evidence in the thriving field of targumic creation. Nevertheless, postulation of a systematic reconstruction of the development from the proto-Onqelos stage to that of the final targums is an endeavor that requires a comprehensive historical survey from all the required parties, as once suggested by Goshen-Gottstein.[65] The genetic relationship established by the parentage of Proto-Onqelos in the present analysis of HL serves as a case in point to affirm the validity of the idea of a "targumic tradition" that is commonly found in studies devoted to the Aramaic exegetical literature.

65. See Goshen-Gottstein, "Language of Targum Onqelos."

Bibliography

Aberbach, M., and B. Grossfeld. *Targum Onkelos to Genesis: A Critical Analysis Together with an English Translation of the Text*. New York: Ktav, 1982.

Albright, W. F. *Yahweh and the Gods of Canaan*. New York: Doubleday, 1968.

Alexander, P. S. "Jewish Aramaic Translations of Hebrew Scriptures." Pp. 217–54 in *Mikra: Text, Translation, Reading, and Interpretation of the Hebrew Bible in Ancient Judaism and Early Christianity*. Edited by M. J. Mulder and H. Sysling. Philadelphia: Fortress, 1988.

———. "Targum." *The Anchor Bible Dictionary CD-ROM Edition*. New York: Doubleday, 1997.

Barr, J. *Comparative Philology and the Text of the Old Testament: With Additions and Corrections*. Oxford: Clarendon, 1968.

Ben-Sasson, H. H. *A History of the Jewish People*. Cambridge: Harvard University Press, 1997.

Berlin, A. *The Dynamics of Biblical Parallelism*. Bloomington: Indiana University Press, 1985.

Blau, J. "Hapax Legomena." Columns 1318–19 in vol. 7 of *Encyclopaedia Judaica*. Jerusalem: Keter, 1972.
Casanowicz, I. M. "Hapax Legomena: Biblical Data." Cols. 225–28 in vol. 6 of *Jewish Encyclopedia*. New York: Funk & Wagnalls, 1903.
Cohen, H. R. *Biblical Hapax Legomena in the Light of Akkadian and Ugaritic*. Missoula, MT: Scholars Press, 1977.
Cook, E. "A New Perspective on the Language of Onqelos and Jonathan." Pp. 142–56 in *The Aramaic Bible: Targums in Their Historical Context*. Edited by D. R. G. Beattie and M. J. McNamara. Journal for the Study of the Old Testament Supplement 166. Sheffield: JSOT Press, 1994.
Díez Macho, A. "Las citas del Targum Palestinense en el midras Bereshit Zuta." Pp. 117–26 in *Mélanges bibliques et orientaux en l'honneur de M. Mathias Delcor*. Edited by A. Caquot, S. Légasse, and M. Tardieu. Alter Orient und Altes Testament 215. Kevelaer: Butzon & Bercker / Neukirchen-Vluyn: Neukirchener Verlag, 1985.
———. *Neophyti 1: Targum Palestinense ms. de la Biblioteca Vaticana*. 6 vols. Madrid: Consejo Superior de Investigaciones Científicas, 1968–79.
Drazin, I. "Dating Targum Onkelos by Means of the Tannaitic Midrashim." *JJS* 50 (1999) 246–58.
Even-Shoshan, A. *Concordantzia Hadashah: leTorah, Neviim, uKetuvim*. Jerusalem: Kiryat Sefer, 2000.
Emerton, J. A. "Some Difficult Words in Genesis 49." Pp. 81–93 in *Words and Meanings: Essays Presented to David Winton Thomas*. Edited by P. R. Ackroyd and B. Lindars. London: Cambridge University Press, 1968.
Fernández Vallina, J. "Targum y exegesis contemporánea: Algunos problemas metodológicos." Pp. 513–21 in *Simposio Bíblico Español*. Edited by N. Fernandez Marcos, J. C. Trebolle Barrera, and J. Fernández Vallina. Madrid: Universidad Complutense, 1984.
Flesher, P. V. M. "Exploring the Sources of the Synoptic Targums to the Pentateuch." Pp. 101–34 in *Targum Studies*, vol. 1: *Textual and Contextual Studies in the Pentateuchal Targums*. Edited by P. V. M. Flesher. South Florida Studies in the History of Judaism 55. Atlanta: Scholars Press, 1992.
———. "The History of Aramaic in Judaism." Pp. 85–96 in vol. 1 of *The Encyclopedia of Judaism*. 2nd ed. Edited by J. Neusner, A. J. Avery-Peck, and W. S. Green. Leiden: Brill, 2005.
———. "Is Targum Onqelos a Palestinian Targum? The Evidence of Genesis 28–50." *Journal for the Study of the Pseudepigrapha* 19 (1999) 35–79.
———. "Late Jewish Literary Aramaic and the Sources of Targum Pseudo-Jonathan." Unpublished paper presented at the European Association of Biblical Studies Conference, Copenhagen, 3–6 August 2003.
———. "The Literary Legacy of the Priests? The Pentateuchal Targums of Israel in Their Social and Linguistic Context." Pp. 467–508 in *The Ancient Synagogue*. Edited by B. Olsson and M. Zetterholm. Stockholm: Almqvist & Wiksell, 2003.
———. "Mapping the Synoptic Palestinian Targums of the Pentateuch." Pp. 247–53 in *The Aramaic Bible: Targums in Their Historical Context*. Edited by D. R. G. Beattie and M. J. McNamara. Journal for the Study of the Old Testament Supplement 166. Sheffield: JSOT Press, 1994.
———. "Targum as Scripture." Pp. 61–75 in *Targum and Scripture: Studies in Aramaic Translation and Interpretation in Memory of Ernest G. Clarke*. Edited by P. V. M. Flesher. Leiden: Brill, 2002.

———. "The Translations of Proto-Onqelos and the Palestinian Targums." *JAB* 3 (2001) 1–25.
Freedman, H., trans. *Midrash Rabbah: Genesis.* 2 vols. New York: Soncino, 1983.
Gordon, R. P. "Targum as Midrash: Contemporizing in the Targum to the Prophets." Pp. 61–73 in *Proceedings of the 9th World Congress of Jewish Studies.* Jerusalem: Magnes, 1988.
Goshen-Gottstein, M. H. "The Language of Targum Onqelos and the Model of Literary Diglossia in Aramaic." *Journal of the Near Eastern Studies* 37 (1978) 169–79.
Greenspahn, F. E. "Hapax Legomena." *The Anchor Bible Dictionary CD-ROM Edition.* New York: Doubleday, 1997.
———. *Hapax Legomena in Biblical Hebrew: A Study of the Phenomenon and Its Treatment since Antiquity with Special Reference to Verbal Forms.* Society of Biblical Literature Dissertation Series 74. Chico, CA: Scholars Press, 1984.
Grossfeld, B. *Targum Neofiti 1: An Exegetical Commentary to Genesis.* New York: Sepher-Hermon, 2000.
Hamilton, V. P. *The Book of Genesis: Chapters 1–17.* New International Commentary on the Old Testament. Grand Rapids: Eerdmans, 1990.
———. *The Book of Genesis: Chapters 18–50.* New International Commentary on the Old Testament. Grand Rapids: Eerdmans, 1995.
Hayward, R. "The Date of Targum Pseudo-Jonathan: Some Comments." *JJS* 40 (1989) 7–30.
Hyman, A. *Sefer Torah ha-Ketubah veha-messurah al Torah, Neviim u-Ketuvim.* Tel Aviv: Dvir, 1979.
Jastrow, M. *A Dictionary of the Targumim, the Talmud Babli and Yerushalmi, and the Midrashic Literature.* Repr. New York: Judaica, 1971.
Kaufman, S. A. "Dating the Language of the Palestinian Targums and Their Use in the Study of First Century CE Texts." Pp. 118–41 in *The Aramaic Bible: Targums in Their Historical Context.* Edited by D. R. G. Beattie and M. J. McNamara. Sheffield: Sheffield Academic Press, 1994.
Klein, M. L. *The Fragment-Targums of the Pentateuch according to Their Extant Sources.* Rome: Pontifical Biblical Institute, 1980.
———. "The Masorah to Onqelos: A Reflection of Targumic Consciousness." *HUCA* 68 (1997) 63–75.
Kutscher, E. Y. *A History of the Hebrew Language.* Jerusalem: Magnes, 1982.
Maher, M. *Targum Pseudo-Jonathan: Genesis—Translated, with Introduction and Notes.* Collegeville, MN: Liturgical Press, 1992.
Müller-Kessler, C. "The Earliest Evidence for Targum Onqelos from Babylonia and the Question of Its Dialect and Origin." *JAB* 3 (2001) 181–98.
Nöldeke, T. *Die semitischen Sprachen: Eine Skizze.* Leipzig: Tauchnitz, 1899.
Orlinsky, H. M. *Notes on the New Translation of the Torah.* Philadelphia: Jewish Publication Society, 1969.
Plaut, G. W. *The Torah: A Modern Commentary.* New York: Union of American Hebrew Congregations, 1981.
Rad, G. von. *Genesis: A Commentary.* Old Testament Library. Translated by J. H. Marks. London: SCM, 1966.
Ribera, J. "The Targum: From Translation to Interpretation." Pp. 218–25 in *The Aramaic Bible: Targums in Their Historical Context.* Edited by D. R. G. Beattie and M. J. McNamara. Journal for the Study of the Old Testament Supplement 166. Sheffield: JSOT Press, 1994.

Samely, A. *Interpretation of Speech in the Pentateuch Targums.* Tübingen: Mohr, 1992.
Shinan, A. "Dating Targum Pseudo-Jonathan: Some More Comments." *JJS* 41 (1990) 57–61.
———. "Midrashic Parallels to Targumic Traditions." *JSJ* 8 (1977) 185–91.
———. "The 'Palestinian' Targums: Repetitions, Internal Unity, Contradictions." *JJS* 36 (1985) 72–87.
Skinner, J. *A Critical and Exegetical Commentary on Genesis.* International Critical Commentary. New York: Scribner, 1910.
Speiser, E. A. *Genesis.* Anchor Bible 1. Garden City, NY: Doubleday, 1964.
Sperber, A., ed. *The Bible in Aramaic: Based on Old Manuscripts and Printed Texts.* 5 vols. Leiden: Brill, 1959–73.
Syrén, R. *The Blessings in the Targums: A Study on the Targumic Interpretations of Genesis 49 and Deuteronomy 33.* Åbo: Åbo Akademi, 1986.
Vermes, G. "Haggadah in the Onkelos Targum." *Journal of Semitic Studies* 8 (1963). Reprinted, pp. 92–126 in *Post-Biblical Jewish Studies.* Leiden: Brill, 1975.
Weitzman, M. P. *The Syriac Version of the Old Testament.* Cambridge: Cambridge University Press, 1998.

The Wisdom of the Sages: Rabbinic Rewriting of Qohelet

PAUL V. M. FLESHER

Rabbinic literature shows only occasional interest in the texts or issues of the earlier wisdom movements. Rabbis cite wisdom books only sporadically. Nor do they treat any wisdom figures as heroes—no wisdom figure takes his place among biblical greats such as Abraham, Jacob, Moses, and David. Solomon receives some attention, but only occasionally for his wisdom; condemnation of his penchant for foreign women appears more frequently. Furthermore, the rabbis wrote no commentaries—*midrashim*—to any wisdom book until quite late in the rabbinic period. Nor did they bring into rabbinic theology any issues central to wisdom. Finally, although both the wisdom and the rabbinic movements use the same terminology for their central figure (the *hacham*, the "sage"), the makeup of that category differs. In one, the sage is a master of wisdom: knowledge gained from the surrounding world; in the other, the sage is a master of Torah: knowledge derived from divine revelation.[1]

In the centuries of religious upheaval following the Temple's destruction, Judaism struggled to discover a way of life and world view that did not depend upon the physical existence of a Temple. During this period, the rabbinate largely ignored wisdom or used it sporadically for its own purposes. But toward the end of the rabbinic period, Judaism reached a more secure and mature state, more confident in its own ability to deal with diversity. What happened when this mature rabbinic Judaism confronted a wisdom text whole?

---

1. Travis Hereford has compared the third-century Mishnah tractate Avot to Proverbs and Qohelet, implying that Avot is like these two wisdom texts (Hereford, *Pirke Aboth*, p. 8). But while I will grant that Avot contains many pithy sayings (sort of a "Proverbs" with attributions), the content of Avot's sayings differs radically from the content of Proverbs. Indeed wisdom is an intellectual movement with an identifiable content, not just the repeated use of literary form. Since Avot has none of that content, it should not be considered wisdom.

The Targum to Qohelet (= TQ) provides an opportunity to address this question.² This "translation" of Qohelet into Aramaic is actually a rewriting of the text, departing from the underlying Hebrew more than typical targums such as those of the Prophets or the Pentateuch. Composed sometime after 600 C.E.—after the "publication" of the Babylonian Talmud—but probably before Qohelet became part of the Sukkoth liturgy, the targum recasts this wisdom text by transforming it into a rabbinic text.³ Indeed, whereas earlier targums may have had their origins outside rabbinic circles, the later Targum to Qohelet participates directly in the rabbinic world view. The Qohelet Targum thus represents a rabbinic attempt to address wisdom head on and to absorb it into rabbinic Judaism while at the same time transforming it to fit its categories. The differences between the Aramaic and Hebrew versions of Qohelet provide a window into how the rabbinic world understood the problems with wisdom in general and Qohelet in particular, and then dealt with them.

The targum reveals that the original version of Qohelet caused two major types of problems for rabbinic Judaism. First, Qohelet is often ambiguous; making statements with no clear meaning or with multiple meanings. Such ambiguity is alien to an intellectual movement concerned with precision. In their translation, the targum's writers frequently provide interpretations with clear, straightforward meaning. Second, Qohelet's whole perspective on life and the world "under the sun" challenges the most elementary and fundamental principles of talmudic Judaism. For example, despite Qohelet's distinction between the wise man and the fool, the righteous and the wicked, Qohelet still argues that both have the same end, namely, death. He sees no future beyond that end. Of course, this perspective does not fit that of rabbinic Judaism and must be changed. And change it the targum does.

---

2. The Targum to Qohelet has not received extensive scholarly analysis; the few relevant studies are reviewed by Knobel in the introduction to his translation of TQ for the Aramaic Bible series. The field has yet to produce a translation that matches a readily available text; recent decades have seen the publication of texts without matching translations, or translations without matching texts. A. Sperber published MS Or. 2375 of the British Museum in 1968, but it has never received a translation. Etan Levine in 1978 produced a translation of Codex Urbinates 1 from the Vatican Library in his *Aramaic Version of Qohelet*. Unfortunately, the accompanying text of Urbinates is poorly reproduced and thus virtually unreadable. Knobel, *Targum of Qohelet*, provides the translation for the Aramaic Bible series. Knobel has done the most extensive textual work, having produced a critical, eclectic text as part of a Ph.D. dissertation, but alas it remains unpublished. Finally, Paris 110 forms the basis of the text used by the CAL (which has been republished by several computer Bibles). Hopefully, E. Clem will produce a translation of it in the near future as part of his project to translate all the targums for Accordance Bible Software (http://www.accordancebible.com).

3. See the discussion in Levine, *Aramaic Version of Qohelet*, pp. 68–70. Knobel's review of the scholarship puts the targum's date in the seventh century, roughly the same time frame. See Knobel, *Targum of Qohelet*, pp. 12–15.

How the Targum of Qohelet Fixes Scriptural Ambiguity

The Hebrew Qohelet is laced with and founded upon ambiguity. Its rhetoric alternately allusive, suggestive, and questioning. It rarely makes a straightforward statement when an indirect one will do. The Qohelet Targum assigns specific meanings to many of these passages. Sometimes this happens in a "don't-get-the-wrong-idea" sense. For example, the original text of Qoh 4:11 makes the remark, "If two lie together, they are warm; but how can one be warm alone?" The targum makes a small alteration, "If two sleep together—a man and his wife—they will be warm in the winter."[4] Specifying the two sleepers' identity prevents a reader from interpreting this passage as an endorsement of homosexual behavior.

Other times, the effect of these changes provides the statement with a religious or *halakhic* meaning. In the beautiful—and beautifully ambiguous— passage that opens chap. 3, "For everything there is a season . . . ," the targumist provides several examples of this means of resolving ambiguity. The biblical "a time to be born, and a time to die" (Qoh 3:2) becomes the targumic "there is a special time to beget sons and daughters, and a special time for killing disobedient and wicked children: to kill them with stones by the decree of the judges" (TQ 3:2). "A time to embrace, and a time to refrain from embracing" (Qoh 3:5) becomes "an opportune time to embrace a wife, and an opportune time to abstain from embracing her, in the seven days of mourning" (TQ 3:5). Finally, the scriptural "a time to rend and a time to sew" (Qoh 3:7) becomes in the targum "an opportune time to tear the garment for the dead, and an opportune time to sew together the torn pieces" (TQ 3:7). Although these renderings destroy the passage's poetic beauty, they remove from the reader the opportunity to wonder about the passage's meaning by fixing that meaning firmly within the rabbinic world view and way of life.

This property of ambiguity in the targumist's eyes extends even to the book's statements about its author. The book states that it is "the words of Qohelet, son of David, king in Jerusalem." Although the only person who fits this description is Solomon (which the targum emphasizes), the Hebrew text never says that directly. But this identification brings on a further problem of ambiguity: why should Solomon, of all people, have such a negative view of life and the world? After he was so blessed of God that God gave him his wisdom, God chose Solomon to built His Temple, and so on. If Solomon was so close to God, then why does he have such a negative view of matters?

To answer this question, the writer of the Qohelet Targum provides a context for the work. He positions the writing of the original book in a time after Qohelet (i.e., Solomon) discovers that all the things he has done for God,

---

4. I have taken all targum translations from Knobel, *Targum of Qohelet*, making an occasional small alteration. The biblical citations are from the RSV.

with God, or by himself will ultimately come to naught. Three key factors account for this pessimism: the results of his own past misbehavior, the future treatment of his son Rehoboam, and the future treatment of the people Israel—the latter two of which he discovers through prophetic means.

First, Solomon's encounter with his own fate comes about through the sin of pride, namely, pride in his accomplishments.

> When King Solomon of Israel was sitting upon the throne of his kingdom, his heart became very proud of his wealth, and he violated the *Memra* of the Lord; he gathered many horses, chariots and cavalry; he collected much silver and gold; he married among foreign peoples. Immediately the anger of the Lord grew strong against him. He sent Ashmodai king of the demons, against him who drove him from his royal throne, and took his signet ring from his hand so that he would wander and go into exile in the world to chastise him. He went about in all the districts and towns of the Land of Israel. He wept, pleaded. . . . (Qohelet Targum 1:12)

Solomon starts by discovering the emptiness of his own actions and achievements. They are stripped away from him even during his life, and he is forced to live even without a home.

Second, Solomon is not only concerned with what happens to his own property, he is also worried about what happens to the people Israel and to God's house, for he knows the Temple will be destroyed and the people taken away from it into exile.

> The heart of the sages mourns the destruction of the Temple and is sad over the exile of the people, the House of Israel. (Qohelet Targum 7:4)

Third, most prominently, it is Qohelet's reaction to the events that will overtake his son that upset him.

> And I hated all labor for which I labored under the sun in this world because I will leave it to Rehoboam my son who will come after me, but Jeroboam the son of Nebat will come and take the ten tribes from his hand and possess half of the kingdom. (Qohelet Targum 2:18)

The same sentiments are reiterated later:

> Solomon the Prophet said through the spirit of prophecy from the Lord, "I saw all the living who are going in their foolishness to rebel against Rehoboam my son under the sun, and will divide the kingdom so that it will be given to Jeroboam." (Qohelet Targum 4:15)

As recast by the targumist, the knowledge of these events provides the impetus for Qohelet's book, for as presented in the targum, the coming division of the kingdom under Rehoboam gives Solomon the motivation for this work.

> When Solomon the King of Israel saw through the holy spirit that the kingdom of Rehoboam his son would be divided with Jeroboam the son of Nebat, that Jerusalem and the Temple would be destroyed and the people of the household of Israel would go into exile, he said to himself, "Vanity of vanities is this

world! Vanity of Vanities of everything for which I and my father David labored. All of it is vanity." (Qohelet Targum 1:2)

So what has happened here is that this book with its negative view of life and death has been provided with a specific context. That context is Solomon's disappointments after he learns that everything that he has worked for in his life will be taken away. The kingdom will be taken from the hand of his son, the Temple will be destroyed, and the people exiled. The book of Qohelet, in its targumic version, thus is no longer a general philosophical treatise on life in general but instead comprises a reaction to a specific set of events. It now constitutes a document mourning specific troubles, which removes its wide impact and the far-reaching nature of its comments. This removes the dangerous wisdom statements from the general realm of life and puts them into the context of lamenting specific disasters.

Contradictions with Rabbinic Theology

If the problem of ambiguity was not enough for the rabbis, Qohelet's world view directly contradicts that of talmudic Judaism. Indeed, Qohelet denies a foundational rabbinic belief, namely, the concept of the two worlds (this world and the world to come) and the role of reward and punishment, which the latter plays. He questions and ridicules the resurrection of the dead, life after death, and the notions of God's mercy and punishment. And unlike the book of Job, Qohelet contains no opposing views. In Job, Job's friends and ultimately even God argue against Job, but in Qohelet, no such opposition—human or divine—ever appears to mitigate Qohelet's unrelenting pessimism.

The book of Qohelet is fixated, it seems, on the opposition between life and death. Indeed, one of the text's primary emphases is the dissymmetry between the two states. This imbalance affects the status of the good and the evil. During life, the righteous person stands above the wicked, and the wise is superior to the fool. But at death, they are treated the same.

> wisdom excels folly as light excels darkness. The wise man has his eyes in his head, but the fool walks in darkness; and yet I perceived that one fate comes to all of them.... How the wise man dies just like the fool! (Qoh 2:13–14, 16)

Indeed,

> one fate comes to all, to the righteous and the wicked, to the good and the evil. (Qoh 9:2)

These sentiments do not appear just occasionally, but in fact make up a sizable bulk of the text.[5] But Qohelet does not limit to human beings his discussion of the equalizing nature of death; he also applies it to animals.

---

5. They can be found in Qoh 2:12–17, 3:16–6:12, 9:1–6, and 12:1–8.

> For the fate of the sons of men and the fate of beasts is the same; as one dies, so dies the other. They all have the same breath, and man has no advantage over the beasts; for all is vanity. All go to one place; all are from the dust, and all turn to dust again. Who knows whether the spirit of man goes upward and the spirit of the beast goes down to the earth? (Qoh 3:19–21)

Qohelet emphasizes that there is nothing after death; it ends everything. All (the righteous, the wicked and the animals) turn to dust. They are cut off from their worldly accomplishments. During one's lifetime, then, there is no reason to hope; all is vanity.

This characterization of life and death in the Hebrew Qohelet emphasizes the world in which humanity lives, the world "under the sun." All activity mentioned in the book takes place on earth. Even the dead remain on earth; they "return to dust." Although heaven is mentioned a couple times, it is not seen as a place that has any interaction with the earth; its only feature is that God dwells there. Thus for Qohelet, the only source of knowledge about life and death is the experiences and events of life "under the sun." He learns from watching the lives of people around him. Qohelet wanders the land to observe different people and finally even conducts experiments—purposely follows certain courses of action—to see what they will teach him (e.g., Qoh 2:1–11). For Qohelet, life is the only source of knowledge; he never mentions the importance of learning from Scripture or from a book of any sort. Although proverbs (presumably based on life) are important sources of wisdom (Qoh 12:9), he holds that life is the best teacher, not study: "Of the making of many books there is no end, and much study is a weariness of the flesh" (Qoh 12:12). A collection of ideas less compatible with rabbinic Judaism would be hard to imagine.

The writers of the Qohelet Targum solve these incompatibilities by getting rid of them. In a sense, the targum constitutes an apologetic for the way rabbinic Judaism ignored wisdom during its formative period. In superficial terms, the apologetic can be stated as "we did not ignore wisdom, we have been doing it all the time." But it redefines wisdom, by presenting it as the rabbinic understanding of Torah. There are no incompatibilities because there are no acknowledged differences. This is most apparent in the redefinition of the word "sage," *hacham*, which is a central term in both contexts. In Qohelet, the sage constitutes a master of wisdom, knowledge gleaned from the study of the life and the world. In the Qohelet Targum, the sage is the master of Torah, of revelation from God as interpreted by the rabbinic movement. The targumic sage is thus a master of *halakhah*. Through this redefinition alone, the Targum to Qohelet takes on a different meaning. It no longer focuses on human knowledge but on divine revelation.

At the most fundamental level, the Targum to Qohelet redresses the dissymmetry of the original version. The Hebrew Qohelet, we recall, posited a division between the righteous and the wicked during their lives but held that death treated both the same: they returned to dust. The advantage to righteousness ends at death. The Qohelet Targum fixes this by introducing the concept of the two worlds—this world and the world to come. An individual's behavior in this world determines his or her place in the world to come. Righteous behavior will cause one to enter into the reward of the "Garden of Eden" in the next world, while wicked behavior will send one to punishment in Gehenna. In this way, the Qohelet Targum provides a balance between the righteous and the wicked. Death does not equalize them; the advantage of the righteous continues into the world to come.

> For to a man whose deeds are straight before God, He gave (him) wisdom and knowledge in this world, and joy with the righteous in the world to come. But to the guilty man He gave an evil way. (Qohelet Targum 2:26)

Similarly,

> When goods are many in the world . . . what benefit is there for its owner who collected it, if he does not do charity from it so he will see its reward in the world to come the reward with his own eyes. . . . A man who collects wealth and does not do from it anything good, at the end of days that wealth is kept for him to condemn him in the world to come. (Qohelet Targum 5:10, 12)

So, whereas in Qohelet, there was no hope in the future (since all returned to dust and it was thus all "vanity"), in the targum, the righteous have hope. Righteousness gets them into the world to come and gives them the reward that waits there for them.

The Wisdom of Torah

If righteousness enables one to enter the Garden of Eden in the world to come, what does it mean to be righteous? For the Qohelet Targum, being righteous means "doing wisdom." The content of the term *wisdom* thus determines the activities of the righteous. Understanding the rabbinic definition of *wisdom* will provide the description of righteousness. For the targum, wisdom refers to both Torah (that is, sacred texts) and rabbinic teaching.

On the one hand, the general identification of wisdom is as Torah—Torah in the meaning of Scripture and other authoritative writings. The targumist frequently refers to the "wisdom of Torah," or to the "wisdom of the Torah of the Lord" (TQ 7:23, 5:11). This Torah is not merely the holy books but Judaism's *divinely revealed* holy books. This becomes clear from a passage in which acquiring such wisdom is portrayed as the sages' goal.

> The heart of the sage is to acquire the Torah which is given by the right hand of the Lord, and the heart of the fool is to acquire possession of silver and gold. . . . the words of the Torah were created as a cure in the world so that great sins may be forgiven and forgotten by the Lord. (Qohelet Targum 10:2, 4)

In this way, Torah, as text and as revelation, becomes the source of knowledge. No longer does the focus lie on life experience but on knowledge revealed from heaven. This change stems from the targum's alteration of Qohelet's one-world viewpoint into the perspective of two worlds. When Qohelet could see only one world ("under the sun"), there was only one source of knowledge, life. Now that the targum has introduced a second world (the world to come), there is a corresponding source of knowledge, that of revelation from heaven.

On the other hand, Torah as revealed text does not remain the sole definition of wisdom for the Targum to Qohelet. The targum also transforms wisdom into *halakhah*. When it presents specific examples of wisdom, they are usually concerned with *halakhic* regulations and behavior. For example, Solomon himself speaks of his wisdom in *halakhic* terms.

> And with respect to everything which the rabbis of the Sanhedrin requested from me, to declare clean or unclean, and to declare innocent or guilty, I did not withhold from them the explanations and I did not withdraw my mind from all the joy of the Torah. I was at ease for my mind rejoiced in the wisdom which was given me from before the Lord more than any man. (Qohelet Targum 2:10)

Solomon's examples of wisdom constitute classic concerns of the rabbis, even forming the basis of several important tractates in the Mishnah, the foundational document of rabbinic Judaism, namely, purity and the judgments of civil law. But the targum's evidence goes beyond mere inference to specific redefinition of wisdom as *halakhah*, for the targum indicates that the foremost "sages" are the rabbis who are the masters of the *halakhah*.

> The words of the sages are compared to goads and nails which are fastened to teach wisdom to those empty of knowledge just as a goad teaches the heifer, and the rabbis of the Sanhedrin are masters of halacha and midrash. (Qohelet Targum 12:11)

Following the *halakhah* of the Torah is not just a rewarded practice for men but it affects women as well, in the specific rabbinic category of menstrual purity.

> Through sloth in the matter of the Torah and commandments, a man becomes so poor he has no children, and through despising the commandment which a woman is commanded to observe concerning separation from uncleanness of her blood which she does not observe she is (always) in a menstrual state in her house. (Qohelet Targum 10:18)

So the Qohelet Targum has given wisdom a distinctly rabbinic definition, one that understands it as revealed knowledge from Scripture to *halakhah*. But righteousness requires more than just the knowledge of Torah and its *halakhah*; it requires the individual to put it into practice.

The Practice of Torah as Doing Wisdom

If righteousness is "wisdom" and wisdom is "Torah," then what does it mean to "do wisdom"? "Doing wisdom" takes on two forms: that of studying

Torah and that of performing elements of the behavior described therein. The Targum of Qohelet reveals that participating in both activities enables a person to enter the world to come with the righteous.

The importance of the study of wisdom is expressed as the study of God's Torah. The Qohelet Targum presents Torah study as an important activity in and of itself.

> Be careful to make many books of wisdom without end, and to occupy yourself much with words of Torah. (Qohelet Targum 12:12)

Similarly,

> the righteous and the sages and their disciples who serve them in the manner of the study of Torah are entrusted to the hand of the Lord. (Qohelet Targum 9:1)[6]

Torah study not only has this-worldly benefits, but it also enables the scholar to enter the world to come.

> And what does that poor man have to do but to occupy himself with the Torah of the Lord so that he will know how to walk in the presence of the righteous in the Garden of Eden? (Qohelet Targum 6:8)

Also,

> All of it is vanity. What profit does a man have after he dies from all his labor which he labors under the sun in this world unless he occupies himself with Torah in order to receive a complete reward in the world to come before the Master of the world? (Qohelet Targum 1:2–3)

In this way, the targum has transformed Qohelet's observation-based wisdom into learning based on Torah. A person gains wisdom not by generalizing from life but from studying the Torah. Only the latter activity can enable a person to enter the world to come.

Torah study as a means of entering the world to come is complemented by the activity of doing good deeds. In general, "good deeds" means deeds of Torah, the proper behavior learned from studying. In general, these are deeds of *halakhah*, of obeying the strictures set out in the Torah, as the next two examples indicate. But they also constitute deeds of charity, as the third instance shows.

> And behold that which I saw that is good for people and what is proper for them to do in this world . . . to keep the words of the Torah. (Qohelet Targum 5:17)

Also,

> There is nothing worthwhile for a man except that he eat, drink, and enjoy himself before the people, to obey the commandments of the Lord and to walk in straight paths before Him. (Qohelet Targum 2:24)

Deeds of charity are also included in these "Torah activities."

---

6. Similarly, QT 4:17 states, "Incline your ear to receive the teaching of the Torah from the priests and the sages."

> And I saw that there was nothing better in this world than that a man rejoice in his good deeds ... so that a man should not say to himself, "Why should I waste my money giving charity?" (Qohelet Targum 3:22)

Such activity cannot but help to improve a person's long-range outlook, while not performing the Torah's regulations must entail a negative effect.

> And a man who is lacking in Torah and the commandments during his life, after his death is not permitted to be counted among the righteous in the Garden of Eden. (Qohelet Targum 1:15)

It is one thing to strive to do the right thing—the good deed; it is another thing always to succeed in doing it. Oftentimes, a person sins without meaning to or in a moment of weakness. Such sin, if unchecked, could prevent the righteous from attaining their otherwise assigned place in the world to come. The Qohelet Targum uses another item from the rabbinic arsenal to solve this problem: repentance. The ability to repent a misdeed is an important one for the Qohelet Targum that helps keep the righteous on track.

> For the righteous know that if they sin, they will be considered as dead in the world to come. Therefore, they guard their ways and do not sin and if they sin, they return in repentance. (Qohelet Targum 9:5)

This is doubly emphasized in the context of death.

> Because he goes into the house of mourning, the righteous will repent and take to heart the matters of death, and if he has anything evil in his hand, he will leave it and turn in repentance before the Master of the World. (Qohelet Targum 7:2)

Thus, the mistakes of the righteous do not prevent them from their place in the next world. Although they may spend most of their time studying or performing acts of Torah, even they can do misdeeds. The targum's concept of repentance provides a means for overcoming the consequences of such accidents.

Conclusion

There is much more to study concerning how the author of the Targum to Qohelet rewrote the text using rabbinic concepts. Aspects of the targumic theology of the afterlife found in the Qohelet Targum that could profit from further analysis are the translation's understanding of Gehenna and the Day of Judgment, to say nothing of the power of personal merit and the efficacy of prayer.[7]

Our search for wisdom in rabbinic Judaism—in what should be the heart of rabbinic concern for wisdom, the translation of Qohelet—leads instead to

---

7. Qohelet Targum's afterlife theology is strikingly similar to that found in the Palestinian Targums to the Pentateuch. See Genesis 2–3 and my own analyses of that story: Flesher, "Theology of Afterlife"; idem, "Resurrection of the Dead."

the central emphases of rabbinic Judaism. The document that should be the prime container of wisdom thought has been hollowed out and refilled by a talmudic rabbinism. The self-confident Judaism that developed during the rabbinic period thus assessed wisdom as dangerous, as antithetical not only to its understanding of the cosmos and God but also to the role of Jews within that cosmos. The Qohelet Targum, which as a translation replaced the Hebrew Qohelet for the vast majority of Jews who did not know Hebrew, is no longer the cogent and relentless perpetuator of ideas dangerous to the rabbinic perspective but the purveyor of a compelling statement of the rabbinic world view. The targumic response to wisdom is that it is dangerous; it can no longer be merely ignored but must be replaced.

In the end, the Targum to Qohelet transformed wisdom into Torah. It reshaped a biblical book that emphasized the negative character of life in the present world to a work that emphasized the positive outlook in the world to come of a person engaged with the study and practice of the wisdom of Torah.

Bibliography

Flesher, P. V. M. "The Theology of the Afterlife in the Palestinian Targums to the Pentateuch: A Framework for Analysis." Pp. 1–48 in vol. 16 of *Approaches to Ancient Judaism. New Series.* Edited by J. Neusner. Atlanta: Scholars Press, 1999.

―――. "The Resurrection of the Dead and the Sources of the Palestinian Targums to the Pentateuch." Pp. 311–32 in *Judaism in Late Antiquity, Part Four: Death, Life-after-Death, Resurrection and the World-to-Come in the Judaisms of Antiquity.* Edited by A. J. Avery-Peck and J. Neusner. Handbook of Oriental Studies. Leiden: Brill, 2000.

Hereford, R. T. *Pirke Aboth.* New York: Jewish Institute of Religion, 1925.

Knobel, P. S. *The Targum of Qohelet.* Aramaic Bible 15. Collegeville, MN: Liturgical Press, 1991.

Levine, E. *The Aramaic Version of Qohelet.* New York: Sepher-Hermon, 1978.

Sperber, A. *The Bible in Aramaic*, vol. 4A: *The Hagiographa.* Leiden: Brill, 1968.

Index of Authors

Aberbach, M.   253, 257–258
Albeck, C.   57
Albright, W. F.   254
Alexander, P. S.   109–110, 146, 153, 159, 210, 222, 228–229, 247, 262
Aviam, M.   53
Avigad, N.   xvi, 49–50, 58, 194, 196
Avi-Yonah, M.   50
Azuelos, Y.   233

Bacher, W.   148
Bar Asher, M.   107
Bar-Efrat, S.   91
Barnes, W. E.   xvi, 23–24, 27
Barr, J.   251
Bauckham, R.   23, 27
Bauer, H.   69–70, 75, 77, 79, 83, 89, 93
Baumgartner, W.   127
Bearman, G.   196
Beattie, D. R. G.   222
Bedjan, P.   15
Ben-Sasson, H. H.   249
Bensly, R. L.   xvi, 23
Ben-Zvi, I.   50
Berlin, A.   251
Bernstein, M. J.   xix, 198–200, 203–204, 210–211, 213, 228, 233
Bijovsky, G.   50
Blau, J.   70, 249
Bloch, A. A.   89
Bonnet, M.   16
Botterweck, G. J.   127
Breuer, Y.   220
Brock, S.   43
Brockelmann, C.   15, 24
Brooks, E. W.   45
Burney, C. F.   134
Burns, J. B.   113

Buth, R. J.   77
Bybee, J. L.   xvii, 70–72, 78–80, 94–95

Campbell, L.   70
Carasik, M.   xix, 220–221, 225, 229
Carroll, R. P.   133
Casanowicz, I. M.   249
Cathcart, K.   225
Caubet, D.   72
Chabot, J. B.   34
Childs, B.   136
Chilton, B. D.   119
Clarke, E. G.   158, 227
Clem, E.   270
Clements, R. E.   132
Cohen, D.   70, 73, 76, 83, 93
Cohen, H. R.   248–249, 251
Collins, J.   212
Comrie, B.   71
Conklin, B. W.   175, 187
Cook, E. M.   159, 247
Cook, M.   45–46
Cowley, A.   50
Coxon, P. W.   93
Crone, P.   45–46
Cross, F. M.   209
Cureton, W.   xv, 3–5, 8, 12

Dahl, O.   94
Damsma, A.   62
Davidson, M. J.   233
Davies, G. I.   105
Davila, J. R.   23, 27
Díez Macho, A.   152–158, 253
Dirksen, P.   164
Drijvers, H. J. W.   12
Driver, G. R.   108
Driver, S. R.   157
Duval, R.   45

Eisenstein, J. D.   237
Eissfeldt, O.   136
Endres, J.   113
Evans, C. A.   194

Fernández Marcos, N.   147
Fewel, D. N.   204
Fischer, O.   71
Fitzmyer, J. A.   73, 194–195, 199–200, 205, 207–209
Flesher, P. V. M.   xiii–xiv, xvi–xvii, xx, 33, 69, 105, 107–108, 110, 159, 164, 167, 193, 224, 233, 246–247, 255, 263–264, 278
Flint, P.   209–210
Flusser, D.   233
Fohrer, G.   134, 141
Folmer, M. L.   73
Frend, W. H. C.   38
Friedman, M. A.   60–61, 64
Friedrich, P.   218
Fröhlich, I.   196, 201, 205

Gaster, T. H.   61–62, 151
Geller, S.   218
Glazov, G.   233
Golomb, D. H.   152
Goodwin, W. W.   84
Gordon, C. H.   218
Gordon, R. P.   225
Goshen-Gottstein, M. H.   228, 265
Gray, J.   134
Greenberg, M.   141
Greenfield, J. C.   86, 93–94, 108, 195
Greenspahn, F. E.   248, 250–251, 261
Greenstein, E.   218
Grillmeier, A.   44
Gropp, D. M.   ix, xiv, 73, 94
Grossfeld, B.   217, 223–224, 253, 257–258
Gruenthaner, M. J.   233
Gunn, D.   204
Gzella, H.   70, 73, 81, 83, 85, 88–89

Hainthaler, T.   44
Harrak, A.   43
Harrington, D. J.   121
Hatav, G.   72

Hayward, R.   159, 247
Healey, J. F.   12
Heine, B.   72
Hereford, R. T.   269
Holladay, W. L.   133
Hopper, P. J.   70
Houtman, A.   61
Hoyland, R. G.   35, 41–42, 44–46
Hurvitz, A.   106–107, 110, 117
Hyatt, J. P.   136

Janda, R. D.   70
Japhet, S.   113
Jastrow, M.   118, 256
Jellico, S.   147
Jenni, E.   127–128
Johns, A. F.   83, 89

Kaddari, M. Z.   94–95
Kasher, R.   61–62, 65, 233
Kaufman, S. A.   63, 153, 159, 247–248
Kautzsch, E. F.   69
Klawans, J.   105
Klein, M. L.   146, 153–156, 158, 217, 247, 253
Knobel, P. S.   221, 226, 270–271
Koehler, L.   127
Koester, H.   25
Kogut, S.   220, 228
Kohl, H.   49
Kooij, A. van der   229
Kraft, R. L.   23, 27
Kutscher, E. Y.   79, 107

Lane, E. W.   16
Lange, A.   196, 206
Leander, P.   69–70, 75, 77, 79, 83, 89, 93
Levey, S. H.   120
Levine, E.   270
Li, T.   69
Linder, A.   52
Livnat, Z.   128
Longacre, R. E.   91
López-Couso, M. J.   71
Lowth, R.   251
Lowy, S.   151

Luzzatto, S. D. 221, 223

Magness, J. 53
Maher, M. 159, 224, 228, 253, 257
Maier, J. 113–114
Mannickarottu, S. G. 27
Maori, Y. 107
Marcus, J. R. 52
Matter, A. 23
McIvor, J. S. 118
McNamara, M. 152–154, 157, 217
McVey, K. E. 6, 8–10, 15
Meillet, A. 70
Merz, A. xv, 6, 19
Meyers, C. L. ix, 49–50
Meyers, E. M. xiv, xvi, 49–50, 53, 55–57, 105, 193, 233
Millar, F. 5, 8
Millar, W. 113
Montgomery, J. A. 134
Morgenstern, M. 195, 197, 199
Müller-Kessler, C. 247
Muraoka, T. 70, 73–74, 76, 87, 89, 93–95, 197–198

Naccach, A. F. 59–60
Nau, F. xvi, 33–34, 39, 41–46
Naveh, J. 12–13, 50–52, 58–60, 63
Nelson, R. D. 157
Nickelsburg, G. W. E. 193, 199, 201, 204–206, 211, 213
Nöldeke, T. 14, 16, 72, 76, 245
Norde, M. 71
Noth, M. 136

Ohana, M. 159
Olyan, S. M. 233
Orlinsky, H. M. 112

Pagliuca, W. 70–72, 78–79
Palmer, F. R. 87
Payne Smith, J. 15, 24
Perkins, R. 70–72, 78–79
Perridon, H. 71
Perry, T. A. 218
Peters, F. E. 16
Peterson, S. xv–xvi, 27
Plaut, G. W. 253

Polzin, R. 107
Porten, B. 73, 76, 93
Pritchard, J. B. 142

Qimron, E. 195, 197, 199

Rabin, C. 107, 148
Rad, G. von 253–254, 258
Rahlfs, A. 143
Ramelli, I. 6, 16
Reider, J. 147
Reinink, G. J. 33, 35, 38, 42, 45–46
Renan, E. xvi, 49
Rensberger, D. xv, 19
Ringgren, H. 127
Rogland, M. 81, 83
Rooker, M. F. 107
Rosén, H. B. 69, 76, 82
Rosenthal, F. 70, 83, 89
Rowley, H. H. 93
Rubin, A. D. 73, 96
Rubio, C. G. 233
Rudolph, W. 131, 133

Sachau, E. 33, 42
Saenz-Badillos, A. 109
Safrai, S. 115
Saldarini, A. J. 121
Samely, A. 107
Sasson, J. M. 222
Savran, G. 204
Schäfer, P. 233
Scheidweiler, F. 11
Schulthess, F. 5–6, 12, 14–17
Schwartz, S. 51–53
Segal, J. B. 12–13
Segal, M. M. 106
Segert, S. 70, 75
Seoane, E. 71
Seow, C.-L. 220, 225–226
Shapiro, M. D. 233, 240
Shepardson, C. C. 10
Shepherd, M. B. 70
Shinan, A. 159, 229, 233, 238, 247, 257
Simon, M. 10
Sivan, D. 195, 197, 199
Skinner, J. 258

Smelik, W.   62
Smith, J. Z.   115
Sokoloff, M.   ix, xiv, 63, 127, 148, 152–153, 159
Sperber, A.   149, 153, 221–222, 253, 270
Splansky, D. M.   159
Staalduine-Sulman, E. van   61
Starcky, J.   13
Steiner, R.   196, 199
Stern, S.   50, 56, 63
Stevenson, W. B.   87
Stowers, S. K.   6
Syrén, R.   251

Tal, A.   151
Talmon, S.   91, 217
Thacker, T. W.   86
Thelwall, S.   10
Thompson, S. A.   91
Tieleman, T.   xv, 6, 19
Toews, B. G.   70, 84, 93
Tov, E.   147
Trafton, J. L.   23–30
Traugott, E. C.   70
Traugott, T. C.   70
Treu, U.   10
Trever, J. C.   195
Tropper, J.   75
Tsumura, D. T.   224
Turner, N.   147

Urbach, E. E.   233, 240

Van Rompay, L.   v, ix, xiv, 6, 15, 33, 43, 69, 105, 193, 233
VanderKam, J.   209–210
Vermes, G.   118, 194, 210, 233, 239, 260
Volz, P.   133
Vööbus, A.   45

Waldman, N. M.   107
Walsh, J.   195
Watt, J. W.   43
Watt, W. M.   16
Watzinger, C.   49
Weinfeld, M.   157
Weiser, A.   133
Wertheimer, A.   96
Westermann, C.   127–128, 132
Wevers, J. W.   141
Wiener, H. W.   91
Wilfand, Y.   ix, 53, 58
Wolff, H. W.   132
Wright, W.   15, 18–19, 43–44

Yadin, Y.   194, 196
Yahalom, J.   238
Yonatan, R.   228
York, A. D.   159

Zaehner, R. C.   17
Zimmerli, W.   141
Zuckerman, B.   196
Zuckermandel, M. S.   151

Index of Scripture

Hebrew Bible

Genesis
1–27   165
2–3   276
3:24   235
4:7   217
5:24   239
6:1–4   152
6:3   152
6:14   250, 260
9:25   221
11:6   250, 260
11:7   236
12:10–20   198–201, 211
12:11–13   201
12:12–20   199
12:14–15   203
12:19   201
12:20   192
13:1   204
13:1–12   198–199
13:14   205
13:14–15   204
13:14–17   204
13:14–18   198–199, 204
13:14–20   211
13:16   204
13:18   204–205
14   198
14–15   198
14:1–16   153
14:1–24   198
14:2   159
14:8   159
14:15   252
14:17–24   153

Genesis (cont.)
15:1   153
15:1–4   198
15:2   250–252, 261–262
15:3   252
15:4   173, 192
16:2   127, 142, 145, 152
16:5   152
18:2   142
18:17–33   152
18:21   152
18:24–32   156
18:28   142
18:29   142
18:30   142
18:31   142
18:32   142
19:20–22   159
19:24   159
20:1–28   203
20:3   203
20:7   203
20:17   203
21:16   250, 263
22:10   233
24:5   142, 152
24:21   250, 253–254, 263
24:39   142
24:63   250, 254–255, 260
25   256
25:30   250, 255
26:20   250, 260–261
26:24   135

Genesis (cont.)
27:12   127, 142
28:12   250, 260–261
28:15   135
28:17   173
30:3   152
30:22   233
30:37   250, 260–261
31:43–32:1   153
32   165
32:2–3   154
32:3   233
32:4–22   153
32:8   154
32:11   154
32:21   127, 142
32:25   237
32:26   233
32:27   173
32:29   173
32:31   236
33:10   236
35:10   173
36:24   250, 257, 261, 263
38:25   236
39:6   173
39:9   173
40:11   250, 260
40:14   173, 183
41:23   250
41:43   250, 258
42:15   173
43:11   250, 260–261
43:12   126, 142
45:8   259
46:4   135

Index of Scripture

Genesis (cont.)
47:13   250, 260
47:18   173, 184
48:16   248, 250, 259–260
48:17   260
49:6–7   215, 217, 220–221
49:17   250
50:15   152

Exodus
4:25   233
5:2   236
8:9   110
8:17   173
9:2   173
10:4   174
12:9   174
17:9   217, 227
20:3–4   134
22:12   226
22:22   174
23:22   174
25:34   217
27:9   110
32   133–134, 136
32:4   134
32:8   134
32:30   133, 142, 157
32:30–35   134
32:31   133
32:32   133–134
32:33–34   133
32:35   134
33:19   135
33:23   233
37:20   217, 227

Leviticus
15:23   186
21:2   174
21:14   174
22:6   174
26:41   152
24:10–16   155

Numbers
2:17   154
2:32   154
10:2   154
10:5   154
10:6   154
10:25   154
10:30   174
13:19   154
14:30   174
15:32–36   155
22:6   127, 142
22:11   127, 142
23   165
23:3   129, 142
23:21   135
23:27   129, 142
24:22   174, 180
25:8   239
26:33   174
26:65   174
35:33   174

Deuteronomy
1:28   257
2:21   257
6:4   155
6:4–5   154
7:5   174
9:2   257
9:19   238
10:12   174
11:22   175
12:5   175
12:14   175
12:18   175
16:6   175
29:22   159
31:8   135
31:16   217, 224–225
32   205
32:8   234
32:48–52   205
33:1–29   205
33:2   233–234, 236
34   205
34:1–3   205
34:4   205

Joshua
9:7   127, 142
14:4   175
14:12   128, 142
17:3   175
23:8   175
23:12   175

Judges
15:7   175, 184–185, 187

1 Samuel
2:15   175
3:3–4   118
6:3   129
6:5   129, 142, 145
8:19   175
9:6   127, 142, 145, 163
14:6   128, 142
14:39   175
17:4   154
20:9   175
21:5   175
21:6   175, 183
21:7   175
25:34   175
26:10   175, 186
26:11   186
30:17   175
30:22   175

2 Samuel
3:13   175
3:35   175
5:6   175
7:22   155
12:3   175
13:33   175, 183
14:15   127, 142
15:21   175, 183, 186
16:12   128, 142
17:18   110
18:3   176
19:29   176
21:2   176

Index of Scripture

1 Kings
6:36   110
7:38–40   112
8   103
8:19   176
8:22   112
8:22–23   112
11:29–31   139
12:25–33   134
17:1   176
17:12   176
18:5   127, 142
18:17–40   132
18:18   176
18:27   132, 142, 163–164
20:6   176
20:21   127
20:31   142
21:15   176
22:8   176
22:18   176
22:31   176

2 Kings
4:2   176
4:24   176
5:15   176
5:17   176
5:20   176, 185, 187
7:10   176
9:35   176
10:23   176
13:7   176
14:6   176
17:36   176
17:39   176
17:40   176
17:41   85
18:4   85
18:13–20:19   132
18:26   146
19:4   142
19:18   176
22:3–9   118
23:9   176
23:23   176
24:18–25:21   132

2 Kings (cont.)
24:27–30   132
25:4–7   139
25:27–30   132

Isaiah
1:12   117
6:3   239
8:10   135
10:22   176
20:1–6   139
33:21   176
36–39   132
37:4   142
37:19   176
42:19   176
43:11   155
44:6   155
45:18   155
47   131–132
47:12   131–132, 142
55:10   176
55:11   177
59:2   177
65:6   177
65:18   177

Jeremiah
1:2   130, 138
1:6–7   130
2:22   177
3:10   177
7   137
7:3   137
7:4   137
7:5   177
7:6   137
7:7   137
7:8   137
7:9   137
7:10   137
7:12   137
7:12–14   137
7:14   137
7:15   137
7:20   137
7:23   177
7:32   177

Jeremiah (cont.)
9:23   177
16:15   177
19:1–2   139
19:6   177
19:10–11   139
20:3   177
20:10   127, 142
21:2   128, 143
22:4   177
22:17   177
22:24   177
23:8   177
25:9   130
26   137
26:2–3   137
26:3   143
26:4–5   137
26:6   137
26:7–23   137
26:9   137
26:15   177
26:24   137
27–29   130
27:6   130
31:30   177
36:1   137
36:2–3   137
36:3   143
36:5   137
36:5–7   138
36:7   143
36:9   138
36:9–26   138
36:10   110
37:10   177
38:4   177
38:6   177
39:4–7   139
39:12   177, 183
41–43   130
44:14   177
46–49   131
50–51   130
51   132
51:6–8   131
51:6–10   131
51:8   130–132, 143

Jeremiah (cont.)
51:9 131
51:14 177, 185, 187
52:1–27 132
52:7–11 139
52:31–34 132

Ezekiel
1:1 55, 62, 64, 118
8:16 110
10:8 111
12:1–4 139
12:1–6 139
12:1–16 138
12:2 140
12:3 140, 143–144
12:5 139
12:6 139
12:6–9 139
12:7 139–140
12:8–9 140
12:8–14 139
12:9 140
12:10 139
12:11 139–140
12:12–14 139
12:23 177
33:11 177
36:22 177
39:27 218
40–46 110
43:7–8 118
43:14 108
43:17 109, 116
43:20 109, 120
44:10 177
44:22 177
44:25 177
45:19 109, 120
46:21 110
46:21–22 114, 120
46:22 110

Hosea
1–3 137
8:7 143
9:12 177
11:8 159

Amos
3–6 134
3:7 177
3:14 134
4:4 134
4:13 134
5:1 135
5:4 135
5:5–6 134
5:6 135
5:7 135
5:8 134
5:10 135
5:12 135
5:14 135
5:14–15 134
5:15 135, 143
5:18 136
5:18–20 136
5:19 136
5:20 136
5:22 177
5:24 135
8:11 177
9:6 134

Jonah
1:6 126, 129, 143, 145
3:9 126

Micah
3:10 135
6:8 177

Nahum
1:8 222–223

Zephaniah
1:7 136
1:7–10 135
1:8 136
1:8–12 136
1:9 136
1:14 136
1:14–18 135–136
1:15 136
2:2–3 135–136
2:3 143

Zephaniah (cont.)
3:8 136
3:8–11 135
3:16–18 135

Zechariah
4:6 178
14:9 155
14:14 154

Psalms
1 27
1:1 24
1:2 178
1:4 178
46:8 135
46:12 135
91:11 239
93:1 216, 218
106:20 134
121:4 133

Job
1:5 126, 143
1:9 135
42:8 178

Proverbs
2:3 178
8:22 215
10:7 60
18:2 178
19:19 178
19:20 135
23:17 178
23:18 178
24:21–22 135
25:9–10 135

Ruth
3:12 178
3:18 178
4:5 219–220, 226

Song of Songs
1:7 150
2:12 216
7:1 154

Index of Scripture

Qoheleth
- 2:1–11   272
- 2:12–17   271
- 2:13–14   271
- 2:16   271
- 3:2   269
- 3:5   269
- 3:7   269
- 3:12   178
- 3:16–6:12   271
- 3:19   218
- 3:19–21   272
- 4:10   178
- 4:11   269
- 5:5   150
- 5:10   178
- 7:16   150
- 7:17   150
- 8:15   178
- 9:1–6   271
- 9:2   271
- 9:10   223–224
- 10:6   218
- 11:8   178
- 12:1–8   271
- 12:9   272
- 12:12   272

Lamentations
- 3:27–29   127
- 3:29   143
- 3:32   178
- 5:22   178

Esther
- 2:14   178
- 2:15   178
- 4:14   178
- 5:12   178

Daniel
- 1–6   196
- 2   89
- 2:5   74–75
- 2:7   74–75
- 2:8   74, 78, 80
- 2:10   74–75
- 2:11   80

Daniel (cont.)
- 2:15   74
- 2:20   74
- 2:21   74
- 2:22   74
- 2:23   80–81
- 2:25   75
- 2:26   74, 78, 84, 88, 92
- 2:27   74, 78, 80, 84
- 2:28   74
- 2:29   74
- 2:31   76, 89–90
- 2:31–34   90
- 2:34   89–90
- 2:38   80
- 2:40   80
- 2:43   74, 80, 85, 87, 89, 92
- 2:47   74
- 3:3   76
- 3:4   75, 81
- 3:6   74
- 3:7   78
- 3:9   74–75
- 3:11   74
- 3:12   80
- 3:14   74, 85, 89, 92
- 3:15   74
- 3:16   74–75, 80
- 3:17   74, 78, 80, 84, 89
- 3:18   89, 93
- 3:19   74–75
- 3:20   74
- 3:21   74
- 3:22   74
- 3:23   74
- 3:24   74
- 3:25   74, 77–78, 80
- 3:26   74, 76
- 3:27   76
- 3:28   74
- 3:31   80
- 4   89, 195–196
- 4:1   196
- 4:4   74–75, 79, 84
- 4:4–5   79, 84
- 4:6   80
- 4:7   89–91

Daniel (cont.)
- 4:10   77, 89–91
- 4:10–11   77
- 4:11   74, 77
- 4:14   86
- 4:15   78, 80, 84, 196
- 4:16   74
- 4:16–30   196
- 4:20   75, 77
- 4:22   84, 86
- 4:26   89–90, 92
- 4:27   74
- 4:28   75, 81
- 4:29   84, 86
- 4:31   196
- 4:32   74, 80
- 4:34   78, 80–81, 84
- 5:1   79
- 5:1–2   79
- 5:2   84
- 5:4   86
- 5:5   73, 76–77
- 5:6   76
- 5:7   74–75
- 5:8   78, 81, 84
- 5:9   77
- 5:9–10   77
- 5:10   75
- 5:11   74
- 5:12   74
- 5:13   74
- 5:15   78, 81–82, 84
- 5:15–16   82
- 5:17   74–75
- 5:19   85–86, 88
- 5:21   86
- 5:23   78, 80, 84
- 5:29   88
- 6:1   78
- 6:2–3   87
- 6:3   85, 87, 94
- 6:4   87
- 6:5   73–74, 78, 81–82, 84, 87
- 6:6   75
- 6:7   75
- 6:11   78–79, 86
- 6:12   77

Index of Scripture

Daniel (cont.)
6:13 74–75
6:14 74–75, 78, 80
6:15 79, 86
6:16 75
6:17 74, 80
6:21 74, 80
6:25 90
6:26 80
6:27 85, 88
6:28 80
7 89, 196
7–12 196
7:1 75
7:2 74, 76, 89–90
7:2–9 91
7:3 74, 76, 78
7:4 89–90
7:5 74–75, 78
7:6 89–91
7:7 77, 89–91
7:8 75, 77, 89–91
7:9 74, 89–90
7:10 76
7:11 75, 77, 89–91
7:13 89–91
7:15 196
7:16 74–75
7:19 74, 77, 85
7:20 75, 77

Daniel (cont.)
7:21 76, 89–91
7:22 91
7:23 75
7:28 196
8:1 196
8:15 196
8:27 196
9:2 196
10:2 196
10:7 196
10:21 178
12:5 196

Ezra
4:16 81
4:22 150
6:8 89
6:9 89
6:10 89
6:12 195
6:14 83
7:21 195
7:23 150
7:24 81
7:25 89
7:26 89

Nehemiah
2:2 178

Nehemiah (cont.)
2:12 178
6:3 150

1 Chronicles
2:34 178
9:18 154
13:2 129
15:2 178
23:22 178
23:28 111

2 Chronicles
2:5 179
4:6–11 112
4:9 109, 111–112, 116, 120
6:12 112
6:12–14 112
6:13 109, 112, 120
7:7 111
18:17 179
18:30 179
20:5 111
21:17 179
23:6 179
23:8 111
25:8 179
31:2 154

New Testament

Matthew
22:7 9

John
20:30 35, 37

Acts
18:21 130

1 Corinthians
4:19 130
16:7 130

2 Thessalonians
2:1–10 25
2:2–10 28

Hebrews
6:3 130

James
4:15 130

Pseudepigrapha

Book of the Angel
   Raziel 239

1 Enoch
  Book of Watchers
    (1 Enoch) 239
  9:1 239
  105–6 208

3 Enoch
  4:1–4 240

Jubilees
  13 207
  13:9 207
  13:11–15 203

Psalms of Solomon
  1:1 26
  1:8 27
  2 26
  2:1 26
  2:3 26, 27
  2:9 27
  2:13 27
  2:17 26
  2:38 26
  2:39 26
  3:11 26
  3:13 26

Psalms of Solomon (cont.)
  3:15 26
  4:2 26
  4:9 26
  4:11 29
  4:12 27
  4:21 26, 29
  4:27 26, 29
  12 28, 30
  12:1 26, 29, 30
  12:1–5 30
  12:3 29
  12:4 29
  12:6 27, 30
  12:8 26
  13:2 26
  13:4 26
  13:5 26
  13:6 26
  13:7 26
  13:10 26
  14:4 26, 29
  15:6 26, 27
  15:7 26
  15:9 26, 27
  15:11 26, 27
  15:13 26
  15:15 26
  16:2 26
  16:5 26

Psalms of Solomon (cont.)
  16:8 26, 29
  17 28
  17:6 26
  17:13 26, 28
  17:14 28
  17:15 28
  17:20 26
  17:24 26, 27
  17:26 26
  17:27 26, 29
  17:36 27
  17:41 26
  Syriac MS
    253 26
    655 26
    659 26

Sibylline Oracles
  1.331 10
  1.364 10
  1.379–381 10
  6.1–2 10
  7.69 10
  8.217–250 10
  8.313–314 10

Testament of the Twelve
    Patriarchs
  Naphtali 8–9 236

Index of Other Ancient Sources

Early Jewish, Christian, and Classical Sources

Acta Philippi 16
Acta Thomae 211 16
Acts of Judas Thomas
  chap. 8 15
  chap. 99 15
Acts of Pilate 11
Alphabet of Ben Sira 18a 237
Aquila
  Genesis 16:2 147
  Job 1:5 147
Augustine
  City of God 18:42 145

Baalbek inscription 59, 60
BL MS Add. 14,666 (fol. 56) 45
BL MS Add. 14,731 (fol. 11a) 45
Book of the Laws of Countries 19

Cairo Geniza
  ketubba (Friedman #1) 64
  ketubba (Friedman #39) 60, 61
Canons of George I 45
Chronicle of 640 45
Chronicle of John Bar Penkaye 45
Chronicle of Khuzistan 45
Chronicle of Zuqnin 43
Dead Sea Scrolls
  1QapGen
    1–5 208
    2:3 197
    2:9–11 194
    2:13–18 194
    2:19 197
    2:24–26 194
    5:1 197, 199
    5:9 194

Dead Sea Scrolls *(cont.)*
  1QapGen *(cont.)*
    5:13 198
    5:20 194
    5:25 199
    5:26 196, 197
    6–7 199
    6:2 199
    6:6 196, 197, 199
    6:23 197
    7:7 199
    8:1 199
    10:2 199
    10:13 199
    10:15 199
    11:1 197
    11:9 197
    11:11 197
    11:15–12:1 194
    12 199
    12:3 199
    12:8 199
    12:10 199
    12:13 199
    12:15–17 199
    12:19 199
    15:21 197
    15:23 194
    16:7 200
    16:12 199
    17:15 199
    19–21:21 200
    19–21:22 199
    19:7–8 194
    19:10–20:32 201
    19:10–21:22 201

Dead Sea Scrolls *(cont.)*
  1QapGen *(cont.)*
    19:14   197
    19:14–17   205
    19:14–20:32   203
    19:17–18   194
    19:17–21   195, 196
    19:18   194, 204
    19:19–21   194
    19:21   204
    19:23   204
    19:25   199
    20:9–10   194
    20:10   197, 204
    20:10–11   197
    20:12   204
    20:12–16   194
    20:16   204
    20:16–18   205
    20:18–21   205
    20:22   205
    20:22–23   194
    20:24–26   194
    20:26–28   194
    20:28   205
    20:33   197
    21:5   197
    21:8–10   194
    21:8–22   201, 206
    21:12–14   194
    21:15   197
    21:23–22:26   200
    21:23–22:34   199, 200
    22:16–17   194
    22:18   194
    22:20–24   194
    22:22   88
    22:27–32   194
    22:32–34   194
    22:34   194
  1QM (*War Rule*)   239
    9:16   239
    10   184
    11:1   184
    11:2   184
  4Q158   209
  4Q213–14   211
  4Q215   211

Dead Sea Scrolls *(cont.)*
  4Q364–367   209
  4Q364 3 ii   210
  4Q439   211
  4Q537   211
  4Q538   211
  4Q540–41   211
  4Q542   211
  4Q543–48   211
  4QtgJob (4Q157)   149
  4QtgLev (4Q156)   149
  11QtgJob (11Q10)   149
  New Jerusalem Scroll   118

Homer
  Iliad 14:231–15:34   135
  Odyssey 8:266–366   135

Jacob of Edessa
  Caliph List of 724   45
  Canons of Giwargi   45
  Chronicle of 775   45
  John and the Amir   45
  scribal addition to letter of Athanasius
    of Balad   45
Josephus
  Jewish Antiquities 18.63–64   10
  Jewish War 4.8.4 §§482–85   161
Justin Martyr
  1 Apology 53.2–3   9
  Dialogue with Trypho
    68:7   145
    124:3   145
    137:3   145
  Oratio ad Gentiles   19
Justinian, Code   52

Letter of Aristeas 301–11   145
Letter of Mara bar Serapion
  BL MS Add. 14,645   15
  BL MS Add. 14,658   18
Letter of Mara bar Serapion *(cont.)*
  Sachau MS 222   15
  Sachau MS 315   42
  col. 1 (fol. 183r)   12
  col. 2 (fol. 184r)   12
Letters of Isho'yhab III   45
Life of Theodotus of Amida   45

6 Maccabees   27, 28
  1 (106)   30
  2 (162)   30
  3 (179)   30
  4 (392)   30
7 Maccabees   27
Maronite Chronicler   45
Mibtahiah archive
  TAD B2.8:4–5   83
Moshe bar Kapha, Damascus Patr. 12/18 (fol. 64b)   45

Nabratein synagogue lintel inscription   49, 57, 58, 60, 66

Old Greek version
  Daniel
    2:43   92
    5:8   82
    6:5   82
Origen, The principiis 4.1.3   9

Peshitta
  Genesis
    16:2   165
    18:24   165
    18:28   165
    18:29   165
    18:30   165
    18:31   165
    18:32   165
    24:5   165
    24:39   165
    24:63   257
    27:12   165
    32:21   165
    36:24   259
    40:14   185, 186
    43:12   150, 153, 165
    47:18   186
  Exodus
    32:30   165
  Numbers
    23:3   165
    23:27   165
  Joshua
    9:7   165

Peshitta (cont.)
  Judges
    15:7   186
  1 Samuel
    9:6   165
    21:5   185
    21:6   185
    26:10   188
    26:11   188
  2 Samuel
    13:33   185
    14:15   165
    15:21   185, 188
    16:12   165
  1 Kings
    18:27   150, 165, 166
    20:31   165
  2 Kings
    5:20   189
    19:4   165
  Isaiah
    47:12   165
  Jeremiah
    3:6   165
    20:10   165
    21:2   165
    26:3   165
    36:7   165
    39:12   185
    51:8   165
    51:14   189
  Ezekiel
    12:3   165
  Amos
    5:15   165
  Jonah
    1:6   165
  Zephaniah
    2:3   165
  Job
    1:5   165
  Psalms
    1:1   24, 30
  Qohelet
    9:10   225
Philo
  Life of Moses 2.2–4   8

Philo *(cont.)*
  On Rewards and Punishments 53–
    55   8
Plato, *Euthyphro* 14d–e   137

Qenneshrē Composition
  Chronicle of 1234   34, 40, 41
  Michael the Syrian
    11:8   34
  Qenneshrē Fragment
    section zero (fol. 58a)   35, 36, 40
    section one (fols. 58a–61a)   35, 36,
      37, 38, 40, 41, 42, 46
    section two (fols. 61a–62a)   35, 37,
      38, 39, 40, 41, 42, 43, 44, 46
    section three (fols. 62a–63b)   35, 37,
      38, 39, 40, 41, 44, 46
  Sachau MS 315   42

Record of Arab Conquest of 637   45

Septuagint
  Genesis
    16:2   146, 147, 165
    18:24   165
    18:28   165
    18:29   165
    18:30   165
    18:31   165
    18:32   165
    24:5   165
    24:39   165
    24:63   257
    27:12   165
    32:21   165
    43:12   165
  Exodus
    32:30   146, 147, 165
  Numbers
    23:3   165
    23:27   165
  Joshua
    9:7   165
  1 Samuel
    6:5   146, 165
    9:6   146
    21:6   185

Septuagint *(cont.)*
  2 Samuel
    14:15   165
    16:12   165
  1 Kings
    18:27   147, 150, 165
    20:31   165
  2 Kings
    19:4   147, 165
  Isaiah
    37:4   147
    47:12   147, 165
  Jeremiah
    20:10   165
    21:2   165
    26:3   165
    36:3   165
    36:7   165
    51:8   165
  Ezekiel
    12:3   146, 165
  Amos
    5:15   146, 165
  Jonah
    1:6   146, 165
  Nahum
    1:8   224
  Zephaniah
    2:3   146, 165
  Job
    1:5   147, 165
  2 Chronicles
    4:9   113
    6:13   113
  Tobit
    1:3   198
  Wisdom
    13:6   165
    14:19   165
Sophocles, *Antigone*   25

Tertullian, *Apol.*
  21   9, 11
  26   10
Theodosian, Code   52
Theodotion, Daniel
  2:43   92

Theodotion, Daniel *(cont.)*
  5:8 82
  6:5 82

Vulgate
  Genesis
    24:63 257
    36:24 259
  1 Samuel
    21:6 185
  Qohelet
    9:10 225

Zoar synagogue lintel inscription
  Epitaph C 60
Zoar tombstone inscriptions/
  epitaphs 50, 52

Zoar tombstone inscriptions *(cont.)*
  Epitaph 10 58, 59
  Epitaph 13 63, 64
  Epitaph 14 63, 64
  Epitaph 15 63
  Epitaph 16 63
  Epitaph 17 63
  Epitaph 18 58, 59
  Epitaph 19 63
  Epitaph 24 63, 64
  Epitaph 25 64
  Epitaph 27 64
  Epitaph 29 64
  Epitaph B 63
  Epitaph C 51, 58, 59
  Epitaph D 63, 64

Rabbinic Sources

Mishnah
  Arakin 9:8 56
  Avot 5:6 240
  Bikkurim 1:8–9 124
  Eruvin
    6:1 115
    6:3 115
  Gittin 8:5 56, 60
  Kelim 1:6–9 124
  Maaser Sheni 5:2 56
  Megillah 4:4 148
  Menahot 10:5 56
  Middot
    1:4 115
    2:5 116
    2:6 115, 124
  Moed Qatan 3:6 56
  Nazir 5:4 56
  Ohalot 18:9 56
  Rosh Hashshannah
    4:1 56
    4:3 56
    4:4 56
  Sanhedrin 10:1 227
  Shabbat 24:3 258

Mishnah *(cont.)*
  Sotah
    9:12 56
    9:15 56
  Sukkah 3:12 56
  Taanit 4:6 56
  Zebahim 14:4–8 124

Tosefta
  Baba Qamma
    6.17 258
  Hullin 3.19 258
  Megillah 3.41 151
  Shabbat 13.2 149
  Shebiit 5.11 263

Babylonian Talmud
  Abodah Zarah 3b 240
  Baba Batra
    4a 260
    80b 263
  Bekorot 8a 263
  Berakot
    8a–b 149
    20a 262
    28b 149

Babyl. Talmud *(cont.)*
  Hagigah 15a 239, 240
  Megillah
    3a 148–149, 245
  Moed Qatan 28b 149
  Pesahim 54a 259
  Qiddushin 49a 149, 151, 245
  Rosh Hashshannah
    24a 116
  Sanhedrin
    38b 240, 241
    94a 240
    94b 149
  Shabbat
    33a 238
    115a 149
    152b 237
  Sotah
    12b 238
    13a 237
    36b 262
  Yoma
    52b 219, 223

Index of Other Ancient Sources

Jerusalem Talmud
  Abodah Zarah 40a 263
  Berakot 12b 259
  Demai 22a 163
  Megillah
    4.1 (74d) 149
    71c 245
  Moed Qatan 81d 163
  Shabbat
    6.10 241
    8d 241
    16.1 (15c) 149
  Shebiit
    7.5 (37a) 263
  Taanit 68c 263

Midrash
  Genesis Rabbah
    8 263
    8:5 241
    10 241
    21:9 237
    44:9 254
    49:13 161
    56:11 236
    60:6 256
    68 263
    69 263
    78:1 241
    82:14 259
    90:3 260
    97:3 262
  Exodus Rabbah
    17:2 237
    18:4 240
    27:9 237
    32:30 159
    42:1 236
  Leviticus Rabbah
    6:6 237
  Numbers Rabbah
    12:12 240
    14:10 237
    20:25 241
  Deuteronomy Rabbah
    1:22 236
    2:27 225, 226
    6:4–5 156

Midrash (cont.)
  Ruth Rabbah
    Prologue 237
  Qoheleth Rabbah
    9:10 225
  Lamentations Rabbah
    Prologue 24 240
  Mekhilta de-Rabbi Ishmael
    Amalek 1
    Neziqin 16 228
  Otzar Hamidrashim
    Yelammedenu 4 225
  Pirke Rabbati 3:3 225
  Pirque d'Rabbi Eliezer
    13 240
    14 240
    21 240
    22 240
    27 240
  Zuta Qohelet 9:8 225

Kimhi, David
  Commentary, Ezekiel
    43:17 118

Megillat Taanit 19 119

Pseudo-Seder Eliahu
  Zuta 240

Rashi, Commentary
  Numbers 13:33 240

Sopherim
  5 149
  15 149

Targums—Pentateuch
  Cairo Genizah Frgs.
    Genesis
      6:3 154
      15:1 152, 155
      18:21 154
      24:39 154
      30:3 154
      32:21 152
      44:18–19 158

Targums—Pent. (cont.)
  Cairo Gen. Frgs. (cont.)
    Numbers
      22:6 154
      22:11 154
  Fragment Targums
    Genesis
      14:15 254
      15:1 155
      15:2 253, 264
      15:3 254
      32 167
      32:2–3 156
      41:43 260
      44:18–19 158
      49 224
      49:17 264
    Leviticus 24:12 158
    Numbers 23 167
    Deuteronomy 6:4–5 156
  Targum Neofiti
    Genesis
      1:1 217
      3:5 234
      3:11 163
      6:3 153, 154
      14:1–16 155
      14:15 254
      14:17–24 155
      15:1 153, 155, 161
      15:2 253, 264
      15:3 254
      16:2 154
      16:5 153, 154
      18:1–2 234
      18:21 153, 154
      18:24 152
      18:24–32 152, 155
      18:28 152
      18:29 152
      18:31 152
      18:32 152
      21:16 264
      22:10 234
      24:5 152
      24:21 255, 256, 264
      24:39 152

Targum Neofiti *(cont.)*
  Genesis *(cont.)*
    24:63   257
    25:30   258, 264
    26:16   118
    30:3   153, 154
    30:22   234, 235
    31:22   153, 158, 161
    32:2–3   156
    32:3   153, 234
    32:25   239
    32:25–26   234
    32:29   234
    32:31   234, 238
    33:10   234, 238
    37:15   234
    41:23   264
    41:43   260
    43:12   150, 153
    44:18–19   153
    48:16   261, 262
    49   224
    49:7   224
    50:15   153, 154
  Exodus
    4:24–26   234
    4:26   236
    22:12   228
    32:30   152
    33:22–23   234
  Leviticus
    22:27   234
    24:12   153, 157
    25:31   118
    26:41   153, 154
  Numbers
    21   224
    22–24   224
    23:3   153
    23:27   153
  Deuteronomy
    2:23   118
    6:4   153, 157, 161
    6:4–5   156
    6:5   157
    32–33   224
    32:3   234, 241
    33:2   236, 238

Targum Neofiti *(cont.)*
  Deuteronomy *(cont.)*
    33:2–3   234
Targum Onqelos
  Genesis
    1–27   167
    3:3   150
    3:5   229
    4:13   229
    8:11   229
    9:25   223
    11:4   150
    14:15   254
    15:2   253, 255, 264
    16:14   234
    19:15   150
    19:17   150
    19:19   150
    21:16   263, 264
    24:21   255, 256, 263, 264
    24:62   234
    24:63   256, 257
    25:11   234
    25:30   257, 258, 264
    26:7   150
    26:9   150
    26:16   118
    27:29   229
    30:22   235
    31:24   150
    31:29   150
    31:31   150
    32:12   150
    32:31   234
    36:24   259, 260, 263
    40:14   185, 186
    41:23   264
    41:43   260, 261, 263, 264
    43:12   153
    47:18   186
    48:16   261, 262
    49:6   223
    49:6–7   223
    49:7   223, 224
  Exodus
    1:19   229

Targum Onqelos *(cont.)*
  Exodus *(cont.)*
    4:24   234
    17:9   220, 221
    25:33 (= 37:20)   229
    26:9   63
  Leviticus
    16:4   229
    25:21   63
    25:31   118
  Numbers
    26:9   229
  Deuteronomy
    2:10–11   259
    2:23   118
    5:3   229
Targum Pseudo-Jonathan
  Genesis
    1–27   167
    1:26   234
    3:3   160
    3:5   229, 234
    3:6   234
    3:11   161
    3:22   150, 234
    4:1   234
    4:9   162, 163
    4:13   229
    5:24   240
    6:4   240
    6:20   234
    8:11   229
    11:7   234, 238
    11:4   150
    11:8   234
    14:15   254
    15:1   161
    15:2   253, 255, 264
    15:3   254
    16:2   159
    18:2   234
    18:10   234
    18:15–16   234
    18:20   234
    18:22   234
    18:24   159
    18:24–32   160
    18:28   159

Index of Other Ancient Sources

Tg. Ps.-Jonathan (cont.)
  Genesis (cont.)
    18:29 159
    18:30 159
    18:31 159
    18:32 159
    19:15 150, 160
    19:17 150, 160
    19:19 150, 160
    19:26 234
    21:16 263
    22:1 162, 163
    22:10 234
    22:19 234
    24:5 159
    24:6 160
    24:7 160
    24:9 160
    24:21 255, 256, 263
    24:39 159
    24:63 256, 257
    25:30 257, 258
    26:7 150
    26:9 150
    27 160
    27:11 161
    27:12 159
    27:25 234
    27:29 229
    30:22 235
    31:22 161
    31:24 150, 160, 234
    31:29 150
    31:31 150, 160
    32 160
    32:3 234
    32:10 234
    32:12 150, 160
    32:21 159
    32:25 234
    32:26 234
    32:29 234
    32:31 234, 238
    33:10 238
    35:7 234
    35:22 162, 163
    36:24 259, 260, 263
    37:13 161

Tg. Ps.-Jonathan (cont.)
  Genesis (cont.)
    37:15 234
    38:11 160
    38:23 160
    38:25 238
    41:43 260, 261, 263
    42:4 160
    43:12 150, 153, 159
    45:24 161
    48:16 261, 262
    49:6 224
    49:7 224
  Exodus
    1:19 229
    4:24 234
    4:25 235, 236
    4:25–26 234
    4:26 236
    5:2 234, 238
    12:12 234
    12:13 234
    12:23 234
    12:42 234
    15:2 234
    20:23 234
    22:12 228
    26:9 63
    26:28 234
    29:37 161
    33:1 161
    33:23 234
  Leviticus
    8:15 162, 163
    9:23 162, 163
    11:43 161
    16:4 229
    25:21 63
    25:22 63
  Numbers
    15:40 234, 241
    22 160
    22:11 159, 160
    22:6 159, 160
    23:3 159, 160
    23:27 159, 160
    24:3 234
    25:8 234

Tg. Ps.-Jonathan (cont.)
  Numbers (cont.)
    25:12 234
    26:9 229
    26:46 234
  Deuteronomy
    5:3 229
    6:4 161
    7:17 161
    9:19 234, 240
    10:14 234
    17:16 161
    20:8 161
    22:8 161
    28:15 162, 163
    31:16 227
    32:8 234, 236
    33:2 234, 236
    34:5–6 234

Targum Jonathan to the Prophets
  Joshua
    9:7 150
  Judges
    15:7 186
  1 Samuel
    3:3–4 121
    3:4 119
    9:6 150
    21:6 185
    26:10 188
  2 Samuel
    15:21 188
  1 Kings
    6:36 118
    18:27 150
  2 Kings
    5:20 189
  Isaiah
    1:12 119
    6:3 241
    10:32 119, 121
    47:12 150
  Jeremiah
    32:2 118
    32:8 118
    33:3 154

Targum Jonathan (cont.)
  Jeremiah (cont.)
    36:7   154
    51:14 189
  Ezekiel
    1:1   59, 119, 120
    8:1   63
    40:17 118
    43:7–8 120
    43:8   119
    43:14 117
    43:17 117
    43:20 117
    44:7   119
    45:19 117
    46:21 118
  Amos
    9:1   119
  Nahum
    1:8   224–225
  Zechariah
    3:7   119
  2 Chronicles
    49   118
Targumic tosefta, Ezekiel
    1:1 (Manchester MS
    Gaster 1478)   61,
    62, 64, 65

Targums—Writings
  Job
    1:5   143
  Proverbs
    7:18   263

Targums—Writ. (cont.)
  Ruth
    4:5   221, 222
  Song of Songs
    1:1   63
    4:11   119, 121
  Qoheleth
    1:2   272, 273
    1:2–3 277
    1:12   272
    1:15   278
    2:10   276
    2:18   272
    2:24   277
    2:26   275
    3:2   271
    3:5   271
    3:7   271
    3:22   278
    4:11   271
    4:15   272
    4:17   277
    5:10   275
    5:11   275
    5:12   275
    5:17   277
    6:8   263, 277
    6:10   221
    7:2   278
    7:4   272
    7:23   275
    9:5   278
    9:10   226
    9:17   221

Targums—Writ. (cont.)
  Qoheleth (cont.)
    10:2   275
    10:4   275
    10:6   220, 221
    10:11 221
    10:18 276
    11:3   221
    12:11 276
    12:12 277
  Lamentations
    3:29   143
  2 Chronicles
    4:9   123
    6:13   123
    7:7   118
    20:5   118
    24:21 118
    29:16 118

Esther, Second Targum
    1:2   119, 121

Samaritan Targum
  Genesis 43:12 152,
    153

Zohar
    32a   236
    46b   236
    72b   236
    265b   236
    B.14b 236
    C.4b   236

Eisenbrauns is committed to preserving ancient forests and natural resources. We elected to print this title on 30% post consumer recycled paper, processed chlorine free. As a result, for this printing, we have saved:

3 Trees (40' tall and 6-8" diameter)
1 Million BTUs of Total Energy
268 Pounds of Greenhouse Gases
1,290 Gallons of Wastewater
78 Pounds of Solid Waste

Eisenbrauns made this paper choice because our printer, Thomson-Shore, Inc., is a member of Green Press Initiative, a nonprofit program dedicated to supporting authors, publishers, and suppliers in their efforts to reduce their use of fiber obtained from endangered forests.

For more information, visit www.greenpressinitiative.org

Environmental impact estimates were made using the Environmental Defense Paper Calculator. For more information visit: www.papercalculator.org.